Proceedings
of the
National Association
for Multicultural
Education

Seventh Annual NAME Conference

October 29-November 2, 1997
Albuquerque, NM

Edited
By Carl A. Grant

1999

LAWRENCE ERLBAUM ASSOCIATES, PUBLISHERS
Mahwah, New Jersey   London

1997 Proceedings of the National Association for Multicultural Education

Edited by Carl A. Grant

Copyrighted 1999
by the National Association for Multicultural Education
    1511 K Street N.W., Suite 430
    Washington, DC 20005 U.S.A.

Published
for the National Association for Multicultural Education
by Lawrence Erlbaum Association, Inc.
    10 Industrial Avenue
    Mahwah, NJ 07430-22262

ISBN 0-8058-3420-6

CONTENTS

Introduction
DARING TO EDUCATE FOR EQUITY AND EXCELLENCE: A MULTICULTURAL AND BILINGUAL MANDATE FOR THE 21ST CENTURY

Carl A. Grant
University of Wisconsin - Madison

The National Association For Multicultural Education held its 7th Annual Conference in Albuquerque, New Mexico October 29-November 2, 1997. The Conference theme, **Daring to Educate for Equity and Excellence: A Multicultural and Bilingual Mandate for the 21ST Century**, generated excellent scholarship in the form of keynote speeches and conference papers and stimulating discussions among the membership. The Southwest provided an excellent back drop to discus the interconnections between Multicultural education and bilingual education, as well as provide an opportunity for proponents of both of these important ideas to engage in useful and important discussions.

The essays below capture much of the written record of the Conference. They convey the ideas, beliefs, and research findings that were presented at the formal sessions at the Conference. Just as with NAME's previous Proceedings, it is expected that **Daring to Educate for Equity and Excellence: A Multicultural And Bilingual Mandate for the 21ST Century** will become not only a written record of the conference but a "live curriculum" to help pre/K - College educators to prepare themselves and those they teach for the twenty-first century.

We open this volume with G. Pritchy Smith reverting and engaging keynote address *Who Shall Have the Moral Courage to Heal Racism in America?* The word and wisdom of this brilliant essay inspired those in attendance to strive even harder for the goals of multicultural education.

In *Multicultural Relationships in Organizations: Exemplar Modules for education and Training*, Sharon Chard-Yaron, Jon Kinsgsbury, and Martie Lubetkin write the following: "This paper will serve to describe a presentation whose purpose was to introduce p\participants to education and training modules which emphasize both instructional delivery and content. Prototype modules on the topics of (1) power distance in cross-cultural education settings, and (2) racial consciousness, are utilized to demonstrate the potential of 'module construction' as a learning and assessment strategy, especially for courses that demand and deserve an 'active learning' approach to subject matter" (p. 1, manuscript).

At a time when students of color are becoming the majority in many classrooms and the number of teachers of color are decreasing, Virginia Jones Dixon investigates the relationship between the cultural awareness of teachers and the frequency of behavior referrals for middle school males. Dixon offers the major findings from her study, that race has a significant effect on white and African American teachers behavioral referrals of white and African American male students.

Rebecca Fox and Marjorie Haley provide a two-part argument in their paper entitled *A Celebration of Teaching: A Conference for Students Aspiring to Become Teachers*. The first part addresses the need for teachers of color and the second describes the George Mason University model for recruiting teachers of color.

In Jack Levy's *The VENN View of Diversity: Understanding Differences Through Similarities*, the author discusses a series of research projects which examines diversity and conflict from a common ground standpoint. Levy argues that the VENN project provides an approach to conflict resolution. Karen Spees's study about Perceived Commonalities Among Elementary Boy and Girl Mediators was part of the larger VENN View of Diversity project, but focused on gender and the opportunities for student peer mediators usually segregated by gender in friendships to work with those of a different gender. She recommends practices to counselors, teachers and other educators that mix genders more often to help prevent sexism and gender stereotyping.

Billy Vaughn discusses how "emotions challenge multicultural education instruction" and offers the technique of LLEL (Listen, Lean into Discomfort, Empathize, and Learn) as a communication strategy and multicultural education tool for teachers and all participants in discussions of diversity.

When discussing *Using Sheltered (SDAIE) Instruction from a Multicultural Perspective*, Yee Wan and Sharon Russell focus on using the sheltered instructional approach within the framework of Multicultural education "to address the linguistic and cultural needs of students who do not speak English as a first language" (p. 1, manuscript). Yee and Russell offer a theoretical framework for using such instruction from a multicultural perspective and discuss the steps of instructional sequences they used.

Gwendolyn Duhon-Haynes, Rose Duhon-Sells, Alice Duhon-Ross, Halloway Sells, and Mary Mondell Addison discuss how *Racism Kills Best Educational Efforts*. The authors offer a definition of racism and describe various manifestations of racism. Their discussion follows early historical documentation of the effects of racism on both White and Black children while discussing the implications of racism on the current system of American education. The authors also include an examination of strategies currently employed to "address and combat the problem of racism in various educational settings and among students in those settings" (p. 1, manuscript). They conclude with an outline of the responsibilities of different educators to reduce the impact of racism.

Peggy Anderson conducted a study, *A Multi-Dimensional, Multi-Intelligences Approach to Assessment Is Good Enough For Teachers. Is It Good Enough For Teacher Educators?*, to ascertain the extent to which schools of education are implementing Gatekeeper versus Gateway assessment. The study reports on faculty beliefs about assessment, the importance of modeling for changes in assessment and the struggles that those teacher educators are having who are using multi-dimensional/multi-intelligence based assessment.

Introduction

Within her paper entitled *Mediated Cultural Immersion and Antiracism: An Opportunity for Monocultural Preservice Teachers to Begin the Dialogue*, Paula Bradfield-Kreider discusses how difficult it has been to change the perceptions of European American teachers educating culturally and linguistically distinct children, and how these teachers' changed perceptions often revert to "previously held cultural constructs within a few years after their multicultural course work". The author proposes a mediated cultural immersion experience to "help facilitate and perpetuate teachers' reconstruction of a more inclusive and critical world view" (p. 1, manuscript).

In 1987, Lesley College announced in its newly adopted mission statement that "The goal of a Lesley College education is to empower students with the knowledge, skills, and practical experience they need to succeed as catalysts and leaders in their professions, their own lives, and the world in which they live" (p. 1, manuscript). Ella Glenn Burnett, Sharlene Cochrane, and Patricia Layden Jerabek offered *A Comprehensive Approach to Changing the Culture of a Four-Year College*, in which they trace the path of institutional change and identify important "understandings" that have implications for higher education and other organizations that "seek to create learning environments that better prepare citizens to work and live productively and peacefully in a Multicultural society" (pp. 1-2, manuscript).

Maria Yellow Horse Brave Heart and Judith Bula, in *Women of Color in the Academic Setting: Empowerment Through Mentoring*, examine the dynamics of the mentoring relationship for women of color with mentors from the dominant culture, present their concerns about this arrangement and examine the "barriers to a successful mentoring relationship cross-culturally/cross-racially" and offer their recommendations for such arrangements (p. 2, manuscript).

Gail Cueto and Elizabeth Aaronsohn in *Moving Within the Monolith: The struggle to Make a University Culturally Responsible* offer their findings from the literature review they have done and the anecdotes they have collected in their attempt to make a case for making Universities more culturally responsible to their faculty members of color. The authors' purpose at NAME was to collect additional anecdotal data with the goal of this work leading to a publication in book form about the problems that faculty of color experience in higher education. Their goal is to present these things in an effort to improve the welfare of scholars of color at predominantly white institutions.

Randie Gottlieb's presentation is *When Sparks Fly: Controversial Issues in Multicultural Education*. Dr. Gottlieb's purpose is to help those who "face resistance to multiculturalism" to develop a positive response, to avoid becoming entangled in angry debates, to listen carefully in order to be better prepared to initiate a dialog about the issues, to build consensus among those with different perspectives, and to develop an inclusive process within a cooperative framework rather than a combative one (p. 2, manuscript).

Tonya Huber, Peggy Anderson, Kimberly Ott, Cindy Combs, and Sharon Edwards offer a work in progress that is dealing with a question that has historically haunted US society and increasingly is becoming a factor that must be understood and dealt with in school and society. The question is on of multiraciality. These authors address this question by discussing popular culture, anecdotes from people interviewed and literature about inter- and multi-racial relationships. Their paper, *Guess Who's Coming to Dinner? Race and Gender at the Crossroads*, offers a first look at these authors' research.

The range of preservice and inservice teachers' responses regarding the value placed on using multicultural literature in diverse classrooms was the topic of Catherine Kurkjian, Kenneth Weiss, and Helen Abadiano's paper, *Electronic Exchanges Across Campuses: Forums for Concerns and Issues Surrounding the Selection and Use of Multicultural Literature*. The issues and concerns that preservice and inservice teachers have with multicultural literature selection and use, and the way they come to grips with these issues during the course of a semester, and the possible benefits, drawbacks and feasibility of using electronic mail user groups across college campuses to explore and extend thinking about education issues in general and about multicultural literature in particular were also focus topics for the authors.

Heidi McKenna discusses and defines ethnobibliotherapy as a "pedagogic strategy employing bibliotherapeutic instructional strategies which foster identification, catharsis, and insight using works by authors representing races or ethnic cultures other than one's own for the purpose of the development of racial/ethnic identity" (p. 7, manuscript). The author specifically addresses race and ethnic identity development, and believes that this strategy will make teacher candidates better equipped to bridge race and ethnic barriers in their classrooms.

A partnership between Delano Joint Union High School District and National University is discussed in the paper *Process Meets Product: Where Technology Enhances Staff Development.* Maria Natera-Riles and Nancy Smith-Dramis explain how this partnership was successful in creating a new approach to staff development in general and CLAD (Cross-Cultural Language Academic Development) certification in particular. The participants of their study said in a survey that they acquired "essential teaching strategies for reaching the language minority students and at the same time implemented Internet research skills for classroom use" (p. 3, manuscript). They also benefitted by creating school and teacher home pages on the net.

Ain't Nobody Can Talk About Things Being About Theirselves, by Kimberly Ott, is a paper which addresses the origins of Black English, grammar, structure and sound rule in West African language, and in Black English. Ott also discusses how Black English is not just a matter of words, but is important to the social and psychological identity of a person. Ott discusses Black English's impact in classrooms, interaction of learning styles and dialect, misconceptions surrounding Black English, and concludes that a better understanding of Black English will help teachers develop quality learning experiences for the speakers and writers of Black English in their classrooms.

Transformative Curriculum Development Through Exploration of Identities of Self and Others is a chapter that introduces teachers throughout the elementary grades to experiences which will be helpful in the development of a transformative multicultural curriculum. Irene Shigaki and Kelly Holloran also offer a four-step process for encouraging participants to engage in transformative curriculum development built on exploration of identities of self and others.

Nancy Smith-Dramis, Maria Natera-Riles, and Rosendo Garcia, in *Multicultural/Multilingual University Urban District Partnership That is Working*, offer a description of a partnership between National University's School of Education and Human Services and the Sacramento City Unified School District. They address how the university and the school district worked together to certify the school district's teachers in teaching their multicultural/multilingual students skills in learning English and other subjects.

Write From the Edge, by Derek Smith, is the title of a creative writing seminar designed specifically for students who are "courting the fringes". The author describes this seminar as one that "speaks to youth who will not listen," to youth unmotivated and to youth who have not challenged themselves. Smith states that the educational objective is to "provide an opportunity for teenage to define for themselves what they value and to translate these values into concrete goals". He also states that this work "begins the creative process of self-determination, self-expression and self-actualization" (p. 3, manuscript).

Fred Stopsky, in *Crime: The Neglected Area of Multicultural Education*, examines the relationship between crime and ethnicity and race within American society. He discusses the manner in which values and beliefs of ethnic and racial groups have been criminalized and how the patterns of scapegoating peoples as constituting criminal classes have changed. The author suggests that studying the history of crime enables young people to more accurately understand crime as a social definition by those in power.

In *STAR, (university Students Talk About Race with secondary students)*, Douglas Warring, Sally Hunter, and Kerry Dean Frank describe the STAR program, which was created by People for the American way in North Carolina as a tribute to the university students who led the Greensboro civil rights sit-ins. They outline the program, brought to Minnesota in 1996, and discuss some of the issues and comments made by students and teachers about how the use of such a program in today's schools represents one of the many elements contained in ideas currently being espoused by multiculturalism and critical pedagogy.

Glenn Doston and Samuel Bolden discuss *Classroom Techniques and Behaviors that can be Utilized by Teachers to Meet the Diverse Needs of Students While Enhancing the Teaching Learning Process.* The authors discuss how preparing teachers who are culturally responsible should be at the top of the list in the preparation to deliver and ensure better education for all students. These two authors argue that the goal to prepare teachers to be culturally responsible is necessary to reduce the disparities in achievement among diverse students. Also, Doston and Bolden discuss techniques and behaviors that teachers may use which will at the same time enhance the teaching/learning process.

Angela Paccione and Barbara McWhorter in *Multicultural Perspective Transformation of Teachers: The Impact of Cultural Immersion* review the educational literature examining the arguments and ideas about what it takes to become a multicultural person. They describe Project Promise a program that uses "best practices" from the teacher educational literature to prepare teachers. Based upon their study of the project Paccione and McWhorter argue that "cultural immersion field experiences have the potential to significantly impact teacher preparation programs in the United States" (p. manuscript).

Finally, several have worked very hard to make the publications of these proceedings possible. First it is important to applaud Jeff Bohls for his diligence and scholarly effort in editing the manuscripts. Kim Wieczorek was also helpful in putting together this introductory chapter. Also, a special thanks to Joy Lei for her work on the proceedings. Finally, Jennifer Austin deserves many, many thanks for getting the manuscript camera ready.

Chapter One
Who Shall Have The Moral Courage
to Heal Racism In America?

G. Pritchy Smith
University of North Florida

The arc of a moral universe is long, but it bends toward justice.
Martin Luther King, Jr.

This article is the transcript of G. Pritchy Smith's keynote address at the 7th Annual NAME Conference in Albuquerque, New Mexico on October 31, 1997. At the end of Smith's address, a deeply moved audience spontaneously burst into a standing ovation. The tone of his message is personal and conversational. It speaks to the heart. With the exception of some minor editorial changes, Smith's address is printed as closely as possible as originally spoken.

I want to thank the NAME Planning Committee of the 1997 Annual Conference for this opportunity to share some of my thinking about education in the United States and its role in creating a more fair, just, democratic, and antiracist society. Before I begin, let me say that I consider this opportunity to speak at the NAME conference one of the highest honors that I will ever receive in my career as an educator. I have titled this address "Who Shall Have the Moral Courage to Heal Racism In America?"

Some of you in the audience, at this very moment, may be asking yourselves, "Why in the world is this white boy with the ponytail standing before the microphone? What in the world does he know about racism?" Before I have finished today, I hope I have convinced most of you that "the problem of racism" in the United States is the responsibility of us all, most especially the responsibility of those of us who are white, and <u>absolutely</u> the responsibility of every one of this nation's educators.

The truth is that only a fool would voluntarily choose to speak on the topic of racism at a national conference. After all, racism is a difficult topic to talk about. However, I chose to speak on racism for that very reason and others -- because it is <u>so difficult to talk about</u> and because the conversation about racism <u>must be</u> a part of the broader discipline of multicultural education. I am also speaking on the topic of racism because of something Rose Duhon-Sells, the Mother of NAME, said to me over twenty years ago.

In order to understand the story behind why I am standing before the microphone today, you have to know the bigger story of my relationship to Rose Duhon-Sells. Rose and I became friends about twenty years ago when she heard me deliver an address in Memphis. You see, for many years now Rose has seen me as "that white boy who is good to call on when you need someone to tell white folks what to do so they'll do right for a change." Rose's perception may be true, but I can tell you that I am not before this microphone today <u>just</u> "to tell us white folks what we ought to do." I am here today to talk to <u>all</u> of us. When I say I am here to speak to <u>all</u> of us, I mean every person in this room who has ever felt marginalized, every person who has ever felt locked out, every person who has ever felt like other people considered them "different," low-down," or "no-good," simply because somebody else did not like "who we were" or "what we believed". When I say <u>all</u> of us, I also mean those of us who have often felt confused regarding how to do the right thing about racism. <u>But when I say I am before this microphone today to talk to all of us, I mean, most of all</u> -- those of us who teach. No matter how different we may be from each other, we are here as well-intentioned people who have dedicated our careers to teaching others.

I am going to talk about racism but not about racism alone. Indeed, it is true that racism cuts deeply into the fabric of this society, but it is the bigger beast of bigotry that wields the sword that continues to prune back this nation -- that prevents this nation from flowering into

the full democracy it could become. In my mind, bigotry is bigotry --
whether it is based on race, ethnicity, or culture or whether it is based
on income level, gender, sexual orientation or any other characteristic
that marks one as "different."

Those of you in the audience who have heard me speak before
know that I always do two things. The first is that I always tell a story,
no matter who the audience is, for I believe it is in the voices of
ordinary people that we find the great lessons of life played out. The
second thing I do is tell the audience exactly what I am going to talk
about. So, after I have told a story I am going to ask you to think along
with me on two subtopics: (1) how racism and its peculiar
characteristics play themselves out in the American education system
from public schools through institutions of higher education and (2)
what teachers must do -- what public and private education's
responsibilities are -- to recreate America as an antiracist, more fair,
just, and democratic society.

T.J. and the Education of a White Boy

I am not an authority on racism, but I have been affected by it
all my life from childhood to the present and I have thought about
racism and education since I was an undergraduate student at the
University of Texas in 1959. The story I have selected to provide as a
context for the "meat" of my address is a personal story. My personal
experience, after all, if not the best is the only lens I have for examining
racism. When I first wrote this story a few years ago, I titled it "T.J.,
A Great Teacher: The Education of a White Boy." It is the story of an
experience I had at the University of Texas in the summer of 1959, an
experience that would change profoundly for the rest of my life the way
I would look at the world around me.

I was enrolled that summer in a Foundations of Education
course. In that class was Thomas Jefferson Johnson, who preferred to
be called "T.J." for short. For the most part, schools were still
segregated in Texas. In fact, in all my 15 years of schooling I had prior
to that class, T. J. was my first African American classmate. In the

beginning, perhaps T.J. was only a curiosity to me, but something told me that I wanted to know this young man better. One day when I was on the way to class, T.J. called out to me from where he was sitting under one of those grand spreading oak trees on the University of Texas campus. "Hey, Smith, you want a cup of coffee?" The idea sounded good to me. After all, I was growing up, I was twenty-years old, and I was away at college, drinking coffee now like a regular grown-up man, something college students did in those days whether they really liked coffee or not. T.J. pulled from his briefcase a thermos and poured me a cup of coffee. We began to have coffee together under that oak tree almost like a ritual, sometimes before and sometimes after class. At these meetings where we would drink coffee and talk, I learned that T.J. was a French teacher in a segregated black high school in Abilene, Texas. He was at the University of Texas to complete a degree and get a teaching certificate. I began comparing myself to T.J. I was chagrined that his vocabulary of English words far exceeded mine and that his pronunciation in French seemed flawless to me, a white boy, who even though I had fourteen credit hours of college level French, still pronounced such phrases as "MUR-SEA BOW-COOO, MAY-MWA-SELLE" with those long flat, dipthonged Texas vowel sounds. I could see that T.J. seemed more sophisticated and more intelligent than me. Sometimes T.J. talked about becoming "a great teacher" as if teaching were a special calling. I had never before heard anyone talk about teaching as T.J. did. And he also said things that frightened me sometimes. He used phrases I had never heard before like "the movement" and "freedom for the People."

You see, in order to understand the importance of my encounter with T.J., you have to remember what it was like in 1959. Neither T.J. nor I were really supposed to be at the University of Texas--T.J. because he was black and I because I was what some of the White fraternity boys called "white-trash." After all, I was not the son of a banker, a doctor, a lawyer, or some well-to-do business man. I was straight off the farm. I was so politically naive that it had not even occurred to me that the reason T.J. and I were drinking coffee from a thermos bottle was that there were no integrated cafes or lunch-counters where the two of us could sit down together in the Austin, Texas of 1959.

One Friday night about mid-way through the semester, I was strolling by myself down Gaudelupe Street, known as "the drag" to college students in those days. As I passed the Longhorn Theatre, a movie house, I noticed a strange phenomenon. The line of people in front of the Longhorn Theatre stretched the entire length of the block, and I noticed the line was really a double line of partners, one black and one white. Then I heard someone call out, "Pritchy, over here, over here!" I looked around to see T.J. standing in this unusual line of people. I walked over, and he asked, "Why don't you join us, Pritchy?" I asked in return, "What in the world are you doin'?" He retorted, "We're trying to integrate the theatre, fool. This is how it works. You see, we stand in line in tandem, a black and white, and tie up the line so that people who really want to see the movie give up and go on home instead of standing in line all night to get their tickets. When we get to the ticket window, my white partner here asks if he and I can buy a ticket. Of course, the ticket seller always says no and we go back to the end of the line and start over. It's a kind of boycott. The theatre owner is either going to have to integrate the theatre or go broke."

T.J. asked again, "Pritchy, why don't you join us?" I faltered as I tried to speak. I stammered "I, uh, uh, I don't know. I don't think so. I....uh." After all, at twenty-years old I had never in my life taken a public action against anything. I had never even stood up for myself when I had been done a wrong, much less ever stand _up_ or _against_ authority that had done someone else a wrong. I remember clearly in less than a second the expression on T.J.'s face changed. His smiling face became stoic and hard. His eyes transformed suddenly from the happy twinkle I had known to a piercing, cold, steely stare. With eyes of ice he looked straight into my eyes and said "Pritchy, if you are not in this line, you are in the wrong line." Then he looked away from me. I felt my scalp tighten. I felt chills run up my spine. I began to back away, almost stumbling from the impact of his words on me as I continued walking down the street. As I walked, his words kept ringing in my ears. I kept hearing over and over in my head "Pritchy, if you are not in this line, you are in the wrong line." I thought about those words all weekend, again and again. I tried to understand what was happening inside me. I had no prior social context within which to place this experience. You have to remember that this was prior to Dr. Martin Luther King, Jr. and Montgomery and Selma.

T.J.'s words worried me all weekend. On Monday, I started to class early. I had to see T.J. I went to the oak tree, but T.J. was not there. I went to class. T.J. was not in class. The next class day, T.J. was neither at the oak tree nor in class. A week passed. No T.J. Then the following week, T.J. was seated in the classroom. Acting like nothing had happened the week before, I said "Hi, T.J. Let's have coffee after class." T.J. did not look at me. He didn't speak. He looked past me with the same icy eyes I had seen on that Friday night in front of the theatre. After class, without a word he walked past me and out the door. T.J. had cut me out of his world.

Another week passed. Finally, when I could stand the inner turmoil no longer, I joined the boycott, an experience that was to affect me forever. Some bad things happened before the protest ended. For example, one night policemen leaped from trucks, swinging their nightsticks. I had never seen policemen swing nightsticks as they plunged into a panicked crowd, hitting men and women in their stomachs and heads. I was terrified by the shrieks and cries from the panicked crowd of protesters and even more terrified by the blood that was being splattered on me as the police hit people, coming closer and closer to me where I was pinned by the crowd against the building. I could see that these uniformed men were not just trying to breakup a protest. They wanted to kill us. I was lucky that night. I survived without injury, but it was that night that I realized, for the first time, that police in those days were there to preserve a racist social order, not to protect protesters who were exercising their Constitutional right to assemble peacefully.

Not all of the time T.J. and I spent together was as frightful or even serious, for that matter. Although we worked hard that summer mimeographing and passing out flyers and always making certain we took our turn at the boycott down at the Longhorn Theatre, we had some fun too. Some Saturday nights we would go to Floyd's Blue Note Club on the Hill, one of the black sections of Austin, located near Hustin-Tillotson College, Austin's only historically black college. If we were lucky, we might catch someone famous like Jimmy Reed wailing his own kind of blues, live, at Floyd's. After Floyd's closed about 2:00 a.m., we would cap off the night at Earl's Chicken Shack, an after-hours club where two hungry under-aged young men could eat and get one last drink of whiskey before the sun came up.

On other occasions, T.J. would be in one of his mischievous moods. During these times, he would pull some prank on me, stamp both feet like he was going to laugh himself to death, and then say, "Smith, you are one dumb white boy." I did not mind though. Somehow it did not seem like an insult.

At the end of that hot summer, in August, T.J. and I parted ways. T.J. had to return to Abilene to start a new school year, even though, as T.J. said, "Most of the kids at the Negro School will be picking cotton until the end of September." We met one last time under the oak tree. The Longhorn Theatre was still segregated. We felt surrounded by the kind of sadness a person experiences when he tries as hard as he can but does not win, the sadness of an unachieved triumph. It was the feeling Langston Hughes must have been trying to capture when he wrote about "a dream deferred." As hard as we had tried, we felt like we had failed. We did not know at that moment that it would be nearly another year before the owner of the Longhorn Theatre would stand before the crowd of protestors to announce that henceforth the doors of the theatre would be open to all. It would be a great moment of triumph with the crowd cheering and tossing their caps and signs into the air -- a moment of joy that T.J. would not be there to experience.

We had met at the oak tree to have one last cup of coffee and say goodbye, but we did not know how. When it became time for T.J.

to leave, there was an awkward uneasy moment, as if both of us were groping for some words that would sound right -- like so often happens when men "just don't know how to act." Then, T.J. broke the silence and said, "Smith, you're O.K. for a white boy. You're gonna be alright."

I stood there a good long while watching T.J. grow smaller as he walked down the street toward the bus station. I remember feeling like something in the world had changed that summer -- like I was not ever going to be the same again, like maybe I knew for the first time that people have a choice. They can stand in the wrong line. Or they can stand in the right line.

On that last day I would see T.J., there was no way we could have known that T.J., just five years later, would be killed in the Vietnam war. It was just a few years ago, in fact, that I found myself standing before the Vietnam Memorial in Washington D.C., weeping almost uncontrollably as I touched my fingers to the letters of his name carved in the stone. The only words I could whisper aloud were "T.J., you did become a great teacher."

I learned many things from T.J. and our experience with the boycott, far too many things, in fact, than I can tell about in the limited time I have for delivering this address. However, the most important thing I learned was about myself. I found out that it would take far more than just learning to like the taste of coffee to become a man. I learned that "I could not stand up as a man until I stood up, first, for someone else," that "I would not become a man until I stood against injustice." It was this single lesson that would enable me later on in life to understand the full meaning of Martin Niemuller's famous words when I would read them for the first time. I am referring to Niemuller's passage about his inaction in Nazi Germany when he said:

First they came for the Jews and I did not speak out because I was not a Jew. Then they came for the communists and I did not speak out because I was not a communist. Then they came for the trade unionists and I did not speak out because I was not a trade unionist. Then they came for me, and there was nobody left to speak out for me.

The experience taught me also to question this society. It enabled me to begin to understand what James Baldwin (1963) was saying in his famous 1963 speech, "A Talk to Teachers," when he said:

> Now if I were a teacher...dealing with Negro children...I would try to teach them...that those streets, those houses, those dangers, those agonies by which they are surrounded are criminal... I would teach (the Negro child) that he doesn't have to be bound by the expediencies of any given (government) Administration, any given policy, any given time--that he has the right and the necessity to examine everything. (p.60)

The experience helped me understand what Lerone Bennett, the African American historian, meant when he wrote that "an educator in a system of oppression is either a revolutionary or an oppressor" (as cited in Hale, 1978, p.7). It was my experience at the University of Texas that enabled me not to respond to James Baldwin and Lerone Bennett by calling them "radical" or "militant," as did so many of my peers, but to respond, instead, by beginning to question the injustices in this society.

Ultimately, my experience with T.J. along with other experiences would lead to my belief that education must be multicultural and social reconstructionist. So, therein lies the thesis of my address -- in the story I have just told lies the genesis of my thinking about what the responsibilities are of public and private education, K-higher education, to heal the racism that makes a mockery of this democratic society. Many times since I first met T.J., over thirty-seven years ago, I have asked myself why I learned more lessons about racism outside the classroom than in the classroom at The University of Texas. I have asked myself, "Why has racism been a taboo topic in a teacher's education?" I have asked, "Why has the study of racism and antiracism not been a part of the civic education of young people in our schools?"

Who Shall Have the Moral Courage to Heal Racism in America?

Today, there seems to be a considerable amount of disagreement in our profession as to what a teacher should know and believe about racism.

So, let me turn from the story of T.J. to the substance of my address, which is an attempt to answer the question, "Who shall have the moral courage to heal racism in America?"

Who Shall Have the Moral Courage to Heal Racism and Bigotry in America?

Before we can begin to answer the question -- Who shall have the moral courage to heal the racism and bigotry in America? -- we must examine the nature of racism, not only with regard to how racism has played itself out in the history of the United States but also some of the *peculiar* characteristics of racism.

The first peculiar characteristic of racism is its historical tenacity. Racism is a very old problem. It has been with us in the Americas since the first Europeans set foot here. Despite the presence of some European Americans who always fought against racism, it has found expression in the official U.S. government policy of genocide in the treatment of First Americans, the enslavement of people of African descent, the Chinese Exclusion Act, the internment of Japanese Americans and the seizure of their property during World War II, and the almost continuous resistance to civil rights for people of color in the United States. Although it is an old problem that has been ignored, particularly in our history books, it has not gone away. Loewen's (1995) study of the twelve most frequently used high school American history books in high schools found that only one linked the causes of slavery to white racism. I suspect that, when W.E.B. Du Bois (1968) said 100 years ago that "the problem of the 20th century is the problem of the color line (p.221), he had no idea that the color line" would also be the great problem of the 21st century. Racism seems not to be the type of problem that goes away if we ignore it.

In addition to being a very "old problem," a second peculiar characteristic of racism is that it is a problem that so many people deny even exists, no matter how much experiential or empirical evidence proves its existence. On the one hand, people like Morris Dees (1996) of the Southern Poverty Law Center and news reporters remind us almost daily that racism and bigotry run rampant in our American society. Consider these recent events in our public schools:

> In suburban Greenwich, Connecticut five white high school students encode the words "kill all niggers" into the school's yearbook captions.

> Some students at Manhattan's Norman Thomas High School send a Jewish teacher a note that includes a swastika and the words "kill all the Jew."

> The principal of Randolph County High School, Alabama, in 1994 threatens to cancel a high school prom because interracial couples might attend and refers to a mixed race student as a "mistake" her white and black parents should not have made.

> In Lake County, Florida the school board, controlled by Christian Fundamentalists, votes that teachers *must* teach that "America is a superior culture."

Consider, also, that hate crimes and harassment based on race have steadily been reported since the mid-1980s with increasing, not diminishing frequency on university and college campuses, some of which are considered the most prestigious of our Big Ten and Ivy League institutions (Lennon, 1988).

Consider this list of events in our larger society:

> The FBI reported over "7,000 victims of hate crimes in 1994 alone." (Dees, 1996, p.4).

Studies continue to show that prestigious banks and loan institutions continue to disapprove mortgage loan applications on the basis of race.

Television sting operations continue to expose employment agencies, realtors, and property and rental companies that discriminate on the basis of race.

In February, 1996 a white law enforcement officer in the State of Maryland refuses to give mouth-to-mouth resuscitation to an African American woman and she dies.

No sooner than the horrifying images of the Rodney King beating begin to fade, we see on our televisions uniformed men beating our Latino brothers and sisters along a California freeway. Then, this year in 1997, police officers in Brooklyn's 70th precinct station house allegedly sodomize with a toilet plunger Abner Louima, a Haitian immigrant.

National leaders show no shame in showing their bigotry in public. As Dees (1996) notes, "Republican Senator Alphonse D'Amato mocks 'little Judge Ito'" (p.4); Republican "House majority whip Dick Armey refers to his Congressional colleague Barney Frank as 'Barney Fag';" and "Republican Presidential contender Bob Dornan calls some of his political adversaries 'lesbian spear chuckers'" (p.4).

GOP Presidential Primary candidate Pat Buchanan says in a 1996 campaign speech, "Women are simply not endowed by nature with the same measures of single-minded ambition and the will to succeed in the fierce competitive world of Western capitalism.

With this kind of misguided moral leadership among political leaders, who shall have the moral courage to heal racism in America?

On the other hand, despite the evidence to the contrary, a majority of white Americans deny the existence of racism and bigotry and deny the resulting effect of discrimination. For example, the National Conference (1994) found in its survey on intergroup relations, titled Taking American's Pulse, that a majority of white Americans believe the citizens of color in the United States simply are not discriminated against. The same poll, however, found that African Americans, Latino Americans, and Asian Americans believed just the opposite -- that bigotry and discrimination continue to be the reality.

In addition to being a very old problem, and a problem that people deny exists, a third *peculiar* characteristic of racism is that it is a problem that no one seems to own. Although the same National Conference poll found that prejudice against other racial groups exists in all ethnic and racial groups, most of the research tells us that it is only a minority of Americans who will admit to being prejudiced. White Americans are less likely than persons of color to own up to and admit their prejudices. For example, another poll found that only 21% of white Americans would go on record as considering themselves biased against people of other races but that twice as many African Americans (41%) would claim their prejudices (Edwards, 1995).

Well, there you have it -- the enigma and irrationality of racism. In short, what I have just said is that racism is *a very old, non-existing problem that no one owns.* So, who shall have the moral courage to heal this "old, non-existing problem that no one owns."? If the answer to this question is educators, let us examine the students in teacher education programs for a moment.

Teacher Education Students

By now those of us at this conference who are teacher educators can almost quote from memory Nancy Zimpher's (1989) well-known and often referenced profile of the "typical preservice teacher." That is, the typical preservice teacher is a monolingual white female from a low-middle or middle class suburban or rural home who wants to teach children who are just like herself. Other demographic profiles tell us that 90% of our preservice teachers are white and less than 10% are students of color (AACTE, 1987). Research tells us that many of our preservice teachers simply do not have the prerequisite attitudes or lifestyles patterns regarding diversity that would enable them to teach children who are different from themselves (Ahlquist, 1991; Beyer, 1991; Ladson-Billings, 1991). In fact, most preservice teachers say they don't want to teach minority children, *except as a last resort* (Contreras, 1988). In truth, most of our students were socialized by their families to live monoracial and monocultural lifestyles as the preferred norm. Some of the studies tell us that a majority of our preservice teachers believe that the home background of minority public school students is so bad that it just can't be overcome by education. Personally, I am far less worried about the home backgrounds of minority students in schools than I am about the "backgrounds" of cultural and racial illiteracy of our teacher education students. Finally, another body of research literature tells us that the attitudes and lifestyle patterns of preservice teachers are extremely resistant to change (Grant & Secada, 1990).

Some of us are shocked -- astounded sometimes -- by the depth of bigotry among so many of our preservice teachers presently in training. My own assessment of today's preservice teachers in undergraduate training is that among them is the largest, most outspoken group of racists I have encountered since the beginning of my teaching career at the university level in 1967, almost thirty years ago. Not all of our students are racists, of course, but too many are. From my own university classroom experiences, my estimate is that about one-third of our teacher education students are *hard-core intractable racists*. Another third of them I would classify as *moderate racists*, young people who are relatively unaware of their racism, who, in fact, are blind to their own racism, and have not even given much thought to their racial attitudes. Another twenty percent I would classify as *non-racists*, young people whom we might describe "as good kids who want to do the right thing" but are rather passive and quiet about their thoughts on race. Another ten to twelve percent, perhaps 3 or 4 out every class of 30, arrive in my classes as *antiracists*, young people who have the prerequisite belief system to become social reconstructionists -- young people who want to reconstruct a fairer, more just, anti-racist democracy. This profile of the preservice teacher begs us to ask the question: "Who shall have the moral courage to heal racism in America?"

Ourselves, Educators

Let us turn from our students for a moment and look at ourselves -- the public and private school teachers and the college professors. If we are honest with ourselves, we are very much like the preservice teachers. Ninety-five percent of professors of education are white European Americans; and as Haberman (1992) has noted, less than 5% of us have taught in an "urban" school and only 10% of the universities where we work are located in the great urban centers of racial and cultural diversity. With respect to other college professors and K-12 teachers, most of us are monolingual and live monocultural lifestyles. Our closest friends are likely to be of the same race. We are likely to attend same-race churches, live in same-race neighborhoods, and, particularly if we are white, send our children to predominately white, middle class suburban schools with limited racial integration. Yet, like the teacher education students and other college students, some of us depart from this profile norm.

Who, then, shall have the moral courage to heal racism in America? If the answer to this question is "those of us who teach," what, then, must we do?

What Must Educators Do?

Many of us assembled here at this conference agonize over this "race thing." Those of us who teach teachers in the universities agonize over the moral dilemma we face each year when we graduate teachers whose racism and other forms of bigotry are so strong and deep that they cannot help but do damage to the children they will teach.

What must universities and teacher educators do to prepare antiracist teachers for diverse classrooms? I can tell you it will take far more than just "culturally diverse field experiences" prescribed by the NCATE standards. First, we must take ownership of this problem, this disease we call racism and its related viruses that constitute the many mutations of bigotry, and we must set goals and missions for our teacher education programs that clearly state our moral intent that we are not willing to accept the minimum standard of teachers who are just tolerant and without bias but that we intend to graduate teachers who are antiracists, who are social activists against bigotry --teachers who will create a new world order where racism and bigotry are unacceptable. My point here is that our mission statements should express the moral imperative that we are not preparing teachers to teach in the world as it is but we are preparing teachers to change that world.

The second thing we must do is infuse what I call "the knowledge bases for diversity" into the center and forefront of the teacher education and liberal arts and humanities curriculum. Limitations on my time today, do not enable me to describe all thirteen of these knowledge bases in detail. Let me simply refer you to the description of these knowledge bases in the forthcoming book sponsored by AACTE[1]. I must, however, take enough time to describe two of these thirteen knowledge bases.

The first knowledge base I speak of is the one I have called in my writings "Knowledge Base 8: The Foundations of Racism." No teacher should graduate from a teacher preparation program without having thoroughly studied *the foundations of racism.* In this knowledge base,

---

[1] The knowledge bases for diversity referenced in the text of this address may be found in Knowledge Bases for Diversity in Teacher Education, a manuscript presently targeted to be published as a book by the American Association for Colleges of Teacher Education (AACTE) in 1998.

(a) preservice teachers must study the true history of prejudice, discrimination, and racism in the United States;

(b) they must study the theory and research on how racism is integrated into one's identity and personality structure;

(c) they must study the effects of racism on members of the dominant white culture and on members of minority cultures;

(d) they must study the theory and research on "changing bigoted attitudes"; and

(e) they must examine a variety of anti-bias and antiracist curricula that have been developed for use in the K-12 school curriculum.

In addition to the knowledge base on racism and other forms of bigotry, we must infuse into our teacher education programs the knowledge base on the educational policies and practices that are harmful to minority and low-income students -- what I have called "Knowledge Base 9" in my scholarship. This knowledge base enables preservice teachers to understand institutionalized racism and other forms of institutionalized bigotry in the educational system. In this knowledge base preservice teachers must study the research on the harmful and inequitable effects of using standardized tests to allocate educational opportunity, tests that favor the white middle class students and disproportionately disfavor minorities and low-income students. They must study the use of ability grouping and curriculum tracking to segregate students by race under the same school roof. They must study the negative effects of racially segregated schools. They must study the use of inequitable funding formulas that cheat minority and low-income students out of equal opportunities for high quality education and the use of school choice, privatization, and vouchers to create even greater inequities and racial segregation in the educational system. In short, this knowledge base exposes attempts of those who have power and privilege to create a meritocratic rather than a democratic educational system. As we teacher educators and other college professors present these two knowledge bases, we must own up to our own absence of courage to root out the racism and bigotry institutionalized in our own admission and certification policies that use standardized instruments that have no predictive validity but have, as my own research has found, eliminated over 100,000 minority candidates from the teaching profession.[2]

If educators do not do these things, then who will have the moral courage to heal racism in this society?

Finally, let me turn to what educators must do at a personal level -- as individuals. Over the long term, what we teach may not be nearly as powerful as what we model. It is likely that long after our students have forgotten the specific facts, the formal theories, and skills, what they will remember most of all is how we teachers lived our personal lives. So it is important that we model a multicultural and multiracial lifestyle. It is important for our students to see us having interracial friendships. It is important for our students to see that not only do we believe that a racially integrated education is superior to a segregated education but that we actually send our children to integrated schools. And, most important of all, our students must see us not merely as non-racists, but they must see that we are antiracists, actively engaged in our communities fighting racism and other forms of bigotry. In the final analysis, we must look into ourselves -- as Ghandi put it, "We must be the change we wish to see in the world."

---

[2] More information regarding research on the use of admission tests and certification tests to eliminate minority teachers can be found in the following citation: Smith, G.P. (1988, Spring) Tomorrow's white teachers: A response to the Holmes Group. Journal of Negro Education, 58 (2), 178-194.

A Final Word

We multicultural educators have a vision of what America can become. We believe that education can be a powerful force to make this a more democratic society. That vision is in danger today. I do not have to tell the committed in this audience that these are turbulent political times and, as Carl Grant (1992) has said, "We are in a war for the minds of our children." Neither do I have to tell you that new, foul breezes are once again flapping the banner of racism over this nation. I do not have to tell you that the banner of racism is flying proudly over the right wing halls of the Republican-controlled Congress in Washington at this very moment. I do not have to tell those of you who know your history that much of the "Contract with America," the assault on affirmative action, and such initiatives as California's Proposition 209 are nothing more than a thinly disguised package of Jim Crow laws just like those passed by Congress and state legislatures to reverse Reconstruction after the Civil War. You know that. I know that.

America stands at a crossroads today. We shall either become a great multicultural society -- the first truly multicultural and multiracial democracy on the planet -- or we shall revert to our most sinister persona that describes the worst part of our historical past, a compassion less society in which only the elite have power and privilege and in which we judge people not by the content of their character but by their race, their culture, their gender, their exceptionality, or their sexual orientation. We can be a better nation than that.

It will not be easy to do what we must do. But if we change the knowledge bases that teachers study and if we, ourselves, model an antiracist lifestyle, we will give the next generations of teachers and students the moral courage they need to do likewise. No one has described what we must do any better than Robert F. Kennedy (1966) when he said:

> Each time a person stands for an ideal, or acts to improve the lot of others, or strikes out against injustice, he or she sends forth a tiny ripple of hope. And crossing each other

from a million different centers of energy and daring, those ripples build a current that can sweep down the mightiest walls of oppression and resistance.

Few are willing to embrace the disapproval of their fellows, the censure of their colleagues, the wrath of their society. Moral courage is a rarer commodity than bravery in battle or great intelligence. Yet it is the one essential vital quality for those who seek to change a world that yields most painfully to change.

So, who shall have the moral courage to heal racism in America? The answer is "us" -- we multicultural educators, we social reconstructionists. It is the only answer we can afford to give. It is from us that the next generation of teachers and their students must learn the simple lesson that T.J., "that great teacher," taught so well -- "If you are not in this line, you are in the wrong line."

References

Ahlquist, R. (1991). Position and imposition: Power in a
     multicultural foundations class. Journal of Negro Education, 60
     (2), 158-169.
American Association of Colleges for Teacher Education, (1987).
     Teaching teachers: Facts and figures. Washington, DC: Author
Baldwin, J. (1963, December 21). A talk to teachers. Saturday
     Review, pp. 42-44, 60.
Beyer, L.E. (1991). Teacher education, reflective inquiry, and
     moral action. In B.R. Tabachnick and K.M. Zeichner (Eds.),
     Inquiry-oriented practice in teacher education (pp. 113-129).
     New York: Falmer Press.
Contreras, A. (1980). Multicultural attitudes and knowledge of
     education students at a midwestern university. In C.A. Heid
     (Ed.), Multicultural education: Knowledge and perceptions (pp.
     63-78). Bloomington, IN: Indiana University, Center for Urban

and Multicultural Education.

Dees, M. (1996, spring). Break the chain. Teaching Tolerance, 5 (1), p. 4.

Du Bois, W.E.B. (1968). The souls of Black folks. In Three Negro classics (p. 221). New York: Avon (Original work published 1905).

Edwards, A. (1995, November 10). Race in America. Family Circle, pp. 83-84, 86-87.

Grant, C. (1992). Unpublished speech. ATE Summer Workshop, University of Wisconsin, Parkside.

Grant, C.A., and Secada, W.G. (1990). Preparing teachers for cultural diversity. In W.R. Houston, M. Haberman, and J. Sikula (Eds.), Handbook of research on teacher education (pp. 403-422). New York: Macmillan.

Haberman, M. (1992). Unpublished speech. ATE Summer Workshop, University of Wisconsin, Parkside.

Hale, J. (1978). Cultural influences on learning styles of Afro-American children. In L. Morris (Ed.), Extracting learning styles from social/cultural diversity (pp. 7-27). Norman, OK: Southwest Teacher Corps Network (Grant No. G007-700-119, Teacher Corps, U.S. Office of Education, Department of Health, Education, and Welfare).

Kennedy, R.F. (1966, June 6). Day of Affirmation address. South Africa: University of Capetown.

Ladson-Billings, G. (1991). When difference means disaster: Reflections on a teacher education strategy for countering resistance to diversity. Paper presented at the annual meeting of the American Educational Research Association, Chicago, IL.

Lennon, T. (Producer), (1988). Racism 101 [video recording]. (Available from PBS Video, Alexandria, VA)

Loewen, J.W. (1995). Lies my teacher told me: Everything your American history textbook got wrong. New York: New Press.

The National Conference (1994). Taking America's pulse: A

summary report of The National Conference survey on intergroup relations. New York: Author

Zimpher, N. (1989). The RATE Project: A profile of teacher education students. Journal of Teacher Education, 40 (6), 27-30.

Chapter Two
Multicultural Relationships in Organizations:
Exemplar Modules for Education and Training

Sharon Chard-Yaron
California School of Professional Psychology
San Diego, CA

Jon Kingsbury
United States International University
San Diego, CA

Martie Lubetkin
United States International University
San Diego, CA

==============================

Introduction
This paper will serve to describe a presentation whose purpose was to introduce participants to education and training modules which emphasize both instructional delivery and content. Prototype modules on the topics of (1) power distance in cross-cultural education settings, and (2) racial consciousness, are utilized to demonstrate the potential of "module construction" as a learning and assessment strategy, especially for courses that demand and deserve an "active learning" approach to subject matter.

The modules utilized in this presentation were developed by doctoral students in multicultural education as projects for a course entitled "Multicultural Relationships in Organizations," designed and taught by the lead presenter. It was hoped that the course, offered through the School of Education, would model strategies that would lead from mindless memorization towards goals of retention, understanding, and active use of knowledge. Inherent in the structure of the course were the following non-yielding parameters:

1. the course would emphasize a linkage between course content area and a repertoire of corresponding teaching/training methodologies,
2. assessment of student learning would be interwoven within the context of teaching and would be based on the "construction" of a product, i.e., a one-stop resource module for education and training that contained *both* substantive content and guidelines for instructional delivery, and
3. the product was to serve as a proactive response to educators who claim we warn them to stay away from "drill and kill" and "stand and deliver," but don't tell them how.

Instructions for the Module Project, featuring the various components along with the criteria for assessment, are reproduced in Figure 1.

Figure 1: Instructions for Module Project I. Introduction
*   this section establishes the purpose, focus, and rationale for the material to come, and desired outcomes;
*   the following phrases may be helpful in organizing your introduction:

"The purpose of this module is to _____"

"The subject is important or significant because _____"

"This module focuses on _____"

"Following active participation in this module participants will be able to _____"

II. Self-Assessment Exercise

- to allow participants to discover what they already know, what their attitudes are, and to identify existing gaps/aspects of your topic that need attention
- may be an inventory, pre-test, critical incident format (if you are not using a critical incident format in part III), etc.

III. Key Concepts, Including Short Literature Review

- presentations of key concepts that should provide participants with concepts/knowledge and frameworks related to your topic
- from the material you write for this section, one should be able to prepare short lectures without having to do extensive additional research; additionally, this material should be able to serve as assigned reading

IV. Case Studies, Critical Incidents

- mainly to promote in participants feelings of empathy and/or identification
- provides the opportunity to have your module come alive - here you allow participants to, in effect, become part of the action

V. Exercise for Application

- may include simulation, role play, group discussions, game board, film clip (if you provide the film clip), etc.
- topics to be included in this section:

    + goals of the exercise   +   time requirements

    + materials   +   instructions

Figure 1: Instructions for Module Project (continued)
VI. Guide for Debriefing

- you do not have to repeat section IV., but include here some guide for the debriefing process (i.e., possible answers to discussion questions, what the teacher/trainer should bring up to participants after completion of the actual exercise, etc.) to make this component less unpredictable for teacher/trainer.

VII. Suggestions for Homework Exercises/Student Projects

- types of homework, research, or collaborative projects might enhance student learning?

VIII. Selected References

- suggested readings. . . additional resources (texts, films, videos, etc.)

Criteria for Assessment of Module Project

1. Were the different components of the module completed on time?
2. Did you fulfill your editing responsibilities to your classmates? to yourself?
3. Did you provide accuracy and depth of information, quality of each component?
4. Did you follow the guidelines? Did you turn in all versions of your work, marked accordingly?
5. Is there evidence of original synthesis in application component?
6. **Oral Presentation:** Did you use the time to gain optimal feedback on all components? Were you ready?
7. **Final Revision:** Did you address the issues/critiques/suggestions of the group? Did you address editing suggestions of group members brought up during the course of the term?
8. The degree to which you have demonstrated (through this project) mastery of outcomes described in the course syllabus/objectives.

The topics represented in the two prototype modules that were part of the presentation are:

1. *Who's in Charge Here?: The Phenomenon of Power Distance in Cross-Cultural Educational Settings,*
2. *What Are You?: Increasing Racial Consciousness Through Biracial Teachers' Ethnographic Narratives.*

These sequences include exemplar strategies for assessment of prior knowledge or opinion along with a short literature review and other topical information to facilitate an instructor's utilization of the material as a "one-stop resource." In addition, active learning and strategies for interaction are modeled utilizing case study analysis, critical incident design, and/or experiential exercises. Guidelines for debriefing and suggestions for additional activities are also provided. It was hoped that by the end of the presentation participants would be able to:

1. articulate an understanding of the subject matters covered in the presented prototype modules,
2. identify "active learning" instructional strategies related to teaching the above mentioned module topics, and
3. apply similar modular design to their own teaching/course construction.

In addition to the topics represented in the presentation as described, other students worked on projects related to areas often omitted from standard texts and based on domestic multicultural environments, such as: a cross-cultural view of leadership, motivation, and decision making; cultural differences and specifics in the acculturation process; attribution theory and world view; risk and resiliency: a multicultural perspective; and cultural differences in conformity, compliance, and obedience. The finished products, two of which are included here, represent a successful alternative to frontal teaching and the ubiquitous term paper. They serve to confirm the potential of "module construction" as a learning and assessment strategy, especially for courses that demand and deserve an "active learning" approach to subject matter.

Prototype Module #1: Who's in Charge Here?:
The Phenomenon of Power Distance in Cross-Cultural
Educational Settings
A cross-cultural training module by Martie Theleen Lubetkin

I. Introduction

> Hofstede (1991) defines power distance as a measurement of the extent to which the less powerful members of institutions and organizations within a country expect and accept that power is distributed unequally." (p. 28). Furthermore, he notes the distinction between institutions (basic elements of society: family, school, and community) and organizations (places where people work). In education, the power structure is quite obvious,...

Educational systems are historically composed of hierarchies of personnel who are organized from most to least powerful. In most cases, the members with the least power are the consumers, i.e., the students and their families. This is especially true of newly arrived immigrant families, who are both unfamiliar with the American educational system and often culturally disposed to trust in the judgments of professionals. The purpose of this module is to explore Hofstede's (1980, 1991) cultural dimension of "power distance" and its effect on the relationship between educators in the United States and recent immigrant students and their families.

Hofstede (1991) defines power distance as a measurement of "the extent to which less powerful members of organizations accept the unequal distribution of power" (p. 28). Furthermore, he notes the distinction between institutions (basic elements of society: family, school, and community) and organizations (places where people work). In education, the power structure is quite obvious, with the hierarchy moving down from state and federal lawmakers to school boards, district and school administrators, to teachers. In this schema, the students and their families are often left out completely. If they are included, they often perceive themselves as having little authority, if any at all, in the planning and execution of the educational program for their children.

This module focuses on the perceptions of power distance held by two distinct groups, who are generally expected to be advocates for children. They are the teachers and the families of recent immigrant students who arrive with limited ability to speak English and who have qualified for Special Education services.

II. Self-Assessment Exercise

Assume that you are an American educator, currently employed in a district whose population has been gradually changing over the past decade from a majority of fluent, native English speakers to approximately 50% fluent, native English speakers and 50% recently-arrived immigrants who speak little or no English. Respond to the following statements as best you can, indicating the degree to which you agree or disagree by circling the number which best expresses your opinion.

1. Because teachers are trained in educational theory and practice, their input is usually more appropriate than that of parents concerning the best program for their students.

5	4	3	2	1
strongly agree	agree	not sure	disagree	strongly disagree

2. In planning the appropriate educational program for a student, his/her cultural background and expectations should be considered.

5	4	3	2	1
strongly agree	agree	not sure	disagree	strongly disagree

3.   It is most important for students to remain at their home school.

5	4	3	2	1
strongly agree	agree	not sure	disagree	strongly disagree

4.   When a student qualifies for special services, the program at the school should be adjusted to meet the needs of that student, and every attempt should be made to avoid busing students to other sites.

5	4	3	2	1
strongly agree	agree	not sure	disagree	strongly disagree

5.   "Full Inclusion" is an appropriate strategy for all special education students.

5	4	3	2	1
strongly agree	agree	not sure	disagree	strongly disagree

The preceding statements were designed to make you think about your own attitudes concerning the authority teachers should have in relation to that of the parents in planning educational programs for students, to explore your feelings toward special education programs, and to examine some of your own attitudes toward the involvement and aspirations of immigrant parents concerning their children's success in school.

III. Key Concepts

Since the passage of PL 94-142 (The Education for All Handicapped Children Act) in 1975, the involvement of families in educational planning has become a major goal for professionals working with students with identified handicaps (Hallahan and Kauffman, 1994). School personnel continue to report a lack of involvement by parents in planning and implementing Individualized Educational Plans (IEPs) for their children (Fradd and Weismantel, 1989). Despite the fact that "informed consent" of the parents is required by law, the perceived apathy of the parents by educators has tempted the educators to overlook at best, or to disregard at worst, the desires of the parents.

For new immigrant families, the U.S. educational system may seem particularly complex and intimidating, as special education services may have no parallel in their home country. In general, newly-arrived immigrant parents may feel that educational decision-making is the purview of the school personnel, with the result that their lack of involvement is interpreted by the school staff as a lack of interest or lack of caring (Fradd and Weismantel, 1989). These parents also experience a sense of loss when their child is diagnosed as learning disabled, and they may be less well prepared to understand the implications of the label than are their second and third generation counterparts who were schooled in the very environment in which their children are now being labeled as "different."

Because these two advocates for the child have, at the outset, a fundamental misunderstanding of the role of the other, the parents relinquish authority to the educators, who are perceived as being the "experts," and the educators, therefore, perceive themselves to be even more powerful.

Hofstede (1980, 1991) identified five "Dimensions of National Culture." One of the ways these dimensions can be valuable to educators is in understanding the behavior of students and their parents, especially in cases where the values of the families' cultures are quite different from those of the teacher. A synopsis of the characteristics of these dimensions can be found in Figure 2, and more complete descriptions are available in texts referenced in the bibliography which follows. It is important to note that Hofstede's (1989, 1991) studies measured the collective national cultures and not individual personalities, although these characteristics may be within individuals to varying degrees (Brislin & Yoshida, 1994).

The mismatch described above, between the expectations of the parents and the perceptions of the teacher, fall within Hofstede's dimension of Power Distance. The United States is generally considered to be a culture where the Power Distance Dimension is a small one. That is, people are felt to be interdependent, superiors should be accessible and not flaunt their power, and cooperation is valued, even among persons of unequal power. Hofstede's (1991) description of small Power Distance includes such characteristics as minimized inequality in society, a hierarchy of unequal roles established for convenience, equal rights among superiors and subordinates, and legitimate use of power subject to judgment of its ultimate good or evil. In societies of small Power Distance, superiors and subordinates each consider the other to be a person just like they are, with little distinction of perceived class. Teachers raised and trained in such a society expect that parents, as advocates for their children, will actively participate in the making of decisions which will affect the child. They would assume that parents would question any concepts which they did not understand, and object to those with which they disagree.

Figure 2: Hofstede's Dimensions of National Culture
(Adapted from Bislin & Yoshida, 1994)

Individualism
Collectivism
- degree of importance placed by a society on competition vs. cooperation
- highly individualized society - personal achievement is highly prized ... people define themselves as individueals, rather than as members of a group
- collective society - tradition & group membership are more valued ... working toward a collective goal is more common

Uncertainty
Avoidance
- degree to which a society seeks to avoid situations that are ambiguous & uncertain
- in such a society, structure & rules are important ... deviation from the accepted norms is not tolerated

Masculinity/
Femininity
- extent to which a society revolves around assertiveness, ambition, task achievement, & issues regarding materialism/acquisition rather than quality of life & social service
- in a highly Masculine society, gender roles are much more rigidly defined than in more Feminine societies

Power
Distance
- degree to which less powerful members of a society accept the unequal distribution of power
- titles, status, and formality have great importance in societies where the Power Distance is high
- in school settings, the teacher as "sage on the stage" is the

common practice, & students do not speak unless spoke to
- teachers and schools enjoy high status, and are not to be questioned

Confucian
Dynamism
- developed in response to sudden economic growth among Asian countries ... values emphasized or de-emphasized
- emphasized - persistence/perseverance ... respect status relationships ... thrift ... having a sense of shame
- de-emphasized - personal stability ... protecting face ... adherence to tradition ... reciprocal giving of favors and gifts
- educators - appreciate persistence in students ... students who respect professor-student relationship ... students who are shamed if assignments are not completed

In the Latino culture, however (Spain and Mexico, for example), the dimension of Power Distance is described as "large." This means that superiors have a privileged position, and are not expected to be accessible, or equal to their subordinates. They are expected to render decisions without requesting or considering the opinions of their subordinates, and in fact, to do so would undermine their authority and standing in the eyes of those subordinates (Kolb, Osland, & Rubin, 1995). Hofstede (1991) describes relationships in a large Power Distance society as characterized by an order of inequity in the world, where everyone has a rightful station, where most people tend to be dependent on a few independent people, and where judgment of the use of power for good or evil is irrelevant. In such a society, superiors and subordinates see themselves and each other as being inherently different from each other, with superiors being entitled to certain privileges by virtue of their station alone, and where the powerful and the powerless engage in a constant, if subtle, struggle against each other. Parents raised in such an environment would expect that their child's teacher, as a well-educated expert and respected community member, is looking out for the child's best interests, and would never question the decisions made by the school team, even if they did not understand or were not in agreement. Such parents would never insult professionals of such high status by disagreeing with them, or even by suggesting that they (the professionals) had not made themselves completely understood.

IV. Critical Incident
The Rebounding Student

Two elementary schools have been built within a block of each other in a very densely populated urban school district. Because of their proximity, the two staffs have worked together to meet the needs of all their students.

Near the end of the school year, a newly-arrived Hispanic student from School B is evaluated and determined to be eligible for Special Education placement. Although this school does offer a Special Education program, all those students are being served in the "full inclusion" model, which means that they spend their entire day in a regular education class with extra help being given by the Special Education teacher and her assistant. Because of the extent of the child's disability, it is felt that this program will not be sufficient to meet his needs, so the child is sent to the neighboring School A, with the principal's and receiving teacher's consent, to be assisted in a class where the students spend most of their day with only 10-15 children, and the full time attention of the Special Education teacher and her assistant.

In the following school year, many personnel changes have taken place, including a new principal for School A, and a new psychologist, assistant principal, and Special Education teacher for School B. About three months into this new year, the Special Education teacher from School A requests that a meeting take place between the administrators and Special Education teachers from both schools, in order to discuss the possibility of returning the child to his home school. Since the principal of School B and the teacher from School A are the only people in attendance who were present when the placement originally occurred, the teacher is able to convince the group that the student is now ready to succeed in School B's full inclusion program. When asked by School B's principal, she insists that the child is now ready and able to succeed in the full inclusion environment.

However, when the entire School B Special Education staff meets with the parents to facilitate the change, a completely different picture emerges. The parents admit that the School A teacher was "rude" to them and to their child and complained often to them of the fact that School B has its own special education program and should be handling its own students. They also indicate, in addition to their relief about their child returning to School B, some confusion because the teacher had phoned them a week before the meeting was even requested to prepare them for the fact that their child would be returning to School B, which was, in her words, "reclaiming" their students.

Once the new placement is made, it appears that the student may not be as ready as his former teacher claimed. On his first day back at School B, he refuses to separate from his mother, cries and protests, and is calmed only by the offer to spend the day with the Kindergarten teacher in whose class he was before the referral was made for assessment the year before. Gradually, he meets and develops a comfort level with his new teacher and his classmates, some of whom he remembers from Kindergarten, but as days pass it becomes clear that, not only is he unprepared academically for a regular class, but is also struggling emotionally with the changes he continues to experience. Two months later, he feels safe with his new teacher, but resists leaving his classroom for any reason, whether for instruction with the Adapted Physical Education Specialist, or to go to Speech/Language Therapy with the same specialist who worked with him the year before.

Questions:

1. What assumptions did the teacher from School A make concerning the cultural dimensions of Power Distance as experienced by the parents? How do you think these assumptions affected her behavior toward them?

2. Imagine that you are the parent of the child who is to be moved. Enumerate and describe the emotions you feel as this story unfolds. How do you feel when your child is moved from his home school? How do you feel about your experiences with the School A Special Education teacher? How do you feel when

you learn that your child is to be moved again? Do you feel that you have the ability to impact on the decision being made concerning your child's academic program? Why or why not?

3.   Imagine that you are the Special Education teacher at School

A.   What factors are you considering as you plan to move the child back to School B? How do you think the staff will react? What response do you expect to get from the parents? Do you believe that the change will be easy or difficult to accomplish? Why?

V. Exercises for Application

The purpose of this exercise is to experience the feelings of the major players in the scenario and to try to work out a compromise solution which will meet the needs of the teachers, and still honor the feelings of the student and his parents. You will form three groups, one of which will represent the "sending" teacher, one of which will represent the "receiving" teacher, and one of which will represent the parents. It is recommended that the information for each character be written on separate pages, so that each can be disseminated only to the participants in that group without revealing information about the other characters. Read the information sheet provided for your character and as a group, brainstorm some of the most important issues for that person. Knowing what you now know about "power distance," please take into consideration the differing perspectives of all the characters in the scenario, and try to respect their disparate cultural customs in planning your responses. Decide which areas are negotiable and which are non-negotiable, depending on your impressions of this person's perceptions and state of mind. Then choose one person to represent your group in the role-play exercise.

Information for "sending" teacher: You have been a special education teacher for 15 years. In that time, you have seen your program change from a very specialized environment for children with substantial learning disabilities with a small student-to-teacher ratio to a program which you now consider to be a "dumping ground." The state has rescinded the law which limited the number and type of children you may serve, and the students now placed with you have a multitude of problems interfering with their ability to learn, including emotional disturbance, mental retardation, and physical disabilities, in addition to serious learning disabilities. This year's class is made up of many more boys than girls, and they all exhibit much greater variance in their skill levels than you have faced before. You are concerned because your training was insufficient to prepare you to handle the variety of needs you face each day. You feel frustrated by your perceived inability to enable them all to succeed, and powerless to change your situation.

Information for "receiving" teacher: You are new to this school district, but not new to your profession. Over the seven years that you have been a teacher, you have been assigned to regular classrooms as well as a variety of special education programs. Because you have already experienced both pull-out and self-contained curricula, you were excited about trying the "full inclusion" schema in place at your new school. You appreciate the innovative ideas which are being tried in order to meet the needs of the students, and enjoy being part of a team, instead of working alone in a classroom. You understand that "full inclusion" is not appropriate for all students, but believe that it can work for many students and are committed to keeping as many as you can in regular classrooms with assistance. Your new student has, by now, adjusted to his new class, and is beginning to bond with his new teacher. You are concerned that the information which was presented by the other teacher concerning the student's ability to perform in a regular class is in opposition to the proficiency that you and his classroom teacher have observed in the classroom. You wonder whether the contradiction is the result of exaggerated information from her or some inadequacy on your part.

Information for parents: You and your family have lived in the United States for ten years, although both you and your spouse were born and raised in Central America. You both attended, but did not finish, high school in your country of origin. You are both employed outside the home, and work opposite shifts so that one parent is always at home with the children. This critical incident, which concerns your seven year old son, your oldest child, has given you your first experience with the educational system of this country. You are both concerned about your child's ability to succeed in school (which you see as an important factor in his ability to get a good job) and his ability to adjust to the many changes which the schools have forced on him. You worry about his shyness, and feel that changing schools so many times has made it even more difficult for him to concentrate on his work. However, you have strong feelings about the way both you and your son were treated by the School A teacher, and because of this you are happy that your son has transferred back to School B. Your main concern is to find a place for your son where he will do well, and be happy.

When your representative is prepared, she/he will meet the other teacher in the front of the room for the role-play.

Instructions for the role-play: It is now two months after the student has been reassigned to School B. You are all required to meet because the student's Individual Education Plan (IEP) is about to expire, and, by law, his Goals and Objectives must be revisited annually, and adjusted according to progress made and expectations for continued improvement. The meeting starts out with a focus on business, but as it progresses, it is clear that all of the participants have unspoken concerns about what has taken place, and what they perceive is the best course of action for this child.

Your goals are to:

1. Clear the air, and express as many of your feelings as possible (within the constraints set by your cultural dimension of Power Distance) concerning the change of placement and all of the events which preceded it.

2. Determine if there were alternative solutions to the problems caused by each of the moves of the student, and describe how

these alternatives might also have met the needs of the student, while still working within district and legal constraints and protecting the feelings of all concerned.

VI. Guide for Debriefing

When the group has completed its performance, ask each person to write a summary of their feelings before, during, and after the role-play, from the point of view of the character their group represented. Depending on the composition of the groups, a variety of responses would be possible from their representatives in this role-play. It is hoped, however, that by "walking a mile in their shoes," the participants will gain an understanding of the characters' behavior and how it was shaped by their cultural perception of Power Distance.

This basic mismatch between the dimension of Power Distance as experienced by the American teacher and the Latino parents resulted in the contrary actions of these two parties. The parents, trusting that the school personnel knew best, were hesitant to express their feelings about the change of placement discussed at the original meeting. Having grown up in a culture where great value is placed on the profession of teaching, they would never have presumed to tell the school personnel that they disagreed with either of the two changes of placement suggested for their child. Neither would they have expressed concern about the treatment they and their son received at School A unless and until they had established a genuine "comfort level," as they would have considered themselves to be subordinate to the teacher, and would have only felt comfortable keeping to their "rightful place."

The Special Education teacher from School A, having grown up in the Low Power Distance environment of the U.S., would have expected the parents to speak up if they felt discomfort with the process at any step of the way, and in fact, would probably even have requested input from the parents as to their feelings about the changes for their son. As the parents would likely have responded that everything was "fine," she would have taken them at their word and felt that she had done exactly what she was expected to do in giving them an opportunity for input. It is also possible, if she understood the different perception of Power Distance held by the parents, that she knew they would not oppose her suggestion, and so the child would be removed from her class without dispute.

VII. Homework Exercises/Student Projects

1. Imagine yourself as the mother or father of the student described in the module. Create a diary as it might have been kept by this parent, describing your true feelings about the events as they unfolded and your reactions to and perceptions of the people and decisions made concerning your child.
2. Rewrite the scenario, but instead of a newly-arrived, non-English proficient immigrant family, describe the process as it might have occurred in an upper-middle class neighborhood school where most of the parents were professional people with some college education. Which events might have occurred in the same way? How would the scenario have been different? In what way(s) would the teachers, parents, and principals involved have behaved differently, in your opinion? If done as a group project, it might be interesting to act out the scenario in this new way, and compare and contrast the two characterizations.

VIII. Selected References

Adler, N. J. (1991). International dimensions of organizational behavior (2nd ed.). Boston: PWS-Kent Publishing.

Brislin, R. W. (1991). The art of getting things done: A practical guide to the use of power. New York: Praeger.

Brislin, R. W. (1993). Understanding culture's influence on behavior. Fort Worth, TX: Harcourt, Brace, Jovanovich.

Brislin, R. W. & Yoshida, T. (Eds.). (1994). Improving intercultural interactions: Modules for cross-cultural training programs. Thousand Oaks, CA: Sage Publications.

Cushner, K., & Brislin, R. W. (1996). Intercultural interactions: A practical guide (2ⁿᵈ ed.). Thousand Oaks, CA: Sage Publications.

Fradd, S. H., & Weismantel, M. J. (Eds.). (1989). Meeting the needs of culturally and linguistically different students: A handbook for educators. Austin, TX: Pro-Ed.

Garcia, E. (1994). Understanding and meeting the challenges of Boston: Houghton Mifflin.

Hallahan, D. P., & Kauffman, J. M. (1994). Exceptional children (6ᵗʰ ed.). Boston: Allyn and Bacon.

Hofstede, G. (1980). Culture's consequences: International differences in work-related values. Beverly Hills, CA: Sage Publications.

Hofstede, G. (1986). Cultural differences in teaching and learning. International Journal of Intercultural Relations, 10(3), 301-320.

Hofstede, G. (1991). Cultures and organizations: Software of the mind. London: McGraw-Hill.

Hofstede, G. & Bond, M. H. (1988). Confucius and economic growth: New trends in culture's consequences. Organizational Dynamics, 16(4), 4-21.

Kolb, D. A., Osland, J., & Rubin, I. M. (1995). Organizational behavior: An experiential approach. Englewood Cliffs, NJ: Prentice-Hall.

Prototype Module #2: What are you?: Increasing Racial Consciousness through Biracial Teachers' Narratives

A cross-cultural education module by Jon Kingsbury

I. Introduction

Since the repeal of the last antimiscegenation laws in 1967, there has been a dramatic increase in the number of biracial and multiracial births in the U.S. despite a census form that has not accounted for biracials (President Clinton recently approved the checking of multiple boxes for the year 2000 census.). This racially-mixed population is challenging the way we perceive race and our own identity. And since, as Carter and Goodwin (1994) point out, "Every student, teacher, teacher educator, and administrator brings to the educational enterprise his or her unique racial identity resolution" (p. 314), there exists a need to gain greater understanding of the role racial identity plays in the teacher-student relationship. The purpose of this module is to increase our racial consciousness through the exploration of our own racial identity and its development. Narratives from biracial elementary teachers will be utilized as vehicles for raising that consciousness.

Carter and Goodwin (1994) point out that although current demographic trends may lead us to a more multiracial complexion within our student population, the population of our teachers continues to be predominantly White, which results in cross-racial interactions between students and teachers being commonplace. Thus, the understanding of the roles of race and racism, whether individual or institutional, is extremely critical to the overall effectiveness of the education process for all students, particularly our students of color. Racial identity development theory provides researchers and practitioners with a framework for understanding how individuals view not only themselves but others within a racialized context. Carter and Goodwin (1994) indicate that racial identity theory influences teachers' perceptions of the competencies and capabilities of their students. The differential treatment afforded students of color, although certainly influenced by other factors such as resource distribution and assessment patterns, "can be exacerbated by teacher expectations, attitudes, and perceptions" (p. 316).

This module focuses on biracial teachers' ethnographic narratives as vehicles for exploring our own racial identity and its development both on an individual and group level. Furthermore, the module is designed to not only increase the participants' level of racial consciousness, but to also allow for personal and group exploration into how it effects their interactions in social settings, be it classrooms, staff development meetings, or parent-teacher sessions.

Given the sensitive and personal nature of this topic, a safe and nurturing classroom environment is of the utmost importance and essential for a productive engagement. Participants must feel comfortable in sharing their personal beliefs and perceptions.

II. Self-Assessment Exercise

The following statements are meant to introduce you to, and to get you thinking about, the topic of this module —racial consciousness. Respond to the following statements as best you can, indicating the degree to which you agree or disagree by circling the number which best expresses your opinion. There are no right or wrong answers, these statements are intended to merely provide you with opportunities for self-reflection.

1.　　I like to think of myself as being "color-blind."

5	4	3	2	1
strongly agree	agree	not sure	disagree	strongly disagree

2.　　In general, stereotyping is a bad thing, however, some stereotyping can be positive.

5	4	3	2	1
strongly agree	agree	not sure	disagree	strongly disagree

3.　　Members of specific racial groups tend to exhibit similar learning styles and behaviors.

5	4	3	2	1
strongly agree	agree	not sure	disagree	strongly disagree

4.　　Because of the way our society is, biracial individuals tend to have a more difficult time developing their racial identity than individuals of one race.

5	4	3	2	1
strongly agree	agree	not sure	disagree	strongly disagree

5.   Children with one white parent and one parent of color will generally tend to identify with the parent of color.

5	4	3	2	1
strongly agree	agree	not sure	disagree	strongly disagree

This exercise allows participants to assess their attitudes about race and racism. The process of increasing racial consciousness may prove to be unsettling for some individuals, given that each brings her/his own unique personal experiences into the discussion, and thus each may be able to identify with certain specifics of the ethnographic narratives. Participants are reminded that this exercise and subsequent discussions will be performed in an environment of mutual respect with a willingness to listen to others as they share their feelings and reflections. It is critical that ample time be available for classroom discussion of possible meanings for all the responses across the Likert scale. This exercise may also prove to be an excellent introduction into the theory of racial identity development.

III. Key Concepts

Racial identity development theory has its roots in multicultural counseling and therapy and more recently has been applied to education research (Rowe, Behrens, & Leach, 1995). Racial identity can be defined as "a sense of group or collective identity based on one's perception that he or she shares a common racial heritage with a particular racial group" (Helms, 1993, p. 3). It is an identity woven from a combination of personal identity (PI), reference group orientation (RGO) and an ascribed identity, a balance of "who I am as an individual" with "to what extent and for what reasons do I feel I belong to a certain group," and its development is influenced by a combination of cognitive, affective, and behavioral processes from various social experiences (Rowe et al., 1995). Critical to those experiences, and their influence, is how the individual is positioned racially within the social system. The experience will be viewed differently by a member of the dominant group as opposed to a member of a subordinate group.

Racial consciousness refers to the awareness that one's RGO can influence one's PI and vice versa, or as Helms (1993) states, "one's racial awareness may be subliminal and not readily admitted into consciousness or it may be conscious and not easily repressed" (p. 7). This awareness can bring with it an evaluative component, be it positive, negative, or neutral, about racial groups. It is the quality of the awareness and the various ways in which that awareness may occur that determines the level of racial identity or identity resolutions. Racial identity theory states that various racial identity resolutions can exist within a racial group, so that racial consciousness should not be viewed as "dichotomous, present, or absent, but rather is polytomous" (Helms, 1993, p. 7).

The racial identity typologies in Figure 3 are based on the stage theory of development, where an individual moves from lower to higher stages as she/he experiences social interactions. Common to most typology models is the assumption that the lower levels are characterized by naiveté and a simplified world view. It is through life's diverse experiences that one progresses to higher levels and a more complex and realistic world view. An individual's particular level of development, even the achieved-status level, is subject to change when specific experiences create knowledge that is in conflict with previously embraced beliefs, resulting in a lack of certainty or commitment regarding one's attitude, what is called "dissonance" (Rowe et al., 1995). Tatum (1992) points out that although the typologies are linear in their formation, each model can be viewed in "spiral form" (p.12), where an individual, given a particular experience, may return to a lower level of racial identity for a period of time. It should also be noted that the stage delineations are blurred, existing on a continuum both between and within the stages. Finally, from a conceptual perspective, the higher the level an individual achieves, the less likely she/he will exhibit prejudice and racist behavior (Ponterotto & Pedersen, 1993).

Within the biracial model, Poston (1990) begins with a similar sense of naiveté from a lack of experiences and moves to a second stage where the individual is forced to make a choice of group identification. This choice is essential within our monoracially racialized society and it is only recently that we have begun to break away from that perspective and to view individuals as biracials or multiracials. Such a choice is predicated on several factors, such as personal (physical appearance), social support (acceptance), and status (economic). This choice process is critical to the individual's overall racial identity development because of the potential impact reference group orientation attitudes can have on personal identity indicators. Poston refers to it as a period of "crisis and alienation" (p. 153) and it is followed by guilt and confusion resulting from choosing one parent's identity over the other. At this point, the individual may evolve to accept and appreciate her/his multiple identity and develop further to fully recognizing and acknowledging that multiplicity. Poston views this highly developed individual as having a secured and integrated identity.

Biracial elementary teachers' ethnographic narratives are used to facilitate the increase in racial consciousness for several reasons. First, these narratives provide "real life" experiences of a former student and current teacher for classroom discussion purposes, thus the discussion focuses on real issues with practical comments and solutions.

Figure 3: Typologies of Developmental Stages

Racial Identity: Dominant Group
(Helms, 1990)

(1)	Contact	• first contact w/Blacks naive curiousity, use White criteria
(2)	Disintegration	• admits Whiteness & benefits in racist society, moral conflict

Figure 3 (Cont.): Typologies of Development Stages

(3)   Reintegration   • racist identity, protect preserve White privilege, guilt + anger

(4)   Pseudo-Independence   • sees Whites' role, uses White view, may perpetuate racism,

(5)   Immersion/Emersion   • re-education process, unlearn myths, "emotional catharsis"

(6)   Autonomy   • seeks diversity, flexible open ... acts against ALL oppression

Racial Identity: Nondominant Group
(Atkinson et al., 1993)

(1)   Conformity   • acculturate/assimilate to dominant - values, norms

(2)   Dissonance   • begins to question, transition, state of flux & confusion

(3)   Resistance & Immersion   • embraces own group's values, rejects dominant - negative attitude

(4)   Introspection   • conflict PI + RGO, question previous attitude - both own & dominant

(5)   Synergetic Articulation & Awareness   • sense of self-fulfillment, high level of personal autonomy
    • pos./realistic RGO, open to selective dominant elements ... to end ALL oppression

Racial Identity: Nondominant Group
(Boston, 1990)

(1)   Personal Identity   • little or no association with any group
    • lacks experiences

(2)   Choice of Group Categorization   • period of crisis/alienation
    • choice factors - personal, social support, social status

(3)   Enmeshment/Denial   • period of guilt/confusion - choosing one group over the other

(4)   Appreciation   • evolving appreciation for multiplicity of identity

(5)   Integration   • wholeness/integration of multiple identity

Author's Note: These typologies were selected from a diverse body of work done by many authors in the field of racial/ethnic identity development. They serve as **examples** only.

Second, these real narratives are chosen to promote empathy and/or self-identification among participants which can heighten their racial consciousness (Jalongo & Isenberg, 1995). Third, the narratives allow for some necessary "distance" when discussing the actors in the vignettes. As noted earlier, race and racism discussions can be unsettling for some individuals and these vignettes provide some cushion for participants by focusing on the actual players in the narratives and not directly on the participants. Finally, the narratives of biracials' life histories provide the participants with a glimpse of what it can be like to live biracially in a highly racialized monoracial society, thus allowing traditionally "silenced voices" to be heard by diverse audiences.

When discussing narratives there is no one right method, for each participant may key on a different phrase or word. What is important to remember is to provide each person with ample opportunity to explain why she/he may find that particular phrase or word compelling.

IV. Ethnographic Narrative

The following ethnographic narrative was selected from several the author has collected over the past few years. It was selected for this presentation because of its relative brevity, and its setting (school) and actors (principal, parent, and child) within the narrative which offers a variety of micro relations that can be specifically discussed.

Nathan, 32, whose white mother is of Irish and German heritage and whose black father is from Jamaica, teaches at the sixth-grade level. He shares an experience from his early childhood (Note: All names have been altered to protect the informant's anonymity).:

> *When my father changed jobs, I was sent to another school . . . this was fourth grade . . . and I was kind of excited about it. But within the first couple of weeks, that excitement turned to anger and pain cause of the other kids. One day I got into a fight with a white kid who*

called me "nigger" . . . it's funny, since a few days before I was called "honky" by some black kids. . . . I guess I got the better of him cause I was sent to the Principal's office and he went to the Vice-Principal's. I had to call my parents and my mom came to school. You could see on the Principal's face that he was really confused, but my mom was real cool . . . she explained it to him. The Principal explained what happened and how fighting was not tolerated at his school, and when my mom asked about the name-calling, he said that it was just a case of "boys will be boys." I found out later that the other kid's parents were never called.

Questions to consider:

These questions are provided to initiate group discussions. Facilitators should be comfortable in developing spontaneous questions based on the ongoing discussions. Facilitators are again reminded to allow as much time as possible for all participants to adequately express their thoughts, emotions, and opinions.

1.   How do you think Nathan felt after this experience? If you were Nathan, how would you feel after this experience?
2.   If you were Nathan's mother, what are your feelings? What would you have done?
3.   How do you think this experience has influenced Nathan's teaching?
4.   If you were the principal, how would you have handled this situation?
5.   Are there other issues you wish discuss regarding this experience? Does this narrative trigger any past experiences for you?

V. Exercise for Application

This exercise is structured for a group of up to 20-25

individuals. Because of the topic, any larger groups may not be adequately served by this module. The exercise begins in small groups and moves its way to the overall classroom:

- Participants are organized into small groups of 3-5 individuals, each group gets the biracial teacher's narrative vignette to read and discuss.
- Questions, directing the participants to view the vignette from the actor's perspective, are provided to initiate the discussion.
- Groups would then share their findings with the other groups for an overall classroom discussion.

VI. Guide for Debriefing

The emphasis to facilitators is the importance of creating and maintaining a safe and secure environment in which the participants feel comfortable in sharing their personal experiences. It is very difficult and dangerous to generalize as to how any one individual may react to a discussion of this nature. Facilitators should be competent in handling multicultural group interactions.

Debriefing considerations:

- Prior to the exercise, the facilitator should make every effort to ensure a safe and secure environment for all participants. Such an environment is characterized by mutual respect and support, and a willingness to not only share one's own thoughts and feelings, but also a willingness to sincerely listen to others share theirs.
- Participants should be given articles on racial/ethnic identity development to read and discuss prior to this exercise. An example is Beverly Tatum's (1992) account of her classroom experiences teaching the psychology of racism.
- Participants are reminded that each person brings her/his own unique experiences into the discussions, and thus, there must exist an atmosphere of mutual respect among all participants.

- Given the sensitive nature of the topic, the debriefing process should include ample opportunity for individuals to express their feelings/reflections about the exercise. Expression can include classroom discussion, personal journals, and reaction papers, all of which are opportunities for further reflection.
- Facilitators should be aware that participants will exhibit a wide array of reactions in the discussions, and thus it will be difficult to anticipate all possible responses. The above mentioned racial ethnic identity development models may serve as conceptual frameworks for potential responses. However, facilitators are cautioned against making any broad generalizations with regard to individual participants and specific racial groups.

VII. Homework Exercises or Student Projects

The following two projects have proven to be very successful for both the students and the facilitator in the exploration of their own racial consciousness. The personal history project should be offered in such a way as to promote the creativity of the participants, such as the use of poetry, song, and art in the detailing of their life experiences. The interview exercise should be prefaced with an in-depth discussion on interview techniques and ethical and philosophical issues related to this research methodology.

- *Personal History: Examining your own racial identity development.*
  You will write a narrative essay about your life, describing those experiences that have helped to shape your views of race, culture, and diversity.
- *Ethnographic Interview: Exploring the experiences of others.*
  You will interview an individual who will share her/his experiences that have helped to shape her/his racial identity. Such interviews may be focused on specific experiences and/or specific social settings.

VIII. Selected References

Atkinson, D. R., Morten, G., & Sue, D. W. (Eds.). (1993). Counseling American minorities: A cross-cultural perspective (4th ed.). Dubuque, Iowa: William C. Brown.

Carter, R. T., & Goodwin, A. L. (1994). Racial identity and education. In L. Darling-Hammond (Ed.), Review of Research in Education, Vol. 20, (pp. 291–336). Washington, DC: American Educational Research Association.

Goodson, I. F. (1992). Studying teachers' lives: An emergent field of inquiry. In I. F. Goodson (Ed.), Studying teachers' lives (pp. 1–17). New York: Teachers College.

Funderburg, L. (1994). Black, white, other: Biracial Americans talk about race and identity. New York: William Morrow and Company.

Hacker, B. (1996). Advice for teachers on racism and oneness. In N. Rutstein & M. Morgan (Eds.), Healing racism: Education's role (pp. 187–203). Springfield, MA: Whitcomb Publishing.

Helms, J. E. (1990). Toward a model of white racial identity development. In J. E. Helms (Ed.), Black and white racial identity: Theory, research, and practice (pp. 49-66). New York: Greenwood Press.

Helms, J. E. (1993). Black and white racial identity: Theory, research, and practice. New York: Greenwood Press.

Jalongo, M. R., & Isenberg, J. P. (1995). Teachers' stories. San Francisco: Jossey-Bass.

Ponterotto, J. G., & Pedersen, P. B. (1993). Preventing prejudice: A guide for counselors and educators. Multicultural Aspects of Counseling Series 2. Newbury Park, CA: Sage Publications.

Poston, W. S. C. (1990, November/December). The biracial identity development model: A needed addition. Journal of Counseling & Development, 69, 152–155.

Root, M. P. P. (Ed.). (1996). The multiracial experience: Racial borders as the new frontier. Thousand Oaks, CA: Sage Publications.

Rowe, W., Behrens, J. T., & Leach, M. M. (1995). Racial/ethnic identity and racial consciousness: Looking back and looking forward. In J. G. Ponterotto, J. M. Casas, L. A. Suzuki, & C. M. Alexander (Eds.), Handbook of Multicultural Counseling (pp. 218–235). Thousand Oaks, CA: Sage Publications.

Tatum, B. D. (1992). Talking about race, learning about racism: The application of racial identity development theory in the classroom. Harvard Educational Review, 62(1), 1–24.

Zack, N. (Ed.). (1995). American mixed race: The culture of microdiversity. Lanham, MD: Rowman & Littlefield Publishers.

Chapter Three
The Relationship Between the Cultural Awareness of Teachers and the Frequency of Behavior Referrals Among Middle School Males

Virginia Jones Dixon
Fort Valley Middle School, Fort Valley, GA
South Carolina State University, Orangeburg, SC

=============================

INTRODUCTION

The changing demographics of the United States society create a critical need for teachers to become knowledgeable about and skilled in multiculturalism. In a great many of the schools across the nation, racial and language minority students (African Americans and Latinos) constitute a majority of students

Zintz (1969), in his research and writing in the area of multicultural education, pointed out that different cultural groups have significantly different views and different systems of values and beliefs; and, that they have different ideas of the ways in which people should relate to one another. Zintz further suggested that the views, values, beliefs, and relations that are characteristic of minority students often clash with those of their teachers. He stated that teachers, even those from minority groups themselves, reflect the basic views, beliefs, and values of the middle-class Anglo society. These clashes strongly impact discipline.

Teachers have the responsibility to recognize cultural differences and establish, within the framework of these differences, an environment that encourages all of their students. There is a concern of whether or not teachers have been adequately prepared to establish a learning environment that is fair and encouraging to students from a variety of cultural and racial backgrounds. Teachers who are ill-prepared to meet these challenges may inadvertently establish differential expectations and discipline patterns which are actually discouraging and detrimental to some groups of students.

The purpose of the study presented here was to investigate the relationship between the cultural awareness of teachers and the frequency of behavior referrals for middle school males. It is hoped that further research into this problem will provide guidance for developing multicultural training programs which will sensitize teachers to their impact upon student behavior and ultimately reduce the number of suspensions among these students.

CONCEPTUAL FRAMEWORK

When teachers ridicule students for not participating in academic activities and convey to students that they expect nothing more from them, students withdraw. These students retaliate by becoming non-communicative or totally disruptive, both explosive fuels for classroom confrontations and behavioral referrals (Sheets & Gay, 1996). Given the indicated effect of teachers' own expectations on their treatment of students, it is reasonable to assume that the negative attitudes of culturally uninformed teachers toward African American males may result in referrals, and thus in suspensions, in disproportionate numbers. In interactions between teachers and students where disciplinary action occurred, the following patterns have been observed: males of all groups were disciplined more frequently, publicly, and severely than females, and African Americans (both males and females) were disciplined more than other ethnic groups (Sheets & Gay, 1996). The order of disciplinary actions by ethnic group, from most to fewest, was African Americans, Latinos, Filipinos, and Caucasians.

The majority of school behavior referrals are written on African American male students. A review of reported discipline problems and the relationship between behavior, ethnicity, social class, and grade level was conducted by Moore and Cooper (1984). The results of their study indicated that pupils who were most different from their teachers (that is, from poorer homes and lower social class backgrounds) were perceived most often as being behavior problems. Teachers of these students tended to use more severe punishments, such as suspension, than teachers who were more like their students in socio-economic background.

The implications of these studies are that when teachers are relating to students in the classroom, they do so on the basis of perceived social characteristics, and that these perceptions apparently affect the choices of discipline that teachers use to control or punish behavior (Bickel & Qualls, 1979).

African American students are twice as likely as whites to be suspended from school, to be physically punished by authorities, or to be labeled as mentally retarded (Mitgang, 1988). It is suggested that teachers tend to overreact to blacks, especially African American males. This is even true with African American teachers. Overall, African American males account for eighty percent of instances of corporal punishment and for seventy percent of suspensions.

Woolridge and Richman (1985) reported that the differential treatment of African American and white male students begins in elementary school and may contribute to the reinforcement of maladaptive behavior of African American male students. Young African American males are reared to be more responsive and perceptive to interpersonal relationships than are Caucasian males (Lewis, 1975). At the same time, African American males are expected to behave in the classroom in a manner that is ascribed to all male students. It is possible that the message that they receive from teachers' verbal and nonverbal feedback results in negative self-concepts and behaviors (Weitz, 1972; Woolfork & Woolfork, 1974). Teacher expectancy has been demonstrated to be a reflection of the race, socio-economic status and previous academic history of the student (Bennett, 1976; Eaves, 1975; Brophy, 1983).

An analysis of disciplinary problems in school suggests that (a) the frequency and severity of infractions correlate positively with the ethnic identity and gender of the students, with African American males being affected most significantly; and (b) as grade level increases so does the frequency of disciplinary problems for the students affected (Sheets, R. & Gay, G. 1996). The American educational system has not been effective in educating African American children. The emphasis of traditional education has been upon molding and shaping African American children so that they can fit into an educational process which is designed for Anglo-Saxon middle class children (Hale-Benson, 1986).

Even so, teachers' attitudes may be amenable to alteration. In order to change the manner in which the behavior of African American males is perceived, teachers who are culturally limited must be trained in cultural diversity. The results of this study may provide insight for developing multicultural training programs which will sensitize teachers to the negative impact teacher perceptions have on student behavior and, perhaps, ultimately reduce the suspension rate among these students. This study has further significance because, globally, society suffers a loss when capable young men terminate their educations early.

The negative attitudes and low expectations held by school officials are sensed by African American students who respond by assuming a negative view of classroom performance and school work. As young African American male students experience failure in formal school work, they seek recognition among their peers in non-academic areas (Hare, 1987). Hale-Benson (1986), states that a dual socialization is expected of African American students. They must be prepared to imitate the "hip," "cool" behavior of the culture in which they live and, at the same time, take on those behaviors that are necessary to be upwardly mobile. She further postulates that the ability of an individual to readily adjust his or her behavior to the norms of two cultures depends upon the extent to which these cultures share values and norms for prescribed behaviors. An important factor in the dual or bicultural socialization process is the amount of conflict there is between the remaining values that are not shared.

Teachers' verbal and nonverbal communications to students were studied by Simpson and Erickson (1983). Their sample was African American and white female elementary teachers of first grade students. The observers noted that the teachers directed more verbal interaction toward boys and that more negative feedback was directed toward African American males. These behaviors were independent of the race of the teachers. The observers also noted that there were real behavior differences between males and females, and that there were minor differences between African American males and White males. These differences may reflect different cultural influences on behavior. The researchers concluded that the teachers might have been responding to these behavioral differences rather than to racial differences. Simpson and Erickson argue that if this is the case, then teachers must become more sensitive to their responses to culturally determined behaviors and must consider carefully what their responses will be.

The vast majority of public elementary school teachers are females--predominantly White females. Yet the majority of students in many of these schools are non-white (Harry & Anderson, 1994). Most teacher preparation programs do not address the implications of differential experience based on race and gender. Harry and Anderson (1994) implied that several traditional features of African American males' behavioral profiles exacerbate the average White female teacher's negative view of them. The high physical activity level of African American males, as compared to girls, has been documented by numerous scholars (Hale-Benson, 1986; Kunjufu, 1985). Tension emanates from American Whites' fear of African American male physicality, and usually this fear is transmitted to Black boys and young men (Harry & Anderson, 1994).

Kunjufu (1985) has observed that the aggressive verbal "volleying" of African American males is interpreted as hostile and threatening by the White female culture of schools. Teachers who don't understand Black culture may interpret the behavior as "fighting" when they are "woofing," which is a verbal ritual that relieves tension in lieu of fighting (Hale-Benson, 1986). Cultural preferences for both physical and verbal behavior have a compelling influence on teachers' perceptions, which are the source of the initial referral of children for special education evaluation (Harry & Anderson, 1994).

The Relationship Between the Cultural Awareness of Teachers

In a study by Cornbleth and Korth (1980), White teachers rated White students higher than African American students in terms of potential achievement and classroom behavior. The study indicated that White students were rated as more efficient, organized, reserved, industrious, and pleasant while African American students were rated as more outgoing and outspoken. Overall, the teachers perceived the White students more favorably than the African American students. Cornbleth and Korth (1980) also concluded that responsiveness to the teacher, especially volunteering responses to teacher questions, is more highly related to teacher perceptions of African American students than White students. The extent that the relationship between the teacher ratings and student behavior differed for Black and White students suggests that teachers interpret the same student behavior in different ways depending on the students' race. The presence of differences in the relationship between student behavior and teacher perceptions of African American and White students has important implications for teacher education and classroom practice.

In the educational arena, teachers' knowledge is heavily informed by the premises and categories of psychology, which has developed primarily from studies of Euro-Americans and which focuses on individual psychological factors rather than on cultural factors. From a cultural (rather than psychological) perspective, a student's behavior is understood to be influenced by institutional norms, the student's definition of school success, conflicts between the cultures of the student's world, differences in patterns of expected social interaction, and messages embodied in school artifacts. Teachers bring their own cultural assumptions, goals, values, and beliefs to their classrooms. When teachers do not perceive the relationship of their own culture to the culture of their students, this blind spot can create conflicts and misunderstandings in their perceptions and interpretations of the behavior of students from other cultures. It is imperative that teachers change their behaviors, attitudes, and assumptions that are biased (and most often discriminatory) and thus detrimental to students whose cultural backgrounds are different from their own (Jacob,

Johnson, Finley, Gurski & Lavine, 1996). Teachers should acquaint themselves with the values, views, and beliefs of the students they teach. Perceptive teachers, those who recognize and understand cultural differences and their implications are able to remain alert for behaviors that may be potential areas of concern (Charles, 1981).

METHODOLOGY

The design for this study was correlational research. The study included collecting demographic data by questionnaire surveys from 178 seventh grade teachers, and comparing the number of behavior referrals made on males across ethnic groups. The targeted population for this study was seventh grade teachers and seventh grade male students from seventeen schools located in rural and urban areas of Florida and Georgia. One hundred sixty-five (165) teachers' scores were used. This represented all of the Caucasian and African American teachers: 45 males (31 Caucasians and 14 African Americans) and 120 females (71 Caucasians and 49 African Americans). Of the teachers whose scores were not included, 13 were either of several ethnic groups or chose not to specify their ethnicity, and the others were from other ethnic groups and made no referrals.

The instrument, the Ethnic Awareness Survey (Project Reach, 1994), was designed to systematically describe the extent to which teachers were aware of and knowledgeable about the cultures of a diverse population of students. The ratings were based on a correct answer from five choices. The survey instrument contained 54 questions concerning different cultures.

Data collected from the questionnaire surveys, teachers' demographic information and student referrals were used to test the hypotheses. A t test, a Two-way Analysis of Variance (ANOVA), and a Pearson Correlation of Coefficients were utilized to determine significant relationships.

FINDINGS

The major findings generated by this investigation are summarized here and followed by a discussion.

The data analysis revealed that the number of male students referred for behavior was not significantly affected by the level of culture awareness of teachers.

- The mean score on the survey was 30.612.
- The mean score was 30.60 for males (45), and 30.71 for females (120). The mean score for Caucasians (102) was 31.69, and the mean score for African Americans (63) was 29.05.
- The number of behavior referrals of Caucasian students provided a mean of 6.884.
- The number of behavior referrals of Hispanic students provided a mean of 4.611.
- The number of behavior referrals of African American students provided a mean of 10.547.
- Pearson Correlation of Coefficients between the teachers' cultural awareness score on the Hispanic subscale of the survey and the number of Hispanic student referrals presented a probability of .697, which is not significant at the .05 level.
- The Pearson Correlation of Coefficients between the the teachers' cultural awareness score on African Americans subscale of the survey and the number of African American student referrals produced a probability of .205, which is not significant at the .05 level.
- The analysis of the behavioral referrals for White male students yielded a statistically significant difference between White and African American teachers' referrals ($t = 2.96$, $p = .004$).
- The difference between White and African American teachers' referrals of Hispanic students indicated no significant difference ($t = 1.97$, $p = .052$), although the disparity was only slightly above the .05 level. Similar results were obtained for the behavioral referrals for African American male students ($t = 1.97$, $p = .054$).
- The t test analysis yielded no statistically significant difference between male and female teachers' referrals for White male

students (t = 1.79, p = .075), Hispanic male students (t = .46, p = .647) or African American male students (t = -1.71, p = .090).

- The analysis of the main and interaction effects of teachers' gender and race on White male students referrals yielded a statistically significant main effects for race (F = 6.067, p = .009). No significant main and higher order interaction effects were found for gender (F = 1.970, p = .162) and gender/race (F = 1.783, p = .184).

Table 1
Analysis of Variance of the Main Effects and Interactions of Race and Sex of Teachers and the Behavior Referrals of White Males

Source	Sum of Squares	DF	F of F	Sig
SEX	135.858	1	1.970	.162
RACE	480.387	1	6.967	.009*
SEX / RACE	122.955	1	1.783	.184

*p = .05

The analysis of the main and interaction effects of teachers' gender and race on Hispanic male students' referrals yielded no statistically significant effects for gender (F = .019, p = .891), race (F = 2.382, p = .125), and gender / race (F = .010, p = .922).

The analysis of the main and interaction effects of teachers' gender and race on African American male students yielded a significant main effect for race (F = 4.490, p = .036). Other main and interaction effects of gender (F = .486, p = .487) and gender / race (F = 1.878, p = .172) were not statistically significant. (See Table 2.)

Table 2
Analysis of Variance of the Main Effects and the Interactions of Race and Sex of the Teachers and the Behavior Referrals of African American Males

Source	Sum of Squares	DF	of F	F	Sig
SEX	55.847	1	.486	.487	
RACE	515.544	1	4.490	.036*	
SEX/RACE	215.630	1	1.878	.172	

*p = .05

The results of these findings indicate that race has a significant effect on White and African American teachers' behavioral referrals of White and African American male students. However, the interactions for sex and race and behavioral referrals for all three ethnic groups presented probabilities that were not significant.

DISCUSSION

The survey information demonstrated that there are more females (72.5%) than males (27.5%) at the middle grade level and that there are typically more Caucasians (57%) than black teachers (35%). Much of the literature has indicated that many of the teachers are working with students who are culturally different and that teachers tend to react to students based on their culture.

On the Hispanic sub-scale of the survey, Caucasian teachers had a higher cell mean score and on the African American sub-scale of the survey, Caucasian teachers had a lower cell mean score than African American teachers. However, according to the Pearson Correlation test, the level of knowledge of the cultures as demonstrated by the surveys, had no significant effect on the number of behavior referrals of either group.

Although the findings were not significant, they did imply that Caucasian females referred more males, both Caucasian and African American, than any of the other groups. Caucasian females also referred more Caucasian males than the other groups. A study by Woolridge and Richman (1985) indicated that Caucasian female teachers were more apt to recommend severe punishment for male students than females and that the punishment was most severe when the offender was a Caucasian male. Examination of the behavior referrals inferred that while teachers tend to refer more African Americans students than their counterparts, African American teachers tend to refer more African American students and very few Caucasian students and no Hispanic students. One explanation may be as Spindler and Spindler (1993) suggested, that teachers bring into the classroom their own culture and expect all students to fit that "mode." Some African American teachers have been Eurocentrically acculturated and, thus, they too tend try to make African American students fit the "mode" of their Caucasian counterparts. African American teachers who are acculturated tend to punish African American students more harshly for a misbehavior than a Caucasian for the same misbehavior.

Another explanation could be that both Caucasian and African American female teachers expect better behavior from students of their own culture.

The statistical analysis found no significant interaction between teachers' gender and race as it pertains to Caucasian, Hispanic, and African American student referrals. However, further examination of the data in the ANOVA indicated that there was a significance of a separate component of the interaction of race in the main effects (.020). This is supported by Sheets and Gay (1996) in which the analysis of disciplinary problems in school shows that the frequencies and severity of infractions correlate positively with the ethnic identity and the sex of students with African American males being most significantly affected.

CONCLUSIONS

The study suggests that there is no relationship between the cultural knowledge of teachers and the behavior referrals of students of different ethic origins. The data indicate that males and especially African American males are referred more often than other students.

The discrepancy indicates that it is not enough to simply be aware of other cultures, but attitudes and sensitivity need to be addressed. Therefore, I would recommend that the study include an attitudinal assessment to address the issue of race.

To be more effective in the classroom, teachers must become more sensitive to the cultural differences of their students. In order to do this, it might be necessary to spend time with the families of these students to gain insight as to their values and customs. Teachers must be willing to adjust and change their attitudes and pre-conceived ideas and biases. Training without willingness to change is fruitless in today's heterogeneous classrooms.

REFERENCES

Bennett, C. (1976). Students' race, social class, and academic history as determinants of teacher expectation of student performance. *Journal of Black Psychology, 3*(1), 71-86.

Bickel, F., & Qualls, R. (1979). The impact of school climate on suspension rates in Jefferson County public schools. *The Urban Review, 12*(2), 79-86.

Brophy, J. E. (1983). Research on the self-fulfilling prophecy and teacher expectation. *Journal of Educational Psychology, 75*(5), 631-661.

Charles, C. M. (1981). *Building classroom discipline.* New York: Longman, Inc.

Cornbleth, C., & Korth, W. (1980, Spring). Teacher perceptions and teacher-student interaction in integrated classrooms. *Journal of Experimental Education, 48*(3), 259-263.

Eaves, R. (1975). Teacher race, student race, and the behavior problem checklist. *Journal of Abnormal Child Psychology, 3*(1), 1-9.

Hale-Benson, J. E. (1986). *Black children: Their roots, culture, and learning styles.* Baltimore: The John Hopkins University Press.

Hare, B. (1987). Coping with double-barreled discrimination.

Journal of Negro Education, 56(1), 100-110.

Harry, B., & Anderson, M. (1994). The disproportionate placement of African American males in special education programs: A critique of the process. *Journal of Negro Education, 63*(4), 602-619.

Jacob, E., Johnson, B., Finley, J., Gurski, J., & Lavine, R. (1996). One student at a time: The cultural inquiry process. *Middle School Journal, 27*(4), 29-34.

Kunjufu, J. (1985). *Countering the conspiracy to destroy black boys.* Chicago: African American Images.

Lewis, D. K. (1975). The black family: Socialization and sex roles. *Phylon, 36*(3), 221-237.

Mitgang, L. (1988, December). *Black students more likely to be punished.* The Macon Telegraph, 1A.

Moore, W. L. and Cooper, H. (1984). Correlations between teacher and student background and teacher perceptions of disciplinary techniques. *Psychology in the Schools, 21,* 386-392.

Project Reach. (1994). *Ethnic Awareness Survey.* Seattle, WA: Reach Center.

Sheets, R. H., & Gay, G. (1996). Student perceptions of disciplinary conflict in ethnically diverse classrooms. *National Association of Secondary School Principals, 80*(580), 84-94.

Simpson, A. W., & Erickson, M. T. (1983). Teachers' verbal and nonverbal communication patterns as a function of teacher race, student gender, and student race. *American Research Journal, 20*(2), 183-198.

Spindler, G., & Spindler, L. (1993). The processes of culture and person: Cultural therapy and culturally diverse schools. In A. L. Davidson & P. Phelan (Eds.), *Renegotiating cultural diversity in American schools* (pp. 27-51). New York: Teachers College Press.

Weitz, S. (1972). Attitude, voice, and behavior. A repressed affect model of interracial interaction. *Journal of Personality and Social Psychology, 24*(1), 14-21.

Woolfork, R., & Woolfork, A. (1974). Effects of teachers' verbal and nonverbal behaviors on students' perceptions and attitudes. *American Education Research Journal, 11*(3), 297-303.

Woolridge, P., & Richman, C. (1985). Teachers' choice of punishment as a functions of a student's gender, age, race, and IQ level. *Journal of School Psychology, 23*, 19-29.

Zintz, M. (1969). *Education Across Cultures.* Iowa: Kendall & Hunt.

Chapter 4
A Celebration of Teaching: A Conference for Students Aspiring to Become Teachers

Rebecca K. Fox
George Mason University, Fairfax, VA

Marjorie H. Haley
George Mason University, Fairfax, VA

==========

Part I: The Need for Teachers of Color
Introduction

Over the past ten to fifteen years, there has been a simultaneous decline in the number of African-American, Hispanic, Asian, and Native American teachers in our nation's schools and an increase in the number of students among these same groups of people of color. A shift in the demographics of our nation coupled with special attention toward our nation's educational goals as we approach the year 2000 have created a fertile opportunity for creating change in our teaching force in order to meet the needs of the classrooms of the twenty-first century. At the same time that this demographic shift has directed national attention to a number of concerns that surround the issue of how many teachers of color there are currently in the teaching force and how many will be needed in the future to equal the percentage of students of color, we must continue to recognize the tremendous value that diversity brings to us. Our schools must work diligently to expand the scope of this situation beyond the issues surrounding number balancing and bring out the positive value gained from a diversity that reflects the population of this democratic nation.

This project is divided into two parts. Part I is a literature review of current issues and trends appearing for publication within the past few years. First, I will examine some of the national demographic changes that have come about in recent years with regard to the student population in the United States and then present information about what has been happening with the representation of teachers of color within our teaching force over the past two decades, including projections for the early twenty-first century. I will discuss the significance of diversity in our nation's schools and examine some of the issues surrounding the need for preserving and advancing diversity in the schools of today and the next century. The next section of the paper will look at the reasons why the number of teachers of color is steadily declining. The last section will discuss the need for targeted teacher recruitment efforts in the area of students of color entering the field of education. The demographics of various areas of the United States show unique population characteristics which have an impact on the needs of schools in those areas. Many different approaches and university-school partnerships serve as examples of the innovative types of models for teacher recruitment and retention that are being implemented around our nation.

Part II will describe a pilot effort at George Mason University in Fairfax, Virginia. As part of Project Diversity, the Graduate School of Education has, with the help of a National Education Association grant, initiated their *Celebration of Teaching: A Conference for Students Aspiring to Become Teachers,* where the University has joined forces with seventeen schools from four surrounding school divisions to reach out to students of all races and ethnicities to encourage them to become teachers. Of particular interest in this pilot teacher recruitment program are the joint planning model involving university and public school personnel, the follow-up contact and coordination planned by the office of Teacher Education with the high school counselors and students who attended the conference, and the targeted outreach to neighboring two-year community colleges. Reversing the trend of declining numbers of teachers of color is a national concern that must not be ignored. It is a trend that will simply not change without concerted, society-wide attention and collaborative efforts.

An Overview of National Data

During the 1970's many educators began to recognize the development of a downward trend in the number of teachers of color in the United States while the corresponding student population in grades K-12 was increasing (Betty, 1990). This trend of decreasing teacher force and increasing student population, in general, did not change in the decade following. In a national survey conducted in the 1980's, statistical analysis showed definite numerical disparities between African American, Hispanic, Asian, and Native American teachers and White teachers Snyder (1987). The National Education Association (1987) published data showing that Whites comprised 89.7% of the teaching force in the U.S. and 71.2% of the student population, whereas African Americans, Hispanics, Asians, and Native Americans, collectively, made up only 10.3% of the teachers and little more than 30% of the student population. Looking at the student population more closely, it is important to note that in 1987, 16.2% of the students in U.S. schools were African American and only 6.9% of the teachers were African American, 9.1% of students and 1.9% of teachers were Hispanics, and Asian/Pacific Islander students represent 2.5% and teachers only 0.6% (Snyder, 1987).

In a 1996 publication by the National Education Association, reports showed that at the beginning of the 1990's slightly over 13% of the teaching force was composed of people of color, while more than 30% of the student population was of color. Another way to look at these percentages is to represent them in actual numbers, such that, with a teaching force of color of 340,412 and a student body of color of approximately 11 million, "there is one minority teacher for every 32 minority students. (With [W]hites, the ratio is one white teacher for every 12 white students)" (NEA, 1996). For the twenty years spanning from around 1970 until 1990-1991, the percentage of teachers of color fluctuated between a low 8.5% and a high of 13.3%.

Table 1
Percentages of Ethnic Minority Students and Teachers for 1991
(National Education Association, 1996, p. 4)

	Students	Teachers
American Indian/Alaska Native	1.0	0.9
Asian & Pacific Islander	3.4	1.4
Black	16.4	8.0
Hispanic	11.8	3.0
White	67.4	86.8

By the year 2000, it is projected that the number of African Americans, Hispanics, Asian/Pacific Islanders, and Native Americans will comprise well over 30% of the student population and probably 6% or less of the teaching force (AACTE, 1990). "The United States is currently experiencing the greatest level of racial and ethnic diversity since its inception . . . and 500,000 legal and approximately 200,000 illegal immigrants have contributed to the population increases [of the current decade]. By 2010, minorities will constitute one-third of the nation" (American Council on Education, 1988, in AACTE, 1990). The minority school-age population is actually expected to increase to far more than 30%, and the statistical projections reflect even higher minority school populations in certain regions of the U.S. (Betty, 1990).

However, the number of teachers of color is on the decline. Furthermore, these percentages and numbers represent an imbalance in our schools that goes beyond what the statistics and the numbers can convey. At this time, there is a heightened awareness of the need for a more accurate representation of our country's actual demographic distribution of ethnicity and race in the teaching force. There is also an immediate need to prepare all teachers to meet the needs of the increasingly diverse student population as we simultaneously try to increase the number of teachers of color in our teacher pool.

Significance of Diversity in our Nation's Schools

A tremendous challenge facing the education community today is helping people understand that diversity is an asset to our nation, not a hurdle to overcome. A value of and an appreciation for cultural diversity encourages diversity and richness of thought--it paves the way for the exchange of different ideas and ways to approach and solve problems. The teaching force needs professional role models to promote education for all students that includes equity and excellence. Just as the lack of teacher role models for children of color to emulate is a recognizably serious problem for them, likewise, White students who do not have the benefit of learning from teachers of varied ethnic backgrounds are equally deprived of a complete education (Michael-Bandele, 1993). At the 1990 National Symposium on Minority Teacher Supply and Demand, presenter Charles Reed, Chancellor, State University System of Florida said that White students who are never given the benefit of experiencing teachers of many ethnicities will be less prepared for the real working world where diversity is a reality and is ever growing (AACTE, 1990). "To deal with diversity, we must abandon the quest for cultural homogeneity and define cultural values that we share as a nation, while simultaneously recognizing and embracing our important differences as a diverse people" (AACTE, 1990).

Teachers of color serve as vital links to understanding and appreciating the cultural differences present in our country today. As the work force becomes more and more culturally diverse, the ability of all citizens to work effectively with people from many cultures becomes essential. Teachers of color can contribute to students' attainment of this skill (Michael-Bandele, 1993). Schools that educate pupils effectively in a positive human relations climate demonstrate appreciation of diversity while focusing on academic achievement and on mutual acceptance and respect among teachers, students, and staff (Mabbut, 1991). Research on prejudice reduction shows that by introducing multi-cultural elements, approaches, and perspectives to schools' curricula, to learning, and to school life, schools can make measurable progress toward creating true social equality (Pate, 1995).

Moreover, teachers not only create the experiences for and shape the attitudes of their students, but they influence their colleagues, as well. For positive changes to occur in our educational system, teachers of all ethnicities and races must confront their own attitudes and knowledge levels about others. The presence of teachers of color in the teaching force can positively influence the attitudes of others and provide a positive impact on diversity awareness in the existing teacher population.

Teachers of color embody the idea that all people can hold positions of leadership in our society. They bring rich perspectives to the schools in which they teach and to the curricula of those schools and school districts. Effective teachers of children of color understand their students, have high expectations of them, and do not categorize them based on social class or standardized scores. "Multi-cultural course development is a very logical response to the abundance of research that indicates a strong relationship between student success and curriculum relevance" (Michael-Bandele, 1993). Teachers of color bring an understanding perspective to the schools in which they teach and can help those schools transform the teaching and learning there to meet the present and future needs of students.

Declining Numbers of People of Color in Education

If the need is so great for diversity in the teaching force, then why is there such a shortage of teachers of color, and why are the numbers continuing to decline? There is not an easy answer to these questions. To provide the reader with an idea of just how drastic the decline has been, in 1976, African Americans earned just over 14,000 undergraduate degrees in education, but by 1989, the number had dropped to approximately 4200 (Haselkorn & Calkins, 1993), while the numbers of other degrees earned increased. The current shortage of and continuing decline in the number of teachers of color is the result of several occurrences over a relatively short period of time. During the 1960's and 1970's, after *Brown vs. Board of Education,* and after desegregation was mandated, many teachers of color were forced to move from teaching in the classrooms of schools they had known into the previously all-white schools, where so many of them were made to feel unwelcome, or were actually not re-hired. New positions were often not filled by African Americans. At the same time that this was happening, many job opportunities that had been previously unavailable to the African American community opened up to them. With the effects of affirmative action, the equal rights movement, and the women's movement, in combination with the low salaries being paid teachers, many people of color left the field of education for a wider spectrum of professional opportunities, many of which were perceived to have more respect and prestige than did teaching (Michael-Bandele, 1993). Salaries are low for teachers as compared to many other professions, and many teachers have left the profession due to "burn out" or discipline problems. There is also a perceived lower social value associated with the teaching profession. Many areas have a low population of people of color, resulting in few representatives who might even consider teaching as a career (NEA, 1996). In addition, many critics of teacher competency tests feel that people of color have been discriminated against by built-in test bias leading to lower test scores on teacher licensing tests (Haselkorn & Calkins, 1993), ultimately resulting in these individuals not even beginning a teacher education program. Figures show that 93% of the White examinees of the National Teacher Exam (NTE) passed in 1983-84, where only 39% of the African Americans and 74% of the Hispanics earned a passing score (Michael-Bandele, 1993). Furthermore, there appears to be a declining number of students of color in high school courses that prepare them for college admission. The lack of adequate preparation in elementary and high school for a higher education track often puts students of color at a disadvantage, so they are less likely to attend college at all, much less consider a teacher education program. If students of color are able to enter college, there has often been a lack of financial help available to them. While the factors above are not a complete representation of all the reasons why there is a decline, they do represent some of the most apparent ones. Many factors have contributed to the current state, but change is underway.

Strategies for Increasing the Number of Teachers of Color, or So, Now What Can We Do?

"The changing demography of the U. S. charges educators to embrace the strengths that a culturally diverse classroom demands. Preparation for this challenging and monumental task demands a sincere commitment from institutions of higher learning" (Larke, Taylor, James, & Washington, 1993). Efforts are currently underway nationwide to develop strategies for the identification, recruitment, and retention of teachers of color. Some of these include programs that identify prospective candidates early in their schooling. Follow-ups to early identification include workshops, summer work on college campuses, financial assistance, counseling, and in-school tutoring. Mentoring in the high schools and colleges has proven to be effective. Many high schools are now sponsoring future teacher clubs or offering teacher cadet classes. Active efforts are being organized to recruit teachers from two-year community colleges into teacher education programs at four year institutions. People of color are also recruited to teaching from business and the military, thus they bring the expertise of their previous professions to classrooms. Financial incentives, including both scholarships and forgivable loans, seem to be attracting more students to teaching. Some of these strategies are combined and used in unique ways in different regions of the U.S. Universities are creating innovative programs. State education associations are taking a close look at their demographic trends and are helping universities create programs which aim to meet the needs of particular regions.

In California, pilot programs sponsored by California State University in the Los Angeles area work with both high school and middle school students during the summer at a Future Teacher Institute held at the Dominguez Hills site. Teams of students work with teachers, mentors, and faculty from the Teacher Education Department. The ethnic mix of this program over the first five years has been 39% Latino, 31% Asian/pacific Islander, 26% African American, and 4%

Caucasian. Other schools throughout the state of California have followed similar models. Supervision and mentoring of these students continues during the school year by teachers at their schools (Braun et al., 1996).

The Aide-to-Teacher Project is a teacher recruitment and preparation project for culturally diverse classroom aides which was also initiated at California State University, Dominguez Hills, in 1987. The program offers financial, academic, and personal support to a special group of paraprofessionals who have been working in the schools as classroom aides. These individuals are representative of the language-diverse population of the area, the students of which may speak any of more than ninety languages including Spanish, Vietnamese, Cantonese, Cambodian, Tagalog, Armenian, Farsi, Korean, or Portugese. Despite their lack of formal training, classroom aides are often the ones who provide day-to-day academic instruction, take over when teachers are absent, translate for the teacher, or negotiate interactions with non-English speaking parents. It is the aim of this special initiative to help this group of paraprofessionals become credentialed teachers by offering financial aid and help in English and mathematics courses that will enable them to complete college degree requirements. In some cases, even child care is considered part of the aid package so that children will be cared for while parents attend classes.

In Arizona, demographic data have indicated that Native Americans, Hispanics, and African Americans have higher dropout rates than Whites. Special programs are being put into place in the Phoenix school district to aid in retention and to encourage students of these ethnic groups to enter the field of education (Betty, 1990).

Xavier University in New Orleans has initiated a Teacher Mentorship Program as part of a comprehensive future teacher development project supported by local public and private funds. It includes future teacher clubs, mentoring, a summer enrichment program, and a parent involvement initiative. The summer enrichment program is held on the university campus and includes college preparatory classes in mathematics, the sciences, language arts, and teacher education. This program serves African Americans almost exclusively, but the description of the program states that there is diversity in the social class and educational backgrounds of the participants.

Minnesota has a rather unique situation, as do several other northern and mid-western states, in that there is only a small (but increasing) population of people of color. Because the student population over the past fifteen years has contained few students of color, the pool of college teacher candidates representing people of color remains small. Yet, there is a need to draw these individuals into the teaching force of the school districts. Minneapolis and St. Paul city schools have seen sharp increases in the enrollment of people of color-- a 70% increase in the past ten years--while the enrollment in the remainder of the state shows a small, but steady, increase. Targeted efforts are underway to meet the current needs and to raise teacher production rates (Betty, 1990).

In New York State, where there is a large urban population and a large percentage of people of color, the State University of New York has numerous projects aimed at encouraging and retaining students in teacher education. One such effort at SUNY Old Westbury is called "Apoyando" (a term which means the act of supporting), a project encouraging Latinos to enter the teaching profession. A particular challenge in this program is Latino teacher. Another SUNY initiative is at Oswego, where the Teaching Assistant Project includes academic advisement, tuition support, and education courses that incorporate urban education issues. Another such initiative aimed toward urban teacher education is a combination project of the Center on Urban Education and the Urban Teacher Opportunity Corps. It provides for current school district teaching assistants and teaching aids to receive financial and educational support to complete a degree in education. Urban education projects are unique to high density population areas and carry with them certain challenges not experienced by other projects. Collaborative efforts of many institutions, school districts, and businesses help to widen the circle of participant inclusion, but there are administrative problems associated with such rapidly expanding programs.

An initiative at George Mason University in Fairfax, Virginia is aimed at recruiting all students, but particularly students of color, into the teaching profession. It is part of a larger effort entitled Project Diversity, whose goal is to form partnerships for improving the education of students in the public schools of Northern Virginia by establishing a system of early identification, recruitment, and financial and academic support which will bring the percentage of minority teachers trained at GMU into alignment with the minority enrollment of the university and the public schools.

All over the United States, from remote and rural Southern regions to the vast mid-western plains, from rugged southwestern states to sprawling cities with highly diverse populations, there is much to be done to meet the goals and objectives of teacher and student recruitment and retention projects. Since we must look at the successes and challenges of projects nationwide and assess their outcomes, we should also take the time to assess these projects from another perspective--on a more individual level. That is, we should also look at some of the personal successes and professional growth experienced by individuals who might not have had such opportunities had special programs not existed. We are all too ready to think only in large numbers, because large change needs to take place. However, if change is to become a reality, it does not occur overnight, or even in a decade. It is the consistent effort and commitment, the education of our society, the collaboration of universities and school districts with businesses and parents, and ultimately the meeting of many needs that will make the important difference in our teacher recruitment initiatives promoting equity and excellence.

Part II: A Close Look at a Multi-Cultural Teacher Recruitment Project at George Mason University

On March 11, 1997, a special conference took place at George

Mason University in Fairfax, Virginia, entitled *A Celebration of Teaching: A Conference for High School Students Aspiring to Become Teachers.* Supported by a National Education Association grant, the *Celebration* was part of the Graduate School of Education's *Project Diversity,* whose goal it was to form partnerships for improving the education of students in the public schools of Northern Virginia by establishing a system of early identification, recruitment, and financial and academic support which will increase the percentage of minority teachers trained at GMU (currently 11%) along with the overall percentage of minority students enrolled at GMU (currently 26.2%). The primary purpose of the conference, now in its second year, is to work in collaboration with surrounding school systems to increase the interest of high school students in the field of education and to increase the number of students of color in the teaching profession and in the teacher education program at George Mason University. Begun as a pilot in 1996, the conference invited students from five area high schools with highly diverse populations. The conference was such a success in its pilot stage that the repeat effort was expanded to include 17 large-minority population high schools in four school districts, and double the number of attendees and presenters.

Despite efforts at George Mason University to increase the number of students of color in its teacher education program over the past several years, the diversity of the program population still did not adequately reflect the proportion of students of color in the public schools in the area. In an effort to remedy this situation and to meet the challenge of a recent NEA policy stating that American students must learn the academic, personal, and social skills they need to function adequately in the multi-cultural workplace of the future, George Mason University has taken several steps to help meet the increased needs and expectations of the 21st century. First, it has begun to form partnerships for improving the education of students in the public schools of Northern Virginia by establishing a system of early identification, recruitment, and financial and academic support which will bring the percentage of minority teachers trained at GMU into alignment with the minority enrollment of the University and the public schools in the area. Second, it is communicating with minority students, parents, and counselors about the benefits of teaching. Third, it has begun work with surrounding school systems and their school administrators to establish Teacher Cadet courses or other organizations for future educators. *A Celebration of Teaching* embodies all of these goals and is helping our university to reach out to the schools to meet the challenge of equity and education for all students.

How Was it Done?

This day-long conference included students, teachers, administrators, and educational personnel from four school districts and George Mason University. Different ethnic, racial, and cultural groups were represented in the planning committee, the attendees, and the presenters. It is the aim of *A Celebration* to be inclusive of all and to model equity and excellence in all facets of the project. The conference program reflected the same richness of cultural diversity in its presenters. For example, the keynote speaker was an African American woman who is the Principal of a local high school. The story she shared with the students was not only compelling, but was an example of how mentoring teachers and positive role models, financial assistance and determination can help an individual reach her dream. Presenters in the small group sessions shared information on "Student and Teacher Diversity in our Schools," "Financial Aid and Other Support," and "Teachers as Leaders." Information was provided to students about what other career path options exist in the field of education other than being a classroom teacher, such as counselors, school psychologists, school administration, and curriculum developers. Because skills learned in education are transferable to other professions, one small group session talked about some of the options open to graduates of teacher education programs. Three schools who already have active teacher clubs presented their programs and made plans to share ideas with the schools forming new clubs. Students had been permitted to choose, in advance, two sessions they were interested in attending, one in the morning and one after lunch.

All students and teachers received packets which included information for them to take home concerning financial assistance at George Mason University and in Virginia generally, teacher salaries in the area's school districts, teacher licensure in Virginia, as well as a few souvenirs and the program of the day's activities. The overall atmosphere was one of genuine enthusiasm on the part of students and teachers alike.

Evaluation of the *Celebration*

Everyone attending the conference was asked to complete an evaluation form. The adults attending the conference rated it a 4.5 out of a possible 5, 1 being the lowest rating (poor) and 5 being the highest (excellent), with a 51% response rate. The students attending rated the conference a 5, on the same scale of 1 to 5, with a 79% response rate.

Since we wanted to see how the conference might have affected the attitudes of those attending, we asked for attendees to share information about what they learned, what they liked best about the conference, and how the conference might have changed their minds about teaching. We also wanted them to take information back to their schools about teaching and about the conference, so we asked them to share some of the ideas they had gleaned from the day's experiences that they might take back to their schools to share with fellow students. We used the information from our evaluation survey form in two ways: (a) to include the students' ideas and perspectives in the planning process for next year's *Celebration*, and (b) to provide a forum for dialogue between the students and our university in order to provide support, answer questions, and address concerns the students might have about teaching in general. Answers and information were provided to the students after the conference via mail to their schools. In one case, a student asked if someone from the university could come to speak at the monthly meeting of their "Grow-A-Teacher Club." We were able to comply with that request, visited the school, and have maintained contact with club members through its officers and sponsor. In addition, a newly created teacher cadet course is now being offered for academic credit at that high school. This school will be one of our presenting groups at the 1998 *Celebration*. In general, the evaluation responses provided excellent feedback about the conference and created an opportunity for ongoing contact with several of the participating students and schools.

Afternoon Recruitment Seminar

In addition to the *Celebration of Teaching* conference program, an afternoon seminar was held for principals and career counselors of the attending schools. The purpose of this seminar was to bring together some of the principals and career counselors of the attending schools to discuss how we could all better respond to the diversity in our schools. It was an effort to continue dialogue with important role models and administrators at the schools who might have on-going contact with the students who attended the conference. All four school districts were represented, but not all schools. Some of the recommendations that were put up for further discussion included:

1. Providing university faculty as mentors for any partner school that establishes pre-teaching activities.
2. Following up the day's conference with personal communication to each participant (both students and adults).
3. Include students on the Planning Committee for next year's conference.
4. Recruit Student Teachers of America members at the university and at the community college campuses to serve as mentors to high school students.
5. Build on high school activities designed to provide academic, experiential and motivational support to minority students.
6. Involve groups of male high school athletes in elementary school tutoring and mentoring.
7. Explore ways to increase the availability of scholarships and

other financial support for teacher preparation in shortage areas, e.g.:

(a) lobbying for increases in funding for the Virginia. Teaching Scholarship Loan Program, which provides forgivable loans for teacher preparation in critical shortage areas such as Special Ed., Spanish, Physics, Chemistry, Technology, males for elementary/middle schools, and minorities for all licensure areas,

(b) apprising students of the availability of the many small scholarships available for support of teacher education and of the Virginia Transfer Grant program,

(c) establishing GMU Foundation accounts for contributions from GSE faculty to support scholarships for course work leading to licensure, and

(d) Establishing or utilizing school division or regional foundations to collect and disburse tax-exempt contributions for teacher preparation.

8. Contact educational publishing companies as a source of support for recruitment activities.

9. In recruitment, stress the marketability and transferability of teaching skills.

There was a follow-up action plan established that would enable university organizers, school administrators and teachers, and students to remain in contact with one another as a result of the *Celebration*. A list of applicable materials, free or for a fee, about minority teacher recruitment and retention, future teacher clubs, and other support information was compiled and sent to each meeting attendee. The University was to also initiate a plan for establishment of Student Teacher Associations at the nearby community college campuses. A resource file of scholarship opportunities was to be established as a nucleus for an expanded data base at GMU. Plans for a third *Celebration of Teaching* were discussed, and a date was set for an evaluation critique meeting of the second conference. Follow-up letters were sent to each school contact thanking them for their participation and including information about the University and its teacher education program. The results of the formal evaluation of the conference were included.

Where Do We Go Now?

Plans are already underway for next year's conference. The date has been set and the Planning Committee has been contacted. A time line for accomplishing a larger and more ambitious effort has been established, and meetings will begin in late September. There is much more to do that will reach out to students encouraging them to enter the profession of teaching so that they can help our nation make a difference in the education of our future citizens.

If we believe that all people deserve a rich and equal education and if we are committed to the development of a new social order that is inclusive and just, then we have much important work to do. We must strive for diversity in teaching as if our very lives depend upon it. (A. Lin Goodwin cited in AACTE, 1990, p. 3)

Bibliography

American Association of Colleges for Teacher Education. (1987). *Recruiting minority teachers: A practical guide.* Washington, DC: Author. (ERIC Document Reproduction Service No. ED 315 416)

American Association of Colleges for Teacher Education. (1990). *Minority teacher supply & demand: The next level.* National Symposium Proceedings & Policy Statement. Washington, DC: AACTE Publications.

Betty, S. (1990). *New strategies for producing minority teachers: A technical report.* Denver, CO: Education Commission of the States.

Braun, J., Felder, C., Lane, M., Marini, N., Kennedy, J., & Woolfolk-Millette, T. (1996). Strategies for encouraging minority high school students to consider teaching careers: A panel presentation by the consortium for minorities in teaching careers. In E. Middleton, E. Basualdo, F. Bickel, S. Fleury. H. Gordon, & E. Mason (Eds.), *Proceedings of the ninth national Conference for Recruitment and Retention of Minority Students* (pp. 20-32). Oswego, NY: State University of New York at Oswego.

Doston, G. A., & Bolden, S. H. (1993). Public School/University Partnerships for the Recruitment and Retention of minorities in teacher education: New programs, a descriptive assessment. In E. Middleton, F. Bickel, E. Mason, D. Jones, W. Stilwell, & A. Frederick (Eds.). *Proceedings of seventh national Conference for Recruitment and Retention of Minority Students* (pp. 81-91). Lexington, KY: Center for Professional Development, College of Education, University of Kentucky.

Education Commission of the States. (1990). *New strategies for producing minority teachers: Plans & programs.* Denver: ECU Distribution Center.

Haberman, M. (1989). More minority teachers. *Phi Delta Kappan, 70* (10), 771-776.

Haselkorn, D., & Calkins, A. (1993). *Careers in teaching handbook.* Belmont, MA: Recruiting New Teachers, Inc.

Haynes, B. P. (1993). A collaborative and comprehensive approach to recruiting and retaining minorities in teacher education. In E. Middleton, F. Bickel, E. Mason, D. Jones, W. Stilwell, & A. Frederick (Eds.), *Proceedings of seventh national Conference for Recruitment and Retention of Minority Students* (pp. 37-44). Lexington, KY: Center for Professional Development, College of Education, University of Kentucky.

James, J. R. (Ed.). (1993). *Recruiting people of color for teacher education.* (Hot Topics Series.) Bloomington, IN: Center for Evaluation, Development, and Research.

Larke, P. J., Taylor, G., James, F. G., & Washington, S. (1993). Minorities interested in teaching conference: A response to the shortage of minority teachers. In E. Middleton, F. Bickel, E. Mason, D. Jones, W. Stilwell, & A. Frederick (Eds.), *Proceedings of seventh national Conference for Recruitment and Retention of Minority Students* (pp. 22-28). Lexington, KY: Center for Professional Development, College of Education, University of Kentucky.

Mabbut, R. (1991). *Prejudice reduction: What works?* Boise, ID: Idaho Human Rights Commission. (ERIC Document Reproduction Service No. ED 355 303)

Michael-Bandele, M. (1993). *Who's missing from the classroom: The need for minority teachers.* (Trends and Issues Paper No. 9). Washington, DC: Eric Clearinghouse on Teacher Education, American Association of Colleges for Teacher Education.

National Education Association. (1987). *Status of the American public school teacher, 1985-86.* Washington, DC: Author. (ERIC Document Reproduction Service No. ED 284 330)

National Education Association. (1996). *National directory of successful strategies for the recruitment and retention of minority teachers.* Washington, DC: NEA.

Pate, G. S. (1995). *Prejudice reduction and the findings of research.* (Tucson): University of Arizona. (ERIC Document Reproduction Service No. ED 383 803)

Smith, A. P. (1993). An early intervention model: Addressing the academic, social, and identity issues that affect the advancement of African-American students. In E. Middleton, F. Bickel, E. Mason, D. Jones, W. Stilwell, & A. Frederick (Eds.), *Proceedings of seventh national Conference for Recruitment and Retention of Minority Students* (pp. 6-11). Lexington, KY: Center for Professional Development, College of Education, University of Kentucky.

Snyder, T. D. (1987). Digest of education statistics, 1987. Washington, DC: U.S. Government Printing Office. (ERIC

Document Reproduction Service No. ED 282 359)

Snyder, T. D., & Hoffman, C. M. (1991). *Digest of education statistics, 1991.* Washington, DC: National Center for Education Statistics, U.S. Dept. of Education. (ERIC Document Reproduction Service No. ED 330 086)

Vaughn, J. (1996). Integrating the recruitment preparation and retention strategies of persons of color in teaching. In E. Middleton, E. Basualdo, F. Bickel, S. Fleury, H. Gordon, & E. Mason (Eds.), *Proceedings of ninth national Conference for Recruitment and Retention of Minorities in Education* (pp. 9-19). Oswego, NY: State University of New York at Oswego.

Warshaw, M. B. (1993). *Aide-to-teacher project.* Los Angeles: California State University, Dominguez Hills, Consortium for Minorities in Teaching Careers.

Chapter Five
The VENN View of Diversity:
Understanding Differences Through Similarities

Jack Levy
George Mason University, Fairfax, VA

===========================

Rationale

The current debate on diversity and multiculturalism in education has become fractious due to an over-emphasis on differences between groups. What is lost is the realization that people are members of many sub-cultures, and they frequently have as much in common as not. True appreciation of diversity -- and the opportunity to take mutual advantage of it -- can only be achieved after initial unifying bridges of similarity are built.

The VENN View of Diversity is a series of research projects which examine diversity and conflict from a "common ground" standpoint. Though it takes different forms according to context, the common ground process features dialogue (as opposed to debate) in a search for shared viewpoints. It encourages connective thinking, the sharing of personal experiences, the formulation of genuine questions, and a joint activity which emerges from the dialogue. Its goal is to develop or strengthen community through a relationship in which similarities soften differences to the point of tolerance (and, hopefully, appreciation).

Writing about the common-ground approach as applied to the abortion conflict, Jacksteit & Kaufmann (1995) described it as,

> "... a matter of emphasis, focusing attention on areas of commonality rather than on areas of difference. It is developing the rapport and safety to struggle respectfully with the tough questions

> that are at the heart of . . . conflict. It is an effort
> to reach understanding, not necessarily
> agreement. It is building an agenda to address
> issues that need the cooperative effort of both
> sides. (p. 2)

In various forms, the common ground strategy for conflict resolution is as old as conflict itself. The idea is especially relevant within the context of the struggle between postmodernism and structuralism, which has clearly contributed to the splintering of U.S. society. Though the affirmative strand of postmodernist thought espouses pluralism, the U.S. is unfortunately a long way from achieving this goal. For example, despite admirable objectives, multicultural education is noted more for controversy than acceptance.

Nonetheless, thoughtful professionals in many fields have successfully employed common ground techniques to build cross-cultural respect and resolve conflicts. The following are a few examples.

There have been a number of efforts to apply common ground thinking to the most glaring areas of need -- race, ethnic and gender relations, stereotyping, and prejudice. Multicultural educators have compiled an impressive research record (see Banks & Banks, 1995), as well as a library's worth of curricular and instructional ideas to enable students to develop balance between perceptions of difference and similarity (see Nieto, 1992; Tiedt & Tiedt, 1995; Bennett, 1994). Some specific common-ground classroom approaches have been described by Van Steenbergen (1994), Batt (1988), and Stover (1990), among others. Recent race-specific treatments of common ground approaches have been described for conflicts between Blacks and Whites by Hill (1993) Native-Americans and Whites by Whaley and Bresett (1994), Arabs and Jews by Divine (1992), and Koreans and Blacks by Nakama (1993).

The legacy of cultural separation produced by the conflict between postmodernism and structuralism has fueled a discussion on the disappearance of community in the U.S. Popularized in The Habits of the Heart (Bellah, Madsen, Sullivan, Swidler, & Tipton, 1985) and more recently espoused by the Communitarian Movement (Etzioni, 1993), the problem has been described as abandonment -- or rejection -- of the mutually-agreed upon, shared morals which hold groups together. This is especially true in urban areas, and the use of a common-ground approach to rebuild our cities has been commented on by Anderson (1990), Mirel (1993), and Nakama (1993). The decline in community (and corresponding weaknesses in the role of family and education) has contributed to the popularity of the Character Education and Moral Education movements in schools.

Possibly no greater use of the common ground approach has been made than in the fields of organizational behavior and management. A number of popular theories -- participatory management, Quality Circles, Theory Z, The Learning Organization -- rest on the assumption that all employees will find common ground in the organization's well-being. Case studies on the common ground approach to management and organizational behavior are provided by Firth (1991), Lanham (1992), and Khermouch (1994), among many others.

The Venn projects apply the common ground approach to education. The title for the research theme comes from the VENN diagram, which depicts the relationship between two concepts or categories. Normally presented by two or more circles which overlap, it describes in graphic form the differences and similarities between the concepts. The diagram was developed by John Venn in the 19th century.

VENN features a series of studies whose central theme is the perception of cross-cultural commonalities. This paper will report on four studies spanning different student populations: sixth and eighth graders, elementary gifted and talented (G/T) students, students in conflict, and university freshmen (see Notes for other papers in the series).

Sixth-Eighth Grade Students

One class of sixth grade students and three classes of eighth grade students were asked to think about someone who is different from them in race, ethnic background, age, gender, religion or anything else which seemed important. The results are reported separately for each grade level.

Sixth-Grade Class

Method. During the last week of school in 1996, a class of 26 sixth graders from a Northern Virginia elementary school were asked the following questions in writing (for homework):

> Think about someone you have met or worked with either in school or out of school who is <u>different</u> from you. What did you learn about how you and the other person are <u>alike</u>? Name as many things as you can that you have in <u>common</u>. How are you going to <u>use</u> this knowledge about what you have in <u>common</u> with people from different groups for next year?

Of the 26 students there were 18 girls and 8 boys. Among them were one Latina, five African-Americans (all girls), three students of mixed parentage, and 17 whites. (NOTE: Identification was made by the teacher; the children were not asked, nor were school records reviewed.) The children's answers are illuminating from several viewpoints: the types of group differences they found important, the commonalities they identified, and the use they would make of the new knowledge.

1)   Different Groups. The children identified people who were different from them in many ways. Some would seem to be inconsequential (e.g., "uses scrunchy's and long pants for PE"), while others seemed more profound (religion, skin color). Most of the students didn't clarify which differences were important and unimportant (and they were not asked to do so). This was

noteworthy, and may indicate their inability to differentiate significant and insignificant characteristics. It might mean, however, that they've considered all these differences and they all seem to have equal weight in determining the behavior and characteristics of the identified other. Finally, it might mean they misunderstood the assignment and did not associate differences with groups. (In some of the VENN studies which followed, students were asked to select the important differences.) A few examples, some excerpted from narratives and others from lists, follow. The first group was contributed by girls, the second by boys.

Girls

- "The person I chose is different than me because she dresses different, uses scrunchy's . . . , long pants for PE, different religion, different color, and she paints her nails."
- "He is a male, he's sweet, mean, nice, thoughtful, shorter than me, he's giving, loving, playful, funny, he's fun, and he sometimes has temper tantrums."
- "My friend is very different from me. She is tall . . . she likes to read . . . she has a good opinion [sic] . . . I can't stand skirts, but she loves them. . . . she has much longer hair . . . she doesn't play football, now what kind of person is that? A very weird one."
- "I'm African-American, she's Caucasian. She works. I go to school. She seems to always be calm and yet I am fifty/fifth. She is an adult. I'm only a child. She has her own car. I have my own bike. She has her own house. I have my own room."
- "She's black, I'm white, she listens to R&B, I listen to alternative, she has a lot of patients [sic], I don't."
- "He is a boy, he has 3 sisters and he's in the 7th grade."
- "My friend likes basketball, I don't like basketball that much. My friend can be a troublemaker . . . my friend lives

with their grandparents, I live with my parents. My friend is male, I'm female."
- "She came from a different country. She is a different color. And she has a different religion than me."
- "My friend is different in a lot of ways, mainly that he is male."

Boys

- "He loves football and baseball. I like baseball a bit but I hate football. He also has 2 brothers and I have 1."
- "He uses a computer to write because his hand writing is bad. He likes playing video games all day, but I prefer going out and exploring. . . . He hates to do new things, I'm a little more daring."
- "We are different in ways like we dress different, we hang out with different people, we sometimes disagree on things, and we like to play with different toys."
- "He's black and I am mixed with black and white. And he is smaller than me."

2) Similarities. As expected, the pattern of grouping seemingly important and unimportant characteristics together was also found in the students' views of things they have in common. Once again, the girls' excerpts are presented first:

Girls

- "We are in common because we have same friends, rings, skirt and glasses. We sometimes both wear shorts on hot days. We are alike and different in many ways, and we are special for that."
- "We're both the same color, we're also the same race (black). We're both nice and mean and we both like basketball . . . we both have the same shoes."
- "X and I are alike in many ways. Both of us have temper

tantrums sometimes, we're both mean, nice, playful, loving, giving, we both like to play basketball, we both have nice hair, both of us have a brother, we like go-go and rap, we like laughing, we both go to Y school, we care about people, both of us can be kind at times, we're greedy and we can be annoying too."

- "Even though X and I are very different, we are still very much alike. Both of us are females. Both of us work at Y school (only she gets paid). We both like nature. We both love helping people and we both are very busy people. I learned so much about X because sometimes we would just talk and talk. She tells me things and I tell her things."

- "We both like to talk on the phone, both like to work on the computer, both of us like to camp, we both like to play sports . . . and ride bikes."

- "We're both girls. Both our names start with 'L', we both have pierced ears, we're both in the same class."

- "We both love cats and have 3 cats. He is also caring and nice and I think I'm pretty nice and caring too."

- "We're both short . . . both wear earrings, have dark hair and have younger siblings. We both share well with others, and we both like helping out with different things, but most of all, we love to laugh."

- "We love sports, movies, to laugh, to talk in general and we are both hyper."

Boys

- "We're both funny, in the 6th grade, like to eat, like sports, both males."

- "We like to play magic . . . like sports . . . to skate . . . music . . . we both have a brother and we're both boys."

- "We are both 11 right now and we both like pushing our brothers down the stairs."

- "Like to explore old houses, likes Star Wars, video games,

watch movies."
- "Likes sports, don't like our brothers, we both get mad at one person in particular, both are in band, both boys, both 11, same hair color."

3)   Future Application of Knowledge. Most of the students felt that their new knowledge would help their understanding of other people (not just the person they identified). Some excerpts:

Girls
- (Speaking about a male) "I think I'll understand better what's going on in there (sic) heads. I'll be able to relate to them about sports easier."
- "It's good to have 'different groups' because you get to know different opinions and feelings."
- (Speaking about a male) "Every time I meet someone I think of this person and use this paper to see if I want a friend like this person, or do I want to have a different type of friend, but keep some of the same qualities this person has."
- "Try to keep things right and to do things their way sometimes."
- (Speaking about a male) "If I was to meet someone I would want them to have the same qualities as X or at least have a couple of qualities that X has. The number one quality I am looking for in a friend is for someone to bring out the best in me and X is the person who brought out the best in me."
- (Speaking about an adult) "I will use the knowledge that I learned from X. Don't judge anyone, keep self-control, etc. by keeping calm, keep my temper under control, be a good student by turning in my work on time, try to stay out of trouble, try not to give into peer pressures and not to judge anyone by their race, religion or actions."
- "She has taught me to give everyone a chance and not to

disinclude anyone because they are different."
- "I will be able to use these (knowledge of commonalities) to make new friends and may be more patient."
- "I have learned to be friends with anyone who wants to be friends with me, no matter their color, race or sex."
- "I'll be able to make new friends, stay in touch and in step with a lot of people . . . I'll try to stay understanding and listen to people."
- "I'll understand differences and what we have in common. I'll show how much I like a person by being nice to everyone. I'll have fun! Stay in the right groups, learn about the people you're around."
- (Speaking about an older student) "I've learned you shouldn't judge people, who they hang with, what their race is, and what they do. And I'll have some more things in common with my friend next year. Like we'll ride the same bus, we'll go to the same school, and we'll both get back from school at the same time."

Boys
- "So I know who to hang out with."
- "Working with him taught me not to judge someone by who they hang out with or how they dress."
- "To accept others that are different to be your friend."
- "The way I'm going to apply this is first going to find out how they act and try to get on people's good side."
- "He spends more of his time studying than I do so I think some of that should rub off on me next year."
- "I will be friends with people no matter what their color or race or sex."

Eighth Grade Classes
Method. In May, 1997, three classes of eighth grade students in a Northern Virginia middle school were asked to think about someone

who is different from them, and identify the three most important differences and commonalities. They responded to the following two questions (in writing):

- How will this information impact the way you will think or behave the next time you meet or are with someone who is different from you?
- What do all people have in common?

Of the 57 students, there were 38 girls and 19 boys. Among them were 19 Hispanics, 18 Whites, 14 East or Southeast Asians, 2 South Asians, 2 African-Americans and 2 Middle Easterners. (Once again, identification was made by the teacher.) As with the sixth graders, the children's answers are illuminating from the standpoint of differences, commonalities and future use of the knowledge.

1)   Differences. Of the 173 differences identified by the group, more than one-third (60) focused on race/skin color, ethnicity, language, gender, or religion. Another 25% (44) identified interaction style and temperament, including differences in personality, values, and way of thinking. While it isn't possible to generalize from four groups of students, there is a clear demarcation between the sixth and eighth graders in the types of differences they identified. The directions to the two groups were virtually the same, and one reason the eighth graders concentrated on race, ethnicity, etc., may have been the mindset created by the teacher. Nonetheless, the instructions did not include any reference to personality or temperament. A clear majority of the older students felt that the groups one belongs to and the way one views the world are quite meaningful in terms of relationships.

While age and maturity (and the teacher's directions) might have contributed to this result, it should be noted that the eighth grade group was much more ethnically diverse than their younger peers. Focusing on ethnic, racial, language and gender differences might easily be expected in such an atmosphere.

2)   Commonalities. The eighth graders felt they were most similar in the same categories they identified above -- race, ethnicity, gender, language, religion, and interpersonal style/worldview. When thinking of commonalities, however, they also identified physical characteristics (facial characteristics, size, age) and hobbies and mutual interests, such as sports or music. Once again, they differentiated themselves from their sixth-grade counterparts in the types of characteristics they considered important.

3)   Future Application of Knowledge.   In perhaps the most interesting outcome of this phase, the majority of students stated that this information (an understanding of differences and commonalities) would have no impact on the next time they meet someone who is different from them because they already treat people in an equitable manner (my phrasing). Some examples:

- "Will act the same; don't care what race they are."
- "Won't impact me when I meet someone because I look at everyone the same as they would to me."
- "I might have an extremely small impact or no impact at all because I always knew this."
- "This won't because I look at our small difference."
- "I think I will be the same."
- "Probably won't, but if it does, I usually try to think the best of him."
- "Won't impact the way I treat another person that's different from me because I realized that everyone should be different and that it's good, so that people have a sense of belonging."
- "Won't change the way I behave or what I think."

- "Won't impact me in any way. Don't care how someone looks."

There were some noteworthy comments from individual students. One student thought about someone who is different from her in terms of race, <u>but is the same skin color</u>. When asked how she might use this information in the future she responded "I'll try to find the things we have in common before I jump on them for being so different than me; I would get to know them."

A handful of students felt that they would use the information toward relationship-building:

- "Being myself, I would like to be with someone different for I could see what they are like."
- "Act friendly and try to get to know that person."
- "Maybe I will consider some of this facts so I can understand that person so we can get along."
- "Won't affect anything. Usually I try to get used to their differences and get to know them better if they are nice to me and willing to accept my differences."
- "I think from now on when I meet someone with different appearance I should consider their inside. Maybe they have lots of things in common with me that I don't know."

In general, the students' responses seemed to indicate an understanding of the need for fairness in developing relationships. (This outcome was similar to the sixth-grade girls' responses). Whether these students have actually internalized this equity-oriented attitude or view it more as a response to a test item is difficult to discern. Nonetheless, it is heartening to realize that, for the most part, these eighth-graders seem to cognitively understand the concept of equal treatment.

Implications

While this study is only a snapshot of two age groups within four classes, it does provide some instructive direction for future analyses. The eighth graders identified consistently more "significant" (by my determination) commonalities and differences than the sixth-grade class. Further, both groups showed clear evidence of understanding the basic tenets of pluralism and equity. Finally, the types of similarities identified can help teachers in grouping, assignments, and individual interactions with students. They can also play an important role in avoiding conflict, building confidence, and increasing motivation in class.

Elementary Gifted/Talented Students

Five classes of gifted/talented students also participated in the project. An ethnic/gender description for each class appears below:

Grade	Total	Boys	Girls	Ethnicity
4	12	8	4	8 - White; 2 - African American
				1 - S/E Asian; 1 - Mixed
4	13	4	9	11 - White; 2 - S/E Asian
5	10	4	6	4 - White; 4 - African American
				1 - S/E Asian; 1 - Mixed
5	12	6	6	10 - White; 2 - S/E Asian
6	14	6	8	12 - White; 1 - S/E Asian; 1 - Mixed
Totals	61	28	33	45 - White; 6 - African American
				7 - S/E Asian; 3 - Mixed

Except for one fifth grade class, none of these groups were diverse ethnically, and they were basically evenly divided in terms of gender. Their task was essentially the same as previous groups; the teacher, however, asked them to both list as many commonalities and differences as possible and identify the three most important from each list. They were then asked to think about how this information might be helpful in the future.

1)   Differences. Though closer in age to the sixth graders, the G/T students' responses resembled the eighth-grade classes. They consistently identified race/skin color, ethnicity, language and gender as their most important differences. While it might be said that they (and the other participants described above) were

led to these conclusions by the nature of teacher directions, their answers clearly differed from the sixth graders (a general education group). They diverged from the eighth-grade participants in one significant aspect: the G/T students did NOT identify interaction style, temperament, personality, or worldview as important differences. They basically stuck to the categories provided in the directions.

2) Commonalities. The latter pattern (of not recognizing interpersonal behavior or attitude) was displayed in the G/T students' identification of similarities. They mostly identified hobbies and mutual interests, or physical characteristics such as gender, size, facial characteristics, and the like.

When asked to think about commonalities, many of these 61 students were not only creative in their reflection, but in their written descriptions. Some examples:

- "We wear the same clothes, read the same books, like the same animals, like the same people, enjoy the same activities, go to the same places and buy the same things without know it." (6th grade)
- "Make new friends easily, male, kids, learning and teaching ability, niceness, outdoor sports, games, indoor sports, Star Wars interests, creativity, language, and feel." (5th)
- "Allergic to pollen." (5th)
- "Friendly ... smart ... happy ... pessimists." (5th)
- "We play cops and robbers together ... his background ... we're both outspoken." (4th)

3) Future Use of Knowlege. As with previous groups, the G/T students generally felt that different people should be treated with respect and dignity. Once again, some of their answers are presented in a colorful manner.

- "We use it to make our relationship unique and better. It's fun to (be) different and same at times. It never stops us though with people and each other because we are equal." (5th)
- "Never talk about religion." (4th)
- "I don't think it will change the way I behave, but maybe the way I think. I think of him differently then I do now. I used to think of him as a rat, but he's really a snob." (5th)
- "I never realized we were so different. I will from now on realize that differences don't matter. And that I should write to my friends more often." (4th grade)
- "I know that if someone I knew was different from me I wouldn't care about what they looked like or what background they came from. I'd notice more of the way they act and their personality." (4th)
- "I will really try to respect her talents and hobbies. Our differences won't affect our friendship and our similarities will make us get to be better friends. Now that I recognize these difference and similarities I will grown to understand her better." (4th grade)
- "I will really try to respect her talents and hobbies. Our differences won't affect our friendship and our similarities will make us get to be better friends. Now that I recognize these differences and similarities I will grow to understand her better." (4th)
- "I will never 'judge a book by its cover' or not like someone because they're different. We've all the same inside; you can't figure out someone's disposition or personality by their appearance." (5th)
- "I sometimes don't like playing with him when he knocks on the door, but I'll remember that he only lives with his mother and I will try to make it easy for him." (6th)
- "You can't expect people to be exactly the same type as you. I think that I won't ever (at least I'll try not to) judge

people before I know them. A lot of people are alike in most ways if you look on the inside." (6th)

Implications

The classroom implications of the G/T students' perceptions are not significantly different from those of the other elementary/middle school participants. They clearly differ, however, in their manner of reflection and written expression. They tended to cite characteristics which were more detailed and unique (e.g., "has tadpoles (mine died)"). Since they also identified a great number of commonalities (on average), this provides a broader base for teachers in terms of building community through grouping. This attribute (of being able to name many commonalities) will also appear in the next study.

Students in Conflict

As mentioned, the Venn project is based on a common-ground approach to conflict resolution. The third study describes the common-ground perceptions of elementary and middle school students who had just agreed, after partaking in a peer-mediation process, to end their conflicts. While more than fifty pairs of students participated, for purposes of this paper the results for only 32 pairs (64 students) are reported. Each of the 32 pairs represent cross-cultural conflicts, in the sense that disputants were different in either ethnicity, gender, or both. There were four overlapping pairs where students differed in both categories, and results will therefore be presented for 36 pairs of disputants.

The students proceeded through a standard peer-mediation process prior to being asked about their commonalities. Each was asked to provide his/her story, followed by an attempt by the mediators (there were two for each conflict) to facilitate a signed agreement to end the dispute. Once the conflict was resolved, each disputant was individually interviewed by a mediator who had been trained for this additional phase of the process. Each student was asked to reflect on the process s/he had just completed, and to think about what s/he learned about the other disputant. The student was then asked to think about "things" s/he had in common with the other party, or in the case of the younger children, "how you and X are alike." Finally, students were asked how they might use this information in the future.

In an additional segment to the study, a sample of elementary mediators and four students who had been in a conflict were extensively interviewed. The results for this piece will be reported in a separate paper.

The results described below are preliminary, and data collection and analysis will proceed throughout this coming academic year. The results have been divided in two parts: commonalities between males and females, and those between students from different ethnic backgrounds. Only the commonalities will be reported on; the questions pertaining to what disputants learned from their peers, and how they will use this information have not been included in this analysis.

Data were analyzed according to the total number of commonalities mentioned by each student, and the types of commonalities which were mentioned by both disputants/mediators. Commonalities were grouped according to the following categories (a full list appears in the Appendix). The categories were determined after an analysis of all students' entries (rather than being decided before the data was reviewed).

1. FOOD
2. SCHOOL CLASSES/SUBJECTS/ACTIVITIES
3. HOBBIES
4. PHYSICAL CHARACTERISTICS
5. INTERACTION STYLE/TEMPERAMENT
6. CLOTHING, APPEARANCE
7. COLORS
8. RACE, ETHNICITY, RELIGION
9. MUSIC
10. FAMILY

11. MISCELLANEOUS

1)   Male-Female Commonalities
Seventeen pairs of disputants were asked about perceived commonalities. The following grades were represented:

Grade	# Pairs	Grade	#Pairs
1	1	5	0
2	2	6	1
3	2	7	4
4	2	8	3

Few patterns were uncovered in the data analysis. Both males and females described an average of about five commonalities they shared with their "partner." Most chose obvious similarities: school activities (such as the same class, grade, teacher) or hobbies (sports). There were no real differences between age groups. The younger students selected school activities and hobbies similar to those of their older peers, and they did this at the same rate. Of the 20 pairs, 14 identified one or more commonalities in common (there were 18 identified in all). In these cases each student accurately perceived the other as sharing the same interest or characteristic. Most of the time this occurred, however, students generally stated that they were in the same class or grade. In one instance the students also perceived that they belonged to the same ethnicity (African-American), and in two cases students named interaction styles/temperament commonalities (both "fight" and "get angry").

2)   Cross-ethnic commonalities
There were 16 cross-ethnic disputes during the year, with two at the elementary level and the remaining 14 in the middle school. A breakdown of conflicts according to ethnicity appears below, ranked according to frequency.

Disputants	# Pairs
Hispanic-African American	6
Hispanic-White	4
White- African American	3
White-Middle Eastern	1
Middle Eastern-Hispanic	1
African American-Asian	1

Once again, few patterns emerge from the data. The approximate average number of commonalities identified by students was 4.8, similar to the male-female results above. There seemed to be a slight difference in the often-cited commonalities between the ethnic and gender pairs. Students in cross-ethnic conflicts identified a greater number of hobbies that they had in common with their counterparts, whereas the gender groups were more evenly divided between school activities and hobbies. Once again, common enjoyment of sports was mentioned more than other hobbies, though not to a significant degree.

Results were further analyzed by cross-ethnic dispute. In other words, Hispanic-African American disputes were examined separately from Hispanic-White and White-African American. As before, no significant patterns emerged.

Implications

While no significant patterns emerged, some of the results are noteworthy. It is heartening to learn that students who have just been through a conflict can still manage to name nearly a half-dozen interests and characteristics they share with their fellow disputants. While this might be a testament to the power of peer-mediation, it is also a valuable source of information for teachers and counselors. Further, the most-frequently mentioned commonalities were school activities and hobbies. It should not be difficult for teachers and counselors to learn which hobbies students have in common (participants named more than forty) and use this information in instruction, grouping, and conflict resolution.

Further, it didn't seem that disputants were very aware of similarities they shared with their counterparts. In other words, students did not often identify the same commonalities as their partners. While this might indicate inaccurate perceptions, it probably does not. If student A says that s/he shares characteristics 1, 2 and 3 with student B, and if student B says that s/he shares characteristics 4, 5 and 6 with student A, they are probably basing their perceptions on observations or real experiences (e.g., as a witness to a class or school activity, or hobby). Thus, the fact that both students perceive different commonalities provides educators with an expanded pool of shared characteristics from which to select.

Finally, it's instructive to note that the commonalities identified by the disputants were more obvious and non-substantial than those cited by the previous student groups. This might be due to the effect of conflict, which might highlight aspects of disagreement at the expense of those of common ground.

National Coalition-Building Institute (NCBI)

The NCBI leads prejudice-reduction workshops in a variety of work settings. Participants come to an understanding of institutionalized racism by experiencing a series of personal and small group explorations. The program seeks to identify and decrease stereotyping, beginning by having participants explore their first thoughts about specific groups. They meet in pairs and select an ethnic, racial, gender, or religious group to which neither partner belongs. With each taking a turn, one partner says the name of the group; the other, without hesitation, free associates and says his or her first uncensored thoughts. When these thoughts are shared in a large group it becomes readily apparent that everyone has internalized negative stereotypes about some group. The advantage of this process is the common discovery that everyone harbors negative stereotypes; no one person or group is singled out for blame.

Next, the program has participants focus on their own groups, identifying first internalized stereotypes and then characteristics of which they are proud. Finally, there are a series of exercises in which individuals and groups share incidents of racism and discrimination. The overall effect is quite powerful, and the program concludes with a skill-development segment on assertive behaviors to build coalitions and avoid stereotyping.

Method. The normal duration of the NCBI workshop is eight hours. Due to time limitations, the program was condensed to two hours for the 175 first-year George Mason University students who participated in fall 1996 and 1997. While much of the intensity was diminished, the students were nonetheless able to focus on racism, discrimination, and stereotyping, both within and outside of their own groups. Although no specific ethnic identification was made, approximately one third of the group was non-white -- African-American, Latino, Asian, and international students. At the conclusion of the session, students were asked to respond to the following question:

> "One of the goals of this program is for you to realize that you share certain characteristics, attitudes, needs, skills or knowledge with people from other cultures. Sometimes we emphasize differences between groups, and sometimes these get in the way of building coalitions. Please think back over your experience today. Did you realize that you had some things in common with people from other cultures? Which were the most important? How did you come to this realization? Do you think this learning will help you in the future? How?"

Results. One hundred thirty two (132) responses were received from the students. Nearly two thirds (84) of the respondents realized they shared two characteristics with members of other cultures: they are stereotyped, and they don't like it. They do not want to be falsely judged because of their culture. For many of the students, hearing the stereotypes that the groups detested created an awareness of how stereotyping affects all cultures.

Some comments:
- "I realized that people from all cultures resent stereotypes about their culture."
- "Everyone is really hurt by the assumptions that others make at or against them."
- "I noticed that I did identify with some other cultures such as the fact that we are all stereotyped."
- "We all disliked being stereotyped because of our race, religion or gender."
- "For example, just as I feel singled out when I am surrounded by people of different races, those same people feel similar when surrounded by people of my culture."
- "The most important similarities between the various cultures were our concerns about how our groups are often misrepresented. We all wanted to be judged on an individual basis, not on what only a few people from our culture do that would cause people to have negative opinions about our group."
- "I really found what the white youth group had to say very informative. They talked about how they aren't anti-black or anything like that, they were just proud of their people's accomplishments in the past like the Constitution and proud of themselves. Many tend to think by the color of their skin especially Caucasian, that they hate other races. They kind of opened my eyes to the fact that this is not always true. I can actually relate with grouping on account of racial pride because I was in the black female group."

The students gathered in self-selected groups to identify the stereotypes they disliked the most. These examples were taken from the hundreds of statements expressed by the participants.

Women: Weaker sex, use PM to advantage, too emotional, need a man to be happy, sluts, naive, controlled/taken advantage of, need affirmative action, not good enough/capable, expected to be perfect, judged by looks, violent feminists, gold diggers, dumb, dependent on men, cheap, lazy, gossipy, vain, non-athletic, inferior, materialistic, burden, expensive, complainers, superficial.

Men: Immature, lazy, bossy, horny, nonromantic, mean, slobs, cold-hearted, stubborn, pigs, jocks, unimaginative, uncommitted, stupid, violent, ignorant.

Foreigners: Fighters, smelly, incompetent, come only for welfare, "go back to your country", speak funny, degrading to women, terrorists.

Asians: Shy, take all the jobs, know martial arts, excellent in math, too short, can't see clearly through eyes, eat rice every day, give paychecks to parents.

Hispanics: Gang members, illegal immigrants, Jose/Maria, lazy, do or sell drugs, sex fiends, violent, women pregnant and already have a dozen kids, play soccer, eat tacos, "wetbacks".

Americans: Lazy, no discipline, selfish, arrogant, dominant, carefree attitude, stupid, global cops, violent (gangs), not family oriented, greedy, materialistic, watch too much TV, immoral.

Bisexuals: "Not real love", "Make up your mind", sluts - will sleep anywhere, sick, controlled by devil, have AIDS.

Single Mothers: On welfare, irresponsible, sluts, stupid, unmotivated, not respectful of themselves, pro-life, problem childhood, high school dropouts, no family values.

As can be seen, some common stereotypic themes run across groups. Most feel they are stereotyped as lazy and incompetent. All feel victimized in one way or another, even the groups which are thought to be on top -- men (most of which were White) and Americans.

Approximately 10% of the participants felt that shared values was another characteristic common across cultures. The students stated that all cultures hold beliefs which are important to them, and in many cases these beliefs are similar across groups. Responses included "The most important thing is that all groups share values" and "The values we all shared about our family and just life itself was important." Future studies will focus on this aspect of cross-cultural commonality, since it is often at the heart of misunderstandings and conflicts.

In terms of usefulness of their learning for the future, more than one third of the students (39) stated that the workshop would help them be more understanding and empathetic with people from different cultures. Some examples:

- "This will help me understand other cultures in the future and not judge people."
- "I hope that this knowledge will help me to express a better understanding of other cultures and to respect them more, but also to respect whatever they have to say, their ideas and views."
- "I think that this will help me in the future when I am working with or see people from other cultures, and will give me a better understanding and respect of/for other cultures."
- "I have a better understanding and know that everyone needs to be treated the same"
- "If I could put myself in others' position to understand them better, then I can live and work in harmony."
- "It will remain of help to me during group collaboration,

understanding others views and fears, and remaining
perceptive during group conflict or possible situations of
anger."

Approximately 20% of the respondents (19) felt that the
workshop had helped them be more open-minded to cultural differences
in the future. They stated that they were now more willing listen
without reservation or preconceived notions. Some examples:
-   "It will give me more confidence to open up more to other
    types of people and cultures."
-   "I will be more open-minded towards other cultures."
-   "Learning to understand and be open and acceptable . . . will
    help open up new relationships and friendships, and also
    help you to be a better well-rounded person."
-   "I believe that this will help me in the future by reminding
    me to be open-minded to all kinds of people and their
    lifestyles."
-   "I think this will help us in the future as in not to stereotype
    other races and to keep an open mind."

Approximately 10% of the students (10) felt that the workshop
improved their communication skills. They stated that as a result of the
training they would be able to express themselves more clearly and have
better interaction with people from different cultures. Sample
responses:
-   "I definitely think that this will help me in the future because
    of the communication skills I'm learning and the fact that it
    is possible to have many things in common with members of
    the same/different cultures."
-   "It will help me communicate better with others and tell
    them how I feel rather than saying something I might regret
    or even saying nothing at all."
-   "It will teach me to better communicate in groups."

Implications

It seems clear from this study that beginning college students (and probably high school students as well) across cultures feel stereotyped and don't like it. Since "perception is reality," it can be inferred that certain statements or behaviors by other people (or the media) have led them to feel victimized. Further, if all groups feel victimized it stands to reason that they are also causing this reaction in other groups. Thus, they are both victim and perpetrator, being stereotyped while they stereotype others.

What does this mean for the teacher? First, it presents a danger signal for all interactive classroom activities, be they large or small group. The instructor must continually monitor his/her own attitudes, as well as students' attitudes toward each other. Further, one way to address stereotypes is through disclosure. Employing cooperative techniques, empowering students to play a more active role in class learning, and diversifying assessment and instructional techniques to address different learning styles are all examples of methods the teacher can use to address the stereotyping issue.

Finally, for the teacher and the school counselor, the realization that students feel victimized by misunderstanding helps explain conflict as well as points the way toward resolution.

Conclusion

The four studies described in this paper were designed to identify cross-cultural commonalities which can be used in education and conflict resolution. Clearly, the studies have accomplished that purpose; well over a hundred commonalities were uncovered, ranging from superficial similarities such as hobbies, clothing, and food to more substantial factors involving personality, identity, and lifestyle. This rich database provides a useful pool of knowledge for the astute educator.

The research also produced some unexpected and important results. The study of college freshmen, for example, resulted in the noteworthy revelation that the students didn't understand the extent and danger of stereotyping. A comparison of the third study with the first two demonstrated the power of conflict to diminish perceptions of commonality, as the similarities identified by the disputants were much more obvious and non-substantive. These outcomes provide a dramatic endorsement for proactive educational measures to avoid conflict and misunderstanding.

The Venn project is continuing into its third year. Extensions of these four studies are planned, and readers of this paper are invited to participate.

NOTES

Other papers in the VENN series are:

Ransom, Deborah. (1997). *VENN 2: Perceived Commonalities of Middle School Students From Different Ethnic and Language Backgrounds.* Unpublished manuscript.

****NOTE TO EDITOR: THE FOLLOWING PAPER IS IN THIS PROCEEDINGS. PLEASE UPDATE REFERENCE****

Spees, Karen (1997). *VENN 3: Perceived Commonalities Among Elementary Boy and Girl Mediators.*

Jackson, Cheryl. (1997). *VENN 4: Perceived Commonalities Among Caseworkers and Social Service Clients.* Unpublished manuscript.

Bibliography

Anderson, E. (1990). Streetwise: Race, Class, and Change in an Urban Community. Chicago, IL: University of Chicago Press.

Banks, J. & Banks, C. (1995). Handbook of Research on Multicultural Education. New York: Macmillian.

Batt, K. (1988). We're All in the Same Boat. A Multi-Cultural and Pre-Vocational ESL Curriculum for Intermediate ESL Students. Unpublished manuscript. (ERIC Document Reproduction Services Number ED 327 859).

Bellah, R., Madsen, R., Sullivan, W., Swidler, A., & Tipton, S. (1985). Habits of the Heart. Berkeley, CA: University of California Press.

Bennett, C. (1994). Comprehensive Multicultural Education (3rd ed.). Boston, MA: Allyn & Bacon.

Divine, D.R. (1992). Arab-Israeli Conflict: Little Common Ground. Middle East Journal, 46(3), 513.

Etzioni, A. (1993). The Spirit of Community. New York: Touchstone (Simon & Schuster).

Firth, J. (1991). A Proactive Approach to Conflict Resolution. Supervisory Management, 36 (11), 3-4.

Hill, L. (1993). Common Ground Race Relations Study Guide. A Study Guide for Small Group Discussions on Race Relations. New Orleans, LA: Southern Institute for Education and Research, Tulane University. (ERIC Document Reproduction Services Number ED 373 003).

Jacksteit, M. & Kaufmann, A. (1995). Finding Common Ground in the Abortion Conflict. Unpublished manuscript. Washington, DC: The Common Ground Network for Life and Choice.

Khermouch, G. (1994). Brands overboard. Brandweek, 35(33), 26-35.

Lanham, M. (1992). Encouraging Shared Identity: USAir's Message to Employees. Unpublished manuscript. (ERIC Document Reproduction Services Number ED 355 577)

Mirel, J. (1993). The Rise and Fall of an Urban School System. Detroit, 1907-81. Ann Arbor, MI: University of Michigan Press.

Nakama, E. (1993). Building common ground--The liquor store controversy. Amerasia Journal, 19(2), 167-170.

Nieto, S. (1992). Affirming Diversity. New York: Longman.

Stover, L. (1990). Using Young Adult Literature as Artifact to Gain Insight about the Adolescent Experience in Other Cultures. Unpublished manuscript. (ERIC Document Reproduction Services Number ED 327 859).

Tiedt, P. & Tiedt, I. (1995). Multicultural Teaching (4th ed.). Boston, MA: Allyn & Bacon.

Van Steenbergen, N. (1994). Controversy: Advocacy or Coalition Building? Writing Notebook: Visions for Learning, 7(4), 16-17.

Whaley, R. & Bresett, B. (1994). Walleye Warriors: An Effective Alliance Against Racism and for the Earth. Unpublished manuscript. (ERIC Document Reproduction Services Number ED 368 528).

Appendix
VENN Codes - Commonalities

1. FOOD (like to eat)
   a. Pizza

     b.   Candy

2.   SCHOOL CLASSES/SUBJECTS/ACTIVITIES
- a.   Like Recess
- b.   Like PE
- c.   Like Art
- d.   Same Class
- e.   Do well on tests
- f.   Like school
- g.   Extended Day
- h.   Dislike music
- I.   Same grade
- j.   Dislike school
- k.   Like teacher
- l.   Dislike teacher
- m.   Like science
- n.   Dislike science
- o.   Like math
- p.   Dislike math
- q.   100 points for walking in hall
- r.   Same bus
- s.   Same table
- t.   Same school
- u.   Same grades
- v.   Dislike reading
- w.   Likes social studies
- x.   Drama
- y.   Team
- z.   Cheerleading

3.   DON'T LIKE HOMEWORK

4.   HOBBIES/INTERESTS
- a.   Sports

    1)   Soccer
    2)   Basketball
    3)   Kickball
    4)   Tennis
    5)   Football
b. Parties
c. Writing
d. Reading
e. Dolls
f. Easter eggs break
g. Play pretend games
h. Birds
I. Dress up
j. Star Wars
k. Beanie Babies
l. Drawing
m. Play instruments
n. Talk on phone
o. Watch TV
p. Sleep over
q. Movies
r. Talk
s. Sing
t. Play together
u. Swimming
v. Push swing
w. Pets
x. Dancing
y. Dislike reading
z. Play
aa. Dislike singing
bb. Summer camp
cc. Computers
dd. Chores

ee. Cooking
ff. Bike riding
gg. Rollerblade, skating
hh. Sleep
ii. Video games
jj. Pool
kk. Outdoor people
ll. Fans of same team, like same organization (college)
mm. Same interests
nn. Shopping
oo. Travel

5. PHYSICAL CHARACTERISTICS
   a. Hair color
   b. Gender
   c. Run (a lot, fast)
   d. Jump high
   e. Eye color
   f. Wear glasses
   g. Age
   h. Size (big or small)
   I. Smile
   j. Facial characteristics
   k. Height
   l. Brain size

6. INTERACTION STYLE/TEMPERAMENT
   a. Making fun of each other, "gross people out"
   b. Bad temper
   c. Scream a lot
   d. Weird, crazy
   e. Sensitive
   f. Joke around, mischievous
   g. Call names

h.   Get angry
I.   Happy
j.   Sad
k.   Same personality
l.   Same feelings
m.   Sense of humor
n.   Is nice, sweet, kind
o.   Is friendly
p.   Is helpful
q.   Dislike name calling
r.   Will stop fighting, will solve problems, separate
s.   Feel like outsider
t.   Fight
u.   Dislike others talking about him/her
v.   Cursing
w.   "Steppin"
x.   Confident (think highly of ourselves)
y.   Confused
z.   Active
aa.   To be in groups
bb.   Be disciplined (self control)
cc.   Serious
dd.   Smart (Intelligence)
ee.   Caring
ff.   Don't talk to each other
gg.   Attitude
hh.   Like each other
ii.   Non-racist
jj.   Act the same
kk.   Deal with our problems
ll.   Do well in school and life
mm.   Hyper
nn.   Talk a lot
oo.   Don't like fighting

pp. Stick to goals
qq. Outspoken
rr. Attributes, qualities
ss. Pessimistic
tt. Apologetic
uu. Learning and teaching ability
vv. Creativity
ww. Think alike, way of thinking
xx. Funny

7. CLOTHING, APPEARANCE
   a. Shoes
   b. Dress/skirt
   c. Jeans, pants
   d. Watch
   e. Makeup, cosmetics
   f. Shirt, blouse
   g. Hair (same)

8. COLORS

9. RACE, ETHNICITY, RELIGION, BACKGROUND
   a. Jewish
   b. Skin color
   c. African American
   d. Same non-English language (usually Spanish)
   e. Hispanic
   f. Religion
      1) Religion conversions
   g. Race
   h. English
   I. Country
   j. Ethnicity
   k. White

      l.   Both Bilingual

10.   Music

11.   MISCELLANEOUS
- a.   Names (both have an "e" in name)
- b.   Laughing
- c.   Pass notes
- d.   Food
- e.   Same friends
- f.   Like weekends
- g.   Same bus
- h.   Want to be patrols
- i.   Like Army
- j.   Like animals
- k.   Like stuffed animals
- l.   Like presents
- m.   Like money
- n.   Like holidays
- o.   Both have friends/or both have boy/girl friends
- p.   Same neighborhood, living area
- q.   Same situation
- r.   Know same people
- s.   Same building
- t.   Immigrants
- u.   Same taste, opposite sex
- v.   Same taste in things
- w.   Supportive, loving friends and family
- x.   Same handwriting
- y.   Citizen

12.   Family
- a.   Both have a brother/sister
- b.   Like family

    c.   Live with mom

    d.   Don't like our parents

VENN Codes - Differences

1.   FOOD
    a.   Pizza
    b.   Candy

2.   DIFFERENT SCHOOL/CLASSES/SUBJECTS/ACTIVITIES
    a.   Not into schoolwork, grades as much
    b.   Misses school a lot

3.   LIKE/DON'T LIKE HOMEWORK

4.   DIFFERENT HOBBIES/INTERESTS
    a.   Sports
        1)   Soccer
        2)   Basketball
        3)   Kickball
        4)   Tennis
        5)   Football
    b.   Parties
    c.   Writing
    d.   Reading
    e.   Dolls
    f.   Easter eggs break
    g.   Play pretend games
    h.   Birds
    I.   Dress up
    j.   Star Wars
    k.   Beanie Babies
    l.   Drawing
    m.   Play instruments
    n.   Talk on phone

o.   Watch TV
p.   Sleep over
q.   Movies
r.   Talk
s.   Sing
t.   Play together
u.   Swimming
v.   Push swing
w.   Pets
x.   Dancing
y.   Dislike reading
z.   Play
aa.   Dislike singing
bb.   Summer camp
cc.   Computers
dd.   Chores
ee.   Cooking
ff.   Bike riding
gg.   Rollerblade
hh.   Sleep
ii.   Video games
jj.   Pool

5.   DIFFERENT PHYSICAL CHARACTERISTICS
a.   Hair
b.   Gender
c.   Run (a lot, fast)
d.   Jump high
e.   Eyes
f.   Wear glasses
g.   Age
h.   Size (big or small)
I.   Smile
j.   Facial characteristics

k. Height
l. Strength (stronger)
m. Facial expression
n. Different physical abilities (sports)
o. Athletic
p. Voice

6. DIFFERENT INTERACTION STYLE/TEMPERAMENT
a. Making fun of each other, "gross people out"
b. Bad temper
c. Scream a lot
d. Weird, crazy
e. Sensitive
f. Joke around
g. Call names
h. Get angry
I. Happy
j. Sad
k. Different personality, traits
l. Different feelings
m. Different sense of humor
n. Nice
o. Friendly
p. Is helpful
q. Dislike name calling
r. Will stop fighting, will solve problems, separate
s. Feel like outsider
t. Fight
u. Dislike others talking about him/her
v. Cursing
w. "Steppin"
x. Confident (think highly of ourselves)
y. Confused
z. Active

aa.	Attitude, beliefs
bb.	Respect other people
cc.	Stereotypes other people
dd.	Level of intelligence (smarter or dumber)
ee.	Don't like me
ff.	Don't talk to me
gg.	Loud voice (tone of voice?)
hh.	Quieter (doesn't express herself as much)
ii.	Thinking ways (ways of thinking)
jj.	Bravery
kk.	Acts up
ll.	Doesn't like people from other countries
mm.	Different goals
nn.	Into doing the right thing
oo.	Scared of getting into trouble
pp.	Rude
qq.	Mean
rr.	Show off
ss.	Identity
tt.	Hyper
uu.	Independent
vv.	Cool
ww.	Act
xx.	Inner Strength
yy.	Writing ability, style
zz.	Boring
aaa.	Tattle tale
bbb.	Pushy
ccc.	Persuasive
ddd.	Mellow
eee.	Day-day planning
fff.	Sunny
ggg.	Outspoken
hhh.	Funnier, funny

    iii.   Liar
    jjj.   Talents

7.   CLOTHING, APPEARANCE
    a.   Shoes
    b.   Dress/skirt
    c.   Jeans, pants
    d.   Watch
    e.   Makeup, cosmetics
    f.   Shirt, blouse
    g.   Hair (same)

8.   DIFFERENT PREFERENCE FOR COLORS

9.   RACE, ETHNICITY, RELIGION, LANGUAGE, BACKGROUND
    a.   Jewish
    b.   Skin color
    c.   African American
    d.   Language
    e.   Hispanic
    f.   Religion
    g.   Race
    h.   Ethnicity (national origin)
    I.   Asian
    j.   White
    k.   Country

10.   Different Taste in MUSIC

11.   MISCELLANEOUS
    a.   Names
    b.   Laughing
    c.   Pass notes

d. Food
e. Different/more/less friends
f. Like weekends
g. Different bus
h. Want to be patrols
I. Doesn't like Army
j. Doesn't like animals
k. Doesn't like stuffed animals
l. Doesn't like presents
m. Doesn't like money
n   Doesn't like holidays
o. Both have friends/or both have boy/girl friends
p. Neighborhood, living area
q. Situation
r. Know same people
s. Building
t. Immigrants
u. Taste, opposite sex
v. Different politics
w. Has job, different type of job
x. Different abilities
y. Had surgery

12. DIFFERENT FAMILY CHARACTERISTICS
a. Adopted, living w/ foster parents
b. Difference in siblings (#, type)
c. Doesn't care about parents
d. Divorced parents
e. Parent, relative alcoholic

Chapter Six
VENN 3: Perceived Commonalities Among Elementary Boy and Girl Mediators
Running head: Mediator Commonalities

Karen A. Spees
George Mason University, Fairfax, VA

===============================

Rationale

This study is part of a larger study entitled The VENN View of Diversity: Understanding Differences Through Similarities. The VENN project was initiated as a result of the controversy surrounding the concepts of diversity and multiculturalism. It takes the following positions:

> The current debate on diversity and multiculturalism in education has become fractious due to an over-emphasis on differences between groups. What is lost is the realization that people are members of many sub-cultures, and they frequently have as much in common as not. True appreciation of diversity -- and the opportunity to take mutual advantage of it -- can only be achieved after initial unifying bridges of similarity are built . . . .

> The VENN View of Diversity is a series of research projects which examine diversity and conflict from a "common ground" standpoint.

> Though it takes different forms according to context, the common ground process features dialogue (as opposed to debate) in a search for shared viewpoints. It encourages connective thinking, the sharing of personal experiences, the formulation of genuine questions and a joint activity which emerges from the dialogue.
>
> The Venn projects apply the common ground approach to education. The title for the research theme comes from the VENN diagram, which depicts the relationship between two concepts or categories. Normally presented by two or more circles which overlap, it describes in graphic form the differences and similarities between the concepts. The diagram was developed by John Venn in the 19th century.
>
> VENN features a series of studies whose central theme is perception of cross-cultural commonalities. (Levy, 1997 pp. 1, 4)

This study focused on gender; it examined the perceptions of commonality among boy and girl elementary school peer mediators. At the elementary level, most boys and girls choose friends who are of the same gender, engage in gender-based organizations such as scouts, and participate in sports teams that are often segregated by gender. In general, they are accustomed to this segregation and find it normal. Being teamed with partners of the opposite gender and having to work closely with these partners may be a unique experience. It is because of this opportunity to work with someone of a different gender that these mediators were considered appropriate for the VENN project.

Method
Participants

The study's participants are 14 boy and girl mediators in the fifth grade at a Northern Virginia elementary school. There are approximately 500 students at the school, and they generally come from middle- to upper-middle class backgrounds. The vast majority of the student body is white, as were 13 of the 14 mediators who took part in this study. One mediator is of Asian descent.

The Mediation Program

The mediation program at this elementary school is based on a model created by Wampler and Hess (1992). Mediators in this program are in the fifth grade. All students receive mediation training in the latter part of their fourth grade year through a series of ten 45 minute sessions in their Health classes. Mediators are chosen at the conclusion of this training based on a number of factors, including active participation in the training, a final product indicative of their learning and interest in mediation, self-nomination and peer nomination. At the end of fourth grade the newly-selected mediators shadow the incumbent fifth grade mediators, and in the fall of their fifth grade year they take on the full responsibility of being peer mediators. This entails being on duty one day a week, wearing T-shirts with the mediator logo, and performing any mediations that are referred to them. Mediators work in teams of two, helping two disputants reach a solution to their problem. If more than two people are involved in a dispute, the two most involved are asked to come to mediation and pass on the resolution to the others. If this is not satisfactory, then a series of mediations can take place, until all the disputants have a chance to solve their problem. In any case, the model involves only two disputants and two mediators at a time.

The mediations take place in a private area of the school library and without adult intervention. An adult is always within eye and ear range, but the mediations are done by the students alone. Referrals are made through a written form that can be completed by the disputants, or by adults if the disputants are too young to read and write. This form asks for the names of the disputants and a general description of the problem. Disputants can self-refer, or be referred by others, including teachers, playground assistants, the principal or a mediator. Involvement in a mediation is voluntary, and sometimes disputants decline.

Upon completion of a mediation, the mediators ask the disputants to sign their names to a report form which states the terms of the agreement (assuming the problem has been resolved; if it has not come to resolution, the form is not signed). Under normal circumstances, the mediation process terminates at this point. For purposes of the VENN Project, however, an additional step was added. Once the agreement is signed, the mediators each take a disputant to a private area to ask him or her to reflect upon what the disputants may have learned about each other and what they may have in common with each other. (The perceptions of commonalities from the disputants is described in a separate paper Levy (1997)). Their responses are recorded on paper and they are then escorted back to class by the mediators. After the disputants are taken back to class, the mediators then finish completing the report form, indicating whether there were any problems in the mediation, and if they think the solution will work. The referral forms, reflection forms and report forms are then submitted to me, the program coordinator.

Data Collection

In early June of 1997, I interviewed 14 fifth-grade peer mediators. These mediators had had a full school year of experience working in teams of two to help other students solve problems or disputes with each other. During this time, all of the mediators had worked with a partner who was of a different gender at least once. Most (12 of the 14) had done so several times, and one girl mediator had worked with boy partners only.

I asked the mediators to reflect upon their experiences working with partners of a different gender and to talk about, list, or describe whatever they thought they held in common with these partners. Because almost all of the mediators had worked with several partners, their answers are most often based on their general experiences, rather than on experiences with specific individuals. The interview protocol appears in Appendix A.

Results

The question about similarities yielded many answers. Several answers were repeated by the mediators or worded in similar ways. I grouped similar answers into one response code and arrived at 56 separate responses that have been divided into seven categories: (a) feelings, (b) values, (c) ideas, (d) interpersonal characteristics, (e) actions/abilities, (f) outside interests, and (g) miscellaneous. Because of the way they were worded, three of the 56 responses fell into two categories, such as values and actions/abilities. Therefore, 59 responses were coded in all.

Feelings

The seven responses that related to the idea that both boy and girl mediators shared similar feelings follow:

1. same feelings about school
2. same feelings in the mediation (e.g., annoyed, wanting to do it, laughing)
3. same feelings about missing recess (neither wanted to)
4. both cared about doing the job
5. both liked being mediators
6. both angry when someone else got to do a mediation they wanted to do
7. both were not embarrassed when working together

Of these seven responses, six related to the job of being a mediator, and five of these six were positive statements about it. The third statement about both mediators not wanting to miss recess relates to the reality that mediations often took place during lunch recess, and mediators sometimes had to give up recess in order to do their job. This seems a natural and honest reaction that was probably true of most (if not all) of the mediators. In the second response, the word "annoyed" refers to how the mediators felt when they were working with disputants who were behaving in ways that made it difficult for the mediators to complete the task effectively. This kind of comment was made quite often, indicating that the mediators wanted to achieve success and were negatively affected when disputants made it hard for them. Again, this speaks to the idea that the mediators felt positively about being mediators and cared about the task. The following statements illustrate this idea:

"Well, sometimes we'd talk about the mediation after like, say something went wrong. We'd talk about it and see if we could make it better maybe for the next time."

"Well we were happy to be mediators. . . . And, um, sometimes maybe we were angry because someone else got to do a mediation that we really wanted to do because we hadn't done mediations as often."

"I think we worked together as a really good team a lot of the time 'cause we would be able to switch off when there was something . . . if I missed something, he missed something I could add it in and we would always just be helping each other out."

Values

The category of values consists of the 10 responses below, and could be considered an offshoot of the Feelings category in that it contains statements that refer to likes and wants, as well as what was held to be important by the mediators (i.e., their goals):

1. both liked working with others
2. both liked helping others solve problems
3. both wanted to get the job done

4. both had the same goal (getting the problem solved)
5. both wanted to do the mediation right
6. both did not care who the disputants were
7. both wanted to be mediators
8. both liked being mediators
9. both did not mind working with each other
10. both liked doing the mediations

All 10 responses in this category relate to being mediators and working with others. As in the Feelings category, these responses convey positive values of mediation and working with each other. They also speak to a sense of community that the mediators shared. They saw themselves as valuing mediation, working with others, and solving problems. They did not care who the disputants or partners were with whom they worked:

"We never didn't want to do a mediation because of a certain person. You know, if it was someone that's been in trouble a lot. . . . We'd do it anyway and, you know, it could really help the person. . . . 'Cause whenever I had somebody (a disputant) that was difficult I always thought that it would help them if they went through a mediation. So I always wanted to do a mediation."

"We didn't, you know, get all worked up and like 'Get me out . . . I don't want to work with him. I don't want to work with her.'"

Conducting mediations, both efficiently and effectively, appeared to supersede personal and/or individual issues. The following statement gives evidence of the tenacity of the mediators and their dedication to the task, despite difficult conditions:

> Well, I do remember one mediation that we had
> a lot of problems with and we had to come do
> it in your (the interviewer's) room because they
> were being, they were not following the rules
> and so . . . um, I remember how we asked them
> to, we took them out and told them to get a

quick drink . . . and then we had them come back and we repeated the rules and we said if you can't remember these, we'll go into Ms. S's room and she'll help us along. You're not going to get in trouble or anything. And I remember when they were getting drinks of water we (she and her partner) talked about how we were going to handle it if they didn't cooperate afterwards. And we were thinking of ideas in case you weren't available.

Ideas

This category includes statements about the ideas and thoughts that mediators said they had in common. The five responses are as follows:

1. same ideas about how to do the mediation
2. both thought being a mediator was fun
3. both knew what questions to ask (level of complexity)
4. same level of thinking (thinking the same)
5. both thought it was better to stay in one place to do the mediation

Of these comments, all but the second apply to how the mediators were working together to problem-solve during the mediations. The mediators appeared to have definite and specific ideas about how to do the mediations and they sometimes mentioned how their thinking was similar: "When you're brainstorming and you come up with . . . a solution that is kind of the same, just like reworded, that's like you're on, you're on her level of thinking and she's on your level of thinking."

These ideas also appeared to take the needs of their disputants into consideration. An example of this is the third response that refers to knowing what questions to ask the disputants: "Well, during the reflections part we both, we knew what to ask them. . . . Like we knew we could ask more complicated questions for the older kids and not as hard for the younger ones. . . . We kind of thought we should do that."

Interpersonal Characteristics

The five comments about interpersonal characteristics were categorized as such due to their emphasis on ways of being that pertained to general personality traits and/or personal attitudes as they related to working with disputants:

1. both were serious
2. both were nice
3. both were responsible
4. both were calm
5. both were sensitive

As so often mentioned above, these responses pertained to how the mediators conducted themselves and portrayed themselves to others when on the job. In other words, the mediators' responses reflect their thinking about the job of being mediators, not other areas and experiences. The concept of being serious arose in several responses, an example of which follows: "And all the people that I worked with they, they weren't those people that fooled around or anything. They were serious and they just wanted to get the job done."

A comment that reflects how a girl mediator was surprised by the sensitivity of her boy partners follows: "I learned that sometimes they can be very sensitive because a lot of boys in class aren't very sensitive at all. They're just yelling out and being very rambunctious and they, they were very sensitive during the mediations and listened."

Actions/Abilities

This category of responses was the largest, containing the 23 comments below:

1.   both tried to get the job done
2.   went through the steps the same way
3.   said the same things
4.   said things the same way
5.   both did the job well (were good mediators)
6.   both able to get the job done
7.   both remembered the steps
8.   both acted normal
9.   both encouraged disputants to speak
10. both took turns (cooperated, shared the job, helped each other)
11. both had the same training
12. both worked hard
13. both forgot to wear the mediator shirts a lot
14. both kept confidentiality
15. both used skills in class (and other places)
16. both acted the same
17. both knew what questions to ask (able to discern appropriateness)
18. both put the idea together
19. both did not laugh or make fun of the disputants (able to hold it in)
20. both went the same speed (pace)
21. were generous to each other
22. both were mediators doing the same job
23. both wore the mediator shirts

Every response in this category referred to the experience of being a mediator, from having the same training, to keeping confidentiality, to doing the job well. Comment number 21, about how they were generous to each other, is explained more thoroughly through this quote: "I thought we were pretty good together because we, we kind of went at the same speed and we would really help each other out, and we, we were really generous to each other. You know, we would offer to . . . leave the room to do the reflections process or . . . we would help each other out a lot. And I think that was really a big part."

Outside Interests and Miscellaneous

The final two categories of responses, outside interests and miscellaneous, include comments that most often fell outside the experience of being mediators, and were ones that were mentioned the fewest amount of times. For instance, only one mediator mentioned that the similarity between her and her male partner was that they both liked sports.

The three responses in the <u>outside interests</u> category were:
1. same interests
2. both like movies
3. both like sports

The six <u>miscellaneous</u> responses follow:
1. same teacher
2. same color hair
3. same color eyes
4. both in the same grade
5. both in the extended day program (after school program)
6. both had difficulty getting out of class to do mediations

These two categories contain statements that might be considered somewhat superficial, such as the reference to hair and eye color. Interestingly, these two responses came from a mediator who specifically asked if she should mention things like hair and eye color. My response was that she could mention anything. She proceeded with those responses then quickly turned to other areas, such as abilities and interpersonal characteristics that she shared with her partners. It was as if she had become stuck, thought about the easy answers, and then moved on to more substantial issues.

Implications

Unlike their disputant counterparts, who seemed most often to find similarities in what might be deemed superficial areas (hobbies, being in the same grade, having the same hair color, etc.), the mediators most often found similarities in more substantial areas such as interpersonal characteristics, values, feelings, and experiences related to being mediators. What made the mediators' answers more substantial? There are several factors to consider. One area to look into is that of the students' individual characteristics. The fact that they chose to be mediators may indicate a tendency toward interpersonal sensitivity. Their maturity, in that they were usually older than the disputants, is also relevant. A second area to consider is that of the mediation process itself. The training and actual experience of doing mediations may have helped them to become more introspective and/or sensitive. The year-long experience of working with each other may have contributed to their ability to find deeper levels of commonality. Also, the manner in which they were asked to reflect on their experience as mediators working with their partners, may have brought the skills and understandings that they learned and shared to the fore. A third influence may have been my own role and involvement with the mediators. Although I assured them that there were no right or wrong answers and that I was interested in their honest opinions, they may have responded in ways that they thought might be pleasing to me.

All of the above are possible influences on their responses. It is interesting to note, however, that all of the mediators had gone through the process of asking their disputants what they thought they had in common with each other (the reflections process). These disputants nearly always mentioned things such as having the same hair and eye color, being in the same grade, liking the same games, etc. Seldom did they mention interpersonal characteristics or values. Yet, despite the mediators' experience with hearing these kinds of answers to the question about similarities, they chose to respond in ways that appear more thoughtful and substantial. The comment by the mediator who wanted to know whether I wanted "stuff like hair and eye color," and her rapid return to more substantial answers, attests to both her experience with different kinds of answers, as well as her preference for her own level of response. As mentioned above, hair and eye color (superficial characteristics) did not seem to be of interest to these mediators.

Another point for discussion is the possibility that the experience of being mediators and working with partners of another gender may have some implications for reducing gender stereotypes.

One of the most interesting findings of this study is that in every case, the mediators indicated that they thought they had more in common than they were different. Remarks such as "we're really the same" and "there's no difference" were made by every mediator.

Because of the proliferation of responses regarding commonalities, as well as the overwhelming sense that the mediators most often found they had much more in common than not, one might think that these mediators had had many experiences working with those of another gender, and that this was nothing new or unusual to them. However, this is not necessarily the case, as is explained in the following quote from a boy mediator: " You know, it's kind of like this is one of the first times 'cause usually even in school you're paired up with other boys when you get into groups."

This mediator went further in explaining why he thought this was a good experience: "You know, like when I get older I'll have to work with girls more often and, it won't be, I won't be like uneasy about it."

A girl commented on what she had learned about working with boys: "Well, I learned that, like in third and half-way through fourth grade, I thought they were kind of gross and, you know, I didn't want to be around them. But when I worked with them as mediators they were normal, just like us, and they worked hard at it. They didn't try and goof off a lot of the time like they do in class."

One of the last questions that I asked the mediators was how they thought that working with a person of another gender and finding things that they had in common might help them in the future. I asked this question in order to find whether they thought they had learned anything helpful through this process that they could apply to future situations. Their answers were enlightening.

One boy made the following comment about working with girls and how that might help him in the future: "Well, it's comforting to know that they aren't different from you, they aren't anyone that'll pick on you or be mean to you. They're just like your friends."

A girl mediator, when reflecting on this question, said, "Well, you need to remember the similarities so you're not always going (thinking that) boys are always rambunctious . . . and you don't hold that against them. You remember that they're a lot like you and they're not just the opposite of you . . . 'cause there are a lot of things that are different but a lot of things are the same." This was the same girl who was cited earlier as having been surprised by the sensitivity of the boys with whom she had worked. She had interpreted rambunctious behavior in class as a lack of sensitivity. She appears to have learned from her experience with her partners that this is not necessarily the case, and that boys are not "just the opposite" of her.

If male and female elementary mediators can identify so many similarities in the ways they work together, think, feel, and act, and if they can come away from their experiences with each other commenting on how much alike they really are, what then does this mean for counselors, teachers, and other educators? It may mean that more activities that involve mixed-gender teams should be incorporated into school programs. Teachers could find ways to have girls and boys working together more often in cooperative classroom activities. Counselors might consider being more open to mixed-gender issue and discussion groups. Certainly, peer mediation programs that do not already incorporate mixed-gender teams may begin doing so.

Opportunities for boys and girls to work together in ways that allow them to get to know and appreciate each other should be provided whenever possible. If students gain positive experiences through this kind of activity, this may lead to a lessening of gender stereotyping and sexism. It could also help in building the sense of community that so many of our schools are working so hard to create.

Recommendations for Further Study

Peer mediation programs have often been studied for their effectiveness in lowering occurrences of violence and serious discipline problems (Johnson & Johnson, 1994), referrals to the principal (Lane & McWhirter, 1992), and suspensions (Miller, 1993). Generally, the findings indicate that mediation programs are effective in these areas. However, more benefits exist than those found through outcome studies of program effectiveness. Qualitative studies are needed to give voice to the students' views of the mediation process and each other, so that educators can build on what the students have to say.

References

Johnson, D., & Johnson, R. (1994). Constructive conflict in the schools. Journal of Social Issues, 50, 117-137.

Lane, P., & McWhirter, J. (1992). A peer mediation model: Conflict resolution for elementary and middle school children. Elementary School Guidance & Counseling, 27, 15-23.

Levy, J. (1998). The VENN view of diversity: Understanding differences through similarities. In C. A. Grant (Ed.), 1997 Proceedings: Seventh Annual NAME Conference. Washington DC: National Association for Multicultural Education.

Miller, R. (1993). In search of peace: Peer conflict resolution. Schools in the Middle, 2 (3), 11-13.

Wampler, F., & Hess, S. (1992). Conflict mediation for a new generation. Harrisonburg, VA: University Press.

Appendix A
Interview Protocol
Perceived Commonalities of Fifth Grade Mediators

Introduce interview subject - perceived commonalities among people.

Ask mediators to reflect on past year's experiences with their partners -- specifically those of a different gender.

Ask mediators to think about the ways they found that they were like their partners.

Sample Questions

How are you similar?

What did you learn about working with (boys - girls)?

What was interesting, good, surprising, etc. about working with someone of another gender?

What did you have in common when doing the mediations?

What did you notice about working with (boys - girls)?

What feelings, ideas, ways of working, etc. did you share?

What else can you tell me that would show how you were similar?

Talk about a particular time when you noticed similarities. What happened?

Wrap up by asking mediators to think about how finding commonalities among boys and girls may be helpful to them in the future.

Chapter Seven
Emotion in Multicultural Education: Application of the LLEL Intercultural Communication Method[1]

Running Head: LLEL Communication Strategy

Billy E. Vaughn
California School of Professional Psychology, San Diego, CA

===================

The O. J. Simpson murder trial verdict was one of the most emotionally-charged events Americans have collectively experienced in recent times. It was by chance that the announcement came shortly before my undergraduate cultural diversity course. The following is an excerpt of one of my student's journals which describes her experience of the event:

> With the verdict given within one hour of our class that week, this served as a timely catalyst for heated controversy. Like countless others, I awaited the verdict in front of the television that morning. I sat, stomach churning, following a sleepless night of restless thoughts during which I reviewed every conceivable outcome and its repercussions. Still, I realize now, in retrospect, how grossly ill-prepared I was for my reaction to the verdict. . . . [My significant other and I] were convinced that O.J. would be charged with the murders. We were fairly comfortable with our certainty, so for several

[1]This work was partially supported by CSPP San Diego Faculty Development Funds. Please send comments to CSPP, 6160 Cornerstone Court East, San Diego, CA, 92121 or e-mail the author at bvaughn@mail.cspp.edu.

incredulous seconds after the verdict was read, neither one of us breathed a word. Shocked into silence, we agreed to talk later. . . .

I drove to school in a distracted daze, arriving shaken and immensely sad. I felt lost, pacing the halls and lounge area, hearing snippets of conversation. Words floated back to me—"verdict," "murderer," "unbelievable," "unfair," and "racial issue." I didn't know where to turn for answers and was unprepared to discuss my reactions with anybody yet. At the same time, I felt that I needed a therapeutic cleansing. The group processing that we engaged in during class that day fulfilled this function and helped tremendously. Knowing that so many others were confused, outraged, and full of questions made me realize that I could explore my own feelings safely and more fully in the group. Although I was still reluctant to verbalize all of the pain I was then experiencing, it helped to hear others and silently commiserate. Despite a difficult morning, that class discussion was a fruitful, timely, and healing process that enabled some closure. The aftermath of the Simpson verdict has left many scars, and many of us reached a new level of awareness about racial tensions.

Laura is a white American graduate student who considers herself liberal and open-minded.[2] Her emotional reaction to the verdict had nothing to do with race from her perspective. Yet, other people in the class thought the reactions to the verdict had everything to do with race. In either case, everyone left the discussion with less anxiety and more knowledge about race relations.

Many students who discussed the verdict before class experienced increased anxiety. The multicultural education instructor

---

[2]Laura is a fictitious name.

---

is faced with managing the accumulated effects of a history of poor American race relations. Students in my classroom benefited from the communication strategies they had learned and the instructor's facilitation. What strategies are needed to manage emotions while simultaneously meeting educational goals?

Teacher Preparation Concerns

Teachers in inner city schools are currently challenged by diversity. This places them in the best position to confront threats to the social fabric of society, but only to the extent that they are trained to plan, apply, and disseminate effective instruction. Diversification of diversity education in the wake of these realities inevitably affects research, practice, and training (Vaughn, 1988; Stricker et al., 1990). The increased inclusion of human diversity courses in the core curriculum holds promise for training in the competencies needed in contemporary professional life.

Americans are not fully prepared to confront their racial attitudes and those in the field of multicultural education are no exception. The laudable efforts to introduce multicultural competency within higher education are inconsistent with the majority of the students' academic expectations and professional goals. This conclusion is based on more than ten years of teaching diversity, scholarly exchanges with other professionals who are dedicated to teaching diversity, intercultural relations research, and knowledge of relevant literature.

Race relations is one of the most emotionally-latent topics in human diversity instruction, and it creates a special challenge to instructors. A lack of appreciation for race relations training among students leads to negative reactions toward mandatory diversity courses, especially when combined with normal ambivalence toward racial matters (see e.g., Gaertner & Dovidio, 1986). Most of my students rationalize their negative reactions by claiming that diversity education is subjective and opinionated, even when the subject matter is clearly grounded in theory and empirical research. Such perceptions are partly derived from the controversy in higher education about multiculturalism in the core curriculum (e.g., D'Souza, 1991) and a poor understanding of teaching emotionally-charged subjects among trainers. The controversy and poor instruction promote resistance.

Teaching strategies for managing emotional responses in race relations courses often reflect the instructor's multicultural competency level, rather than principled instruction based on empirically-driven methodology (Vaughn, 1994a; 1994b). One reason is that the study of emotion has received little focus in cultural diversity research. Insight into emotion management techniques result from recent advances in emotion research. Goleman (1995) provides convincing evidence that emotional intelligence can be more important than IQ. Presumably, the ability to govern one's own emotions and manage those of others' are the hallmarks of higher mental functioning, or rational thinking, in practical life. Insight into the nature of emotion and its implications for diversity instruction is important for developing multicultural competency, developing interventions, and conducting research.

An empirically-based framework describing the relationships among emotional reactions, racial attitude, and learning can stimulate scholarly debate while offering insights into improved instruction. The recent increased interest in the study of emotion has been limited to laboratory studies, most of which are not easily generalized to race relations instruction. This paper contributes to the literature by bridging the psychology of emotion research and cultural diversity instruction. The insights presented in this paper are the result of combining the author's expertise in cognitive psychology, a review of recent research findings, and teaching experiences to build a theory of emotion management.

The Nature of Cultural Diversity Training Resistance

D'Souza (1991) argues that legitimate challenges to the intellectual and moral infrastructure of academia are at the heart of multicultural education resistance and renewed racial tension on American campuses. The Front Line documentary *Racism 101* depicts racial tension on American college campuses as a product of white ethnic Americans'[3] resistance to minority student demands for inclusive education (Frontline, 1988).[4] Doing away with mandatory diversity courses is considered important by many higher education administrators in order to overcome interracial problems on college campuses.

A major problem with introducing multicultural curriculum is the sociopolitical arena in which the subject matter is embedded. White ethnic Americans try to avoid being held accountable for the prejudice and discrimination they feel ethnic minorities lay on them. If feeling attacked by ethnic minorities is a source of resistance for white ethnic Americans, then unwillingness to validate white ethnic Americans' egalitarian values and beliefs is a source of ethnic minority resistance. Many ethnic minorities view multicultural education courses as an opportunity to make whites feel guilty and shameful for being privileged.

Much of the misunderstanding in talk about diversity is the result of well-intentioned White ethnic Americans' efforts to express their egalitarian views with little knowledge about how to do so effectively. Ethnic minorities do not help matters much when they view these egalitarian efforts as signs of the naiveté rather than commitment to change. The multicultural educator's challenge is to provide each side with the knowledge and skills needed to overcome the pitfalls of intercultural incompetence. This can only be accomplished with skillful emotional management.

---

[3]The term *white ethnic American* refers to all Caucasian people who are American and of European decent.

[4]Ethnicity is assumed to be an important part of each and every person's behavior. The term minority refers to a group of people who (a) are distinct in physical characteristics, (b) identify themselves as distinct from other social groups, (c) have less power than one or more majority groups, (d) tend to intermarry, and (e) have less control over their own destiny (Feagin, 1984). Thus, these group characteristics define minority status more than population size.

Emotional reactions to multicultural education demand a teaching style that is necessarily different from that which is used in most courses. Most instructors teach from a positivist perspective which assumes that the information presented represents objective and universal knowledge about human learning (Fried, 1993). The objective-universalistic assumption is shared by students and faculty in most courses. In contrast, diversity course s offer emotionally latent, constructivist instructional contexts in which knowledge is assumed to be bounded by political correctness and ethnocentrism (Fried, 1993). This justifies resistance to such courses. The resistance challenges instructors of mandatory diversity courses in their efforts to coordinate with students. Successful teaching requires learning how to employ emotion management skills. However, the positivist instructional arrangement is not different in reality. The appearance of objectivity and generalizability, along with the perception of legitimacy, disguise the constructive nature of the well-established course (e.g., educational theory). Each teaching style is employed within a socially constructed activity created by people attempting to coordinate with one another in more or less meaningful situations (Kollock & O'Brien, 1994). Differences in emotional reactions to courses are functions of the extent to which a course or topic is considered to be within the curriculum mainstream.

Emotional discharge is inevitable in human diversity courses because Americans lack intercultural competence (Brislin & Yoshida, 1994), especially in dealing with race and homosexuality. A recent Knight-Ridder poll of more than 1300 Americans showed that 3 of 10 Americans oppose marriage between blacks and whites, but are more approving of other combinations of racial mixing (Interracial Unions, 1997). Devine and her colleagues (Devine, Monteith, Zuwerink, & Elliot, 1991) found that their undergraduate subjects averaged higher prejudice scores on a measure of homosexual attitudes in comparison to their scores on a racial attitude measure. Sexual preference probably arouses more emotional reactions because moral indignation toward people of alternative sexual orientations continues to be widely supported, whereas racial aversion can no longer be morally defended (see e.g., Devine et al., 1991). Racial indignation cannot be adequately measured, however, since negative racial attitudes are often disguised as colorblind views of differences. These research findings support the view that race and sexual preference are the most emotionally-latent topics covered in multicultural education. Expertise in managing emotion in discussions of racism and sexual preference can help teachers cover other, less emotionally-charged, topics. The prominence of emotion in race relations training enables the author to simplify the remainder of this paper by narrowing the focus on this aspect of diversity. This is the author's area of expertise, and the author does not intend to convey that race relations is more important than other diversity topics.

The Role of Emotion in Multicultural Education

A racial attitude is comprised of beliefs about racial groups, issues, or objects, affective associations with those beliefs, and corresponding behaviors. Few Americans harbor the stereotypes and aversion toward other races that were prevalent in the 1950s. Rather, poor social skills (Devine et al., 1991), social dominance orientation (Pratto, Sidanius, Stallworth, & Malle, 1994) and ambivalence (Katz, Cohen, & Glass, 1975; Katz, Glass, & Cohen, 1973; Katz, Wachenhut, & Glen Hass, 1986; are characteristics of modern racial prejudice. Diversity trainers must take into account differences in racial attitudes and subtle distinctions that influence corresponding emotional reactions to racial issues.

Recent prejudice research findings provide insight into the nature of emotional responses to race relations training. Patricia Devine and her colleagues investigated emotional reactions to awareness of personal prejudice information among hundreds of white ethnic American undergraduate students (Devine & Monteith, 1993; Devine et al., 1991; Monteith et al., 1993). Devine et al. (1991) provided subjects with scenarios of interracial encounters (e.g., An African American male sits next to you on a crowed bus). They were given a five-point scale to determine the extent to which they agreed with a statement about the scenario. First, they used the scale to rate what they should do in the imagined situation (e.g., African American male sits next to you on a crowded bus. You should feel uncomfortable). They were then instructed to rate the extent to which they would do as they should (e.g., An African American male sits next to you on a crowed bus. You would feel uncomfortable). The majority of their subjects' ratings, regardless of prejudice level, showed a discrepancy between their personal standards (i.e., shoulds) and behaviors (i.e., woulds). The results also showed that the high prejudice subjects had significantly higher should ratings (i.e., they believed prejudice toward Black people in contact situations is justified) compared to their low prejudice counterparts. Low prejudice subjects were more egalitarian in their should ratings, but their higher would ratings revealed more prejudiced behaviors than dictated by their shoulds (i.e., personal standards).

Devine et al. (1991) employed a measure of their subjects' emotional reactions to investigate how awareness of discrepancies from personal standards affected the participants' sense of self. Participants received response feedback informing them of the extent to which their ratings were consistent before stating how they felt about it. Awareness of inconsistencies had emotional consequences that differed as a function of prejudice level and amount of discrepancy. An analysis of the subjects' labels for their reactions resulted in six common factors that account for the differences: Negative self, Discomfort, Positive Feelings, Negative other, Threatened, and Depressed. The overall results support claims that many Americans unconsciously harbor inconsistent racial attitudes and they become uncomfortable with awareness.

Whereas most Americans have egalitarian beliefs, their behaviors are not always consistent with these standards. Poor intercultural skills and poor emotion management help maintain racial distance. Poor multicultural competency is also the basis for avoidance response to mandatory diversity training found even among low prejudice American students. Most distance themselves from other racial group members and discussions about them in order to protect their non-prejudiced self image against the threat of having to show competence. Devine (1996) states that,

> although low prejudice people are highly motivated to respond without prejudice, there are few guidelines for "how to do the intergroup thing well." As a result, many experience doubt and uncertainty about how to express their non-prejudiced attitudes in intergroup situations. . . . Under these circumstances, they become socially anxious; this anxiety disrupts the typically smooth coordinated aspects of social interactions. (p. 11)

Those with poor interracial communication skills tend to engage in nonverbal behaviors, such as decreased eye contact and awkward speech patterns, in intercultural interactions. These are "exactly the types of subtle responses that have typically been interpreted as signs of prejudice or antipathy" (Devine, 1996, p. 11).

Mandatory race relations courses are a source of anxiety for both high and low prejudice Americans. They assume such courses require exposing personal prejudice-related beliefs among strangers. The fear is that they will not be understood, hurt others' feelings, and feel awkward. This is not surprising, given American socialization. We are taught more about what we should not do in intercultural encounters than about how to behave in non-prejudiced ways. In addition, we have few role models to observe, which results in few opportunities to learn "how to do the intercultural thing" from others. Instead, we learn ways to avoid the self reflection needed to expose our belief-behavior inconsistencies. The model offered below is one way to get people to arrest their emotional reactions to diversity and challenge themselves to develop a community of inquiry.

The LLEL Approach

This emotion management strategy is described as the Listen, Lean, Empathize, and Learn (LLEL) model. A good strategy for introducing participants to the strategy is to describe the course as an opportunity to acquire the social competencies needed to manage emotion in difficult human diversity discussions. Then use the Kaleel Jamison Consulting Group's list of learning community behaviors to set up ground rules for class participation. Behaviors such as flexible thinking, risk-taking, and support of others are emphasized (see Table 1).

Table 1
Learning Community Behaviors[5]

Be fully present
Be self-responsible for changing
Listen, listen, listen, and respond
Lean into discomfort
Experiment with new behaviors
Take risks, be ragged, then let go
Accept working through conflict
Be crisp and say what is core
Be open-minded
Honor confidentiality_____

The LLEL strategy is offered next as a way to manage difficult discussions.

Table 2 provides an overview of the LLEL strategy. An ability to listen to and empathize with people expressing controversial views, or points of view different from one's own, is presented as an intercultural competency. Listening is defined as the ability to allow a person to talk while the listener pays enough attention to paraphrase

[5]SOURCE: Kaleel Jamison Consulting Group, Inc., 29 North Main Street, Upton, MA 01568, (508) 529-2338

listening skills. They learn how to refrain from "butting in" in order to "straighten the speaker out." The instructor encourages use of listening skills by creating an atmosphere within which students are allowed to say whatever they think, and offers protection for their rights to do so. Once students take the risk to speak their minds, the instructor models how to employ listening skills. Students who take risks are told by the instructor that their comments are gifts to the class. This encourages others to speak up and disclose private thoughts. The instructor never criticizes or shows disapproval of what a person says.

A classroom rule is that fellow students can ask questions in response to comments in order to get qualification or relate similar beliefs and experiences, but comments criticizing the person are discouraged. Participants must take personal responsibility for how someone's comment made them feel by using self reflection before responding (e.g., "Your beliefs make me realize that I am different from you. This makes me uncomfortable about what you said."). By demonstrating that the instructor can take responsibility for personal values and beliefs while listening to controversial statements, students learn how to listen and lean into their own personal discomfort. Modeling also helps the other students feel that they can trust that the instructor is not interested in punishing those who may have "politically incorrect" views.

Table 2
Listen, Lean, Empathize, & Learn (LLEL)
Intercultural Interaction Strategy

Listen, Listen, Listen.
Lean into the discomfort of listening to beliefs you disagree with.
Empathize with the people who are different.
Learn about yourself and others from the interaction.

Self reflection, listening skills, and emotion management are presented as characteristics of critical intercultural thinking skills. Students are trained to listen empathetically to people with points of view different their own, while leaning into the discomfort differences create. They learn that the first rule in empathizing with someone you disagree with is to trust that most people have good intentions, but lack the competence to show it (Devine & Monteith, 1993). For this reason, most people who know their views are different try not to say things others will find offensive. Empathic critical self reflection, which involves exploring personal reactions to differences from multiple points of view, is also stressed. Students who cannot control their need to take issue with fellow students' disclosures are asked to consider why it is so difficult to listen to views they do not agree with, and how their reaction will affect critical thinking in professional life.

The LLEL approach maintains student self esteem because students are less concerned about having conflicting values or experiencing personal attacks for being different. Even high prejudice participants prefer this teaching strategy because they are able to say whatever is on their minds instead of being silenced by political correctness assumptions. They need evidence that their personal standards are not negatively evaluated by the instructor. It is the author's experience that the high prejudice participants show more personal growth as a result of being included in this way. This is probably because the course is often the first opportunity they have had to explore their views openly and without constraints. This provides a foundation for them to think critically about their views and the extent to which they reflect their ideal personal and professional standards.

Instructional content that presents topics from a balanced perspective provides prejudiced students with opportunities to have their own views validated, thus encouraging critical thinking, risk taking, and increased involvement (see Vaughn, 1994a, for a detailed discussion). The more they believe that their views are heard and validated, the more likely they will trust the process. Not surprisingly, they feel less threatened once they are volunteers instead of compulsory recruits. All students have an opportunity to learn why Americans are different and how much they have in common.

A primary goal of the LLEL model is to provide personal insight into how differences affect you and how to work through it. People who master the LLEL model have better insight into what others do that triggers their emotions, and why such behaviors serve as triggers. This is the real promise of developing the competency. The more one learns about personal racial attitudes, the more one is able to identify one's own personal shortcomings.

The overall goal for employing the method is to provide the entire class of individual students with as much opportunity to get involved in the training as possible. Implementation of the LLEL approach increases empathy for people who are different as evidenced by class discussions and students' journals. The result is greater appreciation expressed in teaching evaluations for the course.

Conclusion

Race relations instructors and trainers are challenged by student emotional responses. Avoiding emotions and the issues that activate them ignores their presence and diminishes instructional effectiveness. At the same time, managing emotion requires understanding differences in racial attitudes. Some instructors have a natural ability to manage student emotions and get them to volunteer to learn in mandatory race relations courses (see e.g., Mayton II, Loges, Ball-Rokeach, & Grube, 1994; Rokeach, 1973; Ponterotto & Pedersen, 1994). Most, however, are ill-equipped for the challenges of race relations training. Without training and experience, intervention strategies are likely to do more harm than good to the students and the course. It is imperative that the instructor has an arsenal of intervention skills to harness emotionally-charged situations for instructional purposes.

The expert provides a supportive context within which students of different attitudes can express and confront their beliefs in a climate of respect and trust (Vaughn, 1994b). This requires allowing students to be heard in a community of inquiry which respects a variety of view points (Ponterotto & Pedersen, 1994). The instructor's ability to diagnose emotions and readily employ management skills is the key to a successful course.

The LLEL approach offers a tool for understanding and managing students' negative emotional responses to mandatory race relations training. It is based on research literature, professional expertise, and classroom teaching experience. Individual differences in emotional reactions to the mandatory course are characterized along with the interaction between intervention strategy and resistance.

References

Brislin, R., & Yoshida, T. (1994). Intercultural communication training: An introduction. Thousand Oaks, CA: Sage.

Devine, P. (1996). Breaking the prejudice habit. Psychological Science Agenda: Science briefs. Washington, DC: APA Science Directorate.

Devine, P. G., Monteith, M. J., Zuwerink, J. R., & Elliot, A. J. (1991). Prejudice with and without compunction. Journal of Personality and Social Psychology, 60, 817-830.

Devine, P. G., & Monteith, M. J. (1993). The role of discrepancy-associated affect in prejudice reduction. In D. Mackie & D. Hamilton (Eds.), Affect, cognition, and stereotyping: Interactive processes in group perception, (pp. 137-166). San Diego: Harcourt, Brace, & Jonanovich.

D'Souza, D. (1991). Illiberal Education: The politics of race and sex on the campus. New York: The Free Press.

Feagin, J. (1984). Race and ethnic relations (3rd ed.). Englewood Cliffs, NJ: Prentice Hall.

Fried, J. (1993). Bridging emotion and intellect: Classroom diversity in process. College Teaching, 41, 4, 123-128.

Frontline. (1988). Racism 101: Racial prejudice on American university campuses. Nova.

Gaertner, S. L., & Dovidio, J. F. (1986). The aversive form of racism. In J. Dovidio & S. Gaertner (Eds.), Prejudice, discrimination, and racism (pp. 61-90). San Diego: Academic Press.

Goleman, D. (1995). Emotional intelligence: Why it can matter more than IQ. New York: Bantam.

Interracial unions rise despite society's same old prejudices. (1997, December 7). The San Diego Union-Tribune, pp. A29, A40.

Katz, I., Cohen, S., & Glass, D. (1975). Some determinants of cross-racial helping behavior. Journal of Personality and Social

Psychology, 32, 964-970.

Katz, I., Glass, D., & Cohen, S. (1973). Ambivalence, guilt, and the scapegoating of minority group victims. Journal of Personality and Social Psychology, 9, 423-436.

Katz, I., Wachenhut, J., & Glen Hass, R. (1986). Racial ambivalence, value duality, & behavior. In J. Dovidio & S. Gaertner (Eds.), Prejudice, discrimination, and racism, (pp. 35-60). San Diego: Academic Press.

Kollock, P., & O'Brien, J. (1994). The production of reality. Thousand Oaks, CA: Pine Forge Press.

Mayton II, D. M., Loges, W. E., Ball-Rokeach, S. J., & Grube, J. W. (1994, Winter). Human values and social issues: Current understanding and implications for the future. Journal of Social Issues, 50, 4, 1-9.

Monteith, M. J., Devine, P. G., & Zuwerink, J. R. (1993). Self-directed versus other-directed affect as a consequence of prejudice-related discrepancies. Journal of Personality and Social Psychology, 64, 2, 198-210.

Ponterotto, J. G., & Pedersen, P. B. (1994, February). Fighting prejudice and racism: A racial/ethnic identity-based intervention program. Paper presented at the annual Teachers College Winter Round Table in Cross-cultural Counseling and Psychotherapy, New York.

Pratto, F., Sidanius, J., Stallworth, L., & Malle, B. (1994). Social dominance orientation: A personality variable predicting social and political attitudes. Journal of Personality and Social Psychology, 67, 4, 741-763.

Rokeach, M. (1973). The nature of human values. New York, NY: Free Press.

Stricker, G., Davis-Russell, E., Bourg, E., Durante, E., Hamilton, R., McHollan, J., Polite, K., & Vaughn, B. (1990). Toward Ethnic Diversification in Psychology Education and Training. Washington, DC: American Psychological Association.

Vaughn, B. E. (1988). Incorporating multicultural issues in professional training. National Council of Schools of

Professional Psychology Newsletter, 3-8. Washington, DC: NCSPP.

Vaughn, B. E. (1994a, Fall). Harnessing the multicultural debate in the classroom. Thought and Action, 2 (10), 37-46.

Vaughn, B. E. (1994b). Teaching cultural diversity courses from a balanced perspective. Exchanges: Newsletter of the California State University System Institute for Teaching and Learning, 2 (5), 17-18.

Chapter Eight
Using Sheltered (SDAIE) Instruction
from a Multicultural Perspective

Yee Wan
California State University, Dominguez Hills, CA

Sharon E. Russell
California State University, Dominguez Hills, CA

===============================

The tide of immigration in the last three decades has brought a rich cultural diversity to American schools. Many school age children come to school speaking a language other than English (Diaz-Rico & Weed, 1995). Diaz-Rico and Weed (1995) report that the U.S. Department of Education estimated that 2.3 million students out of the 40.5 million students in public and private schools have limited English proficiency. In response to this demographic shift of the student population in the public schools, multicultural education is intended to provide equal opportunity for students to achieve academic success regardless of their ethnic, cultural, or linguistic backgrounds. This paper specifically focuses on using the sheltered instructional approach, within the framework of multicultural education, to address the linguistic and cultural needs of students who do not speak English as a first language. A tropical rain forests thematic unit, discussed below, was developed to illustrate how K-12 classroom teachers can incorporate a multicultural curriculum in teaching academic content and English to second language learners. The first part of the paper presents a theoretical framework for using the sheltered instruction approach from a multicultural perspective. The second part discusses the steps of instructional sequences referred to as *Into, Through,* and *Beyond.* Examples of instructional strategies will be utilized at each stage. In addition, their rationale in supporting the theoretical framework will be provided.

Sheltered Instruction Approach from a Multicultural Perspective

Banks (1994) identifies five dimensions of multicultural education: equity pedagogy, content integration, the knowledge construction process, prejudice reduction, and an empowering school culture and social structure. The rain forests thematic unit presented in this paper mainly focuses on the first three dimensions. Equity pedagogy suggests that educators incorporate a variety of teaching modes for students to achieve academic success. Sheltered instruction, which is an instructional approach specifically designed to meet the needs of second language learners, supports the equity pedagogy dimension. It is most appropriate for students at or above the intermediate English fluency level. Sheltered instruction differs from regular instruction in that teachers modify instruction to ensure that all students are able to participate in the learning process. A characteristic of sheltered instruction is to plan instruction around grade-appropriate and theme-based content, so that students can learn content knowledge and English simultaneously. The basic principles of sheltered instruction are to build students' background knowledge and present cognitively engaging content through the use of contextual clues. In addition, scaffolding experiences and schema building are embedded throughout the instructional sequence (Cummins, 1996; Diaz-Rico & Weed, 1995; Peregoy & Boyle, 1997). In our model tropical rain forests unit, students' understanding is supported through the use of posters, pictures, maps, actual rain forest products, graphic organizers, cooperative groups, etc. Finally, students engage in authentic activities that require them to apply the knowledge that they have learned.

Content integration, another dimension of multicultural education, is accomplished through integrating content knowledge from different tropical rain forest locations. Tropical rain forests are found in South and Central America, Central Africa, and Southeast Asia

(Ortleb, 1997). Through studying this theme, students can also learn about the geographical locations, physical characteristics, cultures, natural resources, politics, economy, and environmental concerns in each tropical rain forest location.

The knowledge construction dimension is an integral part of this unit in which students are actively engaged in the learning process and in constructing knowledge. Students are provided opportunities to give input concerning the questions that they want to investigate. They are also involved in analyzing the impact of policies for conserving tropical rain forests, making decisions about possible actions to take, and taking actions based on those decisions.

Instructional Sequence for Sheltered Instruction

The instructional sequence of sheltered instruction is characterized by the into, through, and beyond stages. The "into" stage is primarily introducing the new topic to students and engaging their interests. In the "through" stage, cognitively challenging content is presented. Finally, students have the opportunity to practice or apply what they have learned in the "beyond" stage. Throughout the different stages of the lesson, a variety of sheltered strategies are incorporated, such as schema building, scaffolding techniques, comprehensible input, and cooperative groups. It is important to keep in mind that the instructional sequence does not constrain the teacher in a rigid fashion. Teachers can go from the "beyond" stage to the "through" stage to re-teach some key concepts or to address questions that are raised during the "beyond" stage. Teachers should be flexible in moving back and forth between the different instructional stages when needs arise. The strategies discussed in each instructional stage are examples of effective sheltered strategies. However, teachers can make modifications and create their own strategies based on the needs of their individual classrooms.

When planning for the thematic unit, teachers need to identify the content and language objectives (Diaz-Rico & Weed, 1995; Peregoy & Boyle, 1997). Identifying the learning and language objectives can help teachers organize instruction that maximizes students' learning. The content objectives for our sample thematic unit are:

1.   Students will be able to explain the importance of saving the tropical rain forests.
2.   Students will be able to come up with suggestions to save the tropical rain forests.

The language objectives are:

1.   Students will be able to develop their oral language skills in using academic language through working in various cooperative group settings.
2.   Students will learn how to use arguments in a persuasive manner.

Into

When introducing the topic to students, the focus should be on building students' background knowledge, relating new information to students' previous experiences, and motivating students' interest in learning the materials. Examples of instructional activities that are appropriate at this stage are the mystery bag, guided visualization, and the K-W-L chart.

1.   *Mystery bag.* In a brown paper bag, teachers put different types of rain forest products, such as coffee beans, chocolate candy, a pack of gum, cashew nuts, cinnamon sticks, a piece of wood, etc. Without looking at the products, a student puts his/her hand inside the bag to explore an object. While feeling the object, he or she has to describe its shape and texture. If the student correctly guesses the object, he or she gets to take it from the bag.

This activity can capture students' attention through raising their level of curiosity. Students feel safe participating in guessing the objects inside the mystery bag. In addition, students are rewarded by being given the object that they guessed correctly. This is a fun experience for students across grade levels. The rain forest products placed inside the mystery bag focuses students' attention on the fact that they use rain forest products on a daily basis. This builds a nice connection between learning and the students' lives.

2.   *Guided visualization.*   Prior to presenting a guided visualization, the teacher needs to prepare appropriate instructional materials. These include an excerpt from a book or poem that describes tropical rain forests, a piece of music that contains the natural sounds of the rain forest, and maps, posters, or pictures of rain forests. The teacher displays the rain forest visuals around the classroom, then tells students to prepare to take an imaginary trip through a tropical rain forest. The teacher plays the tape of nature sounds and reads the excerpt simultaneously. After reading the excerpt, students can draw a picture of a rain forest scene of which they have the most vivid memory.

Guided visualization is an effective strategy for building background knowledge. It creates mental imagery that puts students in a learning mode. It also motivates students to learn more about the topic. When students are asked to draw a picture of a rain forest scene, they reiterate the images from the excerpt. Everyone can participate in this activity.

3.   *The K-W-L chart.* Teachers prepare a K-W-L chart (Figure 1) and guide the class to complete it. The K section requires students to share what they know about the theme, the W section requires students to plan what they want to know about the theme, and the L section requires students to reflect on what

they have learned (Peregoy & Boyle, 1997).

The K-W-L is a metacognitive strategy that assists students in planning for their learning. In the K section, students share everything that they know about the topic and their prior knowledge is assessed. In the W section, students propose questions that they still have about the topic. This helps students to set directions for new investigations and learning. Since students themselves decide what they want to know, their ownership of the learning process is increased. Their goal is to find answers to those questions as they study the topic. Finally, students are held accountable for what they have learned by completing the L section. K-W-L charts allow students to focus on topics of their interest, and also enable students to become independent learners.

FIGURE 1 K-W-L Chart

K (What I Know)	W (Want to Know	L (Learned

Through

This stage plays a crucial role in the instructional sequence because it teaches academic content. This stage usually requires students to read text that contains content information which creates a cognitive challenge for students, especially for second language learners. The sample instructional strategies discussed in this stage provide scaffolding experiences to enhance students' comprehension of the content materials. The strategies include word splash, categorization, cued retelling, and jigsaw puzzle.

1. *Word splash.* Word splash is a technique that is used for students to make predictions about the text that they are about to read. Teachers select 10-15 key words from the text and randomly put the words inside a square (see Figure 2). Students work in cooperative groups, discuss the meanings of the words, and write a paragraph using all the words. Each group then shares its paragraph with the class. The teacher then tells the students that they need to pay close attention to the paragraphs to see if the information contained in them is similar to that of the text. After reading the paragraphs aloud to and having students restate the key points, students revise their paragraphs using the information that was presented in the text.

FIGURE 2 Word Splash

Malaysia

heart disease

medicine

wood

rain forests

fuel

American kitchens

coffee beans

resources

Word splash helps students construct meaning with each word and make connections between the words in the text. Through making such a connection and creating the paragraph, second language learners are learning content information and using English in an authentic setting. In addition, students are especially alert to the points that they have predicted correctly. The fact that students have to revise the paragraph will further help them to retain the information.

2.   *Categorization.* Categorization is a strategy that can be used to group similar objects under a general heading. For example, avocado, banana, coconut and mango all are fruits that can be found in the tropical rain forests (Albert & Ling, 1993). Categories are often put in the format of a graphic organizer (see Figure 3). Graphic organizers organize information in a systemic manner which helps students to learn and retrieve information more efficiently. The use of categorization combined with graphic organizers provides visual representation of key concepts, thereby helping facilitate student learning. As students progress through the unit, they can continue to add the newly learned information to the graphic organizer

FIGURE 3 Rain Forest Products Charts
Rain Forest Products

Spices	Fruit	Other Foods	Wood, Fibers, Resins
allspice	avocado	Brazil nuts	balsa
b l a c k	banana	cashew nuts	bamboo
pepper	coconut	chewing gum	mahogany
chili pepper	grapefruit	chocolate	rosewood
cinnamon	guava	coffee	rubber
ginger	lemon	Macadamia nuts	sandalwood
vanilla	mango	tapicoa	teak
	orange	tea	
	papaya		
	passion fruit		

3. *Cued retelling report.* A cued retelling report can help students remember the key ideas from the reading. Teachers have to prepare a cued retelling report form in advance (see Figure 4). Teachers select main ideas from the text and write them down in the Main Ideas column. After reading the text, students work in pairs. Each pair consists of student A and student B. Teachers can ask student A to tell student B everything that he/she can remember from the reading and student A is not allowed to look at the cued retelling report form or the text. Each idea that is recalled correctly is checked in the Free Retell

column. If student A is not able to remember all the main ideas, student B can provide some clues. When student A can recall the ideas with some clues, those points are checked in the Cued Retell column. The same process is repeated with student B being the reteller and student A being the recorder. Teachers may want to let the stronger student be the teller in the first turn, so that the weaker student will be more prepared and have a better chance to succeed when doing the retelling.

FIGURE 4 Cued Retelling Report Form

Free Retail	Cued Retail	MAIN IDEAS

FREE RETELL POINTS _____   CUED RETELL POINTS _____

This strategy provides second language learners the opportunity to listen and use academic language through working with a partner. In addition, students' retention of the text increases because they have to retell what they have read, read the main idea column in the cued retelling report, and provide clues for their partner to retell all the ideas.

4.   *Jigsaw puzzle*. The purpose of using jigsaw puzzles is for students to share responsibility in reading academic content texts. Teachers can divide the text that students are required to read into four parts. The four parts are labeled A, B, C, and D. Students are put into groups of four as their home group. Each group should have an expert responsible for each reading part. Each expert reads his/her part of the text. Then all the experts who are responsible for the same reading part get together to form an expert group. For example, all the experts responsible for reading part A of the text get together to form an expert group on part A (Peregoy & Boyle, 1997). Each expert group has to complete the T-graph (Figure 5). After all the expert groups have completed the T-graph, the experts return to their home group and teach the key concepts to group members.

FIGURE 5 T-graph

Main Ideas	Details
A.	1. 2.
B.	1. 2.

C.	1.
	2.
D.	1.
	2.

Applying the jigsaw puzzle strategy can help students focus on a smaller amount of information each time. While reading the text, students are getting support from their peers in their expert group. Meanwhile, students are held accountable for reporting the key ideas back to their home group. Each student is viewed as an expert in their home group and has the opportunity to teach other group members. This can help students build positive self-esteem. In addition, the T-graph provides structural support for students to record the key points.

Beyond

At this stage of the instructional sequence, students are provided with opportunities to apply the information that they have learned, or to engage in activities that further reinforce their learning. After students acquire the content information about tropical rain forests, their assignments include preparing a rain forest animal speech, and developing action plans.

1. *Rain forest animal speech.* Students select a rain forest animal and pretend that animal can speak in our language. Students then prepare a speech from the animal's perspective to convince people not to destroy the tropical rain forests (Albert & Ling, 1993). For a more dramatic result, students can make a mask

of that particular animal and wear it during the speech.

2. *Develop action plans.* Students might do one or more of the following:

(a) educate others about the resources that are produced in the tropical rain forests and the impact of deforestation (Albert & Ling, 1993). Students can write and illustrate a brochure that they can pass out to reach a broader audience. Students can also design a poster that tells of the rich resources that can be found in the tropical rain forests.

(b) encourage others to become informed consumers. Make a list of products to buy and not to buy (Albert & Ling, 1993).

c) Plan and implement fund raising campaigns such as using rain forest products to make baked goods and raise money to support programs that are working to protect the tropical rain forests (Albert & Ling, 1993).

(d) research, plan, write, and send a proposal to an international tropical rain forests conservation organization to share some alternative ways to save the tropical rain forests.

All of the above assignments require students to use their higher order thinking skills. These assignments can also be used to evaluate students' performance authentically. In the process of constructing action plans, students play the roles of researchers, investigators, problem solvers, and advocates for making changes to improve the current situation. Students have ample opportunities to collect and analyze data, make decisions, and interact with others. Through actively engaging in the learning process, students can develop a sense of ownership in their own learning. They also feel empowered when they know their actions can have a positive impact on others.

Conclusion

This paper demonstrates how effective sheltered instruction can be incorporated within the framework of multicultural education. The tropical rain forests thematic unit is an example of sound educational pedagogy. This unit successfully achieves the goals of teaching rigorous academic content, promoting higher order thinking skills, fostering English language development, and embracing a multicultural curriculum. To ensure effective instruction, teachers need to be flexible in making modifications of existing lesson ideas and coming up with new ideas based on the age level, language proficiency, and interests of their students.

The tropical rain forests unit not only utilizes instructional strategies that provide access for second language learners to learn academic content, but also supports the goals of multicultural education. An important point that teachers need to keep in mind is that English speaking students will also significantly benefit from sheltered instruction that is embedded in a multicultural curriculum.

References

Albert, T., & Ling, G. (1993). *Endangered rain forests.* Greensboro, NC: Carson-Dellosa Publishing Company.

Banks, J. A. (1994). *Multiethnic education: Theory and practice* (3rd ed.). Needham Heights, MA: Allyn & Bacon.

Cummins, J. (1996). *Negotiating identities: Education for empowerment in a diverse society.* Ontario, CA: California Association for Bilingual Education.

Diaz-Rico, L. T., & Weed, K. Z. (1995). *The crosscultural, language, and academic* development handbook. Needham Heights, MA: Allyn & Bacon.

Peregoy, S. F., & Boyle, O. F. (1997). *Reading, writing, & learning in ESL: A resource* teachers (2nd ed.). White Plains, NY: Longman.

Ortleb, E. P. (1997). *Life in the rainforest.* St. Louis, MO: Milliken Publishing.

Chapter Nine
"Racism Kills Best Educational Efforts"

Gwendolyn Duhon-Haynes
Grambling State University

Rose M. Duhon-Sells
McNeese State University

Alice Duhon-Ross
Albany State University

Halloway C. Sells
The Union Institute

Mary Mondell Addison
Houston Texas Independent School District

Racism in the American educational system has been long-standing in our history and in other countries where racial differences exist. Oppressive educational practices are not only devastating to minority students but also to students of the majority race. This chapter will begin with a definition of racism and various manifestations of racism; three of the latter, according to Dube (1985, p. 96), though different, are still parts of the same definition. A discussion will follow on early historical documentation of the effects of racism on the education of White and Black children as well as a look at the implications of racism on the current American educational system. Finally, the authors will examine strategies currently employed to address and combat the problem of racism in various educational settings and among students in those settings. The various responsibilities of educators, administrators, and school systems to address and reduce the impact of racism will be examined and outlined.

The world we live in today is extremely diverse. The world population is 56% Asian, 21% European, 9% African, 8% South American and 6% North American (Hodgekinson, 1985, pp. 14-16). The existing United States social climate does not accept diversity as a reality. Instead, it continues to create pressure on people of color to conform, as well as promoting role confusion, exclusion, isolation, and ethnic and class tension that frequently lead to violent outcomes (Boyer & Baptist, 1996). The diversity of the country is increasing and policy makers are moving further into a state of denial by not addressing the need for a new paradigm. Generating a new paradigm would be an effort to solve the abundance of social problems in the United States. The present educational system is not teaching the vast majority of children of color in a way that prepares them to participate in the larger society. There are politicians who are using these demographics to create an atmosphere of fear among Americans rather than focusing on the positive qualities of each cultural group and offering to improve the fiber of the United States.

In an article entitled, "The Relationship between Racism and Education in South Africa," Dube (1985) asserts a definition of racism. He believes that the concept of racism derives from the myth that mankind is divided into racial subspecies (p. 86). Dube further asserts that there is no credible scientific evidence to support this concept. He defines racism as a psychological phenomenon rooted in the belief that there is a casual relationship between certain inherited physical traits and certain aspects of personality and intellect. This definition includes the notion that some "races" are inherently superior to others. Superiority is believed to be a biologically inherited trait common only to the "virtuous" races. Dube (1985) uses this definition to identify three types of racism: covert, overt, and reactive. The first part of this definition characterizes covert and overt racists; the second part describes the groups labeled as reactive racists. Overt racism is open and up front; covert racism is very subtle and therefore not easily identified. Reactive racism may be seen in the exclusionary tactics displayed by people who themselves have been or may still be victims of racism (Pollard, 1989, p. 9).

McCarthy (1988) discusses the concept of racial ideology in educational structures. He stated that racial ideology manifests itself unevenly in educational structures and in the formal and informal practices of school life(p. 46). Curricula and programs that seek to address racial antagonism in schooling must take into account, for example, the discriminatory effects of what Kevin Brown (1985) calls "White non-racism." "Non-racism" refers to the covert use of racial evaluation, apparently neutral but using coded rhetoric or criteria to discuss minorities, for example, the use of code words such as "over-crowding," "welfare mothers," "the lack of experience," or "strain of current resources."

Racist ideology is often interwoven in the schools. Specifically, with regards to art education in the public schools, Chalmers (1992) proposed that the art curricula and much of art education thinking are or have been ethnocentric, which he states is an implicit part of racism (p. 102). He provides a definition of ethnocentrism by Le Vine and Campbell (1972):

A familiar word most generally understood, in parallel with "egocentrism", as an attitude or outlook in which values derived from one's own cultural background are applied to other cultural contexts where different values are operative. In the most naïve form of ethnocentrism, termed "phenomenal absolutism" by Segall, Campbell, and Herskovits (1965, p. 4) a person unreflectively takes his own culture values as objective reality and automatically uses them as the context within which does not occur to such a person that there is more than one point of view. At a more complex level is the ethnocentric attitude or outlook that takes account of multiple points of view but regards those of other cultures as incorrect, inferior or immoral. (p. 134)

Ethnocentrism displayed by a teacher providing instruction to students of differing cultural backgrounds can have devastating effects on the students' self-esteem and academic abilities. This form of racism diverts minority students' attention and interests from academic pursuits. Because racism is a strongly negative emotional experience for these students, they are more likely to spend time and energy responding to it in an emotional and nonproductive ways (Pollard, 1989, p. 62). Pollard (1989) further asserts that some educators need to overcome their ethnocentrism and open themselves and their students to the achievements and experiences of other cultures.

One Black/White historical example of the problems associated with racism and its effects on American public education is found in the *Brown vs. Board of Education* decision of the Supreme Court of the United States. Clark (1988) cites the following statement from that court decision that described some perceived effects of segregation on Black children:

To separate them from others of similar age and qualifications solely because of their race generates a feeling of inferiority as to their status in the community that may affect their hearts and minds in a way unlikely ever to be undone. *(Brown vs. Board of Education*: 1954, p.34)

Clark (1988) documents another passage from the *Brown* decision, which voiced concern for the effects of segregation and racism on the academic welfare of Negro children:

A sense of inferiority affects the motivation of a child to learn. Segregation, with the sanction of law, therefore, has a tendency to retard the educational and mental development of Negro children and to deprive them of some of the benefits they would receive in a racially integrated school system. *(Brown vs. Board of Education*: 1954, p. 36)

The *Brown* decisions, most importantly, provided explicit educational and human assertions of the damage that racism causes to students in both the minority and majority races.

In schools across the country, there are educational practices, programs, and activities that serve to foster ethnic awareness among students. Thomson (1989) asserts that building tolerance and understanding is important at each level of learning, including early childhood (p. 89). She believes that young children learn through hands-on experiences and through active involvement with materials and people. Therefore, activities to foster ethnic awareness must involve both their hands and their minds. As an early childhood teacher, Thomson (1989) has developed activities that she believes will help them develop racial tolerance by, "pretending to be Martin Luther King, Jr., in a bus boycott role-play, by choosing between the unknown contents of a beautiful box and a dirty carton, and by encountering discriminatory signs in a classroom activity" (p. 114).(p. 78)

Thomson (1989) states that the open-ended nature of these activities allows for queries from children as well as teachers' questions, and that both encourage critical and creative thinking (p. 92). The aims made by educators to intervene early in the lives of students in an effort to combat the effects of racism is an important step in reducing the impact of racism on students as they proceed and progress through the educational system.

Another effort to foster ethnic awareness was developed by two principals in Connecticut: one at a Black school in Hartford and the other at an all-Anglo school in West Hartford. The principal in Hartford was concerned about racial isolation and the principal in West Hartford feared that unless her students really got to know some Black students, they would accept the stereotypes of the past (Foster, 1989, p. 20). The project that resulted was entitled "Across the Lines," and its major goal was to bring students from the two schools together. The student contacts focused on academics, affording students opportunities to study together. The school psychologist used an "imaging" study to assess students' attitudes and expectations. The findings showed that many Black students believed Whites had a negative perception of them in social and academic areas. This was confirmed when White students reported negative expectations. Anglo students' perceptions of Blacks included poor grammar, bad manners, low intelligence, flashy clothes, project housing, no college plans, poor behavior in school, and the like (Foster, 1989, p. 64).

Upon completion of the project, post-testing indicated that many students were pleasantly surprised by these encounters: most faults they expected in the other group did not exist. Students acknowledged that some faults they had expected in others also existed in their own groups. Some Black students were still skeptical of the White students, but they felt they could enter a mostly White gathering with less apprehension (Foster, 1989, p. 20). This exercise was instrumental in not only breaking down racial isolation but also in breaking down stereotypes that the students had of each other. This kind of activity allows students to see firsthand how inhibiting stereotypes can be as well as the number of commonalties that exist between races. Most importantly, this program allowed students to make their own decisions about individuals. As Dube (1985) asserted, children who see firsthand the contradiction between social stereotypes and reality, are not likely to embrace those stereotypes.

Nikki Giovanni, noted poet and professor of English at Virginia Polytechnic Institute and State University, offers advice to Black students in how to effectively deal with racism at predominantly White institutions. She offers some rules to follow that may help:

1. Go-to-Class. It is important to have a consistent presence in the classroom. If nothing else, the professor will know you care and are serious enough to be there;

2. Meet-your-Professors. Put them on notice that you are serious about getting good grades;

3. Do assignments on time;

4. Go-back-to-see-your-Professor. Ask early what you need to do if you feel you are starting to get into academic trouble;

5. Understand that there will be professors who do not like you; there may even be professors who are racist or sexist or both;

6. Don't-defeat-Yourself. Cultivate your friends. Know your enemies. You cannot undo hundreds of years of prejudicial thinking. Think for yourself and speak up. Raise your hand in class. Say what you believe no matter awkward you may think

it sounds. You will improve in your articulation and confidence; and

7. Participate-in-some-Campus-Activity. Join the newspaper staff. Run for office. Join a dorm council. Do something that involves you on campus. You are going to be there for four years, so let your presence be known, if not felt. (Giovanni, 1994, p. 20).

Although Giovanni's advice was specifically for Black students attending predominantly White institutions, these guidelines are applicable to all minority and majority students.

Educators themselves bear a crucial responsibility to address and reduce the impact of racism on students. Pollard (1989) addresses the behavior of school boards, superintendents, building administrators, principals, and teachers. When setting expectations, school boards, and superintendents of school districts can work actively to reduce racism by:

1. Articulating a clear statement of expectations regarding racism;
2. Establishing and enforcing a series of consequences for violations of those expectations; and
3. Providing rewards for those who strive to reduce racism in their schools and classrooms. (p. 73)

Pollard also addresses the behavior of teachers in mitigating racism in their classrooms. She listed a number of strategies for addressing this problem:

1. Teachers need to assess how they interpret the behavior of both minority and White students;
2. Teachers should confront behavior that may be either intentionally or unintentionally racist;
3. Teachers need to carefully monitor their own behavior. One way to do this is for them to invite a friendly and honest

colleague to observe their classroom interaction and ask for informal feedback; and

4. Finally, in assessing student performance, teachers need to be sure to give both minority and majority students encouragement and specific suggestions about how to improve academic work. (p. 74)

With regard to the specific role of educators in combating racism, Clark (1988) holds educators to a high standard in their responsibility to appropriately address racism. He asserts that a "truly educated person (specifically educators) must be prepared to assist this fellow human beings through empathy to attain and live by such uniquely human values as justice, kindness, and social sensibility" (p. 129). He further states that "educators are aware of the fact that educational institutions dominated by race damage and dehumanize human beings. Those who remain silent in the face of these clear facts cannot be considered educators, but must be seen as accessories to the perpetuation of this damage on powerless human beings" (p. 130).

In an article addressing the continuing dilemma of racism in the United States, Molnar (1989) describes the important role that schools must play in this struggle against racism:

Schools have an important role to play in this struggle against racism. Schools are not sanctuaries.... Schools can address the interpersonal aspects of racism as well as offer school and classroom activities that teach about the devastating effects oppression has had on minority group members and their cultures while at the same time acknowledging the strengths and contributions of minority group members and their cultures. (p. 72)

Racism in education and in educational practices not only adversely affects students but our society as a whole. Its effects and implications are expansive, but not irreversible. With a concerted effort from educators, students, administrators, legislators, and society, a shift towards racial equality and understanding can take place.

Bibliography

Boyer, J., & Baptiste, H. P. (1996). Transforming the curriculum for multicultural understandings: A practitioner's handbook. San Francisco, CA: Caddo Gap Press.

Brown, K. (1985). Turning a blind eye: Racial oppression and the unintended consequences of white non-racism. Sociological Review, 33, 670-690.

Brown vs. Board of Education. (1954). Text of the Supreme Court Opinions, May 17, 1954, 347 U.S. 483.

Chalmers, F. (1992). The origins of racism in the public school art curriculum. Studies in Art Education, 33(3), 134-143.

Clark, K. (1988). The Brown decision: Racism, education, and human values. Journal of Negro Education, 57(2), 125-132.

Dube, E. (1985). The relationship between racism and education in South Africa. Harvard Educational Review, 55(1), 86-100.

Foster, L. (1989). Breaking down racial isolation. Educational Leadership, 34(2), 76-77.

Giovanni, N. (1994). Campus racism 101. Academe, 21, 19-20.

Hodgekinson, H. (1985). All one system: Demographics of education, kindergarten through graduate school. Washington, DC: Institute for Educational Leadership.

Le Vine, R., & Campbell, D. (1972). Ethnocentrism: Theories of conflict, ethnic attitudes and group behavior. New York: John Wiley and Sons.

McCarthy, C. (1988). Rethinking liberal and radical perspectives in racial inequality in schooling: Making the case for nonsynchrony. Harvard Educational Review, 58(3), 265-279.

Molnar, A. (1989). Racism in America: A continuing dilemma. Educational Leadership, 34(2), 71-72.

Pollard, D. (1989). Reducing the impact of racism on students. Educational Leadership, 34(2), 73-75.

Segall, M., Campbell, D., & Herskovits, M. (1965). The influence of culture on visual perception. New York: Bobbs-Merrill.

Thomson, B. (1989). Building tolerance in early childhood. Educational Leadership, 34(2), 78-79.

Chapter Ten
Multi-dimensional, Multi-intelligences Approach to Assessment is Good Enough for Teachers. Is it Good Enough for Teacher Educators?
Running head: A Multi-Dimensional

Peggy J. Anderson
Wichita State University, Wichita, KS

===========================

The Call for Assessment Reform

The call for reform in assessment is being heard from outside as well as inside the field of education. From outside, The National Commission on Testing and Public Policy published a 1990 report entitled: *From Gatekeeper to Gateway: Transforming Testing in America*. The report recommended that public schools:

• revise how they develop and use human talent by restructuring educational testing,

• limit reliance upon multiple choice testing since it lacks accountability, leads to unfairness in the allocation of opportunity, and undermines vital social policies,

• cease using test scores as the single measure in making important decisions about individuals and their competencies, and

• promote greater development of all Americans with alternative forms of assessment so that testing opens gates of opportunity rather than closing them off.

This study and others have been a "heads up" for school districts and teachers. Educators around the US have implemented portfolios, checklists, and multiple-intelligence-based (Gardner, 1983) assessments and developed a stance of negotiation with learners as reform efforts infuse schools. Teachers have gorged on the theory of multiple intelligences and resources are ubiquitous on the application of the theory (Armstrong, 1994) to teaching and learning.

For teacher educators to take this Commission's recommendations seriously would mean that unidimensional snapshots of individuals from the lens on a faculty member's camera (e.g., using only traditional testing formats such as T/F, multiple-choice, short answer, and essay) would need to be replaced with something that instead looks more like a movie directed by the student (i.e., a multiple intelligences approach would permeate the process).

Traditional tests essentially ask students to think as the testmaker thinks. A multidimensional process lets students demonstrate how they think to the faculty. Are Colleges of Education on the cutting edge of reform in assessment practices as some would expect? Are they modeling this kind of call for change? Are faculty members using the tools already in their hands to create a more democratic environment and catalyze institutional change? The multiple intelligences approach has been available for well over a decade. Green (1993) talked about the need in our time to create "natural habitats of learning, schools . . . that . . . embody possibility" (p. 12). Girding assessment with a multidimensional, multi-intelligence framework is surely one refreshing way to practically embody possibility within higher education classrooms.

Has reform in assessment taken hold in colleges of education? Are teacher educators using a multiple intelligences framework in assessments? Do they model new views of assessment? Are assessments teacher-dominated or negotiated with students? Is it possible to let go of ownership of a course assessment? Some would say such a concept is heretical, but is it? Is the format selected based on what is easy to grade or administer? Is it what has always been done (even if it isn't fair)? Do faculty still rely on these kinds of traditional views of testing so castigated by the National Commission's report cited above. Is reform in classroom assessment good enough for teachers, but not good enough for teacher educators? What is the actual situation? These questions prompted my own experimentation with a variety of alternative assessments in college classes, as well as this study.

Survey of Teacher Educators

To examine what was happening among other teacher educators, this author conducted a telephone and e-mail survey (see Table 1). The survey examined the degree to which a variety of Schools of Education have implemented Gatekeeper versus Gateway assessments. The survey was intended to reveal the kinds of assessments being administered within teacher education classrooms. The survey responses included information on faculty beliefs about assessment, how important the notion of modeling for change is in the area of assessment, what the struggles are for those attempting to use multidimensional/multi-intelligence-based assessments, what formats and approaches have been used, what rubrics have been created, what the relationship of instruction to assessment is, and what perceived impact these may have had on students, other faculty, and/or the institution.

TABLE 1
Questionnaire: Multiple Intelligences
(MI) in the Assessment Process

Classroom Teachers Grade Level/Area: _____	**Teacher Educators** Area of Expertise: _____
Have you used Multiple Intelligences in the assessment of content with your students? _____YES* _____ NO What content area were you assessing? _____	Have you ever used MI as a tool for the assessment of content in your classes? _____ YES* _____ NO

Is It Good Enough For Teacher Educators?

How important is it for Teacher Educators to model the use of MI in assessments in university classes? 0 1 2 3 4 5 6 7	How important is it to model MI in the assessment process with preservice or inservice teachers? 0 1 2 3 4 5 6 7
Have you experienced an MI approach to the assessment of content in any university class? _____ YES _____ NO If YES, what was the name of the course?	If 0-3, why is it not very important?
Describe the assessment briefly.	As a student in a university class or in a professional development workshop, have you experienced an assessment design which utilized multiple intelligences to demonstrate what you knew? _____ YES _____ NO
If YES, were you satisfied that it measured (i.e., gave you a good picture) of what students knew? _____ YES _____ NO If you were not satisfied, what could you have done differently?	If YES, what was the name of the course? _____ If YES, were you satisfied that it measured (i.e., gave the instructor a good picture) of what you knew? _____ YES _____ NO If you were not satisfied, why not?
Did this experience affect your use of MI in your own classroom? _____ YES _____ NO If YES, how?	If a teacher educator wanted to measure the impact of modeling MI with teachers, what would be the best method of doing so?

Twenty professors in teacher training programs in colleges and universities throughout the US and 27 classroom teachers responded to my inquiry. In the area of multiple intelligences and assessment, classroom teachers felt it was important to model multiple intelligences in the assessment of content (an average of 6.0 on a scale of 7) while teacher educators rated it less important to model it (an average of 4.7 on a scale of 7). Among the classroom teachers, 74% had modeled a multiple intelligences based assessment, while only 20% of the teacher educators had (see Table 2).

TABLE 2
Multiple Intelligences (MI) in Content Assessment: Survey Responses Among Classroom Teachers and Teacher Educators

Questions	Classroom Teachers (n=27)	Teacher Educators (n=30)	Differences
How important do you think it is to model MI to your students in content assessment? Scale: 1 (low)-7 (high)	6.0	4.7	1.3
Have you modeled MI in the form of an assessment? (YES)	82% (22)	10% (2)	72%
Have you modeled MI in the form of an assessment? (NO)	18% (5)	90% (18)	72%
Has MI been modeled for you in an assessment context? (YES)	74% (20)	20% (4)	54%
Has MI been modeled for you in an assessment context? (NO)	26% (7)	80% (16)	54%

Was this use of MI satisfactory to you? (i.e. Did it work as an assessment tool? (YES)	85% (17)	75% (3)	10%
Was this use of MI satisfactory to you? (i.e., Did it work as an assessment tool?) (NO)	15% (3)	25% (1)	10%

From within the field of education, the call for reform can also be heard. Rigden (1996) reported on a survey of 600 elementary, middle school and high school teachers. Teachers were asked to describe major flaws in Teacher Education programs, and make recommendations. Teachers faulted schools of education with having "uninspired teaching methods" and "traditional views of schooling." Their recommendations included the call for schools of education to commit to preparing teaching candidates for the practice of teaching and for faculty to teach pedagogy in the context of the academic content (i.e., practice what you profess). Teacher educators, on the other hand, generally perceive their purpose as teaching about pedagogy and passing on theories of teaching and learning.

Implementing a multi-dimensional, multi-intelligence based framework for assessment is a way to bring US classrooms closer to our democratic ideal for schools. Authentic assessments are an attempt to demonstrate what students know instead of what they do not know. They can serve as a Gateway instead of a Gate Keeper. They can move educators from an institutionalized bias in assessment favoring those strong in verbal/linguistic and mathematical/logical intelligences to one in which all learners' strengths are validated by the system--the same message Armstrong gives to teachers (Armstrong, 1994). A multiple intelligence approach to assessment may be a meaningful way to generate institutional change.

A New Review of Multiple Intelligences

Upon Princess Diana's death in September, 1997, a friend of hers remarked in a TV interview that "she wasn't academically bright and she used to kid about it, but she had an intuition that was superior to anything I've seen. She could sense exactly what was needed, how people were feeling, and what was appropriate in any circumstance" (Colborne, 1997). Those who operate out of a multiple intelligences (MI) framework as described in <u>Frames of Mind</u> (Gardner, 1983) would quickly recognize this intuitive ability with people as a form of <u>interpersonal intelligence</u>, one of the eight intelligences that are identified in this philosophy. Is there a way to tap this intelligence in teacher education course assessment?

Irving Berlin had only two years of formal schooling and couldn't write music. He had a secretary record the music that he hummed. This brilliant composer clearly possessed a kind of intelligence that would also not be tapped by traditional IQ measures. In Gardner's terminology, he had a strong <u>musical/rhythmic intelligence</u>. Can this kind of intelligence be incorporated into the assessment of teacher education courses?

I received a letter from a Malaysian woman whose son I had met a few months earlier. In an effort to have me remember her son, she described him this way: "He is quiet and sheepish, although he is nearly 20 years old. He has a tender, inward-thinking character with a deep conscience. He has always known what he wants to do. He is less active in outdoor games and sports." In Gardner's terms, he had a strong <u>intrapersonal intelligence</u>, but was not strong in <u>bodily/kinesthetic intelligence</u>. How can this aspect of intelligence be acknowledged in the assessment of teacher education courses?

The skillful farmers in my home state of Kansas in the USA, as well as those in every country around the world, may well possess <u>naturalist intelligence</u>--the ability to discriminate differences within nature or an acute sensitivity to one's natural surroundings.

Another of Gardner's intelligences is the <u>visual/spatial intelligence</u>. I think of the power of the still photography in the visual renderings of Edward Steichen in his <u>Family of Man</u> (1955). None of these are the two intelligences most often measured in traditional assessments nor are they the ones most often valued in colleges of education for the delivery of instruction or assessment. Instead, teacher education classrooms have valued the verbal/linguistic intelligence and mathematical/logical intelligence in much the same way that public school classrooms have. Assessment reform is happening in public schools with the portfolio movement, the six-trait writing assessment, other alternative assessments, and rubrics; but are teacher education programs ready to reform their assessment procedures?

Beliefs about intelligences are changing. Most people used to think that intelligence was a singular phenomenon that was static, mostly inherited, and set for life. Following Gardner, intelligence has begun to be viewed as a multi-layered reality, dynamic, and capable of being improved, as well as strongly influenced by cultural, societal, educational, and environmental factors. Unlike learning styles, which are often viewed as static, the eight intelligences so far detailed by Gardner, are dynamic and can be fostered. An MI approach provides the practical means for creating what Green (1993) termed "natural habitats of learning, schools . . . that . . . embody possibility" (p. 12).

The theory of multiple intelligences is a way of mapping the wide range of human abilities as eight intelligences: verbal/linguistic, logical/mathematical, musical/rhythmic, bodily/kinesthetic, interpersonal, intrapersonal and naturalist. This perspective takes us far beyond traditional assessment as a way of defining a future teacher to a more powerful means of validating the capabilities of every unique preservice teacher.

The philosophy of multiple intelligences is restructuring the delivery of instruction and assessment for learners in many public schools. MI is a philosophy of teaching as well as a stance toward learning. As a philosophy, MI embodies a paradigmatic shift from a stance that questions which students are smart to one that devises a means to discover how each preservice teacher is smart. It embodies a shift from telling preservice teachers how to think, to devising assessments that allow them to reveal how they think best.

Culture strongly shapes definitions of intelligence (Gardner, 1993, pp. 35-37) as well. As demographics change globally, more and more non-native speakers of English enter public school classrooms.

This pattern is being mirrored in many teacher education programs. These individuals bring with them their particular cultural attributes (intelligences). Western Europeans bring great literary traditions (verbal/linguistic), Native Americans bring story-telling traditions (*also* verbal/linguistic). The cultures of Japan, China, Germany and Switzerland bring the often unrecognized value of precision, accuracy and persistence (mathematical/logical). The geographic regions of Mexico and Texas (and elsewhere) make extensive use of the designs, colors, shapes, and patterns of their environment in their clothing, arts and crafts (visual/spatial). The societies of Australia and Japan have ubiquitous wellness programs integrated into their societies and Eastern Europeans (including Germany) have a strong tradition of excelling at sports (bodily/kinesthetic). Most cultures outside of the US, Canada and Western Europe value singing and music in daily life as well as in traditional celebrations (musical/rhythmic). Canadians rely heavily on cooperative learning groups. The Chinese emphasize mental concentration in schools (interpersonal), and New Zealanders have developed an effective use of journaling as an integral part of reading instruction (intrapersonal). Can teacher education programs afford to ignore the presence of these attributes in the assessment process?

As college and university teacher education classrooms become more diverse and international in scope, viewing assessment though a cross-cultural lens may become a critical strategy for democratizing academe. Cultural attributes represent unique strengths which are generally ignored in the assessment process of most teachers in training. If, however, these intelligences are tapped in classroom activities, they can potentially foster more positive attitudes among different cultural groups, a target goal of multicultural education. Such attitudes may also promote international solidarity--a one-world mentality--as learners see that each culture has unique strengths and that these are equally valued. Incorporating multiple intelligences in assessment provides a bonus--it gives teachers a way of validating cultural strengths as well as individual strengths and differences. Emphasizing cultural intelligences becomes a vehicle for change. If we can model the use of multiple intelligences with preservice teachers, how much better chance would there be for them to model the same concept with young learners?

Over a period of time, in addition to reinforcing cultural strengths, preservice teachers can be provided with opportunities to explore and develop all of their own intelligences. Unfortunately, in many college classroom settings, cultural and linguistic differences often penalize learners. Sometimes educators operate as though poor verbal/linguistic skills (first or second language) presuppose no other talent, or assume that exceptional verbal/linguistic skills guarantee success in other domains. A multiple intelligences perspective toward learning (and teaching) allows teacher educators to leave behind the notion that verbal/linguistic intelligence is all that matters.

Individuals who perform well in academic courses do not necessarily do the same in teaching. The correlation may not be with verbal/linguistic intelligence, but rather with intrapersonal intelligence or some other unique combination of intelligence strengths. Clearly, teaching, like communication in general, is not only a matter of the words we say; but, instead, each interaction with a student might better be characterized as a whole body or gestural act. As early as 1970, Birdwhistell (1970) noted the power of the nonverbal (e.g., facial expression, eye blinks, head movements, gestures, pitch, tone, body language) in communication. He found that communication was nearly 65% nonverbal. If this is the case, then the classroom emphasis on verbal/linguistic skills is indeed misplaced.

When students are less than successful in a teacher preparation program, is it because instruction is delivered in a mode that is contradictory to their intelligence strengths or that they are assessed without regard to these strengths? Someone once said, I like chocolate ice cream, but when I go fishing I use worms because fish like worms.

The Process of Implementation in a College Classroom

As a teacher educator, I have been attempting to assess students through a multidimensional, multiple intelligence based approach. For my Midterm Examination in Second Language Acquisition, a course required for English-as-a-second-language endorsement, I created an assessment process and an instrument (see Appendix A) that has been implemented for three terms with very encouraging results. I have prepared a slide show of students' artistic presentations to demonstrate exemplars at the beginning of the semester, and to share with interested audiences.

On the day I first introduced this format, I asked students to form groups based on what they believed their strongest intelligence was. They formed seven groups, one for each of Gardner's most-noted intelligences. I will add the eighth intelligence (Naturalist) in future semesters. Each group was composed of at least five students. I then gave the students my initial draft of this exam and asked each group to do three tasks: (a) Examine the projects that were listed under the intelligence that their group represented. Together, modify, improve, or completely change the projects so that they might best tap into the designated intelligence which that group represented; (b) Examine the overall scoring rubric and make changes to reflect what they felt was a fair expectation, and (c) set a due date. After approximately thirty minutes, the class reported their changes. I agreed with most, but not all of the changes. In a friendly spirit of negotiation and compromise, we came to a consensus on all issues. For example, under category IV (Bilingualism), one group asked that their particular task only include five of the ten issues. I rejected that on the basis that all of the other intelligence groups had agreed on the importance of including all ten, and that I thought that was very important. In another part of the discussion, one group commented that my original suggestion that the blue ribbon category allow only one departure from the instructions was asking too much. They suggested that it be changed to 1-2 departures. I conceded the point.

The students commented after class that being involved in the process was very meaningful and gave them ideas for how they might do this with their own classes. Others mentioned that they were excited to get started--something I seldom heard in reference to other Midterm exams. Some asked for clarification on the knowledge base. They realized that they could not just memorize the information. They had to understand the concepts in order to do the projects. I was thrilled with these results. Not only have the students enjoyed doing these, but I have enjoyed examining them. As you will notice on the Midterm Ribbon Evaluation form (see Appendix B), students evaluate their own exam, a peer evaluates it (random selection), and I evaluate it. These scores carry equal weight. The average score determines whether they receive a white ribbon, a red ribbon or a blue ribbon. Actual ribbons of these various colors were attached to their final projects. I had more blue ribbons than I could ever have expected! I cannot wait to do this again!

A Paradigm Shift

A paradigm shift in teaching English to speakers of other languages is occurring which, consciously or unconsciously, appears to be incorporating a multiple intelligences philosophy.

Locus of Knowledge. In the old way of thinking, the teacher is the authority (verbal/linguistic). In the new way of thinking, teachers take a back seat in order to scaffold on students' current knowledge (verbal/linguistic and interpersonal intelligence).

Philosophy. In a behaviorist way of thinking, the teacher imparts knowledge primarily through words (verbal/linguistic). In a new, more constructivist view, multiple intelligences provide the framework for both teaching and learning.

Methodology. In the old paradigm, classes are teacher-fronted most of the time[1], direct instruction is followed by practice. Students

---

[1]In a preliminary study I conducted in 1997 involving 27.5 hours of observation in both(a) a two-way bilingual first grade (12 native speakers of Spanish and 13 native speakers of English) and (b) a regular first grade (8 native speakers of Spanish and 17 native speakers of English), I found that the time dominated by the teacher ranged from 53% in the bilingual classroom and over 70% for the regular classroom. In an analysis of the multiple intelligences employed, the following results were found (ranked in descending order):

(a)   Bilingual First Grade

Verbal/Linginistic	63.5%
Bodily/Kinesthetic	30.0%
Mathematical/Logical	26.5%
Visual/Spatial	25.5%
Musical/Rhythmic	16.5%
Interpersonal	10.0%
Intrapersonal	5.0%
Naturalist	0%

(b)   Regular First Grade

Verbal/Linguistic	76.7%
Mathematical/Logical	43.5%

often work alone at their desks (verbal/linguistic). In the new view, classes are student-centered. Students often work together in cooperative groups. Teachers collaborate in instruction. Teachers are not the only ones who can deliver instruction in the new mode. Teachers can include parents, zoo keepers, cooks, farmers, and artists to enhance instruction (verbal/linguistic, interpersonal, intrapersonal, naturalist and more).

Typical Activity. In the old way of thinking, classes involved memorizing dialogues, drill and practice, workbooks and worksheets (verbal/linguistic). In the new paradigm, student activities include problem-solving (mathematical/logical, visual/spatial), information gap activities (interpersonal), reflective journaling (intrapersonal), real-life learning (visual/spatial, bodily/kinesthetic, naturalist), role-plays (verbal/linguistic, interpersonal, bodily/kinesthetic) and hands-on learning and creating (bodily/kinesthetic, visual/spatial).

Assessment. In the old paradigm, tests often measure more about what students do not know than what they do know. They are typically true/false, multiple choice, or essay tests. Standardized tests are common (verbal/linguistic, mathematical/logical). In the new paradigm, the goal is to meaningfully assess the wider world of what students know. Assessment is authentic in nature (e.g., portfolio assessment), and includes multiple measures, potentially engaging all of the intelligences.

Curriculum. In the old paradigm, the English-as-a-second-language curriculum is text-based, grammar-focused, relies on vicarious experiences, and often makes use of artificial or contrived dialogues (verbal/linguistic). The new way of thinking leads to refocusing instruction to a content-based, thematically organized curriculum

Visual/Spatial	29.5%
Bodily/Kinesthetic	14.0%
Interpersonal	5.0%
Musical/Rhythmic	4.5%
Intrapersonal	1.0%
Naturalist	0%

(supplemented with grammar and text). Video, pictures, computers, realia, field experiences and authentic communicative events (e.g., interviews, surveys conducted outside of the classroom) potentially engage all of the intelligences. This kind of shift can also be observed in the teaching methodology for writing, pronunciation and reading.

Technology. In the old paradigm, work was repetitive and done in solitude (verbal/linguistic, mathematical/logical). In the new paradigm, computer-assisted language learning offers interactive communication both at and on the computer. Use of the internet, video conferencing, E-pals, E-mail, and virtual reality are all tools for language learning (potentially engaging all of the intelligences).

A multiple intelligences philosophy provides a framework that broadens the view of language teaching. It calls teachers to present classes and assess students through multiple means (Armstrong, 1994). It challenges educators to move from a drill and practice grammar-based approach to a thematic, content-based curriculum. It challenges educators to move quickly into technology. It is exciting for those committed to equity. Incorporating this kind of shift can deepen our understanding of all levels and venues of teaching--challenging many current practices within teacher education. The old adage, "Smart minds think alike" has to be reevaluated with regard to assessment. In line with a multiple intelligences perspective, "Smart minds don't all think alike," and as teacher educators recognize this, it is truly cause for celebration.

References

Armstrong, T. (1994). Multiple intelligences in the classroom. Alexandria, VA: Association for Supervision and Curriculum Development.

Birdwhistell, R. (1970). Kinesics and context. Philadelphia: University of Pennsylvania Press.

Colborne, M. (1997, September 3). NBC News Hour. New York: National Broadcasting Company.

Gardner, H. (1993). Multiple intelligences: The theory of practice.

New York: Basic Books.

Gardner, H. (1983). Frames of mind: The theory of multiple intelligences. New York: Basic Books.

Green, M. (1993). Beyond insularity: Releasing the voices. College ESL, 3(1), 1-14.

Report of the National Commission on Testing and Public Policy. (1990). From Gatekeeper to Gateway: Transforming testing in America. Chesterhill, MA: Boston College Press.

Rigden, D.W. (1996, Dec. 11). How teachers would change teacher education. Education Week, 4-5.

Steichen, E. (1955). Family of man. New York: Simon and Schuster.

APPENDIX A
Midterm Assessment

Note to Students: This is a summary the Knowledge Base (six content topics) over which you are responsible. On the pages that follow, you will find seven projects for each of the seven topics below. One project is listed for each of the multiple intelligence areas: VL = Verbal-Linguistic, ML = Mathematical-Logical, V-S = Visual Spatial, M-R = Musical-Rhythmic, Inter = Interpersonal, and Intra = Intrapersonal.

Topic I: Studying Second Language Acquisition (SLA) (including the reasons studying SLA matters, the epistemological errors that we have examined, and the three primary categories of SLA theories: Environmentalist, Nativist, Interactionist).

Topic II: Differences/Similarities Between the Various Types of SLA (including evidence that you understand the differences in the four quadrants of this grid relative to language learning).

	Child	Adult
L1		

L2		

Topic III. **Language Input** (including the thirty or more elements of Teacher Talk that have been identified and the research surrounding its use).

Topic IV: **Bilingualism** (including evidence that you understand the ten contact issues we studied that either promote or impede bilingualism and the research evidence about the cognitive consequences of bilingualism).

Topic V: **Learner Language** (including evidence that you understand the following terms: Variability Fossilization, Codeswitching, Interlanguage, Schema.

Topic VI. **The Relationship Between Culture and SLA.**

Topic VII. **Self-Selected Topic.**

I. Studying SLA

VL   Develop a vocabulary matching exercise for the theories and a second one for the reasons/errors.

ML   Write labeled mental formulas to explain the three; Outline the reasons/errors (add detail).

VS   Create six labeled graphic organizers for the three theories; the reasons, and the errors. You may also combine the theories into one graphic organizer if you choose.

BK   Create an interactive exercise or game or hunt in which adults learn about the theories through walking around. This can involve in-class or out-of-class activity.

MR   Create a poem, song or rap for each theory as well as one for the reasons and one for the errors.

Inter   Survey the class for which of the three theories they felt most akin to. Summarize the results.

Intra   Create a two-page questionnaire that would determine which theory someone believed in without directly asking. Take it yourself. Write a three-sentence reflection on how it worked or didn't work. Create a T/F quiz for the reasons and errors. Take it yourself.

II. Differences/Similiarities in Language Learning

VL   Recreate the four-square handout and fill it in with phrases or brief sentences (paraphrased).

ML   Create a series of problems (scenarios) to which the solutions represent each of the four areas.

VS   Do a mind map/web for each of the four quadrants.

BK   Translate each quadrant into a movement routine. Sketch this roughly and explain your choices.

MR   Create a series of sounds (tape) that show the difference in the four areas. Write an explanation for each justifying your choices.

Inter   Design an interview for a person who would be representative of each of the four areas.

Intra   Stand in the shoes (or booties) of a who might be a representative of each of the four areas. Do an believable autobiographical report for each.

III. Language Input

VL   Summarize the issues/research surrounding teacher talk.

ML   Organize the elements of teacher talk into your own self-styled categories and name the categories.

VS   Create a poster to use to teach adults the elements of teacher talk.

BK   Demonstrate with manipulatives (draw boxes or sticks, etc.) showing the patterns inherent in all of the different elements of teacher talk.

MR   Create a song or set of rhythmic patterns that capture the different examples of teacher talk. Use notation paper to record your ideas.

Inter   Find actual examples of teacher talk by visiting an ESL/BE classroom. Show the sentence in which each example is embedded and underline the element found. Summarize how many were identified and list the others that were not found.

Intra   Tape your own classes (if ESL/BE) and identify your use of teacher talk. If you do not find any or only a few, visit someone else's ESL class and proceed with the Inter task.

IV. Bilingualism

VL   Invent a set of slogans that separately capture the ten contact issues.

ML   Create a timeline and place the ten contact issues somewhere on the timeline in conjunction with historical events. Name each contact issue on the timeline.

VS   Use drawings or paintings or mural to illustrate the timeline task listed in ML.

BK   Invent a physical language arts-type game wherein the participants would learn the ten contact issues.

MR   Write a separate verse of a unified song or poem to represent each of the ten contact issues.

Inter   Create an interview (questions and answers) with each of the ten contact areas as though they were guests on a talk show.

Intra   Reflect on changes in your own understanding of each of the ten contact issues are related to second language acquisition. Then, order the ten in the order you think is the most powerful in affecting the acquisition of another language.

V. Learner Language

VL   Define each term and give three examples of each. Using APA format, cite the sources of your definitions and/or examples.

ML   Create five separate labeled symbolic formulas to illustrate the processes leading to each of the concepts.

VS   Develop a labeled flow chart or diagram to show important elements/processes for each concept.

BK   Develop a kitbag containing labeled objects representing the five concepts. On the label, explain the concept and justify why you selected each particular object.

MR   Develop a song or songs that will help adults learn these five concepts.

Inter Create a jigsaw activity that could be used to teach these concepts to your peers.

Intra For each of the five concepts, reflect on the specific pedagogical implications you can draw for your own ESL students or some future ESL students you may have.

VI. The Relationship of Culture and SLA

VL Write a story showing the impact of culture on someone learning a second language. Underline and label in the margin each point about culture that you are including.

ML Compare and contrast your culture with Vietnamese and Hispanic cultures.

VS Represent a set of at least five cultural phenomena in a montage or drawing.

BK Create a set of short cultural role plays representing at least three cultures.

MR Summarize the rhythmic patterns and forms of musical expression that are typical of two other cultures. Explain how these might be outgrowths of other cultural realities.

Inter Develop a series of three classroom scenarios in which the teacher exhibits personal understanding of other cultures (i.e., responds in cultural responsive way). Explain what happened in each one.

Intra In a two-page essay, explore a personal challenge that you have faced or still face regarding culture. Include at least three pieces of information from class that has informed that challenge.

VII. Self-Selected Topic.
Appendix B
Levels of Mastery: Performance Criteria
A Celebration of Learning AboutSecond Language Learning

	White Ribbon	Red Ribbon	Blue Ribbon
Procedural Compliance	>deviations from instructions	2-3 deviations from instructions	0-1 deviation from instructions
Comprehesiveness	70% of points indicated in each knowledge area attempted and/or three of the six areas completed	80% of points indicated in each knowledge area attempted and/or four of the six areas completed	100% of points indicated in each knowledge area attempted and/or six of the seven areas completed
Presentation	Sketchy, unclear or apparent limited time available to put into preparing presentation format	Clear, vivid, eye-catching, nice--something to be proud of. Viewers might say "Extremely nice"!	Extraordinary presentation--beyond the expected. Would make almost any viewer say "Wow"! in amazement at the overall presentation.
Explorations	2-4 different intelligences attempted	five different intelligences attempted	6-8 different intelligences attempted
Linkages	No links or weak links between or across ideas or beyond class to life applications	At least one identifiable link (explained by the author) between or across ideas or beyond concept to life or classroom applications	More than one identifiable link (explained by the author) between or across ideas or beyond concept to life or classroom applications

Midterm Ribbon Evaluation

NAME _____

	Self-Evaluation	Peer Evaluation	Instructor Evaluation	Average
Procedural Compliance				
Comprehensiveness				
Presentation				
Explorations				
Linkages				

TOTAL: _____

AVERAGE: _____

Evaluator: Select the number of points from the ranges available in the Ribbon categories below, and write the numbers in the appropriate boxes above.

	White Ribbon	Red Ribbon	Blue Ribbon
Procedural Compliance	14-15	16-18	19-20
Comprehensiveness	14-15	16-18	19-20
Presentation	14-15	16-18	19-20
Exploration	14-15	16-18	19-20
Linkages	14-15	16-18	19-20

Chapter Eleven
Mediated Cultural Immersion and Antiracism: An Opportunity for Monocultural Preservice Teachers to Begin the Dialogue

Paula Bradfield-Kreider
Western Oregon University, Monmouth, OR

=====================

For decades, we have witnessed the differences in achievement between students within the cultural mainstream and students who are culturally and/or linguistically distinct (Jacob & Jordon, 1987). Among the many reasons for this educational inequity, one continues to surface which is particularly problematic: a significant number of White European American teachers are unable and/or unwilling to provide equal access to meaningful educational experiences for children whose culture is different from their own (Nel, 1995; Finney & Orr, 1995; Fuller, 1992, 1994; Hilliard, 1974; MacIntosh, 1989; McDiarmid, 1990). This problem increases in importance as the nation's demographics change. While over 85% of U.S. teachers are White, the percentage of European American students is decreasing; the "majority" is becoming the minority (National Education Association, 1992; Smith, Rogers, Alsalam, Perie, Mahoney, & Martin, 1994). White preservice teachers, "situated as they are in a racist, stratified society, are isolated from a significant part of the population they are likely to teach" (Finney & Orr, 1995, p. 328). Culturally encapsulated, (Bennett, 1995; Gay, 1977) European American teachers have developed entrenched, ethnocentric identities with little, if any, knowledge about or experience with children whose culture is different from their own; children whom they are ill-prepared to teach (Delpit, 1988; Fuller, 1992, 1994; Hilliard, 1974; McDiarmid, 1990; Nel, 1995).

To further complicate the issue, teachers often are not aware of their lack of knowledge or of their need to resist the educational status quo. Assuming that their cultural heritage is "normal" and cultural backgrounds other than their own are "different" (Cuban, 1984; Baca & Cervantes, 1989; Fried, 1993; Garcia & Ortiz, 1988; Helms, 1990; Noel, 1995; Spradley & McCurdy, 1984), teachers perceive no need to understand the cultural and linguistic learning, communication, and socialization of culturally distinct children. Instead, they envision their role as that of cultural transmitter. Using Eurocentric educational philosophies and other assimilationist constructs, culturally encapsulated teachers believe their role is to mold the different children to the dominant cultural and linguistic norms. In doing so, they expect all children to perform well in an educational environment which is steeped in individualism, meritocracy (Bidell, Lee, Bouchie, Ward, & Brass, 1994; Chávez Chávez, 1995; Freire, 1970; Jennings, 1995; Shor, 1992) and taken-for-granted powers and privileges available only to European American children (Bradfield-Kreider, 1997a; Cochran-Smith, 1995; MacIntosh, 1989; Sleeter, 1993). Because of their color-blindness and efforts to teach all children using strategies and philosophies that are best suited for middle-class European American children, monocultural teachers continue to widen the gap between the haves and have-nots and to perpetuate the oppression of culturally marginalized children (Ogbu, 1995). To whit, we in teacher education have reached an impasse; an overwhelming proportion of our preservice teachers are entering the schools either unwilling or unable to provide what our children need to gain an equal voice and to become participating members of a democracy.

Our children need teachers who, believing all children can learn (García, 1995; Ladson-Billings, 1995), welcome difficult issues, design collaborative activities for heterogeneous groups, and help students apply models of fairness, equity and justice to their world (Nieto, 1996). To accomplish this, teachers require more than content knowledge and methods (Bartolomé, 1994), and cultural knowledge about learning, communication and socialization (García, 1995; Gay, 1993; Ladson-Billings, 1995). They must develop the political clarity to reconstruct classrooms in which all students are simultaneously respected and challenged (e.g., Chávez Chávez, 1997; Freire, 1970; Freire & Macedo, 1987; Jennings, 1995; Nieto, 1996).

Our children also need teachers who not only "encourage academic success and cultural competence [but who also] help students to recognize, understand and critique current social inequities" (Ladson-Billings, 1995, p. 466)--teachers who develop students' critical social consciousness and collective social action strategies to resist the social injustices that face them daily (Chávez Chávez, 1995; Freire, 1970; Giroux, 1988; Shor, 1992; Sleeter, 1996). "To alter a system that is deeply dysfunctional, [children need teachers who] embrace social change as part of the job -- teachers who enter the profession not expecting to carry on business as usual but prepared to join other educators and parents in major reforms" (Ladson-Billings, 1995, p. 494). They need teachers who realize that teaching is about *doing*, and about *teaching against the grain* of European American educational status quo (Cochran-Smith, 1995).

In response to children's needs and rapidly changing demographics, revisions of teacher preparation programs have become "not just necessary, but urgent" (Cochran-Smith, 1995, p. 541). A growing number of teacher educators and other cultural workers who are fighting for educational equity argue for the redesign of teacher education. The redesigned program must create and strategically place multiple opportunities for monocultural teachers to become what children need -- antiracist teachers with a more transformational, critical construct of teaching (Banks & Banks, 1996; Chávez Chávez, 1995; Cochran-Smith, 1991, 1995; Freire, 1970; Giroux, 1988, 1993; hooks, 1994; Ladson-Billings, 1995; Nieto, 1996; Sleeter, 1996; Sleeter & McLaren, 1995).

Despite the persuasive nature of our society's cultural and educational hegemony, progress is being made by various teacher educators and cultural workers. In the following sections, literature and research results will be shared in two areas: students' membership in communities that are pluralistic and committed to antiracism, and student mediated field immersions in communities whose dominant culture is other than their own. In the subsequent section, the two are merged in the creation of mediated cultural immersions; students become members of communities committed to antiracism while immersed as non-dominant cultural members and second language speakers.

Critical Communities and Cultural Identity

One strategy that has had some success in facilitating changes in teachers' ethnocentric perceptions of teaching, learning, and culture is the use of pluralistic communities in which students, educators and community members work together to fight collective educational inequities, to resist the structural status quo (Boyle-Baise & Washburn, 1995; Gay, 1995; Mizzell, Bennett, Bowman, & Morin, 1993; Sleeter, 1996), and to overcome the personal isolation ensuing from boat-rocking (Boyle-Baise & Washburn, 1995). To differentiate communities whose membership is pluralistic and whose purposes are antiracist from others, I have coined the term critical communities. Critical communities offer monocultural teachers a safe environment in which to confront and broaden their ethnocentric cultural and professional identities and to develop the collective social change strategies and support structures to operationalize reconstructed notions of their role in the teaching, and learning enterprise (Chávez Chávez, 1995).

The Impact of Critical Communities on Students' Cultural Identities

Historically, European American teachers have been taught to avoid the acknowledgment of the benefits associated with the cultural mainstream (Spindler & Spindler, 1990; Tatum, 1994). Consequently, an alarming number (Smith, 1997) either "smugly accept their taken-for-granted privileges" (Chávez Chávez, personal communication, 1996) as active racists or, hiding behind racial "color-blindness," have never acknowledged their cultural privileges nor their race (Tatum, 1994). Because of European American teachers' extreme individualism

(Collins, 1991) and belief in the myth of American meritocracy, they narrow their vision to the individual child, thereby ignoring the positive or negative effects that the child's membership in a particular ethnic group, class, gender, or race has on learning, communication, and socialization (Finney & Orr, 1995; Jennings, 1995; Nieto, 1996). Rather than viewing it as a result of collective injustices, culturally encapsulated teachers perceive lack of success as an individual's lack of effort, enabling them to shirk personal or institutional responsibility for growing numbers of educationally marginalized children.

Due to the combination of encapsulated teachers' ethnically naive (Gay, 1977) cultural identities and misinformed, damaging perceptions of the other (Chávez Chávez, 1995), superficial solutions such as exposure to cultural and linguistic differences is not sufficient to change students' perceptions of their role as a teacher (O'Loughlin, 1995). This type of exposure, without accompanying instructional mediation, actually has the reverse effect in many instances; racial insularity, prejudice, and cultural misconceptions are strengthened rather than diminished (Chávez Chávez, personal communication, 1997). In situations such as these, students often experience powerful negative emotions (Cabello & Burstein, 1995) as their perception of "what is" conflicts with the reality of what is. Expressing disagreement and or discomfort through silence (Ladson-Billings, 1996), teachers wait for the experience, dialogue, or course to end, exiting with their original beliefs and tacit knowledge intact.

Critical communities can be used as vehicles to counteract this passive resistance to multicultural change. In these communities, teachers gain direct exposure to the lives and stories of culturally and/or linguistically distinct community members with ongoing instructional mediation from faculty, other community members and cultural workers. As members of such a small community, escape from the unleashing of unpopular things (Britzman, 1991) through silence and/or withdrawal becomes more difficult for teachers. Instead, they encounter a safe environment in which members in various stages of cultural growth share personal narratives and learn from one another.

These include members who are resisting the European American cultural hegemony to regain or retain their cultural and linguistic identity; members who are managing the emotional reactions accompanying the recognition of benefits gained because of race; members who, upon critical examination of their cultural identity, have abandoned their dysconscious racism (King, 1991) cloaked in the euphemism of color-blindness; members who, realizing that non-racism or awareness of injustice without ensuing action is impossible, are transforming from passive racism to antiracism; and members who, as antiracists, are fighting collectively against social injustice while continuing the deconstruction of their own cultural blind spots. In this type of environment, teachers witness members' growth at multiple stages through open engagement in uncomfortable dialogues surrounding race, power, and dominance and ongoing critical examinations of their cultural identities. Gentle pressure from members to become antiracist becomes the norm, rather than silence, complicity, and pressure to perpetuate the dominant cultural status quo. When new members are ready to begin the dialogue that precipitates changes in cultural identities, the community supports the management of initial emotional reactions, hypersensitivity, habitual resistance and/or denial (Ahlquist, 1992; Jennings, 1995; King, 1991; Sleeter, 1992; Ladson-Billings, 1991; Tatum, 1992). In this manner, teachers begin to confront and then critically examine their own ethnocentric and racist cultural and professional identities, and to abandon the accompanying dysconscious or unwitting racism (King, 1991), first steps in the evolution of a cultural worker.

Using Critical Communities to Develop Social Change Strategies

Although powerful, the abandonment of dysconscious racism is still only a first step. At this point in their development, teachers' dysconscious racism becomes passive racism. Aware of their own ethnocentricities, when they are confronted with instances of collective social injustice, they are unwilling to act. Passive racism cannot be replaced with antiracism however, until teachers develop the courage and skill necessary to engage in social action to promote educational equity. To do this, European American teacher educators must discard the construct of multicultural education as human relations work (Sleeter, 1996), and don one that is more critical and active. Unfortunately, many European American teachers are particularly unprepared to do this, due to limited experiences in fighting for racial or cultural privileges and/or power (Sleeter, 1996) and an inability to critically dialogue with community members whose world view is distinct from their own. Many European American teachers' primary form of resistance is silence (Collins, 1991; Ladson-Billings, 1996; Chávez Chávez, 1995; MacIntosh, 1989; O'Loughlin, 1995) and political withdrawal, both of which are strengthened by continual exposure to the ethnocentric cynicism of media, peers, parents, and other teachers (Cochran-Smith, 1995; Collins, 1991; Giroux, 1993), rendering them politically handicapped. Until the cycle of political withdrawal and the focus on the individual child is broken, many teachers will continue to disconnect from other classes and races (Collins, 1991), minimizing the perceived need for teachers to develop strategies for solidarity and collective social action strategies (Mizzell et al., 1993; Sleeter, 1996).

One way to break this cycle is through critical communities which are instructionally mediated by faculty members who possess a more critical construct multicultural education and an understanding of teacher change. In such communities, new members have ongoing opportunities to connect with others who are committed and actively involved in the politics of the teaching and learning enterprise. An ethic of engagement (Loeb, 1995) can be developed by fostering affective connections between and among people who are working toward a common goal (Collins, 1991; Noddings, 1995). With the support of the community, teachers can be exposed to antiracist educators who, viewing teaching as a political act, fight against the dominant political norms (Singer, 1994; Liston & Zeichner, 1987) to reestablish children as subjects in classrooms rather than objects (Freire, 1970; Freire &

Macedo, 1987). The community can provide the gentle pressure necessary for members to become intimately involved in praxis -- becoming open to personal and community critical analysis, critically examining societal race and racism, and then acting accordingly (Burbules & Rice, 1991; Giroux, 1988; Roman, 1993; Welch, 1991). At that point, new members can begin to develop tools and resources to first unveil and then critically examine educational injustices, to become cognizant of their complicity in the perpetuation of those injustices, and to overcome learned political silence -- to become cultural workers who "embrace civic courage, compassion, cultural and social justice, equity, . . . [and] deconstruct dominant and subordinating narratives entrenched in the hidden curriculum of teaching and learning" (Chávez Chávez, 1995, p. 5), and serve as sites of resistance to the rampaging racism threatening culturally subordinated children (hooks, 1990).

Mediated Field Experiences and Cultural Identity
Similar to membership in critical communities, most students who have mediated opportunities to live with and learn from community members in geographic regions in which the dominant culture is one that has been marginalized in the United States gain the knowledge and skills to broaden their cultural identities. This realization came from work done over a two year time span with month-long field experiences in a small liberal arts college in the northwest. In an attempt to broaden the world view of monocultural preservice teachers, I became involved in this institution's four week January term multicultural internships by developing a field experience in Aguascalientes, Mexico in which students were to live with families whose cultural and linguistic norms were Mexican, study Spanish and teach each day in a bilingual elementary school. Using data gathered from students who had similar trips without attending faculty members who could mediate the experience, this field experience was designed to be mediated by a faculty member to help students remain immersed and manage the changes rather than escaping the culture.

Mediated Field Experiences Description: Year One

In brief, the field experience was split into two phases, on-campus and in Mexico. In phase one, preservice students were engaged in 5 one-hour-long, on-campus sessions to prepare them for the trip and to discuss the program goals, which focused on enhanced human relations, intercultural communication, and cultural sensitivity. During the second phase, each student lived with and learned from host families whose cultural norms were Mexican, studied Spanish three hours per day, and taught in Mexican schools three hours per day. Students were placed individually to provide more opportunities to learn from and depend on their host family. Although no formal instructional mediation was built into this term, just-in-time informal mediation occurred throughout. Upon return to campus, neither formal nor informal mediation opportunities were provided; preservice students returned home to "business as usual."

Subjects: Year One

During the first term, all six students who enrolled were middle-class European Americans, two of whom were males in their mid twenties and four were females whose ages ranged from 19 to 35. Since both males had lived extensively in Mexico and were fluent in Spanish, the four females were chosen for the study. All four were elementary education majors with no international travel, little experience with cultures other than their own and wide variations in both oral Spanish fluency and pedagogical knowledge and skills.

Data Collection: Years One and Two

The students were interviewed before, during, and after the term; field notes were collected before and during the term; the on-site instructors and teachers who worked with the students in Mexico were interviewed; and student journals with entries throughout the term were collected. All data was transcribed, categorized, and examined for emerging themes (Bogdin & Biklin, 1992).

Themes: Year One

After the first field experience, the students' entering cultural identities remained relatively unchanged. They maintained color-blind, dysconsciously racist perception of Other. Rather than confronting their loss of taken-for-granted powers and privileges, students attributed the loss and the accompanying negative emotional reaction to homesickness and bided their time until they returned home. In short, students entered and left the experience with their tacit knowledge and assimilationist notions of teaching intact.

The only significant changes from that term were my own (Bradfield-Kreider, in press). Unsettled by the powerful emotions that arose from my own experiences in Mexico, and from the reactions and interactions of my students with each other and community members, I began examining my own cultural constructs while in Mexico and upon return. Through my deconstructions, concentrated multicultural readings, and dialogue with cultural workers, I began to confronted my own ethnic naiveté (Gay, 1977) and dysconscious racism (King, 1991).

Field Experience: Year Two

The second year, the program was similar in structure but different in content in four ways. First, to encourage better communication, socialization and learning in Aguascalientes, preservice students had a prerequisite language proficiency equivalent to a minimum of 1 ½ years of college Spanish. Second, students were all interviewed in both Spanish and English to assess their Spanish proficiency and to encourage self-selection based on commitment to the modified program goals, which were (a) examination of their cultural identities and their taken-for-granted powers and privileges, (b) reconstruction of their perceptions of power and privilege based on the management of their own loss of those privileges in Mexico, © reconstructing their perceptions of families and community members whose cultural norms are Mexican, and (d) immersing in experiences of cultural and linguistic difference, rather than visiting, escaping the culture, or expecting the community to accommodate. Third, by sharing my narrative, students began to explore their own ethnocentrism before and during the immersion. Finally, both formal and informal instructional mediation occurred throughout the program to encourage and support changes in their cultural identities.

Subjects: Year Two

Eleven preservice teachers entered the program, ten women and one man. The man was a 28 year old secondary education major ready for student teaching whereas all of the women were elementary education majors between the ages of 19 and 21 who were at various stages of program completion. Nine of the 11 had little experience with cultures different from their own and had not traveled far from their hometowns. As a group, the students' Spanish fluency was higher than in term one. One student, Marni[1], had some culturally specific knowledge from the small farm communities in which she was raised and from her fiancée, José. Marni, 21 years old and Keith, 28 years old, were the most fluent, the farthest along in their teacher education programs, and the oldest of the eleven.

Themes: Term Two

The themes that emerged from the second term data were several: reconstructed notions of power, privilege and their own racial identity; dissatisfaction with the cultural status quo; dissatisfaction with their preparation for teaching bicultural children; awareness of their dysconscious racism; a more culturally inclusive world view; the abandonment of passive racism; intense loneliness; an increased desire to learn how to teach bicultural children; a willingness to continue the dialogue concerning race and racism; and a longing for a new form of community (Bradfield-Kreider & Chávez Chávez, in progress). Of the aforementioned themes, students' changed perceptions of their own

---

[1] All names are pseudonyms.

cultural identity will be discussed here.

While still on campus, all students entered as culturally encapsulated dysconscious racists (King, 1991), unaware of their racism and espousing a color-blind construct for race; "I am glad we no longer have racism problems, except maybe in the deep South. I mean, we are all the same. Actually, I have never met a racist." (Nancy, pre-interview, 1995). Students also believed that hard work and parental support were the keys to success; "I think the problem is that some cultures do not value education like we do. In our family, we always had to work hard for what we got. Kids can do it if they work hard and their parents support us" (Hannah, pre-interview, 1996).

Similar to term one, students arrived in Mexico with minimal changes in their cultural identity. Through instructional mediation, all students realized early in the immersion that they had become non-dominant cultural members and first language speakers; "I feel so stupid. I am ignored half the time or just smiled at. I cannot do anything for myself and have to ask for help for everything." (Mindy, interview, 1996). Overnight, what students had considered normal was replaced with unfamiliar socialization, communication, and cultural norms.

The cohort community was continued and work was initiated to help them forming community ties with host families, friends and neighbors. With ongoing instructional mediation and invaluable help from the host family community, students began to learn from and depend on community members whose cultural norms were Mexican. This connection provided a safe environment for them to dialogue about uncomfortable issues such as racism, ethnocentricity and social injustice. "I am furious with my complacency. How could I never have ignored what was in front of my face. The children [First and second generation children originating from Michoacan, Mexico] must have learned nothing except that I did try to understand them" (Edna, journal, 1996).

Upon reentry to the U.S., however, students' cultural growth was largely arrested. Without a formal post-phase or instructional assistance in creating and/or maintaining a community supporting their examination of their own identities and their impact on teaching and learning, students lost their safe environment to continue the dialogue; "My friends think I am crazy. They think my new attitudes are because I fell in love down there . . . as if I have no eyes to see injustice and no head to examine it. Why can't I convince them?" (Kathy, interview, 1996).

Previously complacent and dysconscious about social injustices and racism, students returned with a beginning awareness of racist actions. Their anger at comments and behaviors of friends and acquaintances scared them. Many found themselves pulling back from arguments they began with others, surprised and confused at their emotional response and without tools to manage the changes and accompanying emotional reactions. No longer in the vortex of Eurocentrism, the students felt dis-attached -- out of touch with their own culture. Three students attempted to reconstruct a community similar to what they had in Mexico with little success. Unwilling to take a political stand or speak out against friends, family, and community, the students returned to silence; "It is like showing baby pictures. Nobody seems interested in my experiences or what I learned. They keep changing the topic, pretending like it was just a vacation or something. . . . So, I quit talking" (Sarah, informal interview two months after the field experience, 1996).

Although ten of the eleven students had broadened their cultural identities and had become aware of their prior dysconscious racism, they did not progress beyond that point. Without instructional mediation, a supportive community, or knowledge of social change and networking strategies, students had become mired in passive racism -- agonizing over the ethnocentric behavior and ideology they encountered without overtly fighting it (Bradfield-Kreider, in press). When faced with the choice between the loss of community as they knew it (Breitborde, 1996) and their continued growth, all but one student abandoned their progress within three months upon return (Bradfield-Kreider, 1997b). The nine students would not or could not break their silence and political withdrawal surrounding issues of race, oppression and injustice, rendering them unable to effect social or even overt, personal changes (Collins, 1991; Ladson-Billings, 1996; Sleeter, 1996).

Marni, the only student who did continue to change, found community with a professor and a small group of students in the Modern Language department on campus who were committed to Latino/a educational issues. Her new support group defrayed her loneliness and supported her growth toward antiracism. Marni was the only student who replaced her passive racism upon return with a more active, critical stance as she joined the collective struggle to educate all children (Bradfield-Kreider, 1997a).

Although all students discarded their dysconscious racism, they stagnated. None were able to discard the passive racism which replaced their dysconscious racism. A component that appeared to be missing in the above field experiences was ongoing critical community membership -- a support structure for them to continue the critical examination of their own cultural identity and to acquire the political and social action skills necessary to begin their work as antiracist teachers and to have the moral courage to fight racism within their own ranks (Pritchy Smith ,1997).

Mediated Cultural Immersions

Upon return from the second immersion experience, I realized that a great deal had to change for the program to be effective in creating lasting changes in preservice teachers' praxis. Through an ongoing dialogue with Rudolfo Chávez Chávez and research in multicultural education and critical communities, the program was revamped; mediated cultural immersions replaced the simplistic field experience as a structure to promote ontological changes in preservice teachers (Bradfield-Kreider, 1997b; Bradfield-Kreider, 1997c). In brief, mediated cultural immersions were created for preservice students who had met the three entry requirements; they have successfully completed student teaching; they have an assessed proficiency level of one and one-half years of oral Spanish; and they agree in advance to engage in the uncomfortable dialogue surrounding power, privilege and racism. The two core constructs in mediated cultural immersions that promote changes in students' tacit scripts of teaching, learning, and culture include membership in a mediated critical community and the management of their perceived loss of taken-for-granted powers and privileges while living and working as non-dominant cultural members and second language speakers in the interior of Mexico (Bradfield-Kreider & Chávez Chávez, in progress).

At Western Oregon University, a mediated cultural immersion program has been developed as an optional fifth quarter in a four quarter undergraduate/post baccalaureate teacher preparation program (Bradfield-Kreider, 1997c). The overarching goal of the program is to assist preservice teachers in their development as antiracist educators and cultural workers. Since "we rarely have the opportunity to select teacher candidates with a disposition toward activism or social change" (O'Loughlin, 1995, p. 113), antiracist program goals and student expectations are included in the advertising to help students self-select (Goodlad, 1990).

Rather than two phases, mediated cultural immersions consist of three phases, taking into account the follow-up debriefing and support that were lacking in the pilot immersion experience. During the first phase, a cohort of 10-16 preservice teachers study Multicultural Education on campus with antiracist faculty members and local community members. In the second phase, preservice students and an attending faculty member live as non-dominant cultural members and second language speakers with host families in the interior of Mexico as they interact with, learn from, and depend upon Mexican families and their communities. In the final phase, the students return to campus to continue pondering their inter-relationships with power, privilege, language, and race and their commitment to and strategies for teaching culturally marginalized children.

Discussion and Implications

The personal and programmatic implications of using mediated cultural immersions as a vehicle for broadening preservice teachers' cultural identities are several. First, through my work with students, my own critical community, and my readings, the changes in my own cultural identity have been dramatic. Because of my recent entry into higher education and the field of multicultural education, I am continually deconstructing my cultural identity and my role as a teacher educator and cultural worker, confronting biases and blind spots, and filling in the gaps in my knowledge base. Through a critical examination of my own cultural identity and a growing awareness of the collective social injustices facing school children, I am beginning to emerge from my white silence (Ladson-Billings, 1996) to join the fight. I have experienced the dangers of attempting cultural work without a critical community and have fallen victim to the smugness and hermeneutic circling as I convinced myself that I "had arrived."

Currently, I still struggle to fill in my cultural blind spots and conceptual gaps, and to strengthen my social action strategies. My political voice is now heard, but it is weak and I continually fight my fear of taking a stand that pits me against other European American colleagues. Similar to other committed cultural workers, I have joined the ranks of antiracists and am continually learning to confront individual and structural prejudice and racism, and to leave the safe harbor of political withdrawal (Collins, 1991).

The implications for teacher educators who become involved in critical communities, and for European American teacher educators who have the opportunity to manage their loss of power, privilege, and first language status are several. Currently, the majority of cultural work is being done by multicultural education faculty members, assuming there are such faculty. However, there is no evidence that the add-on notion of multicultural education works; no single course can sufficiently change the tacit scripts of monocultural preservice students. With more antiracist faculty members, however, the work can be programatically embedded throughout the course work.

Of ultimate importance are the potential benefits that programs such as our optional fifth term hold for the growing numbers of educationally marginalized children. Mediated cultural immersions offer opportunities for preservice teachers to (a) gain a critical regard for social justice, (b) construct a multicultural vision for educational equity, and (c) develop the accompanying political strategies to begin their cultural work (Boyle-Baise & Washburn, 1995; Sleeter, 1995; Gay, 1995). "The health of a participatory democracy depends on the ability of citizens to voice dissent and to participate actively in the critical reinvention and enactment of democratic possess. Teachers have a powerful role to play in the process of developing an active, critical citizenry." (O'Loughlin, 1995, p. 114)

Together, in networks and coalitions we can help teachers work together "to adjust the power structure so individual and institutional racism -- the 'dream killers', will not feed upon the hope and idealism of our children" (Bradfield-Kreider, in press, p. 23).

References

Ahlquist, R. (1992). Manifestations of inequality: Overcoming resistance in a multicultural foundations course. In C. A. Grant (Ed.), *Research and multicultural education: From the margins to the mainstream* (pp. 89-105). Bristol, PA: The Falmer Press.

Baca, L. & Cervantes, H. (1989). *The bilingual special education interface*. Columbus, OH: Merrill.

Banks, J. &. Banks, C. (1996). Equity pedagogy: An essential component of multicultural education. *Theory into Practice, 34*(3), 152-158.

Bartolomé, L. (1994). Beyond the methods fetish: Toward a humanizing pedagogy. *Harvard Educational Review, 64*, 173-194.

Bennett, C. (1995). Preparing teachers for cultural diversity and national standards of academic excellence. *Journal of Teacher Education, 46*(4), 259-265.

Bidell, T., Lee, E., Bouchie, N., Ward, C., & Brass, D. (1994). Developing conceptions of racism among young white adults in the context of cultural diversity course work. Paper presented at the annual meeting of the American Educational Research Association, New Orleans, LA. (ERIC Document Reproduction Service No. ED 377 270)

Boyle-Baise, M., & Washburn, J. (1995). Coalescing for change: The coalition for education that is multicultural. *Journal of Teacher Education, 46*(5), 351-359.

Bradfield-Kreider, P. (in press). Antiracism and one teacher educator's journey out of the madness of middle class white America. In C. Clark & J. O'Donnell (Eds.), *Becoming white: Owning and disowning a racial identity.* Westport, CT: Greenwood Press.

Bradfield-Kreider, P. (1997a, February). *Mediated cultural immersion and its impact on monocultural preservice teachers' ontological constructs of teaching and learning in diverse cultural constructs.* Paper presented at the 77th Annual Conference of the Association of Teacher Educators, Washington, DC.

Bradfield-Kreider, P. (1997b, July). *Partners in the Americas who are committed to bicultural children: An online, antiracist community.* Unpublished manuscript, Western Oregon University.

Bradfield-Kreider, P. (1997c, October). *Western Oregon University's Bilingual Immersion in Mexico: One application of Mediated Cultural Immersions.* Report to the Provost, Western Oregon University.

Breitborde, M. (1996). Creating community in the classroom: Modeling new basic skills in teacher education. *Journal of Teacher Education, 47*(5), 367-374.

Britzman, D. P. (1991). *Practice makes practice: A critical study of learning to teach.* New York: State University of New York Press.

Burbules, N., & Rice, S. (1991). Dialogue across differences: Continuing the conversation. *Harvard Educational Review, 61*(4), 393-416.

Cabello, B. & Burstein, N. (1995). Examining teacher's beliefs about teaching in culturally diverse classrooms. *Journal of Teacher Education, 46*(4), 285-294.

Chávez Chávez, R. (1995). *Multicultural Education for the everyday: A renaissance for the recommitted.* Washington, DC: American Association for Colleges of Teacher Education

Chávez Chávez, R. (1997). *A curriculum discourse for achieving equity: Implications for teachers when engaged with Latina and Latino students.* Unpublished manuscript, New Mexico State University.

Cochran-Smith, M. (1991). Learning to teach against the grain. *Harvard Educational Review, 61*(3), 279-310.

Cochran-Smith, M. (1995). Color blindness and basket making are not the answers: Confronting the dilemmas of race, culture, and language diversity in teacher education. *Action in Teacher Education, 32*(3), 493-522.

Collins, P. (1991). *Black feminist thought.* New York: Routledge.

Cuban, L. (1984). *How teachers taught: Constancy and change in American classrooms: 1890-1990.* New York: Longman.

Delpit, S. (1988). The silenced dialogue: Power and pedagogy in educating other people's children. *Harvard Educational Review, 58*, 180-198.

Finney, S., & Orr, J. (1995). Preparing teachers for cultural diversity. *Journal of Teacher Education, 46*(5), 327-333.

Freire, P. (1970). *Pedagogy of the oppressed.* New York: Herder & Herder.

Freire P. & Macedo, D. (1987). *Literacy: Reading the word and the world.* South Hadley, MA: Bergin & Garvin.

Fried, J. (1993). Bridging emotion and intellect: Classroom diversity in process. *College Teaching, 41*(4), 123-128.

Fuller, M. (1992). Monocultural teachers in multicultural students: A demographic clash. *Teacher Education, 4*(2), 87-93.

Fuller, M. (1994). The Monocultural Graduate in the Multicultural Environment: A Challenge for Teacher Educators. *Journal of*

Teacher Education 45(4): 269-277.

García, E. (1995). Educating Mexican American students: Theory, research, policy, and Practice. In J. Banks (Ed.), *Handbook of research on Multicultural Education.* New York: Macmillan.

Garcia, S., & Ortiz, A. (1988). *Preventing inappropriate referrals of language minority students to special education.* (Occasional Papers in Bilingual Education 5, pp. 1-12). Washington, DC: National Clearing house for Bilingual Education (NCBE).

Gay, G. (1977). Curriculum for multicultural teacher education. In F. Klassen & D. Gollnick (Eds.), *Pluralism and the American teacher* (pp. 31-62). Washington, DC: American Association of Colleges of Teacher Education.

Gay, G. (1993). Building cultural bridges: A bold proposal for teacher preparation. *Journal of Teacher Education, 45*(3), 164-171.

Gay, G. (1995). Curriculum for multicultural teacher education. In C. Sleeter & P. McLaren (Eds.), *Multicultural education, critical pedagogy, and the politics of difference* (pp. 155-189). New York: State University of New York Press.

Giroux, H. (1988). *Teachers as intellectuals: Toward a critical pedagogy of learning.* South Hadly, MA: Bergin & Garvey.

Giroux, H. (1993). *Border Crossings.* London & New York: Routledge.

Goodlad, J. (1990). *Teachers for our nation's schools.* San Francisco, Jossey-Bass.

Helms, J. (1990). *Black and White racial identity: Theory, research and practice.* Westport, CT: Greenwood.

Hilliard, A. (1974). Restructuring teacher education for multicultural imperatives. In W. Hunter (Ed.), *Multicultural education through competency-based teacher education.* Washington, DC: American Association of Colleges of Teacher Education.

hooks, b. (1990). *Yearning: Race, gender, and cultural politics.* Boston: South End Press.

hooks, b. (1994). *Teaching to transgress: Education as the practice of freedom.* New York: Routledge.

Jacob, E. & Jordon, C. (1987). Moving to dialogue. *Anthropology and Education Quarterly, 18,* 259-261.

Jennings, T. (1995). Developmental psychology and the preparation of teachers who affirm diversity: Strategies promoting critical social consciousness in teacher preparation programs. *Journal of Teacher Education, 46*(4), 243-250.

King, J. (1991). Dysconscious racism: Ideology, identity, and the miseducation of teachers. *Journal of Negro Education, 60*(2), 133-146.

Ladson-Billings, G. (1991). Beyond Multicultural illiteracy. *Journal of Negro Education, 60*(2), 147-157.

Ladson-Billings, G. (1995). Toward theory of culturally relevant pedagogy. *American Educational Research Journal, 32*(3), 465-491.

Ladson-Billings, G. (1996). Silences as weapons: Challenges of a black professor teaching white students. *Theory into Practice, 35*(2), 79-85.

Liston, D. & Zeichner, K. (1987). Critical Pedagogy and Teacher Education. *Journal of Education, 169*(3), 117-37.

Loeb, P. (1995). The Choice to Care: How Teachers Can Encourage Students to Become More Active and Committed Citizens. *Teaching Tolerance 4*(1), 38-43.

MacIntosh, P. (1989). White Privilege: Unpacking the invisible knapsack. *Peace and Freedom, 49*(4), 10-12.

McDiarmid, G. W. (1990). *What to do about difference? A study of multicultural education for teacher trainees in Los Angeles Unified School District* (Research 90-11). East Lansing, MI: Michigan State University, National Center for Research on Teacher Education.

Mizzell, L., Bennett, S., Bowman, B., & Morin, L. (1993). Teaching in an anti-racist school. In T. Perry & J. Fraser (Eds.), *Freedom's plow: Teaching in the multicultural classroom* (pp. 27-46). New York: Routledge.

National Education Association, (1992). *The status of the American*

School Teacher, 1991-1992. Washington, DC: National Education Association.

Nieto, S. (1996). *Affirming diversity: The sociopolitical context of multicultural education* (2nd ed.). New York: Longman.

Nel, J. (1995). From theory to practice: Ogbu and Erickson in the multicultural education curriculum. *Action in Teacher Education, 17*(1), 60-69.

Noel, J. R. (1995). Multicultural Teacher Education: From awareness through emotions to action. *Journal of Teacher Education, 46*(4), 267-273.

Noddings, N. (1995). A morally defensible mission for schools in the 21st century. *Phi Delta Kappan, 76*(5), 366-368.

Ogbu, J. (1995). Understanding cultural diversity and learning. In J. Banks (Ed.), *Handbook of Research on Multicultural Education.* New York: Macmillan.

O'Loughlin, M. (1995). Daring the Imagination: Unlocking Voices of Dissent and Possibility in Teaching. *Theory into Practice, 34*(2), 107-16.

Roman, L. G. (1993). White is a color!: White defensiveness, postmodernism and anti-racist pedagogy. In C. McCarthy & W. Chrichlow (Eds.), *Race, identity and representation in education* (pp. 71-88). New York: Routledge.

Shor, I. (1992). *Empowering Education.* Chicago, IL: University of Chicago Press.

Singer, A. (1994). Reflections on Multiculturalism. *Phi Delta Kappan, 76*(4), 284-288.

Sleeter, C. (1992). *Keepers of the American Dream: A study of staff development and multicultural education.* Bristol, PA: The Falmer Press.

Sleeter, C. (1993). How white teachers construct race. In C. McCarthy & W. Chrichlow (Eds.), *Race, identity and representation in education* (pp. 157-171). New York: Routledge.

Sleeter, C. (1995). White preservice students and multicultural education course work. In J. Larkin & C. Sleeter (Eds.), *Developing multicultural education curriculum* (pp. 17-29). Albany, NY: SUNY Press.

Sleeter, C. E. (1996). Multicultural Education as a Social Movement. *Theory into Practice, 35*(4), 240-247.

Sleeter, C. & McLaren, P. (Eds.). (1995). *Multicultural education, critical pedagogy, and the politics of difference.* Albany, NY: SUNY Press.

Smith, P. (1997, October). *Who has the moral courage to fight racism?* Speech given at the 1998 National Association of multicultural Education, Albuquerque, NM.

Smith, T., Rogers, G., Alsalam, N., Perie, M., Mahoney, R., & Martin, V. (1994). The condition of education, 1994. *National Center for Educational Statistics, 94*(149). Washington, DC: National Center for Educational Statistics.

Spindler, G. & Spindler, L. (1990). *The American Cultural Dialogue and its Transmission.* Basingstoke, England: Farmer Press.

Spradley, B. & McCurdy, D. (1984). Culture and the contemporary world. In J. Spradley & D. McCurdy (Ed.), *Conformity and conflict: Readings in cultural anthropology* (5th ed., pp. 1-13). Boston: Little, Brown.

Tatum, B. (1994, April). *Teaching White students about racism: The search for White allies and restoration of hope.* Paper presented at the American Educational Research Association, New Orleans.

Tatum, B. (1992). Talking about race, learning about racism: The application of racial identity development theory in the classroom. *Harvard Educational Review, 62*(1), 1-24.

Welch, S. (1991). An ethic of solidarity and difference. In H. A. Giroux (Ed.), *Postmodernism, feminism, and cultural politics: Redrawing educational boundaries* (pp. 83-99). Albany, NY: State University of New York Press.

Chapter Twelve
A Comprehensive Approach to Changing the
Culture of a Four-Year College

Ella Glenn Burnett
California State University, Long Beach, CA

Sharlene Cochrane
Lesley College, Cambridge, MA

Patricia Layden Jerabek
Ibis Consulting Group, Inc., Placitas, NM

==========================

Introduction and Background

In 1987, Lesley College announced in its newly adopted mission statement that "The goal of a Lesley College education is to empower students with the knowledge, skills, and practical experience they need to succeed as catalysts and leaders in their professions, their own lives, and the world in which they live." By 1992, it became apparent that the professions, their lives, and the world in which students live were presenting diversity challenges of such significance that, to prepare graduates adequately, the college needed to address the issues more actively. With the support of the Trustees, President Margaret McKenna obtained a grant from a generous Lesley alumna and established The Lesley College Diversity Initiative to prepare students--particularly teachers-- to work collaboratively and productively in a multicultural world.

In order to effectively reach students, faculty and staff have worked inclusively to radically transform the culture of the college to that of a multicultural learning organization. The journey has been challenging, rewarding, and renewing. At the same time, it has been a struggle--a struggle in the recognition that the ideals of social justice may never be entirely achieved, and where moments of success have been cherished long enough to provide the energy to reach for all that has not been achieved. This article traces the path of institutional change and identifies important understandings which have implications for higher education and other organizations that seek to create learning environments that better prepare citizens to work and live productively and peacefully in a multicultural society.

Lesley College, founded in 1909 and with current enrollments of more than 6000 students, prepares women and men for professional careers in education, human services, management, and the arts. A distinctive and fundamental aspect of education at Lesley College is the conviction that people matter, and that the professionals who respond to their needs provide a unique service to society.

Conceptual Model

President McKenna began her career as a civil rights lawyer--influenced by the Civil Rights Movement and believing that race was America's most critical issue. After several career moves in government and education, one of her primary motivations in assuming the presidency of Lesley College was the opportunity to create an institution that would attract and retain students, faculty, and staff from all of America's populations. Early in her presidency, she assumed that with supporting values, intentions, and words, the college community would engage in transformation toward the desired goal. There were committed change agents sponsoring multicultural projects throughout the college, but progress, as within most institutions, was slow. Lesley remained a primarily white institution, and she decided that bolder leadership was needed. She created, in 1990, the position of Special Assistant to the President for Affirmative Action. In 1992, she announced to the deans and search committees a goal that all fifteen open faculty positions were to be filled with people of color as a remedy for historical discrimination. To attract students of color and dramatically alter the applicant pool, Lesley announced that any student of color from Boston or Cambridge who was accepted to Lesley's Women's College would be guaranteed tuition and funds for book expenses. In three years, the number of students of color there increased from 7% to 19%. Costs prohibited continued aid at that level, but by then Lesley was a different place.

With progress in bringing in new populations, the major task of transforming Lesley as an institution remained. The president contended that the mission of the college could not be realized without creating a truly multicultural environment. With a three year grant of $225,000, the president charged the Special Assistant to the President for Affirmative Action and Diversity with coordinating and promoting strong campus wide support for the Lesley College Diversity Initiative. The donors particularly emphasized their interest in preparing teachers to be effective with diverse populations in classrooms. In addressing that priority through systemic change, Lesley simultaneously changed the experiences of graduates in all areas, including management, human services, and the arts.

The Lesley community was invited to a kick-off breakfast meeting where plans were announced and a group of twenty, including faculty, students, and staff , was invited to serve on the Diversity Initiative Executive Committee. Diverse along many dimensions, including level, function, school, race, gender, religion, and sexual orientation, the Executive Committee established committees to carry out its work: Recruitment and Retention, Curriculum and Instruction, Institutional Assessment and Evaluation, Quality of Life, Training and Development, and Student Issues. The chairs of the committees within the Executive Committee formed the Diversity Initiative Steering Committee. The entire structure created a balance between broad inclusion and small groups that could get the work done. Leadership at all levels of the college was then in place.

Inclusion was one of the most powerful and broadly acknowledged elements from the beginning. Faculty, staff, senior administrators, and students worked together to plan and implement a broad spectrum of activities, programs, and initiatives that would address diversity issues. But the process of developing a conceptual model for change was not an intuitive priority of the Executive Committee in the beginning. The group struggled with process, purpose, confidence, and trust. Disciplines of education, management, organizational development, and the arts introduced varying approaches. At a fall retreat, the Executive Committee brainstormed goals, and within a few months there were many requests for a clear statement of vision and desired outcomes. A volunteer sub-group met and extracted the substance of the brainstorming sessions, and drafted proposals for group critique. After four or five rounds, the Executive Committee unanimously approved the Vision and Desired Outcomes statement and recommended adoption to the president. She responded favorably and communicated the document to the college community. The statement is included in this article because of its centrality to all that followed. It has survived the test of time and has been useful in both spawning activity and pointing to deficiencies and gaps.

Diversity Initiative Vision Statement And Desired Outcomes

At the heart of the Lesley College Diversity Initiative is the goal to create a campus living and learning environment to prepare Lesley students to become positive forces for diversity within their communities. Toward this goal, the Lesley College community will achieve increased diversity, value cultural contributions of all its members, strive to enhance multiculturalism in the professions, and serve as a model pluralistic community.

Desired Outcomes

- Lesley College graduates will be culturally aware, engage in practice with attention to diversity, and take active leadership in their professions to contribute positively to a more equitable and pluralistic society.
- Lesley College's curriculum and pedagogy will incorporate knowledge of and perspectives of diverse groups within society.
- The Lesley College academic community will contribute to advancing multiculturalism in academic fields and professions with continual

efforts to develop and disseminate innovative conceptual work and research to affect theory and practice.

- As a learning community committed to issues of diversity, all members will engage in on-going educational activities to assure knowledge of and sensitivity to oppressed individuals and groups.
- Lesley College will seek, recruit, and work to retain persons from traditionally underrepresented groups in higher education to insure wide diversity in all levels of the college community.
- Members of the Lesley College community will address issues of power, privilege, and oppression as they affect self, others, groups, and the institution.
- Lesley College policies and procedures will be equitable for all members of the community.
- Lesley College will make continued efforts to secure and allocate resources to support diversity.
- Lesley College will project its commitment to diversity through all public relations materials, academic documentation, and activities of its members in the larger community.

The outcomes became immediately operational as the bases for committee charges, clearly aligning committee work with the vision and outcomes.

The vision and outcomes reflect conceptual elements from the literature which members of the Diversity Initiative Executive Committee brought from their disciplines, scholarship, teaching, and organizational experience. A range of research findings, some of which have provided the bases for more recent publications, particularly influenced the Diversity Initiative. These were:

1. Diversity is not a new issue but as old as human history and conflict among diverse groups precedes recorded history (Arredondo, 1996). Research has documented the roots, nature, and dynamics of prejudice (Allport, 1988), but denial has permeated socialization and written history. Media attention to diversity

issues in the 1980's and 90's has increased awareness and spawned action to change organizations and communities.

2. Changing demographics have confronted the nation with major implications for education. Foreign born individuals in the United States increased from 4% of the population in 1970 to 8% in 1990. Increasing immigration from Asia, Mexico, and Central and South America created a phenomenon named the "browning of America," with immigrants bringing hundreds of languages and dialects to work, communities, and schools. More than 13% of the United States population speaks a language other than English at home (Esty, Griffin, & Hirsch, 1995); Spanish is the predominant second language of the United States. By the year 2000, nearly 40% of students in American classrooms are predicted to be African American, Hispanic, Asian American, or Native American while their teachers will be white. (Delpit, 1995). And the workforce is becoming more disadvantaged while expanding service jobs demand higher skill levels (Johnston & Packer, 1987).

3. The culture of power in schools creates destructive dynamics. Those with power are frequently least aware and least willing to acknowledge its existence. The world views of the privileged are often taken as the only reality, while others' views are dismissed as inconsequential (Delpit, 1995). This has important implications for teacher education, faculty development, curriculum development, and teacher-student interactions.

4. Broad and inclusive definitions of diversity including age, gender, race, function, religion, class, ability, ethnicity, sexual orientation, and others bring constituencies together and address problems that cut across all dimensions (Hayles & Russell, 1997; Loden & Rosener, 1991).

5. American commitment to democracy makes diversity a central American issue. Diversity issues involve examination of evil, and no democracy can survive without heroic energies of citizens wrestling with legacies of personal and institutional evil. Democracy is about critiquing forms of hierarchy that associate

people who are different with degradation. Americans are trying to decouple difference and degradation, and after more than two hundred years of slavery need to deal with white supremacy. Democracies are rare in human history and tend not to last long. America, as the oldest surviving democracy in the world, has to grapple with increasing distrust among its citizens, especially across racial, gender, and class lines (Cornel West, Lesley College Diversity Day Keynote Speech, October, 1996).

6.   Increased needs for equity and justice for all students require educating communities and professionals regarding race, language, culture, class, gender, sexual orientation, and disability; and giving priority to the development and achievement of ethnic minority students and bilingual education (Nieto, 1996). Education regarding the sociocultural contexts of human growth and development in non-mainstream cultures is essential in teacher preparation (Pritchy-Smith, 1996).

7.   To remain competitive and effective in meeting future demands, American organizations in all sectors need change masters adept at the art of anticipating and leading productive change by reconstructing reality (Kanter, 1983). In higher education, this particularly means serving broader populations by delivering relevant educational services that increase the professional effectiveness of graduates.

8.   Approaches such as affirmative action, valuing differences , and managing diversity, and clarification of the differences between them, create new options for organizational change (Thomas, 1991). Managing diversity emphasizes policies, systems, and organizational practices that capitalize on differences and create effective learning and work environments. Individual, group, and organizational development models and activities are important tools for managing diversity (Hayles and Russell, 1997).

The literature provided rich theoretical frameworks and institutions of higher education provided laboratories of practice.

Through conferences, networks, and the literature, Lesley reached out to learn what other organizations were doing and discovered exemplary practice in areas such as curriculum, faculty development, student recruitment, and hiring, among others. Lesley set out to strengthen all these areas and, further, to accomplish radical change through organizational transformation, creating both multicultural and multi-contextual environments.

Significant Actions and Achievements

With a goal that the college reflect communities in which graduates will work and live, Lesley made *recruitment and retention* of faculty, staff, administrators, and students of color a priority. People of color now comprise: 18% of Lesley employees compared to 8% in 1989; 18% of faculty compared to 7% in 1989; and 16% of administrators compared to 4% in 1989. Students of color in the undergraduate Women's College increased from 7% to 17% from 1987 to 1996, although college-wide only 8% of students are people of color.

The Training and Development Committee has provided an important educational foundation for change, establishing a three tier program with sequential skill and knowledge building workshops, including: Claiming Cultural Identity, Exploring Differences in the Workplace, and Power and Conflict in the Multicultural Workplace; a Diversity Encounter series, with faculty and staff presenting and initiating dialogue on diversity topics; and Home Groups, which involve the creation, coordination and support of networks for discussion on the school or office level. Racism education has been developed in response to Culture Audit findings. Participation in training is voluntary and groups are diverse along many dimensions including level, function, and school.

The Diversity Initiative supported faculty development through summer workshops in *curriculum revision*. Participating faculty worked with multicultural curriculum consultants to revise more than eighty courses and create fifty new courses, aligning curriculum with the vision and outcomes of the Initiative.

The Transformation Project was an exemplary three-year faculty development project, created and led by faculty, to facilitate (a) faculty awareness of cultural identity, power and privilege, (b) infusion of multicultural perspectives into courses, and (c) development of programs and policies to prepare graduates to engage effectively with both mainstream and socially marginalized populations. Approximately forty faculty participated. The first year focused on defining cultural identity through an exploration of the ways in which cultural roots combine with the social-political contexts to shape world views and professional thinking and practice. The second year focused on curriculum transformation. Faculty identified courses to revise, and worked in small peer groups to discuss course objectives, content, and resources. They critiqued theory and practice and introduced readings, case studies, and other pedagogical strategies to reflect diversity in existing courses. At the end of the year, forty participants submitted syllabi for peer review and received feedback. The third year focused on multicultural competencies to be addressed and used in program evaluation.

In 1997, to advance multiculturalism and encourage dissemination of innovative conceptual work and research, Lesley launched *The Journal of Pedagogy, Pluralism, and Practice*, a biannual web-based publication. Additionally, the college sponsored a writing retreat in March, 1997, where faculty and staff writers with expertise in diversity engaged in small groups for peer review and critique of written drafts in a relaxed off-campus rural setting.

Recognizing the potential isolation of adjunct faculty and the importance of their contributions, the college supported *The Adjunct Faculty Project* in 1995 to provide cross-college leadership to assist the four schools in enabling adjunct faculty members to address the vision and desired outcomes of the Diversity Initiative. Several recommendations from the project are incorporated in the 1996-1997 goals of the Diversity Initiative.

The *Culture Audit* was a significant achievement explored in depth in the NAME presentation. Aware that the knowing of self is as challenging for institutions as individuals, the Diversity Initiative established an Institutional Assessment and Evaluation Committee. Lesley's Office of

Institutional Research tracked historical institutional data, which were primarily quantitative in nature. But the committee sought to probe more deeply and broadly, employing qualitative techniques as well. In 1995, at the recommendation of the committee and the Diversity Initiative Executive Committee, the college contracted with Ibis Consulting Group to conduct a Culture Audit to capture the diversity issues of the Lesley community, programs, environment, and policies. The outside consultant was engaged to explore confidential and sensitive issues of diversity from an objective point of view. The findings, which will be briefly summarized here, were reported to the Diversity Initiative Steering Committee and other members of the Lesley Community at the conclusion of the Audit. These representatives of Lesley immediately engaged in dialogue, reflection and discussion of the audit findings which serve as a basis for decision-making and planning. The resulting on-going process is a model for institutionalizing evaluation, planning, and renewal by programs, schools, and departments within the college.

Ibis developed a multifaceted process which included: a written survey, focus groups and individual interviews, naturalistic observations, and a review of college documents. Ibis worked closely with the Institutional Assessment and Evaluation Committee, the Diversity Initiative Steering Committee, and Senior Administrators in refining the audit process, defining focus groups, designing focus group prompts and probes, and designing survey questions and categories. It was essential to take into account the unique qualities of Lesley College and the Diversity Initiative goals statement .

The Culture Audit included collection of internal institutional data by the Lesley College Office of Academic Affairs from sources such as human resources, the registrar, and individual schools. The data collected were primarily quantitative information, creating a snapshot of the diversity of Lesley's people, programs, environment, and policies. This material was forwarded to the consultant.

Focus groups were designed for the purpose of getting firsthand feedback from members of as many constituent groups as possible. The Institutional Assessment and Evaluation Committee recognized many factors to consider when scheduling the focus groups, such as Lesley's class schedules, meetings, faculty work loads, and student, staff, and consultant schedules. Surveys were sent out with self-addressed stamped envelopes from Ibis to a sample of 1200 Lesley community members including students, staff, faculty, contracted workers, and administrators both on and off campus. More than 400 surveys were returned to Ibis to be collated and analyzed.

The Culture Audit, especially the focus groups and surveys, resulted in an enormous amount of data. Ibis collated and analyzed the data as requested identifying twenty-three critical issues and communicating them in an executive summary. From the twenty-three critical issues, the Diversity Initiative Executive Committee and other members of the Lesley Community selected, by democratic process, six priorities for which to develop action plans.

More than 6000 copies of the Culture Audit Summary were mailed to all members of the Lesley Community. The key to the success of the Culture Audit in effecting change is to continue to provide access to all available data for study, interpretation, and planning from multiple perspectives.

The Findings Of The Audit

The Culture Audit findings are expressly designed to be used by the Lesley Community to move toward the Vision and Outcomes Statement of the Diversity Initiative, and the Lesley College Mission as well. The data provided a critically important foundation for answering questions, establishing priorities, identifying directions for change, and strategic planning more broadly.

In the Audit, Lesley College was described positively across all the focus groups as a progressive, dynamic, open, and people-oriented community. Words such as "welcoming," "friendly," "receptive," "comfortable," "supportive," "caring," "committed," "close," and "compassionate" conveyed positive human values supported by the institution. Lesley was viewed as an exciting, innovative, creative, and collaborative learning community by nearly all of its constituent groups.

However, it is important to note that from marginalized groups, rankings were consistently lower and comments more negative.

In the focus groups, Lesley College was seen as having invested tremendous resources into promoting multiculturalism. It is in the vanguard of educational institutions adapting to the demands of the twenty-first century. The consultant notes the following evidence of success:

1) The public commitment to diversity of senior administrators,
2) Student recruitment practices and policies which have produced a far more heterogeneous student body than ten years ago,
3) Hiring practices which have significantly increased diversity among administrators, faculty, and staff,
4) Curriculum development and training which have increased the inclusion of issues of diversity, difference, and multiculturalism into the academic offerings,
5) High visibility for diversity as an informal and formal topic of conversation across the campus, and
6) The Diversity Initiative may be seen as the capstone project. It embraces and formalizes the many efforts and contributions of individuals across the Lesley community who have labored hard to make the institution where they work, teach, and learn the best that it can be.

And yet, the issues involved in diversity are always complex and difficult despite good intentions. The challenge involved in bringing about change is great, and resources are limited. Decisions about where and how to bring about change have inevitably resulted in gaps, mistakes, and unfinished work as well as success. The Ibis team identified twenty-three issues which need attention as Lesley moves forward. Those in italics were selected by the Executive Committee of the Diversity Initiative as ones to address first.

1. *Develop a process to create a shared vision of Lesley (including adjuncts) as a multicultural institution.*

2. *Clarify the priorities of the college as a whole in terms of diversity, i.e., develop a strategic plan of action.*
3. Increase the sense of Lesley as one institution rather than a number of programs.
4. Bring decision-making process, in line with espoused values of empowerment and inclusion.
5. Legitimize expression of all points of view, particularly those opposed to political correctness.
6. Improve communication beginning with the findings of the audit.
7. Create opportunities and structures for dialogue across groups.
8. Provide more diversity training for senior staff and faculty.
9. *Sponsor celebrations of diversity on campus.*
10. Increase visible participation and involvement of senior administration on diversity issues and activities.
11. *Increase access to buildings for the disabled.*
12. Increase resources and support for bilinguals in the community.
13. Maintain attention to gay, lesbian, and bisexual issues (i.e., clearer policies, more permission to come out, training for all on sexual orientation).
14. *Address the concerns of support staff and contract workers, especially about career development.*
15. Provide more supports for international students.
16. Expand women's programs.
17. Increase child care and work/family supports.
18. Provide more support for AHANA faculty (mentoring, etc.).
19. Increase awareness about religions and religious difference.
20. *Provide training on racism.*
21. Address the concerns of administrators.
22. Increase support and programs for Threshold students to integrate them into the Lesley community.
23. Provide additional support to AHANA students.

Even though the Audit was designed to be inclusive, there remained voices that were not heard in focus groups and were obscured by the majority voices in the summary report. The Institutional Assessment and Evaluation committee concluded after serious debate to include an additional section reporting comments from unheard voices submitted to the committee or overshadowed in the original data. The Culture Audit confirmed that the experience of many minority groups is perceived by some group members to be second class. Examples of inequities cited include: benefits, salaries, social opportunities, and acceptance. Assumptions by members of the majority about ability, intelligence, and aspirations of minorities are frequently experienced negatively. The voices of this relatively small number of people were presented in a section of the report called Unheard Voices.

A primary goal is to institutionalize the efforts of the Diversity Initiative, thereby maintaining a general openness to change and continuing the response to the Culture Audit findings. Because of its pursuit of this goal, Lesley College has become more aware of its diversity. To continue this trend, individual schools have committed to evaluating measurable progress, and have developed means to do this.

The concept of *institutionalizing change* was an important but elusive element in the consciousness of the Diversity Initiative Steering Committee. Going out of business represents best success for vehicles of change, but administrative processes established for a particular purpose seek a life of their own. As the Steering Committee discussed actions and change, there was one participating senior administrator whose predictable cant of, "There is an office in the college responsibility for that." brought the committee back on course. In 1997, the college persists in its efforts, as the following few examples indicate:

- Human Resources is training supervisors to work with employees to establish, each year, at least one goal that supports diversity priorities.
- The Deans Group has charged each school to develop at least one adjunct faculty diversity training effort in 1997 that serves at least 25% of the school's adjunct faculty.
- Partnerships with Boston elementary and middle schools provide

immersion experiences in preparation to teach in urban schools and communities serving diverse populations.
- The Spousal Equivalent Policy promotes equity related to sexual orientation by acknowledging same sex relationships and offering health, dental, and tuition remission benefits to partners in such relationships.

Celebration/Recognition and Awards

In October, 1996, Lesley sponsored *Diversity Day*, an educational and celebratory extravaganza to acknowledge what the college has become, and to further enlighten the community. Fourteen hundred participants from all segments of the college attended more than sixty workshops and events from morning to late evening on topics such as: Caribbean Story Time, "Out" in the Classroom: A Faculty Perspective, and Physical, Learning, Psychological, Emotional, and Other Disabilities: Hidden and Obvious. Cornel West's keynote address was thought provoking. Coordination and staff investment in the success of the event were extraordinary. One faculty member of color commented, "The day was amazing. I would not have believed that Lesley was capable of this. The diversity and gifts in our community have never been so apparent to me before."

In December, 1995, Lesley College was honored with a highly coveted *Ray Frost Award* from the Association of Affirmative Action Professionals. The citation lauded the College for "setting high standards and challenging the system in pursuit of affirmative action, equal opportunity and social justice." Lesley was the first institution of higher learning to receive the award.

Budget and Resources

Resources and funding always influence what is possible. Lesley committed resources to this initiative by (a) creating a Special Assistant to the President for Affirmative Action and Diversity position, (b) obtaining grant funds, (c) requesting that all offices and programs cooperate with the Diversity Initiative, and (d) providing work time opportunities for staff to participate and faculty release time for some faculty leadership roles. Basically, these provisions communicated the high priority of diversity work in the college at all levels and for all constituencies.

The Diversity Initiative has been a rich and challenging learning experience for the Lesley community. In reflecting on three years of institutional change efforts, the Lesley Diversity Initiative Executive Committee urges institutions engaging in diversity-related change to consider the following:

1. Recognize that the quest for pluralism is never ending and requires continual learning. Diversity work is relational and the realities of multiculturalism require constant listening, challenging, and changing, both interpersonally and at institutional and societal levels. Doing the work institutionally means "walking the walk personally".

2. In leadership groups, model the pluralistic community that the institution aspires to become, with involvement from all levels and identities within the institution. The group will exhibit social issues that the initiative is addressing. The commitment of members to the vision and outcomes create an important context for challenging contradictions and developing trust.

3. Build on a foundation of clear statements of vision that are aligned with the institutional mission and the principles of American democracy.

4. Establish a broad base of support with committed leadership at all levels to move the organization forward in both real and symbolic terms.

5. Move forward with positive leadership and small victories to gain credibility and confidence. Work for consensus but be strategic in expending energy on minor resistance.

6. Seek and advocate for resources to make available at least the minimal money and time required for efforts to succeed.

7. Continually challenge the institution to improve with detailed project plans for results each year.

8.   Institutionalize changes through existing organizational structures, creating new structures only when necessary.

9.   Assess and evaluate with increasing focus and depth, paying particular attention to silenced minorities.

10.   Differentiate outcomes clearly from goals, intent, and process to evaluate impact and results effectively.

Lesley has made major strides toward the commitments of the diversity vision statement in areas of: increasing diversity among faculty, students, and staff at all levels; valuing contributions of all members; and enhancing multiculturalism in the professions. Also, the college commits to becoming a living and learning environment to prepare Lesley students to become positive forces for diversity in their communities. The real tests are the extents to which (a) graduates are positive forces for change in their communities, (b) the college community, as a model pluralistic community, inspires a transformation of world views, and (c) community members comprehend the challenges of democracy and respond positively. Answers to these questions require dialogue and assessment with groups that have been disadvantaged and underserved as well as with dominant groups who must examine their privilege and choose to change. The American experience is unique in human history and the development of democracy depends on learning by institutions and individuals. Lesley students who increase their knowledge, skills, and practical experience to succeed as social change agents enlarge the circle of hope.

References

Allport, G. W. (1988). *Nature of prejudice*. New York: Addison-Wesley.

Arrendondo, P. (1996). *Successful diversity management initiatives: A blueprint for planning and implementation*. Thousand Oaks, CA: Sage.

Delpit, L. (1995). *Other people's children: Cultural conflict in the classroom*. New York: The New Press.

Esty, K., Griffin, R., & Hirsch, M. S. (1995). *Workplace diversity: A manager's guide to solving problems and turning diversity into a competitive advantage.* Holbrook, MA: Adams Publishing.

Hayles, R., & Russell, A. (1997). *The diversity directive: Why some initiatives fail and what to do about it.* Chicago: Irwin Professional Publishing.

Johnston, W., & Packer, A. (1987). *Workforce 2000: Work and workers for the 21st century.* Indianapolis, IN: Hudson Institute.

Kanter, R. (1983). *The change masters: Innovation & entrepreneurship in the American corporation.* New York: Simon and Schuster.

Loden, M., & Rosener, J. (1991). *Workforce diversity: Managing employee diversity as a vital resource.* Homewood, IL: Business One Irwin.

Nieto, S. (1996). *Affirming diversity: The sociopolitical context of multicultural education.* White Plains, NY: Longman Publishers.

Pritchy-Smith, G. (1996, November). *Knowledge bases for Cultural Diversity in Teacher Education.* Preconference institute at the Fifth Annual Conference of the National Association for Multicultural Education, St. Paul, MN.

Thomas, R. (1991). *Beyond race and gender: Unleashing the power of your total work force by managing diversity.* New York: American Management Association.

Chapter Thirteen
Women of Color in the Academic Setting: Empowerment through Mentoring

Maria Yellow Horse Brave Heart
University of Denver Graduate School of Social Work
Denver, CO

Judith Bula
University of Denver Graduate School of Social Work
Denver, CO

==========================

Introduction

Women of color (defined as women who are American Indian [Native], African American, Latina, Asian American, or a mixture of these) who are in academia face challenges specific to their gender and race, and to the combination of these two qualities. These challenges exist through all phases of the academic process: recruitment, retention, junior faculty expectations, publication, the peer review and merit review processes, progress toward tenure, promotion, senior faculty expectations, and retirement. The challenges include the dual impact of institutional racism and sexism; how differences in teaching and communication style can influence the perceptions of students and other faculty; and facing the reality that faculty of color, responding to their own internalized oppression, sometimes hold higher expectations for people of color than they do for others or for themselves.

The status of women of color in academia has been only moderately examined in the literature. Schiele and Francis (1996) found that, among former Council on Social Work Education Ethnic Minority Doctoral Fellows, fewer women of color were full and tenured faculty. The problem of opportunities and access in academia is still limited for people of color (Peebles-Wilkins, 1996). Wilson identified the double oppression of women of color due to race and gender as well as the barriers for these women historically and in academia. Schiele (1992) noted that more African American women held lower academic ranks and were not tenured in comparison with African American men. Further, women of color who attain doctorates tend to be older, have families, have parents with limited education, and have a longer completion rate (Moses, 1989). Women of color tend to be hired in greater numbers as adjuncts and instructors rather than being supported toward achieving tenure (Schiele, 1992; Moses, 1989).

Because of the underrepresentation of women of color among tenured and full professors (Wilson, 1989), women of color are more likely to be mentored by senior faculty who are European American. In this presentation, we examine the dynamics of the mentoring relationship for women of color with mentors from the dominant culture. While we recognize that some women of color may be senior and may in fact be mentoring junior Caucasion women as well as women of color, our own experience of mentoring is more common where the junior faculty mentee is a woman of color. Here, we present our concerns about this arrangement, examine the barriers to a successful mentoring relationship cross-culturally/cross-racially, and make recommendations.

Dr. Yellow Horse Brave Heart, the mentee, is a Lakota (Teton Sioux Indian) assistant professor in her sixth year, currently applying for tenure, and the first in her large extended kinship network to receive a Ph.D. Phenotypically (skin color and features), she is Lakota, visibly a woman of color. She entered academia with 16 years of post-masters clinical and community social work experience. While she was a proficient and seasoned trainer, public speaker, and presenter, she had limited formal academic teaching experience and only one publication in progress. She entered academia with some admitted naivete about the career and how to be successful. In addition to her disadvantage as a novice, she began her tenure track position with All But Dissertation (ABD) status before she had collected her data and with her tenure clock ticking.

Dr. Yellow Horse Brave Heart came into academia with the goals of completing her dissertation with an Eastern "seven sisters" college, continuing her community service, furthering her service and prevention research on Lakota historical trauma, publishing about her work to benefit Native people, hoping to establish an Indian social work program, and exploring distance learning and linkeages with tribal colleges in the Dakotas. Her own traditional Lakota values are integral to who she is, to her research agenda, and to how she teaches. Her commitment of service to her community is part of her identity and obligation as a Lakota and one actively involved in her traditional spiritual community. Her self-identified mentoring needs included needing support in becoming a successful teacher and scholar in a private graduate school with a predominant European American population while completing her dissertation and furthering her goals for her community.

Dr. Bula, the mentor, is a EuroAmerican associate professor in her seventeenth year as an academic, has been tenured for six years, and is one of four in the past two generations of her extended family to receive a doctorate. Phenotypically, she is "paleface," brown hair and blue eyes, visibly a white woman. She entered academia with 13 years of post-masters direct practice social work experience after completion of her doctorate at an Eastern "seven sisters" college (not the same one attended by Dr. Yellow Horse Brave Heart). A highly influential mentor in Dr. Bula's life, a person who served on her dissertation committee and went on to become a colleague and friend for ten years, was Virginia Satir, one of the founders of the family therapy movement and, herself a social worker. Dr. Bula began her academic career at a large Ivy League university in New York City. Benefiting from a position of white privilege, she was able to complete her dissertation before her tenure clock began ticking.

Dr. Bula's commitment to serving vulnerable populations comes primarily from the modeling of her two parents: her father, a physician; and her mother, a former dietician in a children's tuberculosis sanitorium and active volunteer throughout her life. Dr. Bula's own traditional WASP values are integral to who she is and are frequently in conflict with her research agenda and how she teaches. These conflicts play out, in a general sense, through valuing relationship with others and with self more than individual isolation, valuing process as much as product, valuing cooperation more than competition, valuing equity and "power with" over hierarchy and "power over." Her active commitment to spiritual wellbeing has supported her research agenda and how she teaches. Though she has served as an informal mentor for many years, the relationship with Dr. Yellow Horse Brave Heart is her first formal academic mentoring commitment.

Themes addressed in this presentation, following the definition of mentoring, include the qualities and principles of a successful mentoring relationship (with individual reflections from the mentor in a separate section and from the mentee as integrated in each discussion), the academic stages of development, and challenges and risks for women of color in academia.

Definition

"The origin of the term "mentor" is found in Homer's epic, The Odyssey, where Odysseus gave the reponsibility to his loyal friend, Mentor, of nurturing his son, Telemachus" (Odell, 1990, p. 5). Odysseus then exited the scene to go fight the Trojan War while Mentor educated and guided his son.

> This education was not confined to the martial arts but was to include every facet of his life --- physical, intellectual, spiritual, social and administrative development (Clawson, 1980, p. 144). Modeling a standard and style of behavior is a central quality of mentoring and that mentoring is an intentional, nurturing, insightful, supportive, protective process.
>
> (Anderson and Shannon, 1988, p. 39)

Mentoring transcends the giving of support to the giving of Self. It includes an intricate web of interactions among intellectual development, spiritual growth, personal life and professional life (Clawson, 1980).

Mentors are seen as guides, ones who can lead us along the path of our lives. They have also been seen to function as teachers, sponsors, encouragers, counselors and befrienders (Anderson and Shannon, 1988). Mentors are trusted because they have been where we are wanting to go. "They embody our hopes, cast light on the way ahead, interpret arcane signs, warn us of lurking dangers, and point out unexpected delights along the way" (Daloz, 1986, p. 17). Bruno Bettleheim (1975) identifies the purpose of mentors when he describes them as reminding us "that we can, indeed, survive the terror of the coming journey and undergo the transformation by moving through, not around, our fear" (in Daloz, 1986, p. 17).

Qualities and Principles of a Successful Mentoring Relationship

Our understanding of the major qualities and principles of a successful mentoring relationship was formed by the words of other authors (Bey and Holmes, 1990; Daloz, 1986; Odell, 1990; Parkay, 1988), by considering our own experiences in the past two years, and finally by acknowledging that there are experiences we have had that may be unique to our situation but which might also be helpful to others in mentoring relationships. We found our thinking focusing in the following areas: the selection of a mentor, safety, sense of trust, value congruence, role modeling, time and accessibility, and the capacity of the mentor to serve as an advocate in the broader system. Each one will be discussed then applied to women of color.

The Selection of a Mentor

In a study of proteges' reflections on significant mentorships, Hardcastle (1988) noted that individuals do deliberately search for someone to guide them but mentors and proteges are more likely to discover each other in unplanned ways. It was further determined in this same study that proteges were attracted to mentors who had integrity and who were wise, caring, and committed to their professions. Other personal attributes cited included being "empathic, gregarious, caring, adaptable" and well versed in problem-solving skills (Odell, 1990, p. 13).

Additionally, proteges also viewed as important the mentor's sense of humor, and the mentor's ability to point out specific strengths and motivate the proteges to grow professionally.

> What distinguishes them has little to do with student load, or publications, or even popularity. Nor do they necessarily wear beards, outrageous outfits, or hearts on their sleeves. What makes the difference is their willingness to care --- about what they teach and whom.
>
> (Daloz, 1986, p. 18)

Academic settings vary in structuring the selection of the mentoring relationship between new faculty and senior faculty. Sometimes a formal structure is in place for these relationships to be assigned from the beginning. Other programs prefer for the mentoring relationships to emerge informally. It has been our observation that, overall, the experience of having a mentor assigned during the first year on faculty with the option, later in that year, of choosing one's ongoing mentor has worked fairly well on our faculty. This allows for some guidance to be present around issues of orientation to the new setting plus it gives some time for the new faculty person to get acquainted with the senior members of the faculty before making the selection for a more long term relationship.

Mentors also need to address the commitment involved when saying "Yes" to a mentoring relationship. Because there is a limited number of faculty of color in senior positions at most academic institutions at this time, it is imperative for white faculty to know that it is not necessary that they "have all the answers" when it comes to assuming the role of mentor with a person of color (or with any potential mentee). Qualities that have been found to be helpful are: a willingness to learn as much as possible about multicultural realities, especially those most relevant to the mentee; a high level of tuning in to overt and covert racism, prejudice and bias; and a willingness to laugh at one's self and, hopefully, laugh together as different viewpoints and perspectives are discovered.

Women of color may experience racism in the assignment and/or selection of a mentor. This mentee, Dr. Yellow Horse Brave Heart, at the time of her appointment experienced the absence of a formal mentor selection process and was initially assigned a mentor who was a Caucasian male junior faculty member who, like herself, had not yet finished his dissertation. Contrary to the tenants of a successful mentoring relationship, he was not a tenured senior faculty member, had no pulication record, and was unable to provide guidance on successfully completing the Ph.D. or mastering the tenure process.

It was not until her fourth year that a more formal mentoring system was being instituted. Dr. Yellow Horse Brave Heart was informed about the selection process only after two Caucasian women, both new hires, were given first choice of their mentors. She and a Latino professor, who also had seniority and had been on tenure track for several years, which made mentorship even more crucial, were told they might not get their desired choice of a mentor because the Caucasian women had already made their selections and, consequently, some senior faculty would no longer be available to them. The tenure clocks of the two Caucasion women did not begin until they had completed their doctorates and they began tenure preparation in their first year as full-time tenure-track faculty. In contrast, Dr. Yellow Horse Brave Heart completed her dissertation at the end of her third year while on the tenure clock, losing those three years as tenure-preparation time, and she received no solid mentorship until the beginning of her fifth year. She did receive her first choice in the selection of her mentor.

Safety

The mentee must have a sense of safety in the relationship with the mentor as well as know that the mentor will serve to preserve the safety of the mentee within the wider academic setting. Emotional safety and trust between people of color and persons who are white is conditioned by the historical realities of our legacy of racism and oppression with traditional suspicion on both parts. Both persons must have a willingness to acknowledge and challenge this tradition as well as present multicultural awareness and an openness for learning in the crosscultural experiences which will occur. For women of color, who are regularly subject to both institutional racism and institutional sexism, an alert awareness on the part of the mentor to safeguard against prejudicial and discriminatory behaviors is essential.

Safety within the relationship is communicated through encouragement, unconditional acceptance, and by "allowing the protege to determine the direction and mode of learning" (Parkay, 1988, p. 197). Assurance of confidentiality is of utmost importance as the mentor and mentee establish boundaries around their relationship.

Safety within the wider academic setting is communicated through established working relationships and interdisciplinary connections on the part of the mentor, within the immediate department as well as with other departments of the university or college setting. Knowledge about the resources and the barriers which exist for people of color in these same contexts also adds to a sense of safety for the mentee. The mentor must create an environment conducive for the mentee to report experiences of any threats, negativity and/or comments of a prejudicial and racist nature. The mentee must be convinced of the mentor's willingness to work together to confront such occurrences. Similarly, identifying who supports, encourages, and promotes the work of the mentee can also provide ongoing awareness of safety in the wider academic setting.

Latina faculty report insecurity and self-doubt despite aptitude (Nieves-Squires, 1991). These feelings, a response to the institutional racism in academia, may inhibit a perception of safety in the mentoring relationship. African American women feel neglected, ignored, isolated, and excluded in academia (Moses, 1989). For all women of color, the historical legacy of interaction with racist institutions in society at large can impact their experiences of academia, which is perceived as begin exclusive and Caucasian-male-dominated (Moses, 1989; Nieves-Squires, 1991). Sterotyping and being viewed as outsiders can exacerbate the discomfort encountered by women of color.

For Native women, the historical legacy of an academic institution may be even more intimidating. Dr. Yellow Horse Brave Heart is on the faculty of an institution founded by a man associated with the genocide of Native people. Former Colorado Territorial Governor John Evans was implicated in the 1864 Sand Creek Massacre of Cheyenne Indians, close allies with the Lakota, the same year he founded the University of Denver (Svaldi, 1989). Despite being well versed in Lakota history, Dr. Yellow Horse Brave Heart became conscious of the university's historical association with the genocide of Cheyenne relatives. Her intuitive feelings were validated as she had experienced a lack of safety and the need to be hypervigilant while, at the same time, wanting to empower herself by being more open and genuine with faculty and students. These feelings of a lack of safety, unfortunately, are not unique to Plains Indian women but rather also exist to varying degrees with all women of color, as reflected in the literature.

Sense of Trust

"Ultimately what is sought in the mentoring relationship is a mutual trust and belief in one another" (Odell, 1990, p. 16). Mentor and mentee must trust each other in order to have a successful mentoring relationship. This trust must exist on both professional and personal levels. Professionally, the mentor must be seen as someone who has reached the goals to which the mentee aspires and as someone who is making regular and valuable contributions to the profession.

To create a context of trust, the mentee must be assured that the mentor is in an "assistance" role rather than an "assessment" role. It has been recommended that the assistance and evaluative functions be assigned to different personnel in the school setting (Brooks, 1987).

> Clearly, from the concept of mentoring, only the assistance function is consonant with a significant mentoring relationship. Stated quite succinctly, 'mentors' who engage in evaluations for future employment decisions are not mentoring.
>
> (Klopf & Harrison, 1981, p. 42)

Personally, the mentor must be someone the mentee can trust, in the realm of ethical conduct, to have a distinct and observable quality of integrity. This assumes that the mentee has had sufficient time to observe a potential mentor in a variety of settings prior to establishing the mentoring relationship in a more explicit manner.

While trust is required for an effective mentoring relationship, women of color may find this prospect difficult with a mentor from the dominant culture. The historical legacy of oppression and racism as well as the current institutional barriers for women of color in academia, described in this paper and in the literature (Moses, 1989; Nieves-Squires, 1991), may limit trust. For Native women, the betrayal by European Americans through treaty violations and the traumatic educational experiences in the federal and religious boarding schools (Brave Heart, in press; Noriega, 1992) present obstacles to the development of faith in the academic institution itself and specifically in a European American mentor.

Value Congruence

Another quality believed to be helpful in a successful mentoring relationship is the sharing of a similar value base and having similar styles of thinking about their professional area. Given the authors' commitment to a service profession (social work) we also found that similarities in our values related to the inherent dignity and respect for all people and the meaning of relationships were very helpful. Value beliefs about similarities and differences can be a crucial factor in all mentoring relationships but particularly when the mentoring relationship is a crosscultural one.

An adequate degree of value congruence between a EuroAmerican mentor and a mentee of color may be perplexing. As Nieves-Squires (1991) identified among Latina women, the values of communities of color in concert with different codes for interpersonal behavior may contradict the mores of the academic culture. Further, the probability of misunderstanding and misinterpretation is greater across cultures.

For Native and Asian women, traditional cultural prescriptions for respectful and appropriate formal behavior involve reserve and indirect eye contact particularly with authority figures and males (Hu and Grove,1991; Sodowsky, Kwong-Liem, and Pannu, 1995). This could be misinterpreted as disinterest, aloofness, or ignorance within the academic culture. For the Lakota, traditionally decisions are made through consensus with time for deliberation and for everyone's opinion to be heard, valued, and respected, without interruption. In contrast, academic decorum requires a degree of assertiveness, debate, and interruption which appears rude, intrusive, and domineering from a Lakota perspective. The result is that Native and Asian women may be unable to communicate effectively and be heard in faculty meetings.

Medicine (1988) determined that gender-related behavior was influenced by tribal identity for Native women in academia. Values influence interpersonal demeanor. The Lakota value of humility is often manifested in silent sacrifice or service. In the Lakota way, one serves out of a sense of generosity and commitment, and out of a belief that what one does should help others, rather than simply for personal gain. Yet the tenure process is based on a demonstration of how much one does. The value incongruences cause dissonance and may be reflected in the discomfort of a Native woman sharing her accomplishments. This may result in faculty not being cognizant of the contributions women of color make to the academic institution and may be damaging in the tenure and promotion processes. Further, the woman of color may be perceived as being aloof, disinterested, apathetic, and neglectful.

Neives-Squires (1991) identifies similar issues for Latinas who focus on building relationships, have more indirect and polite communication styles, and value cooperation, group cohesion, and consensus rather than debate. The competitiveness of academia can be a source of anguish for the Latina and many women of color who, immersed in the individualistic world of academia, can feel despair at the isolation which is in stark contrast to their group-oriented and interdependent communities of origin. For African American women, the need to conform to the culture of the institution, something with which mentors can assist women of color (Moses, 1989), is compounded by the incongruence between the

European American academic culture and one's own. These cultural and behavioral differences can kindle negative misconceptions of women of color.

As a woman who is white, in the position of mentor, and committed to social justice, questions arise about this proposed "need to conform to the culture of the institution" and Moses's belief (above) that mentors can assist women of color to do this. The short term challenges of the mentee's meeting the institutional requirements of tenure must be addressed, of course. Beyond this, however, is the larger picture which begs the question, Is this an institutional culture to which I want to conform, let alone assist someone else in conforming to?

Role Modeling

Though the mentor does need to have more experience with the specific goals being sought by the mentee (i.e., promotion, publication, tenure) in order to have a sense of the dynamics of these processes to serve a guiding function, this does not mean that the mentor will always be older than the mentee. Age is not necessarily a determining factor in the selection of a mentor. What is important in creating the successful mentoring relationship is the mentor's level of competence and skill in performing her or his job and in fulfilling the role of educator.

Identifying with a role model involves a process of viewing the other as being sufficiently like oneself. The process of identification involves a degree of positive attachment and valuation of the object and the capacity to integrate aspects of the perceived other into the self (Mitchell, 1988). Further, it requires a sense that the other values oneself and is related to issues of trust. Across cultures or races where there has been an historically hostile and oppressive relationship and where value differences may be quite divergent, this process of identification may be complex and challenging, albeit not impossible.

Women of color often experience pressure to be role models and mentors for other women of color while they themselves lack adequate role models in their institutions (Moses, 1989). This sometimes involves having all eyes upon one as a model for one's community (Nieves-Squires, 1991).

Time and Accessibility

The mentoring relationship must hold a high priority in the life of the mentor. The mentor must be clear that, with the mentee, it is not a matter of *if* there is time. Both must know that the mentor *will make time* to address the needs and concerns of the mentee, regardless of when they occur. This level of accessibility must be seriously weighed before the two people enter the mentoring relationship to prevent its absence from becoming a frustration for one or both of them at a later time. This is not to say that unforeseen and demanding obligations will not arise. However, with the understanding of the importance of mentoring clearly in place, these changes will more easily be dealt with at the time they occur.

Cultural differences in asking for help may undermine the mentoring relationship. For many American Indian and Asian women there are cultural expectations regarding the way to ask for help which is indirect, permitting the other to avoid the embarrassment of having to say no. Consequently, these women of color may make statements about their needs rather than direct requests. Often, European American mentors may miss these hints and may assume that the mentee does not need, does not want, or is resistant to help. The mentee may also be uncomfortable asking for help as well because of the lack of trust or the fear that the Caucasian mentor will once again assume a dominant, paternalistic position. The mentor may also feel discomfort in offering help, not wanting to appear patronizing or condescending. Such communication styles must be openly addressed and a manner for communicating must be agreed upon to avoid such misunderstandings.

Capacity of the Mentor to Serve as Advocate in the Wider System

The advocate is "not neutral but . . . is a partisan representative" for the mentee (Grosser, 1965). "The advocate will argue, debate, bargain, negotiate, and manipulate the environment on behalf of the (mentee)" and "advocacy is frequently directed toward securing benefits to which the (mentee) is entitled" (Compton and Galaway, 1994, p. 434). In order to fulfill the function of advocating for the mentee in the broader academic system, it is helpful if the mentor's credibility and respect can be established within that system prior to assuming the mentoring role. The mentor's activities as an advocate for students and faculty, particularly for students and faculty of color, must be visible to the mentee and must serve as an example for what could occur in a possible mentoring relationship.

The mentor may become stigmatized and disempowered through her association with a member of the oppressed group which then limits her ability to advocate with the institution. The mentor does need a strong sense of commitment to working with people of color and she needs internal strength as well as her own support network which can help her to tolerate the criticism and stigmatization that may come.

A Mentor's Reflections

The above seven qualities and principles of a successful mentoring relationship represent seven key areas for consideration regarding the external dynamics between mentor and mentee and between both of these people and their larger, surrounding systems of department and university. While reflecting upon them, however, I (J. Bula) also became aware of several internal dynamics which have helped to shape this current mentoring relationship. For me these include a commitment to advancing the wellbeing of people of color and to acknowledging my own ignorance; second, a time and place for humility; and finally, friendship.

<u>Commitments to the Wellbeing of People of Color and to Acknowledging One's Own Ignorance</u>

These two commitments are closely tied to each other for me because of the ways in which they inform each other in my mind. It is only when I am most fully convinced about how little I really know (my ignorance) regarding what contributes to the wellbeing of people of color that I believe I can truly hear what they are saying about what is needed.

Calling on the perspective of Christine Sleeter (1995):

White teachers grow up in different locations in the

> racial structure from Americans of color -- often different geographic locations, always a different location of privilege. As a result, the theories they construct about racial inequality fit the dominant perspective and deny a 'minority position perspective.' Whites generally resolve the contradiction between the ideal of equality and the reality of racial stratification 'by minimizing racism' (Wellman, 1977, p. 219), equating racism with individual prejudice and attributing inequality mainly to cultural deficiencies. (p. 419)

This minimization to which Sleeter refers is one aspect of a white teacher's ignorance. If I can welcome my ignorance as my own "teacher" about the next steps I need to take in learning, then I will confront this minimization through actively seeking experiences and information with which I can face white racism, the dynamics of white supremacy, location of privilege, racial inequality and . . . go right on knowing that I will always be ignorant. I will never be able to fully comprehend these realities from the eyes of persons of color. I am reminded of Daloz's (1986) guidance about our first task being that of listening. Listening to what people of color want and need. Listen to the stories. Listen to the whole context, including its pain and anger. Listen.

Humility

The complexity of the issues which we are addressing here is enormous. One mentoring relationship opens awareness to social, economic, institutional, cultural, psychological, spiritual, and global realities. It is humbling to know that there can never be a way to understand it all. Yet, still, we must continue our efforts to understand as much as possible.

Richard Kay (1990) tells his readers that "Mentors should put the growth of their proteges above their own needs except where both can be served without sacrificing the former" (p. 34). Though we go through our lives simultaneously being mentored and providing mentoring to others, it also becomes evident at a certain point that a major life task before us now is to do the mentoring, to place the growth of the next generation above our own. This shift acknowledges one step in the developmental life of an academic and it is one that requires enough humility to get one's self out of "center stage" (or on to other stages) and to invite and support the mentee in that limelight and place of recognition.

Positive recognition of minority junior faculty is not necessarily supported in one's department or university. What is valued in one culture is not necessarily valued in another culture. Statements of disagreement from faculty and colleagues, when one supports the work of a minority faculty member, can be disorienting, disappointing and humbling in the face of what is valued from a multicultural perspective. As a mentor, one must be prepared to address these behaviors by raising consciousness about what is happening and one must be ready to receive whatever consequences might follow.

For white faculty who are (or will be) mentoring faculty or students of color, there is a risk in these efforts toward inclusivity and equity. Though discrimination and racism are widely known phenomena which occur in most academic settings today, it is possible that some colleagues may take offense at being reminded that such behaviors do occur in their own institution. This pain of recognition is an experience shared by all. To them I would use the words of an African American colleague, "Mutual blame brings no gain, but there is much to be gained by joining together to face our present situation as a team. We are not responsible for the actions of those who came before us but we are responsible for what we do about the results of those actions today."

Friendship

As the mentoring relationship develops, mutuality grows. It is increasingly evident that both persons give and both receive. Professional work may bring the people together initially, but the personal lives of the people involved also become vital and important parts of what occurs in their interactions. The professional and personal aspects of the relationship become more balanced.

When the element of friendship is permitted to enrich the mentoring relationship, differences in status largely become irrelevant other than when called on for the specific tasks which promote the wellbeing and career advancement of the mentee. When friendship is present, there is no doubt that it is a gift to have this person in one's life. I am convinced that I am a better person because this person is part of my life.

Several times above it has been mentioned that there are stages through which one progresses on this journey through academic life. An awareness of these stages has also been mentioned in the literature (Odell, 1990) as a desirable quality on the part of the mentor. We now turn to the task of taking a look at these stages and what they have meant in some of the experiences of our specific mentoring relationship.

The Academic Stages of Development

What is education? I should suppose that education
was the curriculum one had to run through in order to
catch up with oneself.

(Kierkegaard, 1954, p. 26)

What does it mean for a mentor to assist a mentee in "catching up with herself"? Even though formal education in the sense of a specific curriculum is not the focus of the mentoring relationship, there is an informal education which does occur. One assumption which is evident in this image of catching up with one's self is the assumption on the part of the mentor that the mentee has everything she needs within herself to make it through this part of her life journey. The task of the mentor, as guide, may be simply to remind the mentee of this fact at timely moments. It may also mean to be sensitive to those times when the best thing the mentor can do is to stay out of the way, but supportively near, as the mentee rediscovers the resources within to address the challenges of the moment.

As the two of us considered academic stages of development, the ones which seemed to be most evident are survival (first year), adjustment (second through fourth years approximately), mature phase (fifth year), and tenure decision (sixth year). The age and experience of the mentee, as well as the type of setting, can determine the degree and quality of mentoring. The eventual goal is for the mentee to become her own best mentor and for her to go on to mentor others.

In her review of the literature, Comas-Diaz (1989) identifies developmental models of cross-cultural translocation. After initial contact with a new culture, a migrant, initially secure in her or his culture of origin, goes through a stage of disintegration which encompasses a growing awareness of difference that may lead to depression, loss of self esteem and self-deprecation. A decision point is then reached as the migrant asserts his or her own cultural self esteem and may reject the new culture. A choice is made whether to remain in the new culture, working toward resolution, or return to the culture of origin. Successful resolution leads to new identity formation, including autonomy and independence which include skills to cope within the new culture and where cultural differences are accepted and even celebrated. However, the road to resolution is fraught with complications when associated with minority group status (Comas-Diaz, 1989). There is an additional adjustment that women of color have to make since they are in an environment dominated by a different culture and gender from their own (see Moses, 1989).

Women of color may be at greater risk for life experiences of trauma. American Indians (Robin, Chester and Goldman, 1996) and African Americans (Allen, 1996) have high rates of trauma. Elevated mortality rates among American Indians (Indian Health Service, 1995) place Indian faculty at greater risk for traumatic losses as well as health problems during their academic careers. High rates of poverty in communities of color also mean that women of color often have fewer family resources and, in fact, may have to financially support other family members which limits available resources to devote to professional growth. This creates additional burdens for women of color and may deplete emotional energy necessary for focus on academic career development.

Challenges and Risks for Women of Color in Academia

Challenges and risks for women of color in academia have been mentioned or implied in earlier sections. The following specific challenges and/or risks will be further discussed below: isolation and marginality; community service; ethnic research and publication; evaluation of performance and tenure; familial and community obligations; the need for special mentorship; and phenotype and the degree of community involvement.

Isolation and Marginality

Due to their small numbers among the ranks of tenure track and tenured faculty, women of color are isolated from colleagues and role models from their own cultures. Being viewed as outsiders by European American faculty, women of color are often excluded from participation in informal and social networks and consequently are not privy to important information often shared at these gatherings, e.g., information concerning the political climate, opportunities for collaboration, and informal news about research and funding sources (Moses, 1989; Nieves-Squires, 1991). In addition to being closed out of the informal network, women of color lack validation of their work and encounter stereotypes as well as cultural and gender barriers (Nieves-Squires, 1991).

As a woman of color, I recently heard of the serious health problems of a colleague's spouse and of the illness of an administrator only well after these events had occurred. This information came from a former Caucasian faculty member who was more included in the network than I. Certainly that serves as an example of the isolation of women of color from the informal news and network. In six years, other than for an official function, I have been invited into the homes of other faculty by two out of twenty faculty members and had coffee or lunch with a handful, most at my initiation. I requested an office move to reduce my isolation from colleagues but my request was initially denied and the office given to a female Caucasian doctoral student adjunct instructor. After one year, I was given the office.

Community Service

Maintaining connections with one's ethnic community is often not only a value for women of color, but also an expectation of the community (Nieves-Squires, 1991). This activity is not adequately valued for tenure and often interferes with time for other forms of scholarship more recognized by the academy, such as publication. Often, the dominant culture in academia fails to comprehend how maintaining these community connections actually enhances the scholarship of women of color. Through these connections women of color contribute in a meaningful way to the community through research and service. Further, many in academia are insensitive to the precarious positions women of color may face in maintaining the trust of their communities, in trying to help those communities, and in avoiding becoming suspected by those communities of representating the dominant society. Connection with community is particularly crucial for women of color as they are so isolated in the academic culture. Often mentoring, advising, and advocating for students of color, activities which are not counted toward tenure, interfere with time for publication and scholarship (Moses, 1989; Nieves-Squires, 1991).

Ethnic Research and Publications

Ethnic research by women of color is often shunned by mainstream researchers (Nieves-Squires, 1991). African American scholarship, such as ethnic research and publications and conference presentations, is not respected and is often devalued (Moses, 1989). Mainstream journals may be less interested in publishing ethnic research by women of color, yet Caucasian researchers often build careers studying people of color (Moses, 1989). An additional issue for women of color who choose to focus their scholarship on their own community is the emotional drain of the topic area. The struggle to apply academic rigor to topics that effect one's extended family and community can be taxing, albeit rewarding.

This mentee's area of research and service is focused on the Lakota response to our traumatic history, and on studying ways to effectively prevent and intervene to ameliorate such responses. While I have been productive in my scholarship and now have a solid publication record, it has not been without a lot of emotional pain reliving our traumatic history and being immersed in the awareness of our condition, including elevated mortality rates from psychosocial problems. This adds an additional burden to our scholarship as women of color. Further, as I write about our genocide from a Lakota perspective seeking to give voice to our experiences, I am always faced with the danger of institutional racism from more conservative journals which might shy away from some of the political implications raised in a discussion of genocide. The genocide of Native people continues to be a taboo topic for many.

Evaluation of Performance and Tenure

Both gender and race influence perceptions and evaluations of performance, with women of color often not being given as much credit as they are due, and having their ideas either not heard or attributed to someone else (Moses, 1989). Problems with promotion exist and women of color are often overburdened with administrative assignments which interfere with their productivity (Moses, 1989). Women of color report that their self-esteem and professional reputations are demeaned (Nieves-Squires, 1991). They cite disrespectful treatment by majority students, staff, and other faculty, and Caucasian students often resist the authority and the expertise of African American women faculty (Moses, 1989).

Differences in cultural style in the classroom, such as less eye contact (Nieves-Squires, 1991), can be misinterpreted as well when coming from faculty of color and can negatively impact teaching evaluations and the assessment of women of color in faculty meetings and on faculty committees. Further, overt racism from European American students has been evident on teaching evaluations and the manner in which these students may handle concerns or complaints. Women of color have to overcome two barriers to positive valuation in the classroom -- gender and race. They have to overcome and often put energy into dispelling stereotypes and educating students about people of color, which takes additional energy and time. Mistakes are often magnified and accomplishments devalued, or one is seen as different from the rest (Nieves-Squires, 1991).

Familial and Community Obligations

Not unlike all parents, women of color in academia are aware of competing obligations between family and work. With women of color, however, family includes a very large and closely connected kinship network -- a community in the true sense of that word: a tribe, a clan. Typically, the response from the academic community is that the work must get done regardless of the other demands on a person's life. Childrearing responsibilities are not likely to be respected and can, in fact, create a professional disadvantage (Moses, 1989).

On the other side of the coin, community and family support for academic goals may be missing, for example, in the Latino community, further exacerbating the sense of isolation and conflict for the Latina academic. Financial pressures from family obligations may be especially intense (Nieves-Squires, 1991) as women of color have fewer resources for child care. Many are single parenting or are supporting spouses with tenuous employment due to the high rates of unemployment among men of color, particularly American Indian and African American men (Indian Health Service, 1995).

Need for Special Mentorship

The women of color who are entering the academic world of higher education today are often the first in their families or even in their extended kinship network, band, clan, or tribe to have received the doctoral degree. This can mean not only isolation but a lack of knowledge about how academic culture functions. Further, it also implies a lack of familial/community resources including financial resources. The female academic of color may find herself unable to locate any trusted person from her own local community with whom she can share and who would understand. Thus, the role of a mentor can become a key factor in her adjustment to and eventual coping with the academic setting. Moses (1989) has emphasized the need for a special mentoring program for African American women, one which could take into consideration the unique needs and support system resources required by women of color.

Phenotype and Degree of Community Involvement

The phenotype and degree of involvement with one's community can result in diversity among women of color and their experiences. For women of color who are visibly not Caucasian, vulnerability increases over women who may be fair enough to pass or be more accepted by the dominant society. Further, the image for women of color who are deeply committed to and involved with their communities has been one of stigmatization as outsiders (Moses, 1989; Nieves-Squires, 1991) and may be even more extreme than their lighter-skinned counterparts. These women of color would most likely have a style of presentation and interaction that is more congruent with their culture of origin and possibly then, more discrepant from the dominant academic culture which fuels their image as being alien.

Recommendations and Conclusions

Combining the above themes found in current research on women of color in academia with our own observations and experiences, several recommendations emerge for improving the culture of the academic environment into which women of color enter. It is evident that these suggestions have the potential for improving these situations not only for women of color, but for all who are involved.

The work of Nieves-Squires (1991) and Moses (1989), with which we concur, and our own work serve as the sources for the following recommendations:

*   To support and promote all activities in academic institutions which emphasize sensitivity to diversity, to differences in cultural style, and to multicultural understanding;

*   To acknowlege biculturality as a distinct strength, resource and skill and to recognize that those who do not have the skills of moving between and living among the people of at least two different cultures are the ones who are disadvantaged and in need of assistance in developing these skills;

*   To provide specialized mentoring programs for women of color upon

hiring;
* To value the uniqueness of the experiences women of color bring to the institution;
* To value and support the community involvement which is an essential part of the woman of color's contribution;
* To recognize the vulnerability of and discriminatory practices against women of color as a stigmatized population at risk, such as the likelihood of receiving biased teaching evaluations;
* To provide safe environments in which white faculty and faculty of color can continue a dialogue about the importance of facing realities of racism and discrimination in the workplace and beyond.

The question was raised earlier about whether or not the mentor's role includes helping the mentee to conform to the culture of the institution. One of the most obvious responses to such an expectation could be, "And what does the institution plan to do to conform to the values and perspectives of its employees of color?" From the wider view of the social order itself, and where academic institutions fit within that order, it can also be an important task to ask ourselves, "Would I not in actuality prefer to be working within an institutional environment where all members are heard, valued and respected; where cooperation is the mode of work rather than competition; where all would immediately call a stop to a process which was causing any one member to experience despair or anguish?" 7Rather than placing expectations upon people of color, upon all people, to conform to a system that may, in many crosscultural aspects, be more damaging than it is helpful, it seems we are long overdue in needing to listen to, respect, value and include these centuries-tested tenants.

REFERENCES

Allen, I. M. (1996). PTSD among African Americans. In A. J. Marsella, M. J. Friedman, E. T. Gerrity, & R. M. Scurfield (Eds.), *Ethnocultural aspects of post-traumatic stress disorder: Issues, research, and clinical application* (pp. 209-238). Washington, DC: American Psychological Association.

Anderson, E. M., & Shannon, S. L. (1988). Toward a conceptualization of mentoring. *Journal of Teacher Education, 39*(1), 38-42.

Bettelheim, B. (1975). *The uses of enchantment: The meaning and importance of fairy tales.* New York: Vintage Books.

Bey, T. M., & Holmes, C. T. (1990). *Mentoring: Developing successful teachers.* Reston, VA: Association of Teacher Educators.

Brave Heart, M. Y. H. (In press). The return to the sacred path: Healing the historical trauma and historical unresolved grief response among the Lakota. *Smith College Studies in Social Work.*

Brooks, D. M. (Ed.). (1987). *Teacher induction: A new beginning.* Reston, VA: Association of Teacher Educators.

Clawson, J. G. (1980). Mentoring in managerial careers. In C. B. Derr (Ed.), *Work, family and the career* (pp. 144-165). New York: Praeger.

Comas-Diaz, L. (1989). Puerto Rican women's cross-cultural transitions: Developmental and clinical implications. In C. T. Garcia Coll & M. Del Mattei (Eds.), *The psychosocial development of Puerto Rican women* (pp. 166-199). New York: Praeger.

Compton. B. R., & Galaway, B. (1994). *Social Work Processes.* Pacific Grove, CA: Brooks/Cole.

Daloz, L. (1986). *Effective teaching and mentoring: Realizing the transformational power of adult learning experiences.* San Francisco: Jossey-Bass.

Grosser, C. (1965). Community development programs serving the urban poor. *Social Work, 10*(3), 15-21.

Hardcastle, B. (1988). Spiritual connections: Proteges' reflections on significant mentorships. *Theory Into Practice, 27*(3), 201-208.

Hu, W., & Grove, C. L. (1991). *Encountering the Chinese: A guide for Americans.* Yarmouth, Maine: Intercultural Press.

Indian Health Service. (1995). *Trends in Indian Health.* Washington, DC: U.S. Department of Health and Human Services.

Kay, R. S. (1990). A definition for developing self-reliance. In T. M. Bey & C. T. Holmens (Eds.), *Mentoring: Developing successful new teachers* (pp. 25-37). Reston, VA: Association of Teacher Educators.

Kierkegaard, S. (1954). *Fear and Trembling.* Garden City, NY: Doubleday.

Klopf, G., & Harrison, J. (1981). Moving up the career ladder: A case for mentors. *Principal, 61,* 41-43.

Medicine, B. (1988). Native American (Indian) women: A call for research. *Anthropology and Education Quarterly, 19*(2), 86-92.

Mitchell, S. A. (1988). *Relational concepts in psychoanalysis.* Cambridge MA: Harvard University Press.

Moses, Y. T. (1989). Black women in academe: Issues and strategies. Project on the status and education of women. Washington, DC: Association of American Colleges.

Nieves-Squires, S. (1991). Hispanic women: Making their presence on campus less tenuous. Project on the status and education of women. Washington, DC: Association of American Colleges.

Noriega, J. (1992). American Indian education in the United States: Indoctrination for subordination to colonialism. In M. A. Jaimes (Ed.), *The State of Native America: Genocide, colonization and resistance* (pp. 371-402). New York: University Press.

Odell, S. J. (1990). Support for new teachers. In T. M. Bey, & C. T. Holmes (Eds.), *Mentoring: Developing successful new teachers* (pp. 3-23). Reston, VA: Association of Teacher Educators.

Parkay, F. W. (1988). Reflections of a protege. *Theory Into Practice, 27*(3), 195-200.

Peebles-Wilkins, W. (1996). Is it time to rethink affirmative action? Yes! *Journal of Social Work Education, 32*(1), 5-11.

Robin, R. W., Chester, B., & Goldman, D. (1996). Cumulative trauma and PTSD in American Indian communities. In A. J. Marsella, M. J. Freedman, E. T. Gerrity, & R. M. Scurfield (Eds.), *Ethnocultural aspects of post-traumatic stress disorder: Issues research, and clinical applications* (pp. 239-253). Washington, DC: American Psychological Association.

Shiele, J. H. (1992). Disparities between African American women and men on social work faculty. *Affilia Journal of Women and Social Work, 7*(3), 44-56.

Shiele, J. H., & Francis, E. A. (1996). The status of former CSWE ethnic minority doctoral fellows in social work academia. *Journal of Social Work Education, 32*(1), 31-44.

Sleeter, C. (1995). Reflections on my use of multicultural and critical pedagogy when students are white. In C. E. Sleeter, & P. L. McLaren (Eds.), *Multicultural education, critical pedagogy, and the politics of difference* (pp. 415-437). Albany, NY: SUNY Press.

Sodowsky, G. R., Kwan, K. L. K., & Pannu, R. (1995). Ethnic identity of Asians in the United States. In J. G. Ponterotto, J. M. Casas, L. A. Suzuki, & C. M. Alexander (Eds.), *Handbook of multicultural counseling* (pp. 123-154). Thousand Oaks, CA: Sage.

Svaldi, D. (1989). *Sand Creek and the rhetoric of extermination: A cast study in Indian-White relations.* New York: University Press of America.

Wilson, R. (1989). Women of color in academic administration: Trends, progress, and barriers. *Sex roles: A Journal of Research, 21*(1)-(2), 85-98.

Chapter Fourteen
Moving Within the Monolith: The Struggle to Make a University Culturally Responsible

Gail A. Cueto
Central Connecticut State University, New Britain, CT

Elizabeth Aaronsohn
Central Connecticut State University, New Britain, CT

==============================

Our review of the literature has identified a gap in empirical research on how faculty of color view their experiences in higher education (MHEC, 1995). Our intent in this paper is to begin to fill that gap. Combining anecdotal experiences and literature based elements, this paper summarizes our initial work, and describes our future plans for focusing on people's actual experiences of diversity in institutions of higher education.

- An untenured female assistant professor receives an unfavorable yearly evaluation, stating, among other things, "students think you are too multicultural."
- An untenured East Indian female faculty member decides not to wear her traditional "sari" to class, in order to avoid negative student comments, to try to eliminate what she has learned is the "baggage" that comes with expressing a culture other than the dominant culture.
- A group of faculty members from diverse ethnic backgrounds and representing a variety of public institutions of higher education describe their working environment as one of "isolation and lack of support."
- A recent report responding to an affirmative action complaint by a faculty member described current instances of

discrimination: "unaware or unwillful racists attempt to avoid interracial interaction whenever possible . . . they frequently express their bias indirectly, by favoring whites rather than discriminating against members of minority groups."

- A group of African American faculty agree that they always feel compelled to "do more," to prove themselves well beyond what faculty of the dominant culture must achieve.

The recent experiences described above seem to indicate that issues of racism, stereotyping, and prejudice are still very much a part of the American higher education scene. Even though there has been a decrease in overt racial hostility in many areas and facets of higher education (Astin, 1993; American Commitments National Panel, 1995), the above anecdotes indicate a clear and disturbing trend: what has not materialized for faculty of color in institutions of higher education is a welcoming campus climate. A current report published by the Midwestern Higher Education Commission (1995) talks about higher education's "chilly climate" toward faculty of color, and lists that climate as an important area that needs to be addressed. Our presentation at 1997 Annual NAME conference attempted to describe, analyze, and engage participants in dialogue about this reality. The responses from participants at the NAME session supported data we had already collected, and themes we had already identified (e.g., dress "codes," insiders vs. outsiders, invisibility), suggesting to us that there is indeed rich data still to be tapped that may establish, through multiple triangulations, a need to document a case for change.

There has already been widespread recognition in the higher education community that racial and ethnic diversity is a reality in the United States, and must be accommodated by a democratic society in numerous ways and on various fronts (American Commitments National Panel, 1995; Hirano-Nakanishi, 1994; Dilworth, 1992). Nevertheless, nationally, faculty of color are significantly underrepresented in institutions of higher education (MHEC, 1995). The most current statistics (U.S. Department of Education, 1996) indicate that 86.4 percent of instructional faculty in public and private institutions of higher education are White, while the recognized "minority" groups (Black, Hispanic, Asian/Pacific Islander, and American Indian/Alaskan) make up the other 13.6 percent.[1]

The above-mentioned demographic characteristics of higher education faculties can subject multicultural education and its proponents to difficulty. For example, according to Grant (1992), faculty of color engaging in research do not experience access to the same resources as their mainstream counterparts. In addition, Grant notes, the criteria used to evaluate scholars of color are many times "not sufficiently independent of the personal interests of the reviewers" (p. 9). In our interviews with groups of faculty members of color from various universities, as well as with White faculty members who attempt to teach from multiple perspectives, respondents have referred to similar experiences, frequently describing them as the dominant culture's having "changed the rules in the middle of the game." While Grant (1992) has clearly identified the problems that scholars of color face, and the issues inherent in engaging in multicultural research, we are finding that being a scholar and teacher of color, and being identified as an openly multicultural scholar/teacher, subjects faculty to numerous forms of institutional resistance and criticism which go beyond research to daily experiences and interactions in the workplace.

In the process of cataloguing these experiences, we found many more cases emerging. People have stories to tell. In fact, we have begun to find that the very telling of those stories to researchers, who themselves have directly experienced the chilly climate, has been useful for the tellers. Seeing that the issues they face are systemic rather than merely personal puts them into perspective for individual faculty and staff who have experienced forms of discrimination within their colleges

---

[1]The issue of how our society defines the term "minority" needs to be addressed, both denotatively and connotatively. The terms "diverse" and "minority" are both understood in this project to be mainstream code for "people of color," which is therefore the term we prefer to use. Faculty of color are the focus of this study.

and universities. Telling, sharing, collecting, analyzing, and publishing the stories can provide a powerful, previously underrepresented perspective to the national dialogue about diversity, an issue currently at the forefront of judicial and political discourse.

Extending our research beyond the NAME presentation, therefore, into the larger framework of a book, we intend to further document the struggles of faculty and staff members of color in their attempts to work within traditional and often resistant institutions of higher education. We are primarily concerned with documenting people's experiences by identifying and examining a) the challenges they confront, b) the strategies they utilize to try to surmount difficulties, and c) any practices that have effectively alleviated institutional bias and induced institutional change as it affects multicultural perspectives, identities, and relations on campus. Overall, then, we hope to begin to answer these broader questions: "What is the academic ideal of diversity? What is the reality? What is the role of multicultural education in making the rhetoric reality?"

The aim of the book will be to provide the readers with a relevant forum for and information about this important social issue through a diversity of voices. Through this collection and scholarly analysis of stories, we hope to include activities and discussion questions that should give readers a range of perspectives about the issues raised. The larger intent is that both contributors and readers will discover ways to transform their institutions through identifying their own and others' real-life experiences.

The plan to write this book actually began with conversations between the authors about the mixed blessing of our commitment to multiculturalism, and our desire to include it as an important component of our redesigned teacher education program. We immersed ourselves in long and difficult discussions about the dilemmas of diversity, multiculturalism and discrimination. Our university governance, climate, and pedagogical concerns included such issues as power; opposing definitions of leadership; misunderstood or competing priorities, cultural styles, and approaches; and the larger complexity of social change faced—or ignored—by our institution within its surrounding community. The disappointment with how some of these issues were excluded from the departmental discourse on curriculum and change led to discussions with colleagues in other institutions, who, it turned out, were encountering similar experiences in their workplaces. As scholars and teachers ourselves, we hope that our approach to this issue from a research perspective will, by contributing to the literature, ultimately help transform the situation.

Working with small groups of colleagues, we talked about our work as multiculturalists within our institutions. We discovered commonalities, and we came up with questions we felt needed to be asked and answered by others like us. We began exchanging outlines and laying the groundwork for a writing project. From the initial collection of individuals' stories of attempts to make their own universities and colleges "culturally responsible," we found reason to believe that the result can be a text for multicultural educators, helping us to move both within our own monolithic institutions and outside, to link our struggles for cultural responsibility nationwide.

Sources

American Commitments National Panel. (1995). *The Drama of Diversity and Democracy: Higher Education and American Commitments.* Washington DC: Association of American Colleges and Universities.

Astin, Alexander. (1993). *What Matters in College? Four Critical Years Revisited,* San Francisco: Jossey Bass.

Dilworth, Mary E. (Ed.). (1992). *Diversity in Teacher Education.* San Francisco: Jossey-Bass.

Grant, Carl (Ed.). (1992). *Research and Multicultural Education: From the Margins to the Mainstream.* Washington, DC: The Falmer Press.

Hirano-Nakanishi, Marsha. (1994). Methodological issues in the study of diversity in higher education. In *New Directions for Institutional Research, 81,* 63–85.

Midwest Higher Education Commission. (1995). *Minority Faculty Development Report*. Minneapolis, MN: MHEC.

U.S. Department of Education. (1996). *The Digest of Education Statistics*. Washington, DC: Office of Educational Research and Improvement, National Center for Educational Statistics.

Chapter Fifteen
When Sparks Fly: Controversial Issues in Multicultural Education

Randie S. Gottlieb
EMPIRE Consortium for Multicultural Education,
Toppenish, WA

=================

* *Diversity is what's wrong with our country! It's dividing the nation!*
* *And multicultural education is anti-American! It criticizes the United States!*
* *There's no diversity at our school; so why do we need multicultural education?*
* *Anyway, we aren't the ones who need to change; they are! Why can't they be more like us?*
* *And why are you trying to revise our history books?*
* *Yeah! The existing curriculum was good enough for me, and it's good enough for my kids.*
* *Besides, what if we don't want our kids to "appreciate" people of other races or lifestyles? We moved out here to get away from all that!*
* *As parents, shouldn't our schools reflect our values?*
* *Also, I'm against inclusion. Why should my kid have to sit in class where half the students don't speak English? The curriculum is watered down and my child looses out.*
* *Anyway, most minorities are criminals; they're all on welfare or in gangs.*
* *I don't want my kids to study their culture. Put them in separate classrooms!*
* *Besides, maybe some groups just don't have what it takes.*

* * * * * * * * * * *

Sound familiar? These are the real voices of teachers, parents, and school board and community members concerned with the introduction of multicultural programs in the schools of our town. Similar protests can be heard in conference rooms and living rooms around the country. The purpose of this presentation was to help those who face resistance to multiculturalism to develop a positive response. Participants were also encouraged to avoid becoming entangled in these angry debates, but to listen carefully so they would be better prepared to initiate a dialog about the issues, build consensus among those with differing perspectives, and develop an inclusive process within a cooperative framework rather than a combative one.

During the conference presentation, small groups were given a series of "attack questions" and were asked to prepare a response based on multicultural ideals. The questions are included below, along with answers developed previously by teachers and administrators from the EMPIRE[1] schools. While there are no ready-made answers appropriate for every school and situation, these responses illustrate the basic democratic principles of liberty, equality, justice, and participation--not just for a few, but for all. Also discussed was the attached Crisis Communication Protocol, which was developed in response to strong criticism of a diversity symposium (see case study below) at one of the EMPIRE schools.

---

[1]EMPIRE is a consortium of elementary and secondary schools from eight districts in the Yakima Valley of Central Washington State. Headed by a leadership team from Heritage College, the goal of this ongoing grassroots effort is to bring together educators, students, parents and community members, in a collborative network to encourage positive multicultural change. EMPIRE is helping to educate staff and students about diversity issues. It has promoted positive race relations, and an appreciation for ethnic and cultural differences, and has encouraged schools to develop learning environments where children of all backgrounds can be successful. Each school is responsible for designing and carrying out its own project in light of local resources and needs.

Case Study

Late last year, a large group of parents expressed concern over the mention of homosexuality during their high school's diversity symposium, which was organized by the EMPIRE site team. Homosexuality had been included as part of a dramatic performance about hate crimes in America, and the parents argued that even in that context it was inappropriate and harmful to their children. Emotions ran high as the school board and the media were contacted by parents and church leaders, and flyers of protest were distributed to the community at large. As coordinator of the EMPIRE Consortium, the author was invited to meet with the superintendent, members of the school board, the district's Diversity Committee, and the concerned parents to help resolve the issue.

EMPIRE's position was that promoting tolerance is very different from promoting homosexuality. Homosexuals are more often victims of hate crimes and violence, and no parent wants their child to be victimized--whether the child is black or white, speaks with an accent, or is homosexual. EMPIRE took the stance that our responsibility as educators is to make schools safe for all children. "Gay bashing" is already a problem on campus, and if schools aren't even allowed to discuss the issue, how can we begin to deal with it responsibly? After a series of meetings, the school administration and the parent group agreed that:

(a)   future presentations and materials will be screened by the school,

(b)   any presentation that promotes homosexuality will be excluded,

(c)   for other presentations that refer to homosexuality, parents will be notified so that students/parents can make a choice about whether or not to attend,

(d)   an alternative activity may be provided by the school for those who choose not to participate, rather than keeping students at home (It is interesting to note that one-third of the student body had boycotted the diversity symposium and stayed home from school that day with the permission of their parents.), and

(e)   the district will develop a position statement on homosexuality to share with all future presenters

While the process was at times difficult, as the discussions progressed the mood became gradually less confrontational and people were increasingly willing to work together to find a solution for all our children. It is felt that these discussions and their resolution represent a significant step towards promoting tolerance and understanding, not only on campus but in the greater community as well.

Challenging Questions About Diversity and Some Answers
(Based on responses from EMPIRE Consortium members)

1.   *What is multicultural education (MCE), why do we need it, and who is it for?*
MCE will divide the nation; it's undemocratic & anti-American as it criticizes our country.

- There's no diversity in our school; why do we need MCE? It's for minority students only.
- We're not the ones who need to change; they are! Why can't they be more like us?
- We already have too much to squeeze into a crowded day; how can we add MCE?
- We need the basics, not superficial frills like MCE.

When was our nation ever truly united? MCE is designed to reduce divisions of race, class, and gender--to build bridges between people. The real threat to national unity is ignorance and prejudice. MCE promotes democratic ideals of liberty, equality, justice, and participation--not just for a few, but for all. Wouldn't it be anti-American not to celebrate our heritage? MCE is for all students--to prepare them to live in a global society. We can't get through life without interacting with other people. There is room in the curriculum if we don't treat MCE as an add on, but an integral part of all subjects. Infusion is the key.

2. *Why do multiculturalists want to change the curriculum?*
    Why do you want to revise our history and social studies textbooks?
    -   Aren't you just trying to make minorities feel good, and whites feel bad?
    -   We'll lose our time-honored Western traditions such as Shakespeare and Dickens, to make room for a bunch of unknown authors and insignificant literature.
    -   The existing curriculum was good enough for me, and it's good enough for my kids.

    We're not revising history, but making our lessons more rich, more accurate; we're not excluding Western tradition, but rather including the missing voices from our past and present. We need to look at history, and other areas of the curriculum, from the points of view of all participants. Lessons should be infused with a more whole, balanced perspective.

3. *Isn't MCE pushing certain values?*
    Aren't we supposed to keep values out of the schools?
    -   Why should we teach tolerance, respect, and appreciation for differences?
    -   What if we don't want our kids to "appreciate"

people of other races, or from different religions or lifestyles? We moved out here to get away from all that! Shouldn't our schools reflect our values as parents and community members?

Is MCE pushing certain values? Yes! Try to visualize what our school would look like if everyone showed respect and appreciation for others. It would be nicer, kinder, friendlier, safer. . . . Now picture what our school would be like without that. What a hurtful place! Which place would you rather be? Now, how can we make that happen? Also, today's graduates will need to work in cooperative groups at job sites or on college campuses, and they'll need to get along with all kinds of people in order to be successful.

4. *Aren't new immigrants lowering the quality of our schools?* I'm against inclusion. Why should my kid have to sit in class where 1/2 the students don't speak English? Instruction is slower, the curriculum is watered down, the teacher pays more attention to the kids with problems, and my child looses out.

   • Most Hispanics are illiterate criminals; they're all on welfare or in gangs. I don't want my kids to study their culture, or to sit next to them in class. Put them in separate classrooms or schools.

   Hispanic and other parents also feel uncomfortable around such attitudes and values as those expressed above. Their children have a right to learn, too. Immigrant students have a lot to contribute to the classroom and the nation. Many educational strategies have already been developed that promote learning for all students. Segregation is inherently unequal. We need to work together to find a better way.

5. *Why do minority kids do worse in school?*

All the statistics show that, on the average, minority kids do worse in school (lower GPA's, higher absentee & drop out rates, more discipline referrals, etc.).
Why is this so and what should be done about it?
- Why should we provide extra help, when they'll never catch up anyway?
- Maybe some groups just don't have what it takes.

Yes, there are differences in school success. The reasons are varied and complex, and not all within our control. But we can create an educational system that is more responsive to the needs of all students. Low teacher expectations and a lack cultural sensitivity can make some students feel unwelcome or discriminated against. We can create a welcoming, supportive environment. Teachers can develop a repertoire of instructional styles to reach diverse students, provide educational materials that are free of bias and stereotyping, and model acceptance of and appreciation for differences. The goal of educational reform is achievement for all students. We believe all students can learn.

Crisis Communication Protocol

(Prepared by the EMPIRE Program, Heritage College, Toppenish, WA).

Following are a few important suggestions to consider when responding to criticism, complaints, attacks, and other negative reactions to multicultural programs.

Steps To Take

1. Immediately inform the program coordinator of the situation.
2. Have the coordinator update all involved, including the school administration and the director of public relations.
3. Devise and implement a plan based on their input.

Basic Principles

1. Respond quickly.
2. Respond accurately.
3. Designate only one spokesperson.
4. Designate the appropriate spokesperson.
5. Don't say "no comment."

In Addition

1. A crisis is also an opportunity to talk about what we believe in and what we're doing, to develop links with the media and find supporters in the community.
2. If the media approaches you, direct them to the designated spokesperson. (e.g., "The one you really need to speak with about this is __. Let me give you her number.")
3. Respond in a positive, educational, non-adversarial way.
4. Don't be upset, defensive, or repeat negative words from the question in your answer. Be sure to get your own positive message across, no matter what questions you are asked.
5. Don't give unnecessary publicity to a negative incident, i.e., don't call the press to initiate a dialogue or issue a denial. Rather wait until they contact you, then decide whether and how best to respond. Many times, the situation will resolve on its own.
6. Each school district should ideally have its own plan for responding to crisis situations.

Chapter Sixteen
Guess Who's Coming To Dinner? Race and Gender At the Crossroads: Preliminary Findings of Retrospective Interviews

Tonya Huber
The Wichita State University, Wichita, KS

Peggy J. Anderson
The Wichita State University, Wichita, KS

Kimberly Ott
Wichita Public Schools, Wichita, KS

Cindy Combs
Cooper Elementary, Newton, KS

Sharon Edwards
Sunset Elementary, Newton, KS

==================================

"I sometimes think the media has dreamed our history up."
Oliver Stone, Boston Globe, May 12, 1994

"A filmmaker of substance understands that a movie is more than a sequence of images; it is a carefully and coherently constructed value system."
Chrisman, 1991, p. 57

In Stanley Kramer's 1967 *Guess Who's Coming to Dinner,*

Spencer Tracy and Katherine Hepburn meet their daughter's gentlemanly Black fiancé, Sidney Poitier. "The audience knew that in the end the family unit would ultimately expand to include him" (Golden & Shreve, 1995, p. 151). A generation later, in Spike Lee's 1991 *Jungle Fever*, Cyrus (played by Lee) responds to his friend Flipper's affair with a white woman (played by Wesley Snipes and Annabella Sciorra) with the emotive expressions: "H-bomb" and "Nuclear holocaust." The exclamations are no exaggeration—in the movie or, seemingly, in real life. Interracial relationships—from holding hands to marriage—continue to be one of the most explosive detonations in America. As photojournalist Renee Brokaw, wife of NBA's Gary Brokaw, explained: "People who are not racist and are liberals still draw the line at couples. Integration for them means that they go to school together, but God forbid your son and daughter should date" (Kroll, 1991, p. 48). "Despite Technicolor and multiculturalism, our lives are still largely segregated—off limits to one another by habit, custom, and choice (Golden & Shreve, 1995, p. 3).

While movie-goers challenged the violence and message of the film, few could doubt that art was imitating life as Lee admittedly mirrored the 1989 murder of Yusuf Hawkins in the plot of *Jungle Fever*. The murder, the lynching of the young Yusuf, was because the Italian youths in Bensonhurst thought he was the black boyfriend of one of the girls in the neighborhood, explained Lee (Kroll, 1991, p. 45). The movie reflected a violent image of "a nation polarized by an unabating obsession with color" (Kroll, 1991, p. 46). If color were not an American obsession, "an equal number of dark-skinned and light-skinned women would be married to successful Black men, and, interracially, Black women and White men would marry as often as Black men and White women do. *That is not the case*. [Emphasis added.] Clear color preferences characterize the romances of African-American men and women, both intraracially and interracially" (Russell, Wilson & Hall, 1992, p. 108).

If these *color preferences* were personal and no different than preferring blonde hair, sleek bodies, long hair, or muscled bodies, this study would not be necessary. But color preferences in America are political (Dyson, 1997), and the outcomes may be determined, in part, and impacted by one of America's largest politicized systems—education (McIntosh, 1989; Kozol, 1991; Banks, 1995; Gould, 1996). In the 1990s, race relations are once again a national preoccupation as renewed debate over discrimination and affirmative action rages. Popular books and trade magazines feature widely differing views caused, in part, by interpretations made without support and lacking a theoretically and empirically informed knowledge base beyond personal perception and bias. As Anthony W. Jackson, co-editor of *Toward a Common Destiny: Improving Race and Ethnic Relations in America,* cautions: "One of the concerns we have is that the discussion of race and ethnic relations be based on knowledge—*not just opinions or anecdotes*" (emphasis added). Serious study of racial and ethnic bias among young people is of urgent interest as we seek to understand the connections made with violence, intelligence, success, and a myriad other factors stated and implied and often without a research base (Brawarsky, 1995, p. 2).

On the 40th anniversary of Little Rock, President Clinton warned that for the first time since the 1950s schools were resegregating and "too many Americans of all races have actually begun to give up on the idea of integration, and the search for common ground" (Enda, 1997, p. 8A). An obvious integration can be claimed by those couples who cross the invisible yet divisive color line—a line preventing the accomplishment of *common ground.* The biracial and multiracial (bi/multiracial) children of these unions continue to be the incarnation of integration.

Although many variations of biracial/interracial/multiracial couples exist in the United States, the present research focuses on African American and European American heritage couples, particularly Black men and White women.[1]

Review of the Literature on Black-White Multiracial Marriages

While many recent studies comment on racial issues, a review of the relevant literature indicates a paucity of both quantitative and qualitative research on relationships and intermarriages between American couples composed of one person of primarily or only African American heritage and the other of primarily or only European American heritage.

According to Kalmijn (1993), who examined the marriage license data for 33 states from 1968-1986 to assess the role of the black/white color line in marriage choice, the demographic data reveals an increase in intermarriages among Protestants and Catholics, Jews and Christians, and members of different European ancestry, but a traditionally maintained color line in marriage between Blacks and Whites. This color line, according to Kalmijn, summarizes the three main features of racial differentiation in American society, is linked to high degrees of racial prejudice as the natural outcome of strong patterns of residential and school segregation, and is in part the heritage of a long history of racial inequality in the economic sphere (p. 119). Kalmijn interprets "racial endogamy" as a "direct indicator of how social interaction in society is structured, . . . Provid[ing] important insights into the nature of contemporary race relations" (p. 120). Kalmijn concludes that "race boundaries are crossed sporadically, and when they are, they are conditional on status considerations" (p. 123). Kalmijn also asserts that qualitative studies could provide better insights and more meaningful interpretations into the motives to intermarry (p. 139).

Yancey and Yancey (1997) propose the study of interracial unions as valuable research in understanding the nature of race relationships. They conclude from their study that biracial relationships seem to form with the same principles as same-race relationships (Yancey & Yancey, 1997). Their analysis of more than 400 personal advertisements led to the conclusion that sex and age were more predictive variables of interracial relationships than race. Their conclusion challenges the historically argued theory of hypogamy (the theory that African American heritage men belong to a lower caste in society than European heritage women and, therefore, will trade personal assets, i.e., money and physical attractiveness, for higher racial caste status in unions with White women). Yancey and Yancey's proposal that hypogamy may have been truer at another time in history points to the need for consideration of historical context in the study of relationships and the review of relevant literature. A caveat in consideration of their findings is that the database may not be representative of mainstream society.

Ernest Porterfield (1978) interviewed forty black/white couples, seven of whom consisted of black women married to white men and thirty-three in which white women were married to black men. The forty couples resided in Illinois (20), Ohio (11), Alabama (7), and Mississippi (2). Porterfield reported that most Black-White couples in his study married for the same reasons as other couples, out of love and compatibility.

Schoen and Wooldredge (1989) studied marriage choices in North Carolina and Virginia in 1969-71 and 1979-81 and reported that White women make greater status gains when they marry outside their racial group, suggesting that acceptance of Blacks in the family may be based on status gains.

Legislating "Loving" and Relating

Since marriage between Blacks and Whites has been a legislated activity, examination of the laws governing interracial marriages informs this study. The year 1967 is often noted as a significant division of the historical timeline in the analysis of demographics related to laws governing interrelationships and marriages. In that year, the Supreme Court decision known as <u>Loving v. Virginia</u> (argued 10 April, 1967, and decided 12 June, 1967) overturned the existing antimiscegenation laws in Virginia and fifteen other states. In the previous fifteen years, fourteen states had repealed laws outlawing interracial marriages (Hall, 1992, p. 513). As Brown (1987) pointed out in his social casework with Black-White couples, "laws do not eradicate sentiments, and strong feelings still persist against Black-White marriages. Color labeling, rather than actual <u>color</u> appears to be the issue. Thus, although Black-White unions are more visible today, vestiges of racist attitudes remain" (p. 24), perhaps most directly traced to the earliest stages of <u>American</u> settlement by those of European heritage.

Departing from traditional English law, in which the status of the child was always determined by that of the father, the colonists voted in 1662 that children in Virginia would have the same status of the mother. Not exactly a victory for women's rights, this statute allowed, even encouraged, owners to increase slaveholdings through sexual misconduct. The law also dashed slave women's hopes that their mulatto offspring might go free.

Not all mulatto offspring in the early years of America were subject to slavery, though. Children born of free Colored parents were free, as were those born of free Colored mothers and slave fathers. In addition, mulattoes born of White females and Black slave fathers lived free, as did most children of mixed Negro and Indian parentage. . . . In the upper South, including Virginia and Maryland, legislators decided that any person with even a drop of Black blood would have the same legal status as a pure African. This early statute became the basis of today's *one-drop rule* (also called the one-drop theory) of racial identity, which has its origin in racist concern about the contamination of the White gene pool; no matter how White looking or White acting someone of mixed ancestry is or how little Blackness is in a person's genetic makeup, that person is considered Black. Even when part of an individual's genetic lineage is Indian, he or she is usually considered Black. (Russell, Wilson, & Hall, 1992, pp. 13-14)

One of the most extreme cases of the one-drop rule emanated from Louisiana, a state that legislated that anyone with a trace of Black ancestry would be classified as black. In 1970, the state enacted the "one thirty-second rule" which translated into anyone with a single Black great-great-great-great grandparent was legally black. Susie Guillory Phipps sued the state in 1982 when she discovered in applying for a passport that her birth certificate identified her as Black, although she had always identified herself as White. The state hired a genealogist and determined Phipps was precisely three thirty-seconds Black because her great-great-great-great-grandmother was the Black mistress of an Alabama plantation owner in 1760. The law remained on the books until 1983 (White, Edwards, Lafferty, and Monroe, 1997, pp. 35-36).

Demographics Related to Multiracial Marriages

Over the last twenty years, the number of bi/multiracial marriages in the U.S. has escalated from 310,000 to more than 1.1 million, and the incidence of births of mixed-race babies has multiplied 26 times as fast as that of any other group (Smolowe, 1993, p. 64). The 1970 Census reported 310,000 interracial married couples. The 1990 Census reported four marriages per 1,000 were mixed with 71 percent between black men and white women, 29 percent white men with black women. The apparent increase in Black-White marriages has impacted Black marriages, as well. In the last 20 years, the incidence of Black marriages has dropped 20 percent (Russell, Wilson & Hall, 1992, p. 119).

The 1993 Census reported 1,195,000 interracial married couples (see Table 1 for national statistics), but some estimates put the number closer to three million (White, Edwards, Lafferty, & Monroe, 1997, pp. 35-36). In the mid-western state from which the participants in our study were chosen, 4.9 percent of the marriages in 1993 were interracial, with the most common combination (345) between a Black groom and a White bride (Center for Health and Environmental Statistics, 1994, p. 121).

Table 1. Interracial Married Couples
Interracial Married Couples: 1960 to Present
(Numbers in thousands)
International Married Couples 1/
Black/White

Year	Total Married Couples	Total	Total	Black Husband White Wife	White Husband Black Wife	White/ Other Race 2	Black/ Other Race 2/
Decennial Census							
1990	50,708	(NA)	(NA)	(NA)	(NA)	(NA)	(NA)
1980	49,514	953	121	94	27	785	47
1970	44,598	310	65	41	24	233	12
1960	40,491	149	51	25	26	90	7
Current Population Survey							
1993	54,199	1,195	242	182	60	920	33
1992	53,512	1,161	246	163	83	883	32
1991	53,227	994	231	156	75	720	43
1990	53,256	964	211	150	61	720	33
1989	52,924	953	219	155	64	703	31
1988	52,613	956	218	149	69	703	35
1987	52,286	799	177	121	56	581	41
1986	51,704	827	181	136	45	613	33
1985	51,114	792	164	117	47	599	29
1984	50,864	762	175	111	64	564	23
1983	50,665	719	164	118	46	522	33
1982	50,294	697	155	108	47	515	27

1993	54,199	1,195	242	182	60	920	33
1981	49,896	639	132	104	28	484	23
1980	49,714	651	167	122	45	450	34

1/All interracial married couples with at least one spouse of White or Black race.
2/"Other race", is any race other than White or Black, such as American Indian, Japenese, Chinese, etc.
Source: http://www.commonlink.com/~chiron_rising/race/stats.html

An issue for continued consideration is the method employed for identifying *biracial, interracial,* and/or *multiracial* people. In the 1980 census, 9.8 million Americans of mixed Hispanic, Asian, African, or European blood checked "other" to describe their racial identity, a 45 percent increase from 1980. While most of those who checked "other" were of Hispanic descent, a growing number of individuals of African ancestry are also beginning to embrace their multiethnic identity. . . . The United States has no legal concept of biraciality. Depending on the state, biracial offspring automatically acquire the race of either the mother, the father, the minority parent, or the Black parent according to the traditional one-drop rule. (Russell, Wilson, and Hall, 1992, p. 78)

The trend seems to suggest that any marriage including a Black spouse has been termed biracial; technically other marriages are biracial, for instance, Asian and European, but may not have been reported as such. The same terminology issue plagues the demographic data on multiracial students.

Demographics Related to Multiracial Students
The demographic data on bi/multiracial students is suspect. In the mid-80s, the number was estimated to be between 600,000 to five million . . . . *Time* magazine noted, in a feature exploring the insensitivity of Frank ("Fuzzy") Zoeller to Tiger Woods,

For many citizens the browning of America means a

disorienting plunge into an uncharted sea of identity. Zoeller is far from alone in being confused about the complex tangle of genotypes and phenotypes and cultures that now undercut centuries-old verities about race and race relations in the U.S. Like many others, he hasn't got a clue about what to call the growing ranks of people like Woods who inconveniently refuse to be pigeonholed into one of the neat, oversimplified racial classifications used by government agencies—and let's face it, most people don't. Are they people of color? Mixed race? Biracial? Whatever they like? (White, Edwards, Lafferty, and Monroe, 1997, p. 33).

Since 1970, the number of multiracial children has quadrupled to more than 2 million (White, Edwards, Lafferty, and Monroe, 1997, p. 33). In addition to those children born of multiracial families are those who are adopted. In 1992, over 8,000 foreign and transracial adoptions occurred, according to estimates from the National Council on Adoption (Steel, 1995).

If the exact numbers on bi/multiracial children are difficult to identify with accuracy, one fact does seem to be clear: "The child who is the product of a black-white union is always viewed by society as being black—a status that does not always follow children of other mixed unions" (Brown, 1987, p. 25). In American society, determination of blackness creates minority status categorization. As Princeton Ph.D. Michael Eric Dyson has highlighted in analyzing American affairs from O. J. Simpson to Colin Powell, gangsta rap to Elvis Presley to jazz, university campuses to school cafeterias, Americans can't deny "the stigma attached to blackness" (Dyson, 1997). Not that Black is the problem, but that people's perception of Black is.

If the exact number of multiracial students in our schools is difficult to access, some of the issues facing them are not. In Randolph County High School, Alabama, 1994, the principal threatened to cancel the prom because a dozen students were planning to bring a date of another race. Revonda Bowen, whose mother is Black and father is White, challenged the principal's stance on interracial dating (Steel, 1995; Jacobs, 1995). The case illuminates the racial divisions and issues that children of multiracial families may encounter.

Playwright Velina Hasu Houston, the executive director of the Amerasian League, is the daughter of a Japanese mother and a father of mixed Indian and Black ancestry. Houston recalls the way her father explained her racial identity. Like other multiracial Americans, Houston refuses to deny the individual parts of herself.

> When I was four years old, I went into the kitchen of my home and I said to my mother, "Mommy, why are you vanilla and why is Papa chocolate?" And my father went out and bought a carton of Neapolitan ice cream and he came back and he said, "You see this chocolate stripe? You see this red stripe? That's me." And he put it into the bowl. And then he said, "Do you see this vanilla stripe? That's your mother." And he mixed it up in the bowl. He showed me the brown mixture and he said, "You see? That's you and your sister." And I said, "Yes." And he said, "Now, can you take that out and put it back into the three stripes?" I said, "No, I can't." (Russell, Wilson, and Hall, 1992, p. 75)

Given America's preoccupation with race issues (Cose, 1995; Gose 1996), with how we identify race (Gould, 1996), and with the labels used to identify children in schools (Leslie, 1995, p. 72), any information that can assist in the untangling of racism in this nation, ultimately in this world, is human knowledge that benefits us all.

> The problem is not only that we must question social systems that insist on maintaining divisions for easy categorization and more efficient social control; it is the problem of what is left out when prepackaged identities

are handed out at birth. How little is communicated about who we are when we are labeled: *Black/White, queer/straight, male/female.*

The tight little boxes of identity defined by our society keep the building blocks of political and economic power in place. How can we gender-bend, race-cross, nature-bond, and love ourselves in our plurality enough to rebel against the deadening crush of identity control? (Filemyr in Golden & Shreve, 1995, p. 187)

The rarity of census reportage of Black-White unions (1 in 1,000 in the 1970 census) negates census data as meaningful beyond the documentation of uncommonness (Kalmijn, 1993, p. 123). As O'Hare reported: "Birth statistics are tabulated by the race of the infant's mother. This decreases the number of minority births because most mixed-race births are born to white mothers and non-white fathers" (1992, p. 7). How, then, do we gain an accurate demographic report for the number of bi/multiracial children in our classrooms?

A brief review of the confusing history of identifying race highlights the multiraciality of an America that has more often considered itself in biracial terms with a clear dividing line between *Black* and *White* (see Russell, Wilson, & Hall, 1992, pp. 10-15) .

Henry Louis Gates, Jr., acclaimed scholar, writer, professor, and chair of the Afro-American Studies Department at Harvard University categorizes race as a *trope*, while acknowledging its impact: "One must *learn* to be *black* in this society, precisely because *blackness* is a socially produced category" (1992, p. 101).

Reasons Given For Multiracial Relationships From A Review of Popular and Professional Literature

Staples states that while the motivation for an interracial marriage may or may not differ from that of an intraracial marriage, certain problems are unique to this type of marriage (1973, p. 125). A list of issues given in both the popular media and in the professional literature documents current research and espoused belief regarding the reasons and resulting issues revolving around multiracial relationships between Blacks and Whites. While the following list is not necessarily exhaustive, it is intended to be comprehensive:

1. "There's an intellectual current in the black community which suggests that interracial relationships are not politically correct" (Kroll, 1991, p. 49), that the *races* should not mix (Brown, 1987, p. 29) and that Black men are "abandoning their race" (Gose, 1996, p. A45) when they date White women.

2. "White males have problems with Black men's sexuality . . . . They think we've got a hold on their women" (Kroll, 1991, p. 45).

3. Resentment by Black women of White women because of a perceived shortage of Black men (Kroll, 1991, p. 49; Brown, 1987, p. 29).

4. Individuals who profess to be liberal may, in fact, be counter conformists who have a desire to act in opposition to socially accepted norms (Kouri & Lasswell, 1993, p. 243).

5. "The black male has always been heavily stereotyped. He has been depicted as a violent, pleasure-oriented person who is brutal in his relationships with women and desirous of possessing white women. He has been viewed as being superficial in relationships, primitive in his thinking, and incapable of developing insight into his problems" (Brown, 1987, p. 25).

6. Media perpetuates myths about the Black male by portraying him "as an irresponsible person who is aggressive, either a pimp or a stud" (Brown, 1987, p. 25).

7. Like many white women who become intimate with Black men, many Black women are latent or unconscious homosexuals—the White man's color and unfamiliarity tend to heighten or excite their sense of themselves as females. Such women simply cannot get along with Black men. In many instances, since he is considered kind, gentle, and compliant, the

White man may psychosexually represent a pseudo-female for an otherwise homosexual, or lesbian-inclined, Black woman (Hernton, 1988, p. 167).

8. *Color tax* parties, common in Black fraternities from the 1920s to the 1960s, required the darker the date the higher the entrance tax at the door (Russell, Wilson & Hall, 1992, p. 30).

9. The *slut concept*, common in the comments of both Black and White men, weighs heavily upon any White woman who marries a Black man (Hernton, 1988, pp. 53-54).

10. It is no mystery why White society is now tending to accept the Black woman more readily than the Black male. First of all, the Black woman, like the White woman, does not represent to the White world as much of an aggressor against the present power structure as does the Black man. Then too, if, as a consequence of integration, the Black woman should marry a rich White man's son (or any White man), the power still remains in the hands of the White man. Not so, if Black males start marrying the bosses' daughters (Hernton, 1988, p. 171). It is not *race* that makes a White man tremble on seeing a Black man with a White woman; it is *racism* (Hernton, 1988, pp. 177-178).

11. Curiosity about those who are different creates heightened sexual interest for some (Kouri and Lasswell, 1993; Grier & Cobbs, 1968) and a *sexual mythology* (Kroll, 1991, p. 45)—or the power of positive stereotypes (Crohn, 1995, p. 48):

    a. The racist *fears* that the relationships between Black men and women are healthier and freer than those between himself and White women. He [the White man] also *fears* that Black men can be better with White women than he is (Hernton, 1988, p. 123). "Black men know how to f—k" (Kroll, 1991, p. 45); "Tell me the truth, it's the dick, isn't it?" (Austin in Russell, Wilson & Hall, 1992, p. 121); "White women are attracted to Black men because they are curious about *zulu d*—k" (McPhail, 1996, p. 134).

b.   "Images of White women being the epitome of beauty and the standard that everything else must be measured against" (Kroll, 1991, p. 45); White women have always been off-limits to Black men and accessible only through girlie magazines which fostered attraction to White women (Russell, Wilson & Hall, 1992, p. 113).

12.   Genuine feelings; the power of love; (Kroll, 1991, p. 46; Smith, 1991, p. 46) "someone whose exterior differences are far outweighed by inner qualities that make them feel truly at home" (Austin in Russell, Wilson & Hall, 1992, p. 118).

13.   Looking for something completely different: "Where they've come from is not where they're going" (Austin in Russell, Wilson & Hall, 1992, p. 118).

14.   Rebels who "have no interest in a conventional, no-risk marriage" (Austin in Russell, Wilson & Hall, 1992, p. 118).

15.   "Black-nanny syndrome" (Russell, Wilson & Hall, 1992, p. 120), a psychological urge in White men raised by Black nannies; If Freudians are right about the Oedipus Complex, it is an equally sound idea to hypothesize a *Dual Oedipus* when we deal with the Southerner. One mother White . . . another *mother* Black—the mammy or maid (Hernton, 1988, pp. 111-112).

16.   Black men eager to "affirm their manhood" by having sex with historically forbidden White women during the Civil Rights movement (Russell, Wilson & Hall, 1992, p. 112).

17.   "In possessing the White woman [the Black man] sees himself as degrading her (a function of his own feelings of degradation), in this instance sharing the community's feeling that a White woman who submits to a Black lover becomes as debased as he. In this way he may feel the gratification of turning the tables on his white oppressor and thus becoming the instrument through which a White person is degraded" (Grier & Cobbs in Russell, Wilson & Hall, 1992, p. 113).

18.   The equality in a relationship between a White female and a

Black male "and the uncertainty of dominance, generate a sexual tension" (Willie in Russell, Wilson & Hall, 1992, p. 113).

19. A White partner in an interracial relationship conveys social status (Russell, Wilson & Hall, 1992, p. 107)—The theory of hypogamy. "A marriage between a white woman and a black man can be seen as a relationship in which the *racial caste prestige* of the wife is exchanged for the socioeconomic prestige of the husband" (Kalmijn, 1993, p. 123).

20. "Working-class Black men who are snubbed by Black women, self-hating Black men who can't deal with Black women" (Kroll, 1991, p. 47).

21. Black men choose white women because they accept the stereotypes of black women as bossy homemakers or strident complainers, according to Larry Hajime Shinagawa, an assistant professor in the Department of American Cultural Studies at Sonoma State University who has studied interracial marriages (Gose, 1996, p. A47).

22. Black men view white wives as *stepping up*: "I've heard guys here [Brown University] say they're going to get their good job, their big salary, their big house, their big cars—and their white wife" (Gose, 1996, p. A47).

23. White women are more likely to marry a Black man when it allows them to marry a man with high socioeconomic prestige (Kalmijn, 1993, p.122; Bernard, 1966; Heer, 1974), and higher educated Blacks are more likely than lower educated Blacks to marry outside the race (Bernard, 1966; Heer, 1974; Schoen & Wooldredge, 1989).

24. "Among whites, and especially white women, the pattern of educational differences is the mirror image of that among blacks: intermarriage declines with increases in educational attainment" (Kalmijn, 1993, p. 129).

25. Lack of kinship controls in urban environments makes personal characteristics more likely to be valued than categorical traits

such as race, ethnic background, religion, or social class (Kvaraceus, 1969).

26. Propinquity or proximity (Brown, 1987, p. 26).

27. "The Human Relations Area Files, an anthropological listing of 312 different cultures, reveals that in 51 cultures skin color is a criterion of beauty, and that in all but 4 of these, lighter skin is preferred" (Russell, Wilson, & Hall, 1992, p. 58). A full 70 percent of the Black women in a study by Bond and Cash (1992) believed that Black men preferred women whose skin was very light (Russell, Wilson, & Hall, 1992, p. 69). As the Harvard psychiatrist Alvin Poussaint has commented:

> The preference for light skin, long straight hair, and keen features comes through most strongly in music videos where dark-skinned Black men frequently choose light-skinned Black women with White features as love interests. Picking this type of woman as an emblem of beauty and desire is a class issue for many urban dark-skinned Black men. (Russell, Wilson, & Hall, 1992, p. 159).

28. The hunger for fusion with someone who will complete us. People from another culture may be seen as offering something missing in the searcher's culture; a person from another culture affords wholeness (Crohn, 1995, p. 44).

29. Sychopathological motives including "exaggerated narcissism, including the phallic significance of the marriage bond . . . Exhibitionism . . . And choices that defend against castration anxiety" (Lehrman, 1967, in Crohn, 1995, p. 44).

30. Higher levels of education and income that lead to exposure to different kinds of people and ideas, including the idea of love outside of one's group. . . . Quite recently some ethnic and religious leaders have argued that, far from being a sign of

deviance, intermarriage is an indication of enlightenment and the path to a better world" (Crohn, 1995, p. 46).

A premise upon which this research effort is based is that this study will be more systematic, rigorous, and research-based than what is often reported as research but is more often a selection of quotes and cases from professional experience. While valuable in highlighting the issues, such reports may actually blur the issues while accentuating the sensational, the unusual, and the unique. While the findings of this study are not intended to be generalizable, the methods employed with the purposive sample of informants will substantiate the interpretations sufficiently to allow for meaningful integration with the other studies that have tackled this difficult topic of study.

Methodology
Recursive, Ethnographic Interviews

Each participant in this study was invited to respond to several surveys dealing with personal attributes, perspective taking, and ego development. After providing informed consent, participants had the option of selecting their own pseudonym for the study. All names are held in strictest confidence. All data are encoded.

In conjunction with the assessments, participants schedule at least two interviews of 90-120 minutes each. Participants are encouraged to reflect on their personal family of origin relationships and intimate relationships in semi-structured interviews. Interviews are taped and transcribed, then returned to the participant/informant for member-checking and verification. Participant confidentiality prevents the investigators from presenting these tapes to any person outside the study without written authorization of the participant. The interviewer's note pad and interviewing microphone are the only instruments used during interviews. The approaches taken in these open-ended interviews employ both strategies detailed by Harry Wolcott (1987).

One approach is to invite informants to tell their life story, with each newly introduced person or event providing the perceptive interviewer a possible topic for future elaboration. The other approach is to ask informants to recount the events of their daily lives and routines. Again, each event offers a point of potential elaboration as the ethnographer probes for underlying themes and patterns. Both approaches provide access and beckon us to view our subjects as people, rather than people as our subjects: to recognize that people live fully contextualized lives. (p. 49)

The life-story approach is taken in the initial interview, and the daily-events approach is used during probes in the follow-up, recursive interviews.

Participants are asked to provide a self-description of their physical characteristics as well as a description of the physical characteristics of the people they have been involved with in their significant relationships. Each participant is also asked to provide the names of relationship partners who may be willing to participate in the study, a snowball methodology that implicitly facilitates triangulation and the obtaining of informants. Participants are asked to tell about their significant relationships from birth to present. Most begin with parents or another family member. In the recursive interviews, informants are asked to talk about their daily lives with partners.

The entire interview process is recursive and analytical. The principal researcher's emerging interpretation of the data is shared with the individual participants and the other members of the research team on an ongoing basis. This process of recursive interviews and informal conversations will ensure a reciprocal exchange of information and opportunities for validation of the ongoing data analysis. Statistical analyses of survey data, ethnographic triangulation of interview data, and microethnographic analysis of discourse provide multiple opportunities for triangulation and rich, thick description.

The Site of this Study

A Midwestern, metropolitan, university city with a population of approximately 300,000 people is the site of this study, and the majority of respondents/informants were living in the city at the time of the interviews. Fewer than 10% of the respondents were living in another Midwestern community during the interviews, but they had lived in the site city during most of their lives.

Purposive Sampling

Initially, the research team targeted forty men of African American heritage, twenty women of European heritage who have been or are their partners, and up to ten African American heritage women. Reflection on preliminary data analysis and ongoing review of literature has led the research team to attempt a sample more representative of the demographics of interracial relationships between Blacks and Whites: about 71 percent Black men and White women and 29 percent White men and Black women. Additional interviews will be conducted with mothers of African American heritage whose children have dated across the color line.

The purposive sampling model employed was utilized to provide a pool of participants with a range of education, age, and background experiences. Participants were carefully selected for inclusion, based on the possibility that each participant will expand the variability of the sample. Purposive sampling increases the likelihood that variability common in any social phenomenon will be represented in the data, in contrast to random sampling. The investigators will control for age (18–46), educational level (high school diploma through advanced degree), and employment (employed or full-time student status).

The concept of *cohort* has also been considered in the purposive sampling process. Ryder defined "each group of people born over a relatively short and contiguous time period as a *generational cohort* that is deeply influenced and bound together by the events of their *formative years*" (Meredith & Schewe, 1994, p. 24). However, Ryder distinguished a generational cohort from a generation since a cohort "can be as long or as short as the events that define it" (Meredith & Schewe, 1994, p. 25), but a generation is defined as 20 to 25 years.

The Research Instrument

As is always the case in ethnography, the main research instrument is the researcher, for it is through her sense and senses that analysis emerges. Lincoln and Guba (1990) recommend:

> Some portion of the methodological treatment ought to comprise reflections on the investigator's own personal experience of the fieldwork (Punch, 1986). Any case study is a construction itself, a product of the interaction between respondents, site, and researcher. As such, the construction is rooted in the person, character, experience, context, and philosophy of the constructor. That constructor, the inquirer, has an obligation to be self-examining, self-questioning, self-challenging, self-critical, and self-correcting. Any case study should reflect these intensely personal processes on the part of the researcher. (p. 53)

From an original think tank series of discussions, a team of six researchers evolved who were committed to interviewing, transcribing, analyzing, and sharing in this exploration. Three faculty and three Masters-level graduate students in the College of Education at a Midwestern university compose the team. The faculty represent the fields of multicultural education, applied linguistics, English as a second language (ESL), teacher education, and developmental psychology. The team has a combined total of 89 years of teaching experience in nine states and three countries. One member of the research team is native to the state in which this study is being conducted. The team spans two generations in age and four cohorts with the youngest member of the team in her mid-twenties and the senior member in her early sixties, a significant feature given consideration of the ages (18-46) and cohorts represented by the participants in the study.

As specifically related to the topic of this study, all six members are female Americans of European heritage. Five members of the team have experienced interracial relationships, and two have married Black men. One is the natural parent of a multiracial child.

Data Collection

The various sources and techniques employed to develop triangulation points include: taped and transcribed recursive interviewing, member checking of transcribed interviews by informant, informal interviewing, self-description, perspective-taking instruments, and researcher journaling. As Wolcott (1988) noted:

The strength of fieldwork lies in its *triangulation*, obtaining information in many ways rather than relying solely on one. Anthropologist Pertti Pelto has described this as the *multi-instrument approach.* The anthropologist himself [sic] is the research instrument, but in his information gathering he utilizes observations made through an extended period of time, from multiple sources of data, and employing multiple techniques for finding out, for cross-checking, or for ferreting out varying perspectives on complex issues and events. (p. 192)

Analysis

The initial step of data analysis begins with the first interview. The researchers maintain researcher logs and face (or cover) sheets on notes for the recording of attitudes (both theirs and the informant's), perceptions, themes, and possible prominent ideas. Each interview is transcribed verbatim. Then, the transcribed interview is returned to the informant for "member checking" and verification of accuracy. Next, the interview is unitized, a process in which each meaningful unit is mounted on a separate index card. The concept of meaningfulness is determined by a simple test: does the word or group of words have meaning in relationship to the context of the study.

After the interviews of twelve informants had been transcribed and unitized, the research team met for phase one provisional category development. The team determined to work with the male informants first (a total of six). A list of prominent ideas was generated and from that list the team determined the prominent idea with which to begin. Prominent ideas were determined by having each researcher identify the idea she determined to have the most substantiation—an indwelling, reflective *feels like* kind of process supported by the transcription references already supporting the idea as prominent (Maykut & Morehouse, 1994). The following ideas were identified as the most prominent:

* racism
* descriptors (of partners)
* complexion
* expectations
* attractiveness

The team determined that all but the first, *racism*, were similar enough to be considered as parts of the same theme, *descriptors*. The second phase of provisional category development began. (See Figure 1 for an overview of the constant comparative method of analysis employed in this study.) As Sutton (1986) notes:

> In qualitative research, data analysis is not a circumscribed stage which always follows data collection. Indeed, the qualitative researcher uses analysis throughout the research to make sense of what is happening in the field and to direct further data collection (cf. Glaser & Strauss, 1967; Bogden & Biklen, 1982). (p. 16)

Figure 1. The Flow of Analysis

(ongoing and recursive)

↓

prominent ideas

↓

phase one provisional category

↓

phase two provisional category

↓

rule of inclusion as propositional statement

↓

category code (phase three)

↓

preliminary outcome propositions

↓

review of lit and triangulation

↓

outcome propositions

↓

report of the research

PRELIMINARY INTERPRETATIONS
Researchers' Assumptions

Each unit card was studied to determine thematic relationships, patterns, and connections. The first two categories that could be substantiated led to the first meaningful outcome. Since the qualitative approach to inquiry emphasizes an emergent research design process (Maykut & Morehouse, 1994, p. 144), these outcomes are viewed as preliminary interpretations that will further guide the research.

Category 1. Initially, 21 units from 4 different cases were identified to determine the first rule of inclusion: "African American heritage men set up comparative descriptors of women that depict white women in positive terms and black women in negative terms." Development of this category lead to 72 units from four of the six male cases:

24 units, 3 cases comparing Black and White women
21 units, 3 cases describing negative characteristics of Black women
7 units, 3 cases describing positive characteristics of White women

Category 2. Initially, 9 units from the same case were identified to determine the rule of inclusion: "In describing attractiveness and what attracted/s them to women, African American heritage men describe both physical and non-physical features of European American heritage women and only physical features of African American heritage women." Next, 21 units from 3 cases were identified to substantiate the category; an additional 7 units were added representing a total of 4 of the 6 cases being analyzed. A possible sub-category emerged, as well: characteristics of the ideal of attractiveness based on 5 units from 2 cases.

Outcome Proposition 1. A theme emerged in several of the informants' cases during categorization of units. Several of the men of African American heritage expressed a sense of *betrayal* by a person of their own *color* and, then, they had experienced a subsequent redemption by a person or persons identified as White. A preliminary interpretation of this cycle is represented by Figure 2. *Abuse* is being employed to include physical abuse, sexual abuse, and extreme discrimination as catalysts in the cycle.

One participant, Al Okinowa (all names are pseudonyms to insure confidentiality), reflecting on his experiences as a young man, explained: "I was really overcompensating for a problem that I, well, I wasn't really acknowledging that I had a problem, but the problem was that I was feeling really serious pangs of an inferiority complex" (AO.1.1848-1853). Al talked about having a crush on his English teacher (AO.1.1108+) and other crushes on "White" females to whom he turned or who "looked out" for him. The same description of "rescue" was described by Victor Demore who cited several "White" female teachers and counselors who provided tutoring and the expense of application fees for him while in high school and college (VD.2.8).

The *betrayal cycle* was also evidenced in the informants' declarations of *aloneness*. Okinowa identified a feeling of "Us against

Figure 2. Preliminary Interpretations of Betrayal

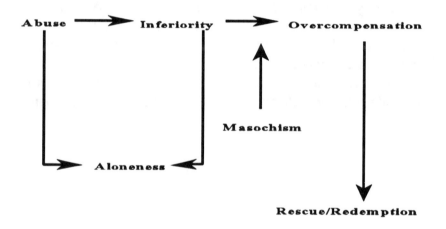

the world" (AO.1.1971-1974), a statement about his best relationships also used by Denny Rodman (DR.1.826-830+). Similarly, Okinowa stressed the importance of having "somebody on my side" (AO.1.2003-2005), a sentiment also expressed by Paul Rodgers (PR.2.395-402).

Where Do We Go From Here?
Issues From Our Data

Like any valid research project, ours has generated more questions than it has answered. Like any valid ethnographic inquiry, questions continue to emerge from new interviews and ongoing analysis. With only one third of the projected interviews completed, much information remains to be gained. Issues and areas for further investigation as the interviews and review of literature continue include the following:

1. Development of a focused questionnaire based on topics and issues emerging as themes (1) from transcription categorization, (2) during analysis discussions, and (3) in the review of literature.

2. Number of times informant has dated *across* the *color line* as compared to times dated within *race*.

3. Does the family tree include bi/multiracial couples and families? If so, where?

4. In at least two of the six male cases to date, as well as in the pilot case and at least one of the female cases, sexual abuse has been reported. Is there a connection between abuse and choices made in about relationship partners? Questions to be included on the questionnaire regarding this topic follow:

   a. Was sexual abuse part of your family's history? Were you aware of this as a child?

   b. Was sexual abuse a part of the family history of any of your significant others? If so, are you aware of this as incidental information (having little importance in the present) or because of resulting issues (having importance in the present)?

5. Relative age (younger/older and by how many years) of each partner discussed as significant, along with three descriptors. *Color* or complexion should be asked for if not given in the

descriptor list. (This question should come in the final interview and be based on all people identified on the list of significant others, as well as those mentioned during the interview who may not appear on the list.)

6. Is it possible that informant AM describes the qualities of his former girlfriend of African American heritage in the same way he does the girlfriends of European American heritage because having been educated in a school for the blind, both have possibly been acculturated into *White (WASP) culture*? Wouldn't this support the MC argument that in a dark room we all *look* the same and that racism has always been about appearances even when it has been in its most evil forms associated with intelligence, behavior, and morals.

7. Is *colorism* a driving force in the attraction of men of color to White women? Of White women to men of color?

8. What impact (if any) does the complexion of a man's mother have on his dating preferences?

9. An important assumption of this research team is that "research should provide new and better understanding of the dynamics of teaching and learning, new perspectives rather than new rules of action" (Shavelson in Kennedy, 1997, p. 10). How do we identify these perspectives as they relate to school issues involving children of multiracial parents? White children? White teachers? Multiracial teachers?

On Our Way To Where?

What drives this extensive exploration? To date (October 31, 1997), a documented 1,127 hours have been invested by the research team on this project. Perhaps Joel Crohn (1995) said it best in the introduction to his work on cross-cultural relationships, *Mixed Matches, How To Create Successful Interracial, Interethnic, and Interfaith Relationships:*

All of us, whether we are intermarried or not, are caught between our need for continuity with tradition and the necessity of adapting to a rapidly changing world. Each of us *takes our own odyssey* [emphasis added] to search for a place and a community we can call our own. And all of us need to learn how to understand, negotiate, and creatively use our differences in an increasingly multicultural world. (p. 19)

We intend that our research effort will aid in the *Homeric journey.*

References

Austin, Beth. (1991, October 6). Regarding your marriage, your honor. Chicago Tribune, Hersay column, sec. 6, p. 11.

Banks, James. (1995). Multicultural education and curriculum transformation. *Journal of Negro Education, 64*(4), 390-400.

Bernard, Jessie. (1966). Note on educational homogamy in Negro-White and White-Negro Marriages, 1960. *Journal of Marriage and the Family, 28,* 274-276.

Bogden, R. C., & Biklen, S. K. (1982). *Qualitative research for education: An introduction to theory and methods.* Boston: Allyn & Bacon.

Bond, Selena, & Cash, Thomas F. (1992). Black beauty: Skin color and body images among African-American college women. *Journal of Applied Social Psychology, 22,* 874-88.

Brawarsky, Sandee. (1995). Toward a common destiny. *Carnegie Quarterly, 34*(4), pp. 1-4.

Brown, John A. (1987). Casework contacts with Black-White couples. *Social Casework: The Journal of Contemporary Social Work, 68,* 24-29.

Center for Health and Environmental Statistics. (1994). *Annual summary of vital statistics, Kansas, 1993.* Topeka, KS: Kansas Department of Health and Environment.

Chrisman, R. (1991). What is the right thing? Notes on the deconstruction of black ideology. *The Black Scholar, 21,* 53-57.

Cose, Ellis. (1996, November 25). Color blind. *Newsweek, 128,* 51-

56.

Crohn, Joel. (1995). Mixed matches: How to create successful, interracial, interethnic, and interfaith relationships. New York: Fawcett Columbine.

Dyson, Michael Eric. (1997). *Race rules: Navigating the color line.* New York: Vintage Books.

Enda, Jodi. (1996, September 26). Keeping the doors open. *Wichita Eagle*, p. 8A.

Filemyr, Ann. (1995). Loving across the boundary. In M. Golden & S.R. Shreve (Eds.), *Skin deep: Black women and White women write about race* (pp. 162-188). New York: Doubleday.

Gates, Jr., Henry Louis. (1992). Loose canons: Notes on the the culture wars. New York: Oxford University Press.

Glaser, B. G., & Strauss, A. L. (1967). *The discovery of grounded theory: Strategies for qualitative research.* Chicago: Aldine.

Golden, Marita, & Shreve, Susan Richards. (Eds.). (1995). *Skin deep: Black women and White women write about race.* New York: Doubleday.

Gose, Ben. (1996, May 10). Public debate over a private choice: Interracial dating at colleges angers many black female students. *The Chronicle of Higher Education*, A45, A47.

Gould, Stephen Jay. (Orig. 1981, 1996). *The mismeasure of man.* London, England: Penguin.

Grier, William H., & Cobbs, Price M. (1968). Black rage. New York: Bantam.

Hall, Kermit L. (1992). *The Oxford companion to the Supreme Court of the United States.* New York: Oxford University Press.

Heer, David. (1974). The prevalence of Black-White marriages in the United States, 1960-1970. *Journal of Marriage and the Family, 36*, 246-258.

Hernton, Calvin C. (1988). *Sex and racism in America* (Rev. ed.). New York: Anchor Books.

Jacobs, Sally. (1995). Wedowee, When an Alabama principal said no to interracial dating, a small community was forced to confront its racist heritage. *Rolling Stone, 708,* 55+.

Kalmijn, Matthijs. (1993). Trends in Black/White intermarriage. *Social Forces, 72,* 119-146.

Kozol, Jonathan. (1991). *Savage inequalities: Children in America's schools.* New York: Harper Perennial.

Lehrman, Samuel R. (1967). Psychopathology in mixed marriages. *Psychoanalytic Quarterly, 36,* 67-82.

Leslie, Connie. (1995). The loving generation: Biracial children seek their own place. *Newsweek, 125*(7), 72.

Lincoln, Yvonna S., & Guba, Egon G. (1990). Judging the quality of case study reports. *Qualitative Studies in Education, 3,* 53-59.

Maykut, Pamela, & Mayhouse, Richard. (1994). *Beginning qualitative research, a philosophic and practical guide.* London: The Falmer Press.

McIntosh, Peggy. (1989, July/August). White privilege: Unpacking the invisible knapsack. *Peace and Freedom,* 10.

McPhail, Mark L. (1996). Race and sex in Black and White: Essence and ideology in the Spike Lee discourse. *The Howard Journal of Communications, 7,* 127- 138.

Meredith, Geoffrey, & Schewe, Charles. (1994). The power of cohorts. *American demographics, 16*(12), 22-28.

O'Hare, William P. (1992). America's minorities--The demographics of diversity. *Population Bulletin, 47*(4). Washington, DC: Population Reference Bureau.

Porterfield, E. (1978). *Black and White mixed marriages.* Chicago: Nelson-Hall.

Punch, M. (1986). *The politics and ethics of fieldwork.* Newbury Park, CA: Sage.

Russell, K., Wilson, M., & Hall, R. (1992). *The color complex, the politics of skin color among African Americans.* New York: Doubleday.

Schoen, Robert, & Wooldredge, John. (1989). Marriage choices in North Carolina and Virginia, 1969-1971 and 1979-81. *Journal of Marriage and the Family, 51,* 465-81.

Smith, Vern E. (1991, June 10). Fact is, Spike Lee's a romantic at heart. *Newsweek*, 46.

Smolowe, Jill. (1993, Fall). Intermarried . . . With children. *Time, Special Issue*, 64-65.

Staples, Robert. (1973). *The Black woman in America*. Chicago, IL: Nelson-Hall Publishers.

Steel, Melissa. (1995, Spring). New colors: Mixed-race families still find a mixed reception. *Teaching Tolerance*, 44-49.

Stone, Oliver. (1994, May 12). Boston Globe.

Sutton. C. F. (1986, April). *Finding a focus: Does it have to be first?* Paper presented at the Annual Convention of the American Educational Research Association, San Francisco, CA. (ERIC Document Reproduction Service No. ED 280 253)

White, J. E., Edwards, T. M., Lafferty, E., Monroe, S., & Rainert, V. (1997, May 5). *Time, 149*(18), 33-36.

Willie, Charles. (1992). Black-White marriages rise, but couples still face scorn. In K. Russell, M. Wilson, & R. Hall (Eds.), *The color complex, the politics of skin color among African Americans* (p. 113). New York: Doubleday.

Wolcott, Harry. (1987). On ethnographic intent. In G. Spindler and L. Spindler (Eds.), *Interpretive ethnography of education: At home and abroad* (pp. 37-57). Hillside, NJ: Lawrence Erlbaum

Wolcott, Harry. (1988). Adequate schools and inadequate education: The life history of a sneaky kid. In R. M. Jaeger (Ed.), *Complementary methods for research in education* (pp. 221-249). Washington, DC: American Educational Research Association.

Yancey, George A., & Yancey, Sherelyn, W. (1997). Black-White differences in the use of personal advertisements for individuals seeking interracial relationships. *Journal of Black Studies, 27*(5), 650-667.

Notes

[1] Note on word choice: The research team in this study prefers

the use of multiracial, as opposed to biracial or interracial, because the term seems to most appropriately represent the multiple cultures from which we have all descended. The term interracial, however, seems to more accurately represent the implication of the two sides of the metaphorical Black-White color line.

Further, while so much has been written about the use of race/color/ethnic descriptors, and a section of this review of literature is dedicated to exploring the contemporary nomenclature, our preference for the use of heritage over color creates the following descriptors: Americans of African heritage, Americans of European heritage. Although grammatically it is appropriate to hyphenate compound adjectives, to avoid creating hyphenated Americans, the hyphen will not be used in descriptors such as European American when used as a noun describing people. (For further discussion of the hyphen in this usage, see Gates, 1992, p. 125.) The implicit intention is to stress that all people in the review of literature and participants in this study are Americans by nationality, though their unique cultural affiliation, racial/ethnic classification, and developmental scripts distinguish them. Black and White will be used when it is specifically the issue of color that is being discussed. In direct quotes and in the context of discussing direct quotes, the original author's word choice has been maintained. (For a review of the findings of studies regarding terms of racial designation, see Russell, Wilson, & Hall, 1992, pp. 70-72).

Chapter Seventeen
Electronic Exchanges Across Campuses: Forums for Concerns and Issues Surrounding the Selection and Use of Multicultural Literature

Catherine Kurkjian
Central Connecticut State University, New Britain, CN

Kenneth J. Weiss
Nazareth College of Rochester, Rochester, NY

Helen R. Abadiano
Central Connecticut State University, New Britain, CN

===

"I am a middle class white American, pretty average. However, I grew up in a house with no central heat, no neighbors within 1/4 to 1/2 of a mile, no town within 7 miles, no rock music, and extremely limited TV (weird, huh? And you wonder why I turned out like I did?) The suburban American experience was pretty alien to me throughout my childhood. I could fillet a fish without a single bone, start a woodstove by myself by age 10, and sleep with an old-fashioned soapstone wrapped in towels at the foot of my bed, but I do pretty poorly at Trivial Pursuit. Am I a minority? Point is, there are as many differences between individuals within a labeled culture as there are similarities, and I think we need to keep our eyes on that."

In this excerpt, Kara reflects on her childhood experiences in sharing her definition of diversity. This kind of self-revelation is uncharacteristic of the kinds of sharing that we generally find in our college classrooms, however, it is precisely this kind of reflective sharing that is helpful in facilitating the development of teachers toward valuing and respecting diversity, and reflecting these values in their classrooms. It is for this reason that, as teacher educators, we decided to explore alternative forums for leading our students to that level of thinking/reflecting and dialoguing about diversity. This decision also led us to choose multicultural literature as a source for content and electronic exchanges as one forum for such dialogue.

Multicultural literature and electronic exchanges: A delivery system package in one

It is recognized that multicultural literature can serve as a powerful component of a multicultural curriculum in that it has the power to touch not only our minds, but also our hearts (Rasinski & Padak, 1990; Sims Bishop, 1992). Multicultural literature has been described as a tool to affirm cultural identity, to promote pride in one's heritage (Tompkins & Hoskisson, 1995), and to develop an appreciation of and sensitivity to differing cultural groups (Walker-Dalhouse, 1992). It is also argued that multicultural literature can influence the way students interact with people in a culturally pluralistic world (Yokota, 1993).

Despite the powerful benefits of using multicultural literature, related literature suggests that there are issues surrounding its definition (Madigan, 1993; Sims Bishop, 1992; Yokota, 1993), availability (Huck, Hepler, Hickman, & Kiefer,1997; Nieto, 1993; Reimer, 1992), and criteria for selection (Nieto, 1993; Sims Bishop, 1992; Yokota, 1993) that are problematic to teachers. These issues have been generating concerns among teachers about selecting and using multicultural literature. Consequently, teachers either shy away from using multicultural literature in their classrooms or do not use it in ways which maximize its powerful benefits (Au, 1991; Rasinski & Padak, 1990; Reimer, 1992).

One way of promoting teachers' understanding of and

appreciation for multicultural literature, as well as their commitment to using it in literacy education, is to provide them with opportunities to collaboratively identify and consolidate individual and collective reactions, feelings, thoughts, opinions and concerns about these issues across diverse teaching and learning communities.   Yet, such opportunities are very limited at best.

Fortunately, the rapid changes in computer technology, and the ever-growing use of telecommunications in particular, have given rise to richer opportunities for social collaborative interactions and cooperation among diverse communities. Proponents of technology agree that it provides essential tools with which to accomplish the goals of a constructivist classroom. Electronic exchanges, e-mail in particular, can provide a means for dialogue, discussion, and debate--interactivity that leads to the social construction of meaning (Willis, Stephens, & Matthew, 1996).

In the related literature concerning the facilitative effects of using e-mail for instructional purposes are studies which focus on: (a) computer-assisted writing instruction as a means of improving the quality of students' writing (Allen & Thompson, 1994; Fey, 1993); (b) literacy dialogue between preservice or inservice teachers and elementary school children (Dunston & Schenk 1996; Moore, 1991; Traw, 1994); (c) electronic communications of high school students with other students around the world in content areas of study (Noden & Moss, 1993); (d) on-line dialogue discussion journals in response to selected multicultural books (Battle, Nicholson, & Sinagra, 1996); (e) unstructured on-line dialogue journals across campuses (Grisham, 1996); and (f) discussions of course readings via e-mail in a large university psychology class with students who were reluctant to speak out in a large class setting (Meacham, 1994). However, there is limited research which focuses on using e-mail as one forum for exploring and/or extending thinking about issues and concerns in the selection and use of literature in general, and multicultural literature in particular.

This paper focuses on one aspect of a major qualitative collaborative teacher research study. The study on which this paper is based is grounded in a social constructivist perspective in which collaboration and cooperation are essential social, economic, cultural, and educational processes (Bruner, 1990, Willis et al., 1996). Cunningham (1992) states that the role of education in a constructivist view is "to show students how to construct knowledge, to promote collaboration with others, to show the multiple perspectives that can be brought to bear on a particular problem, and to arrive at self-chosen positions to which they can commit themselves, while realizing the basis of other views with which they disagree" (p. 36). The primary question posed in the major study is: How can teacher educators provide a fertile ground for a social constructivist approach to issues and concerns surrounding the selection and use of multicultural literature?

More specifically, the study addresses (a) the range of preservice and inservice teachers' responses regarding the value placed on using multicultural literature in diverse classrooms, the issues and concerns they have in its selection and use, and the way they come to grips with these issues during the course of the semester; and (b) the possible benefits, drawbacks and feasibility of using electronic mail user groups across college campuses in exploring and extending thinking about educational issues, in general, and those elated to multicultural literature, in particular.

Process cycles

The project involved two process cycles--the planning phase (Phase I) and the implementation phase (Phase II). Phase I included conceptualizing the design for the pilot project, preparing for project implementation and assessment, scheduling of implementation, preassessing teacher participants, facilitating a project orientation program for the teacher participants, and organizing teacher participants into user groups.

Five user groups were formed out of the 55 inservice and preservice teachers who were graduate students earning either their Master's degree, Teacher Education Certification or Masters plus 30 credit hours in the areas of Reading, Elementary Education, Special

Education, or Computer Literacy. All user group members were enrolled in one of two Children's Literature classes offered at two separate college campuses in spring semester, 1997. Both sites are located on the east coast of the United States and are situated in different states.

At one site, twenty four students were enrolled in all, nineteen of whom were earning their Master's degree either in Reading (15), or in Elementary Education(4). Four of the students were earning first time teacher certification, while one student was working towards thirty credits hours beyond a Master's degree. Among the twenty certified teachers, two were unemployed, and eighteen were currently teaching grade levels ranging from preschool to grade 8, with most working in grades 1-6.

Thirty one students were enrolled at the other site, fifteen of whom were earning their Master's degree either in Reading (8), Special Education (5), or Computer Literacy (2). Sixteen students were earning their first time teacher certification. Among the fifteen certified teachers, grade levels taught ranged from preschool to the secondary level, with most working in grades 1-6.

Each user group consisted of 10 to 12 students, drawn randomly to have representation from both sites. Instructors served as participant observers in each of the 5 user groups, labeled (A to E). After the user groups were formed an orientation program followed. The program included introduction to the nature and objectives of the project, expectations and requirements, and procedural and technical project information.

In order to ensure that all students had access to electronic mail, arrangements were made for students to obtain accounts at respective campuses. At one site, students had to merely sign up to receive an account. At the other, however, the process was more complicated. Prior to receiving an account, students were required to either enroll in a training class offered at limited times or to take a tutorial which would prepare them to take a ten-question quiz. Only those students who had received training or had done the independent tutorial qualified to take the quiz.

The preparation for implementation also involved the coordination of syllabi and semester schedules, as well as the determination of the number of entries to be required per article. In reviewing semester schedules across campuses, we decided to require students to read five selected articles so that discussions would span across the course of the semester.

Phase II of the process cycles included the implementation of the pilot project, selection of articles to be assigned for the e-mail forums, conducting of asynchronous group discussions via e-mail in response to assigned articles, collection of transcripts of e-mail dialogues, and design of a content coding procedure based on identifiable patterns from the transcripts. It also involved an ongoing analysis and evaluation of the project and continuing dialogue among project coordinators.

The instructors at each site dialogued about which articles would be most appropriate. We selected articles which we hoped would stimulate exploration of issues surrounding the definition of what constitutes multicultural literature, its availability, and the criteria for its selection. We selected at least one article which was practice oriented, and one article that spoke to issues of overt and covert censorship. The students in each user group engaged in asynchronous group discussions in response to the five articles assigned throughout the semester.

Each student was required to log on a minimum of two times for each article. In addition to the electronic forum, students engaged in other forums to explore the selection and use of multicultural literature. They engaged in five in-class face-to-face conversation groups which occurred subsequent to their electronic dialogues. At one of the sites the students were also required to write a critique of the article following the electronic and face-to-face conversations with their classmates and colleagues across campuses. At this site students were also asked to keep a dialogue journal with a classmate on ten multicultural books that they jointly selected to discuss.

Scaffolding was to be provided in the form of guiding questions which would serve to focus students' responses. However, this plan was modified after the first three articles. At that point we believed that the students were ready for a more open forum for response, and that in fact our questions seemed to be more of a constraint than a support.

Data analysis & category generation

The data we obtained were in the forms of e-mail entries, field notes, and the critiques and dialogue journals that were assigned only at one of the participating sites, as well as a post assessment survey concerning the feasibility of using e-mail. Data analysis was descriptive in nature. It involved the designing of a coding procedure based on identifiable patterns from datum sources that would organize the data into representational categories and subcategories (Bogdan and Biklen, 1992). Content analysis (Guba and Lincoln, 1981) of transcribed datum sources was also used. Each of the datum sources described was analyzed in order to triangulate findings across data gathering techniques and research questions. Additionally, because analysis is being conducted by several researchers and is ongoing, the reliability of our categories is being assessed across researchers.

Because qualitative data analysis is both labor and time intensive, three of the participating instructors along with three graduate students are in the process of refining our coding procedure across each of the five user groups A-E. This paper presents our preliminary findings from the data for Group A , which consisted of 12 participants--five from one campus and six from the other.

We began our analysis of the data for Group A by organizing the ninety-nine entries for the semester in chronological order. Our first analysis began by analyzing the data in its hard copy form. In this round of analysis we generated broad categories as we moved from the first entry to the last. The process involved asking questions of the data, and was recursive--often moving back and forth among entries. In our second round of analyses, transcripts were imported to our own word processing files so that categories could be further refined and compiled using electronic capabilities. In this round all the data for each category were compiled in order to define and refine subcategories. We then triangulated our findings in our review of our field notes, critiques and dialogue journals, and other artifacts (where applicable).

Currently, transcripts from each of the user groups are being analyzed separately moving chronologically from the first student entry to the last. The researchers began with Group A in developing a tentative coding scheme. In doing so each entry was looked at chronologically and coding was done by making comparisons between similarities and differences in ideas addressed in each entry in an effort to label and group concepts. As each entry for user group A was analyzed, categories emerged which were refined and or redefined in a recursive process of revisiting earlier entries. This process resulted in the generation of broad categories and more specific subcategories. This process is currently being applied to user groups B-E.

In Phase II, the categories generated for each of the user groups will be compared and contrasted in order to further refine and define the range of categories and subcategories across groups. Once again this will be a recursive process which may result in the generation of new categories or the revision of old ones across user groups and other datum sources.

Meanwhile, the categories and subcategories identified for Group A are the following:

1. *Concerns* (C): Addressing the problems and issues that teachers grapple with in connection with culturally conscious literature.

   C_1 keeping up with new books

   C_2 teacher's limited knowledge

   C_3 lack of value for diversity and culture in school/community

   C_4 authenticity, accurate representation

   C_5 time issues involved in book selection and use

   C_6 need for resources

   C_7 difficult topics to broach with children

   C_8 political issues in the of use multicultural literature

   C_9 overgeneralization about groups

C_{10} differentiation between traditions of groups of past and contemporary life

C_{11} which cultures to represent

C_{12} definition of what constitutes multicultural literature

C_{15} impact on existing curriculum

2.   Rationale (R): Explaining the reasons for and benefits of using culturally conscious literature--the *why?*

    R_1 to explore differences and similarities among people

    R_2 curriculum based, knowledge related reasons

    R_3 learning tool for teachers

    R_4 to affirm identity

    R_5 to impact availability of culturally conscious books

    R_6 to take social actions

    R_7 to reduce prejudice, promote understanding

    R_8 to experience enjoyment

Other broad categories defined are:

3.   *Teacher's Job* (J): Discussing the teacher's roles and responsibilities.

4.   *Specific Classroom Practices* (P): Addressing the *how?*-- approaches and activities.

5.   *Sharing Personal Experiences* (E): Relating one's own situation to issues surrounding the use of multicultural literature.

6.   *Technology And Process Comments* (TC): Referencing to e-mail and/or responding to engaging in the process of using e-mail.

7.   *Contingent Responses* (CR): Responses in which students recognize that there is an audience or responses in which student acknowledges what someone else has said.

Three selected coded entries are presented and discussed in order to provide a sample of the kinds of categories described. Excerpt one is in response to Junko Yokota's (1993) article entitled *Issues in selecting multicultural children's literature*. This was the first article to which the students were asked to respond. The following guiding questions were posed to them:

MAIL

Regarding the first article by Junko Yokota, what are the significant issues brought forth in the article? What implications does this article have for classroom instruction? What are your general reactions to the article? The interesting part of this conversation will be signing on to see what others in the group have to say. You may find yourself responding more than once.

Excerpt One

MAIL

Subj: Junko Yokota's article

I read your reply to the first article we read **(CR)**. *I have no experience with kindergarten classes* **(E)**. *I was just wondering if there was a lot of multicultural literature appropriate for children that are so young, or is it hard to find good multicultural lit.?* **(CR)** *I think that that would be a challenging task!* **(C₆)**.

In this short entry Emily is responding to Yokota's article for the second time. She addresses her response specifically to an across campus member of her user group **(CR)**. In doing so, she shares her own background **(E)** and concerns about resources **(C₆)**, and invites a response regarding the availability of good multicultural literature for kindergarten classes **(CR)**.

Excerpt Two is in response to an introductory chapter entitled *Multicultural literature for children: Making informed choices* written by Sims Bishop (1992) appearing in Violet Harris's book *Teaching multicultural literature in grades K-8*. Questions posed to the students for this article were the following:

MAIL

Bishop talks about varying definitions of multicultural literature and provides some guidelines in considering cultural authenticity. She takes a stance concerning who should write multicultural books and makes a variety of recommendations. What is your opinion about these issues? How might you apply these ideas in the context of your own classroom? If you are not teaching, then how might you apply these ideas?

Excerpt Two

MAIL

Subj: Bishop

Hello everyone **(CR)***. Sorry that it took so long to respond to Bishop but I just received the questions again after I'd deleted them* **(TC***). There are a few definitions of multicultural literature in Bishop's article. I had always felt that multicultural literature included groups that were not part of the mainstream in the United States and other countries as well* **(C$_{12}$)***.*

Bishop again brings up the insider/outsider issue. I think my opinion on this issue is becoming less clear. Obviously an insider who takes an active part in their culture can write an accurate book that will be authentic. But what about an "insider" who does not take an active part of their culture? Outsiders, I would hope, have the best intentions when they write a book about another culture. But even with the best intentions they may as Bishop states, be "unaware of the nuances of day to day living in the culture portrayed in the book" (p.41). I feel that insiders who are active participants in their culture can do a better job portraying their culture then an insider who does not participate and outsiders. However, I do not think that they definitively cannot write books about a different culture, I think it more challenging and works out less often **(C$_4$)***.*

The guidelines that Bishop provides will be helpful to me in the future. There were several recommendations that are weaved throughout the article. I really liked the idea of reading a lot of books written from the "inside" perspective. I feel that the more insider books that we read the more we'll understand about that culture **(R₃)**. *Also, it will allow us to notice which outsider books are inaccurate* **(C₄)**. *I do not know a lot about other cultures so this will benefit me in the future when I introduce children's books into the classroom* **(C₂)**.

When I teach, I may present insider books to the students have them study and read them and then present them with outsider books as well as insider books and see if they can pick out which books are accurate and inaccurate and why **(P)**. *I think one of the greatest gifts we can give children is to teach them to look for inaccuracies that misrepresent a culture* **(C₄)**. *What do you think* **(CR)**? *Talk to you soon* **(CR)**, S.

In this entry Susan describes a technical glitch when she talks about deleting questions posed by the instructors to which she was required to respond **(TC)**. She articulates her own view of what constitutes multicultural literature and her recognition that there are varying definitions **(C₁₂)**. She then explores the issue of authenticity when she revisits her original opinion concerning who can write authentic multicultural literature, authors who are "insiders," members of the culture being portrayed, versus those who are "outsiders" or not part of the culture. In this excerpt she takes the opportunity to further consider the nuances of this issue. She comments, "I think my opinion is less clear" and examines the notion of "insider" and "outsider" in more depth **(C₄)**.

She speaks to her concerns about her limited knowledge of particular cultures **(C₂)** and her belief that she can enhance her own learning by reading authentic multicultural literature **(R₃)**. She addresses the issue of teacher practice when she suggests that teachers should encourage students to evaluate authenticity for themselves **(P)**. Finally, Susan invites a response to this idea, when she asks, "What do you think?" and acknowledges her audience with "Talk to you soon"

(CR).

Excerpt Three is in response to the assigned article by Rasinski & Padak (1990) entitled *Multicultural learning through children's literature*. For this article the students were given the following prompt for response:

MAIL

*Rasinski and Padak discuss how multicultural children's literature can be used as a means of moving children to some form(s) of social action. What's your opinion of this? How might this apply (if you are teaching) in your own classroom (if not teaching, if you were to have your own class)? You might also wish to discuss the concept of "empowerment" of children through the use of multicultural literature. ***By the way, it is perfectly okay to keep discussing the first article.*

Excerpt Three
MAIL
Subj: Rasinski & Padak
*Hi, all --***(CR)**

Whew! I had 50 messages when I logged in tonight! A little overwhelming!(**TC**) *Dr. --- I believe I'm supposed to be the secretary this week, and am not sure I'll be able to print this stuff out successfully at home. If you are printing all of our responses anyway, would you mind bringing kidlit-a's to class on Tuesday just in case? I can take them and copy them if we need to have two copies. Thanks... let me know if this is a problem* **(CR/TC)**.

I thought the Rasinski and Padak article was right on target, and at the same time a little idealistic. The first three levels seem very doable in today's public school arena; however, I find the fourth to be a little progressive for the world I see in public schooling today.

I'd love to do things like that -- and would fight for the opportunity to do them (P) -- but I think you'd have to leave things out of the curriculum (C_{13}) in order to do so, and I believe that realistically, you'd meet a lot of resistance (C_8).

My point from my last response remains true in this one: it is critical that we catch kids at a young age when it comes to "helping students learn tolerance and appreciation of other cultures and persons who are members of those cultures." (p. 576, un-APA style!) (CR/J). I think kids need to develop empathy and understanding and curiosity about people who are different from them, regardless of whether that difference is cultural or individual. I agree that literature is a very excellent vehicle with which to accomplish this goal, because even the hardest and most stubborn heart can be reached with a story (R_1, R_7).

Where I think this article becomes a little "pie in the sky" is where it talks about transformation and social action. Please don't get me wrong -- I believe with all my heart that transformation and social action are necessary. However, I think that there's a delicate balance between what's happening in school and what's happening in society. I don't believe that public schools, as servants of a tax-paying public, can stray too far from mainstream society. I don't like this reality -- and might wind up teaching in a private school someday, making half the money, because of it -- but I think we must be savvy and realistic if we are to gain any respect as professionals in our society. The fact is, real change is sometimes (not always) radical, and radical doesn't fly in the averaged-out world of public schooling (C_8). What do you guys think? Any teachers out there who have successfully pulled off radical activities and would like *to prove me wrong?* **(C$_8$/CR)**

I fully and completely believe that children must be empowered in every aspect of their education as much as possible **(J)**. *Once again, I think true empowerment comes from knowing your stuff, in a real, down-to-earth fashion. Come on -- is it fair to let kids think that it will be effective to write to government officials and "argue for an end to actions of this type" (referring to the Japanese internment of "Journey to Topaz")? Kids tend to be idealistic to start with -- instead of suggesting "soft" solutions like this, I'd rather let them face real problems in their school or community and try to find solutions. These still may be controversial with parents, but at least kids will get a feel for the struggle, and may see some real change in their world* **(P, C$_8$)**.
I'm a hard-nose, huh? A couple of years in corporate America will do that to you **(E)**.
Anybody want to argue? **(CR)** -- *Kara*

In this excerpt Kara uses e-mail as a forum to debate and explore issues in a way which conveys her expectation that her work is being read. In her "Hi all !"and her comments to Dr. ---, there is an assumption that she is writing to an audience consisting of her instructor and fellow students. Kara articulates a dilemma that teachers sometimes find themselves in, when she examines beliefs in the importance of using multicultural literature **(J, R$_1$, R$_7$)** and her concerns about the resistance that will be met in its use **(C$_{13}$, C$_8$)**. She goes beyond the definition of this problem when she grapples with issues revolving around the political nature of teaching, and the relationship between school and society. She examines issues that delve into the nature of the role of schools in society, and concerns voiced by progressive and critical educators such as John Dewey (1902) and George Counts (1932). Moreover, Kara brings to bear her own experience in corporate America **(E)** and invites her fellow students to dialogue with her about the political realities of teaching as it relates to the use of multicultural literature.

What we have learned

The process we have undergone with our students has taught us many valuable lessons concerning the use of e-mail technology as one forum for discussion in exploring the use of multicultural literature in the classroom. We have learned about the content and context of the conversations held within these groups, including the positive outcomes, the rich construction of meaning, the sharing of commonalties and belief systems, as well as the negative aspects, the fears, and the misunderstandings.

As we consider the feasibility of using electronic mail user groups, we conclude that they could, and in fact often do, offer another forum for conversation. While we presented some of the more interesting conversations, we also discovered that in some instances, students were merely responding in the mode of "task completion" or going through the motions with minimal personal investment in order to earn a grade. The care and nurturing of e-mail user groups is often cumbersome and time-consuming. We had extremely large numbers of students participating in each of the five user groups, which made maintenance (including reading, responding, and printing) overwhelming. These large numbers of participants per group also made it difficult for the participants to follow and engage in more in-depth conversations surrounding the concerns and issues.

An interesting discovery was made concerning the content of the conversations in terms of perceived vulnerability. Some participants believed they could open up more easily as they did not need to interface directly with other users face-to-face. It was as if they were playing an anonymous role. This meant, for some, that they could discuss the issues openly and honestly, without fear of face-to-face reaction and confrontation. Some students also expressed the fear that they might be making themselves or others in the group vulnerable to outsiders. Many of our students received mail directly over their own subscribed electronic servers and others received their e-mail at work or at school. The concern was that others signing on and/or seeing printed conversations, taken out of context, might put them in some sort of danger if views expressed were not those of the accepted "norm" of others.

Some of the participants could not easily (if at all) determine the tone of the conversations, in terms of honesty, hostility, sarcasm, irony, etc. This was rendered impossible since participants using e-mail were not able to really sense "voice" electronically. Even with the use of "shouting" (USING ALL CAPITAL LETTERS), tone was not conveyed. This annoyed and frustrated some of the participants, because they had trouble perceiving the intent of some of the conversations, and how best to respond.

Another interesting aspect we found was that some of the participants did not recognize the sense of audience (that is, other group members who were participating). They kept their input one-sided and short. They did not often engage in response to what others were saying. On the other hand, many of the participants, after several weeks, had a better sense that they were not out there alone. They slowly began responding back to ideas and concerns shared by members of their group. This led to richer, fuller conversations, where varied levels of constructed meaning were established.

In reflecting on the feasibility of using e-mail user groups as part of constructing meaning around issues and concerns, we found that it can be extremely beneficial as one more forum for discussion. It allowed for conversations centering around relevant issues, drawing on the divergent backgrounds of members outside of the local community environment. The ability to share ideas and concerns with others in another geographical location allowed for the discussion of common issues as well as divergent opinions.

It is important to note, however, that these groups served as only one forum for discussion. Face-to-face conversations were conducted as part of each of the campus classes. These in-class conversations not only allowed for another forum of ideas, but permitted members of different user groups to share ideas--ideas that had been shared previously only among the membership of individual user groups. This opened up rich discussion, which in turn allowed for the addition of more information and more points of view to be shared.

The drawbacks we found included the amount of time needed to establish groups, train students, and monitor the conversations. Although we have come a long way with computers and electronic technology, it quickly became apparent that different operating platforms, different e-mail servers, and students' perceived and actual confidence in their own technology skills, all played direct and important roles in this project. We found many glitches that interfered with the ease of use. This, in turn, led to some degree of frustration on the part of some of the participants as to issues of computer access and availability, time required to complete assignments, and technical errors and problems, as well as their own senses of ability/inability to be a part of the technology revolution.

Where do we go from here?

As we deal with the current array of data collected, we will continue to develop our protocol for the analysis of qualitative and quantitative data. As we read and re-read the data sets, we find that new categories emerge. The wealth and range of data allow us to take what we are finding in many different directions. We are finding out a great deal about the way inservice and preservice teachers choose and use multicultural children's literature. We are encouraging our students to examine their own "baggage" as they discuss issues and concerns among themselves and with their students.

As we look at how we might move from the pilot study to a full scale replication, we continue to develop better strategies and formats for the use of e-mail user groups. We have determined that membership size is a key factor. The smaller the groups, the richer the opportunities for a sense of community. The amount of data needed to be read and responded to will decrease with fewer members in each group. As we move into the expanded study, we have decided to use paired groupings. We will be asking our students to negotiate the selection of ten children's books that are multicultural. Each group will be required to read and respond to their self-selected books as they read articles and participate in class discussions centered around the choice and use of literature for children.

REFERENCES

Allen G., & Thompson, A. (1994, April). *Analysis of the effect of networking on computer-assisted collaborative writing in a fifth grade classroom.* Paper presented at the meeting of the American Research Association, New Orleans, LA.

Au, K. (1991). *Literacy instruction in multicultural settings.* Orlando, FL: Harcourt Brace Jovanovich College Publishers.

Battle, J., Nicholson, S., & Sinagra, M. (December, 1996). *Discussions of multiethnic literature via e-mail between developmental reading students at two universities.* Paper presented at the 46th Annual Meeting of the National Reading Conference, Charleston, NC.

Bogdan, R. C., & Biklen, S. K. (1992). *Qualitative research for education* (2nd ed.). Boston, MA: Allyn & Bacon.

Bruner, J. (1990). *Acts of meaning.* Cambridge, MA: Harvard University Press.

Counts, G. (1932). *Dare the school build a new social order?* Carbondale, IL: Southern Illinois University Press.

Cunningham, D. J. (1992). Assessing constructions and constructing assessments: A dialogue. In T. M. Duffy & D. H. Jonassen (Eds.), *Constructivism and the technology of instruction: A conversation* (pp. 35-44). Hillsdale, NJ: Erlbaum.

Dewey, J. (1902). *The child and the curriculum.* Chicago, IL: University of Chicago Press.

Dunston, P. J., & Schenk, R. (1996). *Preservice teachers and elementary school children use electronic mail to engage in dialogue about literacy.* Paper presented at the 46th Annual Meeting of the National Reading Conference, Charleston, NC.

Fey, M. H. (December, 1993). *Reader response, collaborative writing, and computer networking.* Paper presented at the 43rd Annual Meeting of the National Reading Conference, Charleston, SC.

Grisham, D. L. (December, 1996). *Electronic literacy learning: Teachers' on-line dialogue journals.* Paper presented at the 46th Annual Meeting of the National Reading Conference, Charleston, NC.

Guba, E. G., & Lincoln, Y. S. (1981). *Effective evaluation: Improving the usefulness of evaluation results through responsive and naturalistic approaches.* San Francisco, CA: Jossey-Bass.

Huck, C. S., Hepler, S., Hickman, J., & Kiefer, B. Z. (1997). *Children's literature in the elementary school* (6th ed.). Dubuque, IA: Brown & Benchmark.

Madigan, D. (1993). The politics of culturally conscious literature for children and adolescents: Combining perspectives and conversations. *Language Arts, 70,* 168-176.

Meacham, J. A. (1994). Discussions by e-mail: Experiences from a large class on multiculturalism. *Liberal Education, 80,* 36-39.

Moore, M. A. (1991). Electronic dialoguing: An avenue to literacy. *The Reading Teacher, 45,* 280-286.

Nieto, S. (1993). We have stories to tell: A case study of Puerto Ricans in children's literature. *Rethinking Schools, 8*(2), 20-23.

Noden, H., & Moss, B. (1993). Virtual schools: Reading and writing. *The Reading Teacher, 47,* 166-667.

Rasinski, T., & Padak, N. (1990). Multicultural learning through children's literature. *Language Arts, 67*(6), 576-580.

Reimer, K. M. (1992). Multiethnic literature: Holding fast to dreams. *Language arts, 69,* 14-21.

Sims Bishop, R. (1992). Culturally conscious literature for children: Making informed choices. In V. J. Harris (Ed.), *Teaching culturally conscious literature in grades K-8* (pp. 37-54). Norwood, MA: Christopher Gordon.

Tompkins, G. E., & Hoskisson, K. (1995). *Language arts: Content and reading strategies.* Englewood Cliffs, NJ: Prentice-Hall.

Traw, R. (March, 1994). School/university collaboration via e-mail. *Tech Trends,* 28-31.

Walker-Dalhouse, D. (1992). Using African American literature to increase ethnic understanding. *Reading Teacher, 45,* 416-423.

Willis, J. W., Stephens, E. C., & Matthew, K. I. (1996). *Technology, reading, and language arts.* Needham Heights, MA: Allyn & Bacon.

Yokota, J. (1993). Issues in selecting multicultural children's literature. *Language Arts, 70*(3), 156-167.

Chapter Eighteen
Ethnobibliotherapy: Ethnic Identity Development through Multicultural Literature

Heidi McKenna
University of Washington, Seattle

================================

The Need for Identity Development of Teachers through Multicultural Literature

> Even if we are successful in increasing the percentage of
> teachers of color from the projected 5% [in the year]
> 2000 to 15%, 85% of the nation's teachers will still be
> white, mainstream, and largely female working with
> students who differ from them racially, culturally, and in
> social class status. Thus an effective teacher education
> policy for the 21st century must include as a major focus
> the education of all teachers, including teachers of color,
> in ways that will help them receive the knowledge, skills
> and attitudes needed to work effectively with students
> from diverse racial, ethnic, and social class groups.
> (Banks, 1991, pp. 135-136)

The primary strategy for meeting the needs of our increasingly diverse student population has been an effort to create a diverse core of teachers in the image of the student population. Even if recruitment strategies were to exceed Banks' projected 15%, multicultural transformation would not necessarily follow. Members of our teaching force were successful students themselves, able to negotiate and master the institutional and educational rigors demanded by their secondary and undergraduate educations. Thus, teachers are rarely prepared to understand and accommodate students who have had a dramatically different experience with schools and learning due to differences in class, race, or ethnicity (Cazden & Mehan, 1989; Delpit, 1995; Florio-Ruane, 1994; Heath, 1983, 1992). Lacking a shared cultural and social experience, it is difficult for teachers to help their students bridge home and school cultures. Without a multicultural perspective, educators will continue to construct curriculum and pedagogies from a cultural base quite different from, and often incompatible with, the cultures of students for whom such curriculum and instructional strategies are designed (Erickson & Mohatt, 1982; Vogt, Jordan, & Tharp, 1993).

Literacy, at the core of all education, is also at the core of educational cultural mismatches (Delpit, 1995; Purcell-Gates, 1995). While teaching their students to think and communicate, teachers guide them via literary texts, often assuming a monocultural interpretation of literacy as a monolithic phenomenon, unaware that many of their students may be experiencing intense, internal, value-loaded conflict created when the constructed knowledge of lived experience contradicts the knowledge taught at school. Writes Banks (1993), "Cultural conflict occurs in the classroom because much of the personal/cultural knowledge that students from diverse cultural groups bring to the classroom is inconsistent with the school knowledge and the teacher's personal and cultural knowledge" (p.26).

I propose that the first step toward equipping educators to meet the challenge of teaching diverse cultures is the adoption of a new definition of literacy. Literacy can be defined as the knowledge, skills, and attitudes needed to communicate effectively with people from diverse racial, ethnic, and social class groups. This definition is consistent with the ideas of Judit Kádár - Fülop (1988) who claims the first function of any literacy curriculum is the promotion of cultural communication that enables individuals to meaningfully communicate with a wider circle than family, friends, and cultural intimates. My research into a possible methodology for teacher educators is based on this definition.

Many literary scholars today believe that literacy is a political, cultural and historical construct which defines expectations of competencies, conventions, and styles that a society holds for its members as language users (Florio-Ruane, 1994; Gee, 1992; Giroux, 1992; Shannon, 1992). Contemporary understandings of literacy suggest it is far more than the ability to organize and make meaning of print: it is the ability to pragmatically control the use of language for knowledge construction and transformation (Giroux, 1992). Because, as Florio-Ruane (1994) would remind us, literacy "is a social accomplishment highly influenced by the contexts in which it is acquired" (p.53), people learn and engage in multiple literacies which vary with the social contexts they inhabit. Gee (1992) suggests that various literacies include both a primary discourse acquired in the home and secondary discourses individuals must master to effectively communicate with people and institutions outside their circles of intimates. And since, as Gee (1992) observes, "even among speakers of English there are socio-culturally different primary discourses" (p.25), all literate people must, in essence, be multilingual and multiliterate to exercise pragmatic control of the language and texts they will utilize in the varied contexts of their lives. Beyond the social benefits of a multicultural definition of literacy lies the practical problem of communicating clearly enough with our students so that they might acquire the skills and knowledge they need.

Ethnographic research suggests the more similar the primary, home discourses and the secondary discourses modeled and taught by schools, the more readily students can and will master school literacy (Heath, 1983, 1992; Vogt et al., 1993). In contrast, students whose primary discourses differ substantially from the school literacy they are expected to master may find the languages, cultural practices, and preferred literacy displays of home and school to be incongruent and even conceptually incompatible (Delpit, 1995; Heath, 1983, 1992). These difficulties are exacerbated by cultural misunderstandings as teachers misread student problems in bridging and translating diverging discourses and literacies as inability or unwillingness to learn, or as deficits in their students' home cultures.

Banks (1994) advocates teacher education programs designed

to promote the characteristics that effective teachers in a multicultural society must have:

> To function effectively in ethnically pluralistic environments, the teacher must have democratic attitudes and values, a clarified pluralistic ideology, a process conceptualization of ethnic studies, the ability to view society from diverse ethnic perspectives and points of view, knowledge of the emerging stages of ethnicity in Western societies, and the ability to function at Ethnicity Stage 4 or above. (p.251)

Banks' claim that effective multicultural teachers must be able to function at what he defines as "Stage 4 Ethnicity: Biethnicity" is consistent with others in the field whose work suggests that effective educators must acknowledge their own ethnic identities as resources for their learning while simultaneously affirming the emerging and divergent identities of others (Flood & Lapp, 1994; Florio-Ruane, 1994; Grant, 1991; Hansen-Krening, 1993; Houser & Chevalier, 1996; Sleeter, 1993; Zeichner, 1992, 1993). Teacher educator Hansen-Krening (1993), for example, "engage[s] teachers directly in examining their own cultural perspectives first and the multicultural perspectives of others next" (p.125) as a means of exposing the impact of teachers' cultural perspectives on their teaching. It seems to Zeichner (1993) that "the development of one's own cultural identity is a necessary precursor to cross-cultural understanding" (p.15).

Banks (1994) describes people within this stage of development as having "a commitment to their ethnic group, an empathy and concern for other ethnic groups, and a strong reflective commitment and allegiance to the nation state and its idealized values, such as human dignity and justice" (p.266). Because Banks is speaking of attitudes, the use of affective rather than cognitive language is appropriate and significant. This need to move beyond the cognitive domain and into the affective is echoed in Gay's (1994) description of multicultural education as "fundamentally an affective and humanistic enterprise that aims to achieve greater understanding and appreciation of diverse cultures and peoples" (p.24).

While the task may seem daunting to an academy inclined to shy away from feelings and emotions as part of teacher education, research from the field of counseling psychology suggests a possible strategy for enhancing appreciation of diverse others through racial/ethnic identity development (Carter, 1990; Helms, 1993). Further, while theorists have linked identity development to teacher effectiveness (Banks, 1994; Grant, 1991), preliminary research also suggests a relationship between identity development and decreases in racism (Carter, 1990). Yet, of the four empirical studies cited above (which were identified in the Ladson-Billings' (1995) survey of multicultural teacher education research), none addressed ethnic identity development as a variable of multicultural course work.

Theorists of racial/ethnic development are in agreement that contact with diversity is necessary for the development of a healthy racial/ethnic self-identity (Banks, 1994; Cross, 1991; Gay, 1985; Helms, 1993). Yet individuals engaged in this contact are typically defensive and fearful of difference, retreating into the safety of their own cultural group. While most theorists believe this resistance is unavoidable, guiding potential teachers through resistance toward a positive multiethnic attitude is an important skill to develop in teacher education programs. Banks (1994) refers to this resistance, this voluntary separation and exclusiveness, as "ethnic encapsulation," suggesting the path out of such "psychological captivity" is to be found by an individual exploring basic assumptions of her or his culture in contrast to other cultures (p.224). Creating forums for such questioning is problematic in an America that is increasingly polarized and segregated along racial lines. Gay (1994) writes that even in communities with racially mixed residential areas, "this mixture only appears on the surface" (p. 6). She concludes, "The absence of close and significant interactions across ethnic, social and cultural lines may reinforce stereotypes and cause individuals to be suspicious and distrustful - even fearful - of those who are different" (p.6). It is from this context that eighteen and nineteen year olds arrive at our institutions of higher learning, some of whom have decided to make teaching their life work, as well as older, post baccalaureates returning to earn a teaching credential. How, then, can multicultural teacher education both provide a context for cultural contact and guide students out of their cultural encapsulation? One potential strategy is the use of multicultural literature as a surrogate for direct contact.

Two theoretical traditions suggest how such literatures might support racial/ethnic identity development: reader response theories and bibliotherapy. Reader response theories (Beach & Marshall, 1990; Bleich, 1978; Cox & Many, 1992; Fish, 1980; Holland, 1980; Iser, 1980, 1978; Purves & Beach, 1972; Rosenblatt, 1938/1983, 1985; Sebesta, Monson & Senn, 1995) maintain that readers engage texts in a literary experience which changes their understandings of self and other. Rosenblatt persuasively argues that for a text to become a literary experience, it must entail an aesthetic and efferent response: heart as well as head must engage a text as an expressive synthesis occurs between the reader and what is read. This is remarkably similar to what Helms (1993) writes concerning Whites in the process of immersion: "The person in this stage is searching for the answers to the questions: 'Who am I racially?' and 'Who do I want to be?' and 'Who are you really?'" She concludes, "successful resolution of this stage apparently requires emotional catharsis in which the person reexperiences previous emotions that were denied or distorted" (p.62).

Sebesta et al (1995) have developed a Taxonomy of Reader Response which can be used by teachers of literature to "assess and focus teaching" (p.5) as well as in self-assessment by readers to discern patterns in quantity and quality of aesthetic response. The approach is fundamentally different from the traditional analysis of characterization, plot, and theme. In a classroom using the Sebesta et al. taxonomy, readers of multicultural literatures can learn to respond through evocation, exploring contrasting evocative experiences of others, reflecting on and evaluating them.

Whereas Sebesta et al (1995) start with literature and use affect to bring meaning to the work, one strategy from counseling psychology starts with people's detachment from affect and uses literature as a means to reintegrate emotion. Called bibliotherapy, it is defined as "a process of dynamic interaction between the personality of the reader and literature . . . which may be utilized for personal assessment, adjustment and growth" (Russell & Shrodes, 1978, p.211). Bibliotherapy draws upon psychoanalytic theory to hypothesize a therapeutic effect of identification, catharsis, and insight through reading.

I have combined the theoretical frames of reader response and bibliotherapy into a practical application of identity development theory. I have chosen to call this approach "ethnobibliotherapy," a term first used by Geneva Gay (1985) to describe an instructional technique "which uses literature written from an experiential, personal point of view (such as novels, autobiographies, short stories and plays) to help students learn ways of coping with different ethnic dilemmas" (p. 53). I will further define ethnobibliotherapy as a pedagogic strategy employing bibliotherapeutic instructional strategies which foster identification, catharsis, and insight using works by authors representing races or ethnic cultures other than one's own for the purpose of the development of racial/ethnic identity. By specifically addressing racial/ethnic identity development, I believe teacher candidates will be better equipped to bridge racial/ethnic barriers in their classrooms.

"Cultural identities," declares Toni Morrison, "are formed and informed by a nation's literature" (1990, p.39). Readers of multicultural literature explore the race/ethnicity of Others as, with an insider's view of worlds they otherwise would not know, they gain a better understanding of both their own and others' cultural identities. The intimacies of family, the distribution of power, the role of spirituality, the relationships of men and women -- all these human activities can be seen in particular racial, cultural and ethnic contexts. Readers who come to know and care about fictional and nonfictional characters with fundamentally different world views may begin to see past the differences to the universals which underlie all cultures.

This study seeks to answer the question, "Can the racial/ethnic identity of teachers be developed by reading literature from racially and ethnically diverse authors in classes which use instructional techniques of reader response and bibliotherapy?"

Certain key terms require definition:

Bibliotherapy: Instructional strategies which foster an affective as well as an intellectual identification with literary characters through strategies of reader response. Such strategies may include asking students to re-experience their literary response by: acting out or retelling evocative events, imagining or picturing characters or settings of events from the selection; applying personal experience; applying other readings or media to the work; applying other readers' views to examine their own responses; reexamining the text from other perspectives; and reflecting upon and generalizing the meaning of the literary experience.

Ethnobibliotherapy: A pedagogic strategy employing bibliotherapeutic instructional strategies which foster identification, catharsis, and insight using works by authors representing races or ethnic cultures other than one's own for the purpose of the development of racial/ethnic identity.

Race/Ethnic identity: An individual's sense of self with respect to their membership in and feelings of identification with a distinct cultural subgroup with whom they share certain phenotypic and/or cultural characteristics such as language, religion, and customs which distinguish them from other members of their society.

Race/ethnicity: Socially constructed categories of identification and classification of individuals and affinity groups that are based on cultural and/or phenotypic similarities among members.

Methodology
Site and Recruitment of Participants

The site of this research was a course in Multicultural Adult Literatures offered by a suburban school district and taught by a professor from a major research university in the Northwest. Participants included the instructor, a professor in curriculum and instruction, 20 preschool, elementary, and secondary teachers of literature from the school district hosting the class, and myself. Many of the participants had taken this class before; indeed, some of the participants have enrolled in this class each spring for the six years it had been offered. A majority of the participants (18) were self-identified White and female, with one Asian American female participant, and one Hispanic female participant. Because I am particularly interested in the development of racial/ethnic identity among White, female and middle-class teachers who demographically represent the largest population within the teaching profession, the composition of this class was well suited to my inquiry.

The instructor of this class, Professor Hansen-Krening selects books from diverse cultural perspectives that first and foremost are "good stories," books that tell an engaging story with well-crafted language, strong characterizations, important themes, and literary style. Since one of her goals is to acquaint the class with the wealth of quality literature that exists from cultural traditions with which participants may not be familiar, these representative books must engage the audience in the power of their narratives. Additionally, books are selected that explore a variety of perspectives within a given culture so as to acquaint readers with the range of thought that exists within any cultural tradition.

She organizes book selection thematically, finding common threads between books which invite comparisons. The selections under consideration all dealt with three themes: survival, silence, and generational differences in values, beliefs, and attitudes.

Participants read a minimum of six books by authors of color; one which was assigned to all class members, and the remainder of which were selected by participants from five pairs of books including both fiction and nonfiction options. Participants met biweekly for six two-hour class sessions which included three different instructional strategies: mini-lecture, literature circles, and the viewing of both fictional and documentary videotapes thematically related to each weeks' books. In literature circles, participants who had read the same books gathered in groups of 4 to 6 people to engage in evocative reader response activities. These activities were designed by the instructor to foster: 1) evocation of and identification with the literary characters by reexperiencing parts of the books which were significant to participants through retelling or rereading meaningful passages; 2) generation of alternatives to the original evocation by comparing and contrasting alternative perspectives such as other readers' points of view or applying other readings to the work; 3) reflective thinking through an examination of participants' cultural assumptions by comparing and contrasting personal values, beliefs and attitudes with those presented by the works read; and 4) evaluation of the literature's impact in broadening participants' cultural perspectives and appreciation, knowledge of multicultural literature, and understanding of cultural change generationally and geographically.

For the first class session participants were assigned *A Long Distance Life* by Marita Golden (1989), a book the instructor felt would be an accessible introduction to the organizational themes which would be explored throughout the course. During the remaining class sessions, participants were asked to chose between a pair of books, with three of the four book pairs including fictional and nonfictional options. For the second class session, readers chose between *Secrets of Mariko* by Elizabeth Bumiller (1995) and *A Mature Woman* by Saiichi Maruya (1994); the third session choices were Holly Uyemoto's (1995) *Go* and *A Bridge Between Us* by Julie Shigekuni (1995); for the fourth session, participants chose between two books by Bette Bao Lord: (1990) *Legacies*, and (1981) *Spring Moon*; and session five choices were *Bone* by Fae Myenne Ng (1993) and *Rice Room* by Ben Fong-Torres (1994). All books supported the instructor's three stated purposes for the class: "To broaden cultural perspectives and appreciation, to broaden knowledge of superb literature by authors of color, and to broaden our understanding of cultural changes not only by generation, but by geographical location."

To obtain an empirical measure of the ethnic identities of participants at the beginning of the course, I administered Helms' (1993) White Racial Attitude Identity Scale (WRIAS). These scores were compared both with participants' own post- scores when the scale was re-administered at the end of the class, and with the scores obtained from a control who had not taken a similar course. Treatment participants and the control group were comparable in terms of their gender (all were female), annual household incomes (T = $58,000, C= $53,000), years of teaching experience (T=13.0 years, C=12.2 years) and demographics of current suburban teaching assignments. At the end of the study, I conducted interviews with four participants whose assigned stages of racial/ethnic identity as measured by the WRIAS were at the autonomy level of development, to elicit their experiences of and responses to the class, and to share my emerging analysis. I selected Autonomous individuals for two reasons: first, Autonomy was the one level of racial/ethnic development which showed significant positive change pre- and posttreatment for participants in the study; and second, I was interested in participant perceptions of change, and the ability to metacognate their participation in the multicultural literature class. Taken together, these sources of data illuminated four fundamental questions:

1. What are participants' understandings of race and ethnicity as they participate in literature circles reading ethnically diverse authors?
2. How do participants interpret multicultural literatures in relation to their own culture and ethnicity?
3. What do participants self-identify as critical in any growth in their racial/ethnic identity?
4. How do techniques of reader response and bibliotherapy support racial/ethnic identity development?

Observational data, interviews, and participants' written responses were analyzed and coded using Glaser's (1969) constant comparative method to systematically compare data from multiple sources in order to generate theory.

Findings and Discussion
Measures

Data were collected using the Helms' White Racial Attitude Inventory Scale (WRIAS) at the beginning and after the completion of the multicultural literature course to measure participants' racial/ethnic identity development.

Members of the Multicultural Literature Class completed and returned the WRIAS during the first class session, and again at the conclusion of the course after the final class session. Pre- and posttreatment subscores of treatment participants were calculated and compared for significance, and were also compared with those of the control group. Four participants were selected for interviewing whose posttreatment adjusted stage scores registered at Helms' (1993) autonomous stage of racial/ethnic development.

Three statistical tests were conducted, the results of which are aggregated in four tables. First, an independent samples t-test, the Levene's Test for Equality of Variance, was used to compare for significance of the pre- and posttests of the treatment and control group for all five subscores of the WRIAS (Table 2); second, a paired samples t-test was used to compare for significant differences in pre- and post-scores within the treatment group (Table 3); and third, the Bonferroni Multiple Range Test, a one way ANOVA, was conducted to test for significant differences in post-test scores among participants with the number of times participants had previously enrolled in this course as a factor.

TABLE 1
Summary of Treatment and Control Group, Pre- and Post-Mean Scores on WRIAS Subscales

| | Treatment (n=11) | | | | Control (n=10) | | | |
| | Pretest | | Posttest | | Prestest | | Posttest | |
	$\bar{x}$	SD	$\bar{x}$	SD	$\bar{x}$	SD	$\bar{x}$	SD
Contact	3.17	.38	3.00	.51	3.05	.43	3.23	.32
Distintegration	1.95	.34	1.69	.40	2.01	.45	1.98	.25
Reintegration	1.80	.37	1.77	.41	1.77	.38	1.68	.31
Pseudo-Independence	3.69	.46	3.98	.45	3.86	.56	3.91	.47
Autonomy	3.63	.32	3.93	.40	3.72	.27	3.64	.15

TABLE 2
TEST OF SIGNIFICANCE BETWEEN GROUPS

| | Pretest difference | Levine's Test for Equality of Variables | | Posttest difference | Levine's Test for Equality of Variables | |
	$\bar{x}$	F	p	$\bar{x}$	F	p
Contact	0.1227	0.189	0.673	-0.2300	0.643	0.433
Disintegration	0.0505	1.642	0.215	-0.2936	3.258	0.087
Reintegration	0.0300	0.080	0.780	0.0927	0.874	0.362
Pseudo-Independence	-0.1601	0.749	0.398	0.0718	0.272	0.608
Autonomy	-0.0327	1.074	0.313	0.2918	7.554	0.013

TABLE 3
Test of Significance within Treatment Group

| | Paired Differences | | | |
	x̄	SD	t value	2 tail significance
Contact	-0.0048	0.595	-0.09	0.971
Disintegration	-0.1524	0.406	-1.72	0.101
Reintegration	-0.0571	0.476	-0.55	0.588
Pseudo-Independence	-0.1762	0.486	1.66	0.112
Autonomy	-0.1214	0.466	1.19	0.246

Results

As noted in Table 2, the results indicate no initial significant difference between treatment and control group mean scores for racial/ethnic identity development on the five subscales measured by the WRIAS. Thus treatment and control groups were statistically equivalent pre-treatment. Significant difference in posttreatment mean scores for treatment and control group was found on one subscale measures of the WRIAS, autonomy ($F=7.554$, $p=.013$). While the mean Contact and Disintegration scores decreased for the treatment group posttreatment, the differences between treatment and control groups were not statistically significant with respect to either subscale.

The paired samples t-tests (Table 3) showed that while treatment group participants' paired mean score differences decreased on the WRIAS subscales of contact, disintegration, and reintegration, these differences were not significant at the .05 level of significance; the difference in the mean disintegration score was, however, significant at the .10 level. Also, while treatment group participants' paired mean score differences increased on the WRIAS subscales of pseudo-independence and autonomy, these differences were not significant either.

Analysis of variance procedures were used to examine effects of previous enrollment in this multicultural literature class on the mean postscores of the treatment group on all five subscales of the WRIAS (Tables 4 and 5). While times of enrollment had no significant effect on mean contact, reintegration, or pseudo-independence post-scores, the mean disintegration and autonomy post-scores of those participants who had previously enrolled more than one time showed significant differences at the .05 confidence level.

TABLE 4

Analysis of Variance of WRIAS Posttest Scores with Times Enrolled in Treatment Multicultural Literature Class

	F	p
Contact	1.2230	0.3177
Disintegration	3.6660	0.0462
Reintegration	0.4089	0.6704
Pseudo-Independence	0.0713	0.9314
Autonomy	4.2303	0.0312

TABLE 5
Analysis of Significant Differences in Mean Scores Varied with Times Enrolled in Treatment Multicultural Literature Class

	Total Enrollments in Treatment MCL Class = 1 (n=3) $\bar{x}$	Total Enrollments in Treatment MCL Class = 2 (n=3) $\bar{x}$	Total Enrollments in Treatment MCL Class > 2 (n=5) $\bar{x}$
Disintegration	1.53	1.87	1.98
Autonomy	3.64	3.76	4.08*

*significant at p = .05

There are several sample and design limitations within this research that restrict the generalizability of the findings to larger populations of teachers enrolled in similar teacher education courses. A major limitation is noted in the nonrandom selection and relatively small size of the sample constituting treatment and control groups. In acknowledging the lack of randomization in both treatment and control groups, other plausible hypothesis could explain the changes in racial/ethnic identity development scores from the pretest to the posttest measures. Potential threats to internal validity include interactional effects of the participant election process with other sources of invalidity such as history and maturity. Rival explanations for the outcomes of the study might include the effects of history, maturation, and/or testing effects on posttest performance of participants.

The quantitative data indicate that participants' enrollment in a multicultural literature class had a significant impact in promoting ethnic identity of participants when the context in which the literature was processed was managed by a highly skilled teacher using techniques of reader response and bibliotherapy. The data also indicate that the time necessary for statistically significant identity development may be substantially more than the traditional ten week course. Participants who had enrolled in the multicultural literature course more than two times had statistically significant mean differences pre- and posttreatment in Disintegration scores (X= 1.98 ,p=.05) and Autonomy scores (X=4.08, p= .05), while those who had enrolled only once had statistically insignificant changes pre-and post treatment on all five subscore measures.

Although the results of the research are favorable, there are clear limits to the breadth of possible conclusions we can legitimately draw from the data. While it is apparent that these participants made significant positive changes toward autonomy, Helm's (1993) highest stage of racial/ethnic identity, further research is needed to replicate the findings, as well as to test the hypothesis in settings such as courses in which teachers are fulfilling a degree requirement rather than participating voluntarily in an elective course with like-minded educators. The sustainability of changes and their application within the classrooms in which participants teach is also an intriguing avenue of inquiry. While it may be tempting to assume positive effects in participants' classrooms, further research will be needed to establish what, if any, positive effects are carried over to the classrooms of participants when they resume their roles as teachers with more highly developed identities.

Another threat to validity is suggested in the responses of the participants to the WRIAS. These responses occurred both as refusals to complete the survey, comments written on the WRIAS itself and those volunteered in the concluding interviews. Of the twenty people who initially agreed to participate in this study, five returned a partially or totally incomplete WRIAS and revoked their consent to participate, including the self-identified Asian American participant. When asked about their reasons for withdrawing, all five spoke of their discomfort with the WRIAS. The Asian American participant specifically spoke of her difficulty identifying with the White point of view embodied in the instrument. Five of the eleven participants who completed the WRIAS pre- and posttreatment either refused to respond to statements which they found offensive, changed the wordings of certain statements to more accurately reflect their attitudes and beliefs, and/or wrote and attached paragraphs explaining their actions. According to Helms (1993), each of these constitutes a "nonresponse" indicating participants have not yet reached "the relevant stage of development [and therefore] some items may appear to be meaningless" (p.69). Participants' written comments and interview data suggest that at least in the case of these individuals, "nonresponse" is a singularly inadequate characterization. Contrary to Helms' interpretation, nonresponse may indicate participants have transcended the relevant stage of development and reject the inherent racism embodied in certain WRIAS items.

A primary concern voiced by these outspoken participants was that the WRIAS, in framing racial/ethnic identity attitudes in biracial terms, gives a distorted portrait of participants' multiethnic awareness. One participant painstakingly crossed out each and every reference to "Blacks" and inserted phrases such as "people from different ethnic backgrounds" or "other ethnic groups" to enlarge the lens of the inventory and more adequately and accurately capture her attitudes and beliefs. In her attached notes she wrote, "I am uncomfortable with many of these questions . . . and the exclusive focus on Blacks (one minority)/Whites." Another participant wrote, "The fact that this survey is framed in Black/White questions alters my responses. I cannot consider my thoughts and interactions with Asians, Hispanics, etc. [on this instrument]." Still another claimed, "This survey prevents me from expressing my attitudes and beliefs about race and ethnicity because of its insistence that my world is only Black and White. It's not - it's in Technicolor."

When asked about the utility of the instrument to convey their racial/ethnic identity attitudes, interviewed participants consistently objected to the biracial frame of the survey. Said one woman, "I guess my experience has tended to be broader than that . . . if it had been framed as 'other racial groups' it would have been easier for me . . . I have a little more experience." Another said, "The survey didn't convey my feelings about race and ethnicity and social attitudes because it was limited only to African American perspectives, and didn't mirror the opportunities the class enabled us to explore . . . it didn't capture the experiences that I know and work with and that have helped me . . . It was bicultural and it was just very limited." Still another woman said, "I resented some of the statements on the survey because they didn't allow me to respond in a way that I felt was more honest. They were forcing me to consider just two parameters and I thought that was too narrow. I could have answered differently many times if it hadn't been limited to a bicultural framework."

In keeping with Helms' (1993) directive, these responses were tallied as a "nonresponse." Yet it seems probable that, far from indicating that the participants had not yet reached a relevant stage of development, these responses actually were indicative of multicultural attitudes transcendent of the ability of the instrument to measure. This raises the possibility that the gains noted within the autonomy measures may have been more significant than measured, and that there may have been similar changes in the other four substages beyond the ability of the WRIAS to detect.

This may be an opportune moment within multicultural education for Helms or others with similar expertise to craft an instrument for gauging racial/ethnic identity development more reflective of the multicultural world in which identity is created, perhaps one which tests Banks' hypothesized stages of racial/ethnic identity transcendent of Stage 4: Biethnicity (Banks, 1994, p. 228). As indicated by the participants' responses, Helms' (1993) bi-racial, Black-and-White-only paradigm was problematic when attempting to express the nuances of White racial/ethnic identity attitudes in a multiracial, multiethnic setting.

Professor Hansen-Krening incorporated three distinct aspects of instruction within each classroom experience which interviewed participants identified as critical in the growth of their ethnic identity:

1.   an informal lecture in which she provided background information using handouts and visual aids,
2.   the viewing of and responding to related videotapes, and
3.   literature circles.

These three activities were thematically interrelated and mutually supportive of each session's topic or theme. In terms of the time allocated for each of these class components, the majority of class time was devoted to literary circles: of the total twelve hours of formal class instruction, 58% of class time was used for literary circles, 21% for informal lectures, and 21% for viewing videos. While both the sequencing and the time allotted for each activity changed from week to week, all three aspects were present in each class. To illustrate the structured interdependence of these three components, I will describe one specific and quite typical class session.

The third class session began with an informal talk by Professor Hansen-Krening in which she gave background information pertinent to the assigned readings: *Go* and *A Bridge Between Us*. Since both books focus on generational changes in Japanese American culture, Professor Hansen-Krening explained the names for successive generations of Japanese Americans and discussed challenges faced by Japanese Americans in bridging their two cultural worlds. Issei, first generation Japanese immigrants, were denied both naturalization and the right to purchase land; Nisei, second generation Japanese Americans, comprised the highest percentage of those interned during World War II; Sansei are primarily the children of Nisei, many of whom have never been told by their parents about the internment, and Onsei are the grandchildren of the Nisei. She then introduced the history of the internment as a powerful force which disrupted Japanese American culture and adaptation, describing both the first and second phases of internment in terms of the locations and conditions of the concentrations camps. Population totals for each of the ten camps were given, and the special significance of Tule Lake as a concentration camp for internees deemed criminal for their resistance to internment was explained.

Professor Hansen-Krening then introduced the video, *Tule Lake* (Tsuchitani, 1994) a documentary which explores the experiences of those who were incarcerated within that compound. The film itself features eight different internees and their stories, told against the backdrop of one internee's poetry about the experience. In quiet and understated emotion, those interviewed for the film describe the conditions within the camps, as well as the profound impact the experience has had on their subsequent lives. The response of class participants to this film was powerful and emotional, characterized at first by tears and silence, followed by expressions of shock and anger such as, "How come I never knew?" (fieldnotes 3.14.96). Professor Hansen-Krening then asked class participants to form their literature circles and reflect on both the internment and the function of silence among and between the various generations of Japanese Americans represented in the books they had read.

Interestingly, this particular session itself was characterized by silence on the part of participants who seemed reluctant to talk about what they had experienced while watching the video. Many within the circle were quietly crying, and it appeared that people were attempting to control and process the emotion that had welled up during the video. After about three minutes, one participant remarked on this silence, suggesting that perhaps like those interned, they were stunned by the shame of the internment. Conversation then haltingly and tentatively began.

Within the literature circles, participants began to talk about the role of silence within that session's assigned books, A Bridge Between us and Go. Sometimes reading directly from the texts, sometimes retelling significant passages in their own words, class members related the parts of the story with which they had identified. These readings and retellings piggybacked on one another. As one person offered her significant passage, another would suggest a thematic connection to another part of the book which had similarly impacted her. Of the five members of the literary circle I observed, each member contributed at least three times, with one member contributing five times.

As the conversation continued, participants began referencing both the videotape they had just viewed and other books they had read to find similarities among and contrasts between the perspectives each provided. A variety of comparisons was made between the literary characters' personal experiences of silence, and the cultural silence among Japanese Americans concerning the internment explored in the videotape. Additionally, participants talked of times when they had lapsed into silence relative to especially painful and disturbing events in their lives, and speculated about the psychological functions such silence supports. Said one woman, "Maybe silence is like a scab protecting a raw wound to keep it from bleeding while it heals" (fieldnotes 5.14.96). The participants' cultural assumptions surrounding silence and voice were thus interrogated in light of an ethnic group's cultural experiences and perspectives, including an examination of generational differences in the possible roles and meanings of silence among Japanese Americans.

The other five class sessions were similar to the one I have described. All included background information which related to each week's assigned readings, included either portions of a commercially produced videotape or one of the professor's own videotapes chronicling her experiences teaching in China, and devoted at least one half of the allotted class time to literature circles.

In discussing the results of this research relative to the subsidiary questions I posed, it seems appropriate to address each question in turn, drawing from interview data where appropriate to illuminate and extend my classroom observations.

How do participants interpret multicultural literatures in relation to their own culture and ethnicity?

The presence of community seemed to be critical to the process of racial/ethnic identity development with multicultural literature. Jesus is reported to have told his followers to first take the stick out of their own eye before trying to remove the speck of dust from someone else's eye (May & Metzger, 1962). Apparently it has been true for a very long time that people find it is easier to see the "stuff" in someone else's eyes rather than in their own. This investigation suggests that there is a productive way to exploit this limitation in perspective by joining in community for the purpose of allowing others to examine our "eyes," and to help us in improving not only our vision of Other, but more importantly, our vision of ourselves. Cultural constructs are exposed and labeled as individual cultural values, beliefs and assumptions become visible, sometimes for the first time. Participants can then use their constructs to understand the literature and the culture it portrays. I observed two ways that community significantly contributed to identity development. First, it allowed for confirmation of understandings from which cultural contrast could be explored. Second, the connections between the experiences of the literary characters and the personal experiences of the participants were articulated, sharpened, and shared. This braiding of experience among participants and literary characters established the relevance of the multicultural literature to themes in the lives of participants.

Community for Confirmation and Cultural Contrast

In their watershed book *Women's Way of Knowing*, Belenky, Clinchy, Goldberger & Tarule (1986) established the importance of community both for confirmation of women as knowers, and validation of their experiences. This study lends further support for these functions of community in women's construction of knowledge, and suggest a third role: community for cultural contrast. My examination of both fieldnotes and audiotapes of class sessions reveal that participants were actively seeking and creating a community of readers where their literary tastes and inclinations would be confirmed while their culture-bound perspectives would be challenged.

This course in multicultural literatures for adults was held after school in the library of a local high school. Yet the content of the course spilled far beyond the allotted times and designated place. Participants usually began drifting in 45 minutes early, gathering in groups to share their reactions to the books they had read. As they grabbed a cup of something hot to drink, or helped themselves to the food someone inevitably brought to share, the talk centered on the literary characters they had come to know through their readings. There was an eagerness in these exchanges as people shared and compared their reactions.

The first book that was assigned, *Long Distance Life*, evoked an emotional response among participants; discussion of it began as soon as participants walked through the door. The following conversation which occurred between two participants before the first class was convened was typical:

"What did you think of Nathan? Did you feel Golden developed his character enough so that you really knew him?"

"I think she told us about Nathan, but showed us Logan . . . she revealed his character through his action rather than just telling us who he was, what he was like. I know Logan, I know who he is and what he thinks. For me Nathan was a shadow."

" Was this intentional? Was Golden trying to tell something about her lack of connection with his generation? You know, this 'generation x' stuff of kids without an identity?" (Fieldnotes, 2.15.1996)

As people milled around, greeting friends and colleagues, obviously pleased to be with readers who shared their tastes in books, the conversations centered around multicultural literature. Comparisons were made between the assigned book and texts by other African American authors, recommendations for related books were offered, and titles exchanged. These exchanges continued even after the class was formally convened, with groups of three or four settling at tables to quietly continue their book talk even after the professor had begun her opening remarks. Book-related conversations were the norm; whether the participants were gathered at the coffeepot or waiting in line at the rest room, the talk was about books. Even after the conclusion of each class, participants lingered to continue their conversations about the readings, both in the classroom and as they made their ways out to their cars. When I shared this observation with a woman who remained with a friend to talk about the books, she told me how grateful she was to have a forum for sharing the books she loved: "The people I work with just don't read the same kinds of books I do. This is the only place I know where I can have conversations about literature I love."

This opportunity to "have conversations about literature I love" is such a powerful draw that two of the participants had continuously enrolled in the class each time it has been offered for the past six years; indeed, 12 of the 20 people enrolled had taken the course before. The course seemed to fulfill participants' needs for community which theorists suggest creates the sense of connectedness essential to knowledge construction (Asante, 1987; Belenky et al., 1986; Code, 1991). Participants seem to seek a community for confirming their authority as readers as well as confirming the validity of engaging personal experience and observations as a basis for constructing knowledge. Community thus has the potential to help participants translate "their ideas from the darkness of private experience into a shared public experience" (Belenky et al. 1986, p.205).

Within this community of readers, participants had the opportunity to contrast their interpretations with others who occupied cultural vantage points different from their own, and thus to clarify the cultural values and assumptions which informed their understandings of the books they read. This was especially evident in the discussion of *The Secrets of Mariko* as participants wrestled with the nature of Mariko's marriage and the question of love.

The Secrets of Mariko is an intimate and revealing chronicle of one year in the life of Mariko, "an ordinary Japanese woman at the close of the twentieth century living in one of the richest nations on earth" (Bumiller, p.5). The candid portrait of her twenty-four year marriage to her husband, Takeshi, invites readers to examine the cultural values and assumptions they hold about what constitutes love and commitment in marriage. Participants struggled to make sense of what to many readers seemed like an unhappy, arid, and dysfunctional marriage devoid of intimacy and warmth, to understand what "glue" kept the marriage together. One participant posed the question to her discussion group, "Do you think there was love between Mariko and Takeshi?" The first response was a resounding "No!" from a woman who went on to analyze the relationship in very culturally bound terms, citing the lack of affection, honest dialogue, and power imbalances between husband and wife. Immediately another participant questioned the cultural assumptions inherent in this analysis: "Well, it depends on how you define 'love,' doesn't it? There may not have been intimacy, but there was security in the relationship. And commitment to family" (fieldnotes 2.29.1996). Alternate perspectives enabled participants to question the taken-for-granted values and assumptions they brought to their reading; this community of readers offered one another cultural contrast to examine and bring into focus the cultural constructs which informed their understanding of self and literary other. Said one of the interviewed participants, "What impressed somebody or what they recalled sometimes didn't match up real well with another person, and so it really kind of completed the picture" (Interview 5.1.96).

This process also paralleled Sebesta et al.'s (1995) Hierarchy of Reader Response. Participants began their exploration of the text with evocation, putting themselves in the place of the character of Mariko in an attempt to understand her world and her perspective. Identifying with Mariko, participants "lived through" the year chronicled in the story, retelling events and rereading passages that were particularly meaningful to them. Participants compared and contrasted their experience with the text with those of others in their literary circles, reexamining their original evocations in light of the perspectives offered. Participants then reflected on these contrasting experiences with the text to generalize about the meaning of their literary experience, and to apply this new understanding to their own lives.

I observed in these responses an exploration by participants of cultural commonalties and differences as readers explored their own and each others' stories in relationship to the text. Participants examined the themes of silence, survival, and generational difference to understand both Mariko's search for identity and their own. Drawing upon each others' varied and contrasting perspectives, participants paralleled the content and structure of Mariko's marriage with their own in dialogues about cross-cultural gender inequities to create a shared vision of knowledge through consensus. Consensus in this context does not imply dialogue devoid of conflict and contradiction; rather, it reflects its original Latin meaning of "sensing together." The knowledge thus constructed within this community of readers connected individual's personal, subjective experiences with the shared, communal reality, engaging contrasting perspectives to expand their understanding of cultural identities.

Literary Lives and Lived Experience: Braided Boundaries

Related to the importance of community both for confirmation and cultural contrast is the observation that participants used their literary circles as an occasion to explore personal experiences which paralleled those of the characters they came to know through their reading. Participants drew upon their observations and experiences to make sense of the stories they read, using their lived realities as a context for "living through" the experiences of literary others. As they responded to the text and each other, participants seemed to prefer a reading strategy of "reading into" rather that "reading closely," eschewing direct explication of texts and instead finding connections between the authors' stories and their own.

Participants narrated personal vignettes which related thematically to their reading. When, for example, the question was raised about whether or not Nathan, a character in Long Distance Life, "survived," participants offered a round of "survival" stories which examined the many different levels of survival they had experienced, from physical to spiritual. In their attempt to comprehend what survival might mean to a Black man such as Nathan within a racist, oppressive social structure, participants offered their stories of survival in the contexts of the oppressions they had faced, "living through" Nathan's experience by reliving similar events in their own lives. The telling of personal vignettes thematically related to those experienced by literary characters was present in every literary circle which I observed. Regardless of the book, class participants constructed bridges between their lived experience and literary others through identification.

How do techniques of reader response and bibliotherapy support ethnic identity development?

This identification with the lives of autobiographical others in a personal and empathetic way is remarkably similar to what Rosenblatt (1983) describes as transaction, what bibliotherapists refer to as identification and catharsis, and which both traditions claim is essential for a text to become a literary experience. Rosenblatt persuasively argues that literary transactions entail both aesthetic and efferent response: heart as well as head must engage a text as an expressive synthesis occurs between the reader and what is read. Participants in the Multicultural Literature for Adults class appeared to blend literary and lived realities, engaging heart and head in this synthesis.

Professor Hansen-Krening consistently encouraged participants to reflect upon the ways their cultural identities, with their imbedded assumptions, values, and attitudes, may have shaped their responses to what was read when contrasted with the world as seen through the eyes of characters positioned differently from themselves in society. Evidence from my observations of reading circles supports the speculation that this blending of literary and lived realities contributes to participants' construction of a broader understanding of self and other. Interviews conducted at the conclusion of the class also provide insights into the ways in which identification with literary others supports an expanded sense of self. Said one participant, "these books help me move myself along and be culturally with others . . . I look to move myself. If others want to come along, that's fine with me."

Participants also clearly identified the importance of a highly skilled and experienced instructor in order for the techniques to be effective. Said one participant, "It is very different having someone who can guide the conversation who has had the opportunity to have in-depth knowledge of [this] field of study, and can bring that knowledge to the discussion" (Interview 6.17.96). Said another, "She brings a whole lifetime of knowledge" (Interview 5.29.96).

What are participants' understandings of race and ethnicity as they participate in literature circles reading ethnically diverse authors?

One of the most significant understandings evidenced by participants was an awareness that they, as well as the multicultural Others of whom they read, have a race/ethnicity. Race and ethnicity are all too typically viewed as descriptors of Others, remnants of a reformulated colonial discourse which generates and marks a range of racially/ethnic and culturally irreducible Others as different from an apparently stable White self. This unmarked and unarticulated identity position precludes critical introspective contrast with the marked and articulated categories of Others with which the culturally dominant category is constructed. Ethnobibliotherapy enabled participants to begin a process Frankenberg (1993) calls "*defamiliarizing* that which is taken for granted in White experience and to elaborate a method for making visible and analyzing the racial structuring of White experience" (p. 44). All four of the participants I interviewed spoke of gaining an awareness of themselves as racially/ethnically marked, and pointed to the multicultural literature class as pivotal in making visible their experience as Whites within a racially/ethnically hierarchical society. This process was eloquently expressed by one of the participants I interviewed when asked how she would describe her race and ethnicity:

> I'm a White Northern European . . . my assumption [use to be] that other people should describe themselves and I didn't need to. I think that is a sort of stupidity or luxury that only comes from being a part of a majority group that one can make assumptions like that, [assuming] my group is just a given and I don't need to say anything, but you are an exotic so you ought to

explain yourself . . . race was something that somebody else had, but I didn't . . . it was kind of an unconsidered assumption. (Interview 5.1.96)

Another participant rejected racial categories as social constructions, pointing to the inadequacy of those constructions for capturing and articulating the lived reality of people:

Well, the only people I know that are White are albinos, and everybody else has pigmentation: light dark, or otherwise. I find those categories problematic. I think they don't allow people to be honest . . . children who are fortunate enough to have mixed ethnic cultures are forced to chose one of those [racial] categories . . . I just don't like it. I tell people to not answer that question. (Interview 5.29.96)

Her comment labeling children of mixed ethnicity as "fortunate" shows a sophisticated understanding of the double edge to the sword of economic and political privilege inherent in the category "White," as well as her understanding that racial/ethnic categories fail to match the social complexity we see everywhere within the global village. She rejected the category "White" as inadequate and exclusionary.

While quite different in their stances, both participants had reached a point where the understanding that we all have a racial/ethnic identity was *assumed*. The first claims her identity as a "White Northern European." The second rejects "White" and demands more complexity in order "to allow people to be honest" about who they are. Both of these White female teachers have crossed a threshold into a world where a cultural spectrum is acknowledged and embraced. It is unlikely that either of these teachers would see creating a "color blind" (Schofield, 1986) classroom as either possible or desirable.

What do participants self-identify as critical in any growth in their ethnic identity?

As revealed during the interviews I conducted at the conclusion of this course, participants considered three components of their multicultural literature class to be pivotal in the evolution of their racial/ethnic awareness: 1) participation in literature circles using ethnobibliotherapeutic techniques; 2) viewing and responding to related videotapes; and 3) the professor herself as a role model for multicultural awareness and appreciation. This aspect of instructor as role model is a key attribute in addition to the previously discussed need for the instructor to be skilled in the techniques of ethnobibliotherapy. Comments by two participants during their post-class interviews illuminate the importance of modeling by the instructor.

> She is a role model in the information or perspective that she brings when she discusses those things and the way she puts them together . . . I think most of us-if you asked for the difference between [the class] and just a reading club or a book club-many do read many of the same things, but without someone who has done some study in that area and has reflected and pulled it together. (Interview 5.1.96)

Another woman said:

> I think I see her as a role model. Her emotional ties to the people and her level of concern . . . it is sort of like a validation . . . and partly because she has made such an effort to be knowledge-based. I mean, she's not fluffing around without experience or a knowledge base, but she hasn't lost the emotion. (Interview 5.5.1996)

The significance of these comments by participants is very important in establishing a working hypothesis for further research as to an effective relationship between the instructor, the multicultural literature, and the participants. Remembering that the focus is White female teachers who will continue to constitute the majority of classroom teachers for the foreseeable future is also important. Tatum (1994) tells us that in the absence of "White Allies" (p. 464) to use as role models, White individuals attempting to develop anti-racist values and beliefs have a more difficult time establishing an operational anti-racist stance. In the comments of these participants and their specific reference s to the value of the instructor as a role model there is valuable confirmation of Tatum's claim. Regardless of the race/ethnicity of the instructor, the importance of modeling a confident, anti-racist stance is strongly suggested.

Concluding Comments

The Inuits, a people who have a long and intimate relationship with polar bears, call the animal "he who casts no shadow." I find this to be a useful metaphor for understanding the issue of White identity development. Apparently a lack of pigmentation within the hair follicles of the polar bear makes them virtually invisible to the naked eye, for against an expanse of Arctic ice they cast little shadow by which they might be visually distinguished from their glistening white backdrop. With no shadow, with no contrast, the bear cannot be seen.

Without cultural contrast, White cultural identity may likewise be invisible to the naked eyes of White teachers. White teachers reading literary works from the dominant canon in which the projected values, beliefs, and assumptions are indistinguishable from their personal values, are offered no contrast against which their taken-for-granted values can be discerned, evaluated, and owned. Like polar bears moving amongst the ice floes, White readers moving through a White literary landscape may find cultural boundaries fuzzy or invisible. They may even believe the literature to be value neutral.

Interestingly, in photography, too, the word used to express the degree of contrast is "value." High value in a photo results in stark contrast between clearly defined regions. Thus the polar bear on ice at noon would have almost no value; on a dark riverbank at sunrise, the same bear would have very high value. In the same sense, individual White readers of classic Western literature may perceive neither the cultural values of the work nor their own cultural values, for there is no contrast, no shadow, no discontinuity between the cultural constructions of the White reader and the work. When transacting with multicultural literature in community, readers find that in "feeling through" (Rosenblatt, 1983, p. 182) the literary world of the author and characters, a critical examination and definition of personal values is required. Since "that" world is not "my" world, both worlds can be discerned in terms of the other. In determining just what those terms are, readers look at themselves through the eyes of the "Other" presented in the multicultural literature. The contrast exposes the shape and form of their own values, and readers may be startled to find their own race/ethnic identity emerging magically like the images which slowly appear on white photographic paper submerged in developer.

BIBLIOGRAPHY

Asante, M. K. (1987). *The Afrocentric idea.* Philadelphia: Temple University Press.

Banks, J. A. (1991). Teaching multicultural literacy to teachers. *Teaching Education,* 4, 135-144.

Banks, J. A. (1993). Multicultural education: Development, dimensions, and challenges. *Phi Delta Kappan, 75*(1), 22-28.

Banks, J. A. (1994). *Multicultural education: Theory and practice.* Boston: Allyn and Bacon.

Beach, R. & Marshall, J. (1990). *Teaching literature in the secondary school.* San Diego, CA: Harcourt.

Belenky, M. F., Clinchy, B. M., Goldberger, N. R., & Tarule, J. M. (1986). *Women's ways of knowing.* New York: Basic Books.

Bleich, D. (1978). *Subjective criticism.* Baltimore: Johns Hopkins University Press.

Bumiller, E. (1995). *The secrets of Mariko: A year in the life of a Japanese woman and her family.* New York: Times Books.

Carter, R. T. (1990). The relationship between racism and racial identity among White Americans: An exploratory investigation. *Journal of Counseling & Development, 69,* 46-50.

Cazden, C. B. & Mehan, H. (1989). Principles from sociology and anthropology: Context, code, and classroom. In M. Reynolds (Ed.), *Knowledge base for the beginning teacher* (pp. 47-57). Oxford: Pergamon.

Cox, C. & Many, J. E. (1992). Toward and understanding of the aesthetic response to literature. *Language Arts, 69,* 28-33.

Cross, W. E. (1991). *Shades of black: Diversity in African-American identity.* Philadelphia: Temple University Press.

Delpit, L. (1995). *Other people's children: Cultural conflict in the classroom.* New York: New Press.

Erickson, F., & Mohatt, J. (1982). Cultural organization of participant structure in two classrooms of Indian students. In G. C. Spindler (Ed.), *Educational anthropology in action* (pp. 132-175). New York: Holt.

Fish, S. (1980). *In there a text in this class? The authority of interpretive communities.* Cambridge, MA: Harvard University Press.

Flood, J. & Lapp, D. (1994). *Teachers' book clubs: A study of teachers' and student teachers' participation in contemporary multicultural discussion groups.* Reading research project no. 22. Athens, GA: National Reading Research Center.

Florio-Ruane, S. (1994). The future teachers' autobiography club: Preparing educators to support literacy learning in culturally diverse classrooms. *English Education, 26*(1), 52-66.

Fong-Torres, B. (1994). *The rice room: Growing up Chinese-American, from number two son to rock 'n' roll.* New York: Penguin Books.

Frankenberg, R. (1993). *White women, race matters: The social construction of Whiteness.* Minneapolis, MN: University of Minnesota Press.

Gay, G. (1985). Implications of selected models of ethnic identity development for educators. *Journal of Negro Education, 54* (1), 43-53.

Gay, G. (1994). *A synthesis of scholarship in multicultural education.* Oak Brook, IL: North Central Regional Educational Laboratory.

Gee, J. P. (1992). What is literacy? In P. Shannon (Ed.), *Becoming political: Readings and writings in the politics of literacy education* (pp. 21-28). Portsmouth, NH: Heinemann Educational Books.

Giroux, H. (1992). Critical literacy and student experience: Donald Graves' approach to literacy. In P. Shannon (Ed.), *Becoming political: Readings and writings in the politics of literacy education* (pp. 15-20). Portsmouth, NH: Heinemann Educational Books.

Glaser, B. (1969). The constant comparative method of qualitative analysis. In G. J. McCall & J. L. Simmons (Ed.), *Issues in participant observation* (pp. 216-228). Reading, MA: Addison-Wesley.

Golden, M. (1989). *Long distance life.* New York: Ballantine.

Grant, C. (1991). Culture and teaching: What do teachers need to know? In M. M. Kennedy (Ed.), *Teaching academic subjects to diverse learners* (pp. 237-256). New York: Teachers College Press.

Hansen-Krening, N. (1993). Authors of color: A multicultural perspective. *Journal of Reading, 36*(2), 124-129.

Heath, S. B. (1983). Ways with words: Language, life, and work in communities and classrooms. New York: Cambridge University Press.

Heath, S. B. (1992). Oral and literate traditions among Black Americans living in poverty. In P. Shannon (Ed.), *Becoming political: Readings and writings in the politics of literacy education* (pp. 29-41). Portsmouth, NH: Heinemann Educational Books.

Helms, J. E. (1993). *Black and White racial identity: Theory, research and practice.* Westport, CT: Praeger.

Holland, N. (1980). Unity identity text self. In J. P. Tompkins (Ed.), *Reader response criticism: From formalism to post-structuralism* (pp. 118-134). Baltimore: Johns Hopkins University Press.

Houser, N. O. & Chevalier, M. (1996). Multicultural self-development in the preservice classroom: equity education for the dominant culture. *Equity & Excellence in Education 28*(3), 5-13.

Iser, W. (1980). *The act of reading: A theory of aesthetic response.* Baltimore: Johns Hopkins University Press.

Kádár - Fülop, J. (1988). Culture, writing, curriculum. In A. C. Purves (Ed.), *Language and cultures: Issues in contrastive rhetoric.* Newbury Park, CA: Sage.

Ladson-Billings, G. (1995). Multicultural teacher education: Research, practice, and policy. In J. A. Banks & C. A. M. Banks (Eds.), *Handbook of research on multicultural education* (pp. 747-759). New York: Macmillan.

Lord, B. B. (1981). *Spring moon.* New York: Harper & Row.

Lord, B. B. (1990). Legacies: *A Chinese mosaic.* New York: Alfred A. Knopf.

Maruya, S. (1994). *A mature woman.* New York: Kodansha America, Inc.

May, H. G. & Metzger, B. M. (Eds.). (1962). *Oxford annotated Bible.* New York: Oxford University Press.

Morrison, T. (1992). *Playing in the Dark: Whiteness and the literary imagination.* New York: Random House.

Ng, F. M. (1993). *Bone.* New York: Hyperion.

Purcell-Gates, V. (1995). *Other people's words: The cycle of low literacy.* Cambridge, MA: Harvard University Press.

Purves, A. C. & Beach, R. (1972). Literature and the reader: Research on response to literature, reading interests, and the teaching of literature. Urbana, IL: NCTE.

Rosenblatt, L. M. (1983). Literature as Exploration. New York: D.

Appleton-Century Company.

Rosenblatt, L. M. (1983). Literature as Exploration. New York: MLA.

Rosenblatt, L. M. (1985). The transaction theory of the literary work: Implications for research. In C. R. Cooper (Ed.), *Researching response to literature and the teaching of literature: Points of departure* (pp. 33-53). Norwood, NJ: Ablex.

Russell, D. H., & Shrodes, C. (1978). Contributions of research in bibliotherapy to the language-arts program I. In R. J. Rubin (Ed.), *Bibliotherapy sourcebook* (pp. 211-229). Phoenix, AZ: Oryx Press.

Sebesta, S. L., Monson, D. L., & Senn, H. D. (1995). A hierarchy to assess reader response. *Journal of Reading, 38*(6), 2-9.

Shannon, P. (Ed.). (1992*). Becoming political: Readings and writings in the politics of literacy education.* Portsmouth, NH: Heinemann.

Shigekuni, J. (1995). *A bridge between us.* New York: Doubleday.

Sleeter, C. E. (1993). How white teachers construct race. In C. McCarthy & W. Crichlow (Eds.), *Race, identity and representation in education* (pp. 157-171). New York: Routledge.

Tatum, B. D. (1994). Teaching White students about racism: The search for white allies and the restoration of hope. *Teachers College Record, 95*(4), 462-476.

Tsuchitani, Scott T. (Producer & Director). (1994). *Meeting at Tule Lake* [Video]. (Available from Tule Lake Committee, P.O. Box 170141, San Francisco, CA 94117)

Uyemoto, H. (1995). *Go.* New York: Dutton.

Vogt, L. A., Jordan, C., & Tharp, R. G. (1993). Explaining school failure, producing school success: Two cases. In E. Jacob & C. Jordan (Eds.), *Minority education: Anthropological perspectives* (pp. 53-66). Norwood, NJ: Ablex Publishing Corporation.

Zeichner, K. (1992). *Educating teachers for cultural diversity* (Special

Report). East Lansing, MI: National Center for Research on Teacher Learning.

Zeichner, K. (1993). Connecting genuine teacher development to the struggle for social justice. *Journal of Education for Teaching, 17* (1), 5-20.

Chapter Nineteen
Process Meets Product: Where Technology Enhances Staff Development

Maria Natera-Riles
National University, Sacramento, CA

Nancy Smith-Dramis
National University, Sacramento, CA

Introduction

It is not too often in education that we get two of anything for the price of one! In the partnership between Delano Joint Union High School District and National University, this is exactly what occurred. Forty-one high school teachers and administrators learned crucial teaching strategies (product) for reaching language minority students and at the same time acquired internet skills (process) for classroom use. An added bonus was that the educators created their own home pages to integrate the WWW into the CLAD (Cross Cultural Language Academic Development) curriculum.

This partnership included a collaboration between a private university and a public high school district which provided four special courses to prepare veteran teachers for the instruction of language minority students. At the completion of the four courses, which included English Language Development and Specially-Designed Content Instruction, the previously credentialed teachers and administrators were recommended to the California Teacher Credential Commission which resulted in approval for the CLAD (Cross Cultural Language Academic Development) Certificate.

The CLAD Certificate (Cross Cultural Lanugage Academic

Development) qualified the participants so they could meet the needs of their highly linguistically diverse student population. Since an increasing amount of national attention is focused on connecting high schools to the internet, National University faculty, charged with the responsibility for this partnership, made the decision to combine the teaching curriculum with technology. The partnership coordinators were aware of a lingering reluctance on the part of teachers and administrators to actively use technology, or as one enthusiast put it: "to get on with it." The decision was made to offer two of these classes in their pristine computer lab to remedy participants' lack of experience and confidence in technology. This action resulted in yet another bonus: a tripling of the initial enrollment!

Many comprehensive high schools in California are now connected to the internet; however, less than 25% of the teachers in North California have availed themselves of the opportunities represented by this paradigm (Natera-Riles 1997). National University has completed several pilot programs consisting of four university classes wherein professors work collaboratively with secondary teachers at their school sites. However, this project represented a first effort to integrate the WWW into the CLAD curriculum.

Survey N=41

The forty-one secondary participants completed a followup survey that focused on teaching and learning CLAD on the WWW. Key questions relating to their involvement in the delivery of integrated CLAD/Technology courses were answered on the survey. What follows should be of interest to secondary and university educators because it includes student reactions and corresponding faculty reflections.

Use of Gateways Links to the Internet

The instructor facilitated access to education web sites by providing highlighted Gateways (Education Sites) on her own home page. All that was necessary was that the teachers and administrators click on selected sites. The educators indicated on the survey that they used the Gateways to:

1. check out district/school/teacher home pages throughout the country, and
2. identify and research lesson plans in the appropriate content areas.

Use of the Search Engines

Despite the fact that initially the participants found using the search engines frustrating and fruitless, many did succeed. In order to facilitate the learning process, the class divided into two groups. The secret to success seemed to lie in small group instruction coupled with peet tutoring. In particular, the participants enjoyed discovering lessons that educators from other states and countries were sharing on the web. They also enjoyed finding content lesson plans such as those for math and business. The assignments included finding lesson plans that could be converted into CLAD lessons. Many found lessons that were already in the SDAIE (Specifically Designed Academic Instruction in English) format.

Sharing of WWW Locations with Lesson Plans

The participants exchanged locations which they found with lesson plans in specific content areas. Their original assignment was to create a thematic unit which embodied a series of sequential lesson plans. The plans if not adapted already to the SDAIE format were to be so converted under the direction of the instructor in the methodology classes. Selection Location Addresses can be found in the Appendix of this article.

Strengths of the Technology Program

The general feedback of the participants regarding the CLAD/Technology courses reflected increased skills and enthusiasm for both aspects of the learning. In particular, they expressed appreciation for the accessibility to so much information "in a matter of seconds at the click of a button," a marvelous new tool for teacher staff development. Positive comments were also made regarding the accessibility of the NU instructor and district technical assistance in the form of a fellow computer teacher. Co-teaching was a powerful element of the partnership.

Conclusion/Implications

In retrospect, the partnership between Delano Joint Union High School District and National University was successful in creating a new approach to staff development in general and CLAD Certification in particular. According to the survey results the participants acquired essential teaching strategies (product) for reaching the language minority students and at the same time implemented internet research skills (process) for classroom use. Added benefits included both the creation of school and teacher home pages and a tripling of the participants involved in the staff development process. The internet is truly a dynamic tool! Participants were then more importantly continue to be enthusiastic about the use of technology in the classroom. By understanding the basics of the internet, educators are prepared to face the complexities in classroom instruction that will surely follow.

References

Natera-Riles, M. (1997). Utilization of School-Based Web Pages: A Study in Progress Addresses Challenges for Administrators. Cyber Symposium-Columbia University, Archived in CD-Rom, 7/97. Available World Wide Web: http://nunic.nu.edu/'mnatera/final.html.

Selected Shared Gateways/Links

www.fsci.umn.edu/nutrexp/sh nutrition.htm/
www.yahoo.com.education/k-12/teaching/lesson-plans/
www.wowpages.com/nga/edu/nutrit.htm
http://www.teachnet.com/lesson/heafit.htm/

http://infoserver.eh.vt.edu/~p.e.central

http://www.coedu.usf.edu/~campbell/images/space.html
http://www.coedu.usf.edu/~campbell/images/egypt.html
http://www.jrac.com/cmsa/architechure.html
http://encir.syr.edu/projects/newton/newton.alpha.html
http://www.coe.missouri.edu/~kyle/edu/html

www.teachers.net/lessons/posts/posts.html
http://dpsnnet.denver.k12.co.us/bilingual/lesson/lessonplans
http://www.yahoo.com/education/k-12/teaching/lesson-plans
http://www.coe.missouri.edu/~kyle/ssmexico/timeline.1
Http://city.net/countries/mexico/

http://www.eduplace.com/ss/act/planvac.httn
http://www.amazon.com/exec/obidos/isbn
http://www.mcn.org/ed/cur/liv/units creative writing
http://www.msstate.edu/archives/history/usa/usa.html
http://dizzy.library.arizona.edu/images/palnes/execords.html
http://www.homecentral/ubc/tools/wiring/environment
http://hanksville.phast.umass.edu/yucatan/mayormath.html
http://ofcn.org/cyber.serv/academy/ace/math/cemath
gopher://ericir.syr.eduÖsubject/math
http://www.neufeldmath.com/angles.html

Chapter Twenty
Black English: "Ain't nobody can talk about things being about theirselves."

Running head: Black English

Kimberly S. Ott
Wichita Public Schools, Wichita, KS

====================================

The quote in the title of this paper is taken from research done by Shirly Brice Heath (1982, p. 105). The quote was directed from a third grade boy to his teacher who insisted on asking him questions about a story the class had just completed reading. The child's statement is an example of the lack of understanding about diverse dialects that goes on everyday in communities and schools all around the United States.

The Origins of Black English

"English was not an abstract construction of dictionary makers, but a language that had its basis broad and low, close to the ground."
Walt Whitman (McCrum, Cran, & MacNeil, p. 223)

The above quote by Walt Whitman serves as a reminder that what America's macroculture calls "Standard English" did not originate out of one place or one nation. It's roots are like those of a willow tree, they run shallow and are spread out to better pick up the many flavors of the earth.

Landrum-Brown (1996) cited two major theories of the origins of Black English: the African tradition of Black English, and the European tradition of Black English. The European tradition of Black English states that Black English is traceable to British dialects of old and middle English which Blacks picked up from the Whites who settled in the South during the colonial era. This theory states that Black speech is just archaic White speech that has been sustained by linguistic isolation. This view argues that all traces of African heritage and culture were stripped from the slaves.

The theory that seems to draw the most support is the African tradition of Black English. The African tradition of Black English states that Black English is really Africanized English which can be traced to the formation of English pidgins and Creoles during the slave trade. McCrum, Cran, and MacNeil (1992) refer to Black English as the product of one of the most infamous episodes in the history of our civilization: the slave trade. Black English probably began on slave ships and can be traced back to 1619 when a Dutch vessel landed in Jamestown with a cargo of 20 Africans (Lewis, 1996; Smitherman, 1977). The first extensive exposure to any form of English that these and other African slaves would have experienced would have been on the slave ships. The English spoken on those slave ships was in all probability highly idiosyncratic. Members of the ship crews represented a variety of different nations and had served on a number of ship crews under many crew leaders. The language that would have been familiar to most of these crew members would have been the Mediterranean sea-going lingua franca, Sabir. This was a language developed in the Mediterranean to cope with multiethnic crews (McCrum et al., 1992). Every slave ship that came to America was full of Africans hailing from many nations. Creating such a linguistic mix was intentional, the rational was that if the Africans spoke different languages, it would be impossible for them to communicate with each other, which would in turn reduce the chance that they would be able to unite and overthrow the ship's crew (Lewis, 1996; McCrum et al., 1992; Smitherman, 1977).

Once African slaves arrived in America, the primary task was survival. In order to survive in a new and hostile land it was necessary to learn to communicate. In order to adequately learn any new language a person must have complete access to it. Learners must be given the opportunity to speak it, read it, and write it. For many years, Africans who were brought to this country were not provided the opportunity read or write English. They not only did not have the opportunity to read or write English, but they were forbidden to do so. Thus, the acquisition of English was greatly inhibited. From this perspective, as African slaves attempted to learn English their native language got in the way. This is often called interference--the tendency of people to make the language they are learning conform to the sound and structure of their native language. Therefore, early Black English involved the substitution of English words for West African words, but within the same basic structure and idiom that characterized West African language patterns. The following table contains items from Smitherman (1977, pp. 6-7) to give specific examples of the translations from West African grammar and sound rules to Black English.

Grammar and structure rule in West African Lanaguage	Grammar and structure rule in Black English
Sentences without the form of the verb *to be*	He sick today.
	They talking about school now.
Repetition of noun subject with pronoun	My father, he work there.
Question patterns without do	What it come to?
Same form of noun for singular and plural	one boy, five boy
No tense indicated in verb	I know it good when he ask me.
Same verb form for all subjects	I know, you know, he know, we know, they know

Sound rule in West African language	Sound rule in Black English
No consonant pairs	jus (for just); men (for mend)
Few long vowels or two-part vowels (diphthongs)	rat (for right); tahm (for time)
No /r/ sound	mow (for more)
No /th/ sound	substitution of /d/ or /f/ for /th/; souf (for south) and dis (for this)

Landrum-Brown (1996) gave specific examples of West African languages translated into Black English:

1. *Predication with optional copula.* The sense of complete predication conveyed by a noun, followed by an adjective, adverb, verb, noun, or prepositional phrase. This is common in

many West African languages, e.g., in Kimbundu, "Enc macamba" literally means "They friends."

2.   *Semantic inversion.* Turning a word into its opposite. This feature is familiar in Mandingo, in which "a ka nyi ko-jugu" literally means "It is goodbadly," or "it is so good that it's bad."

3.   *Pronominal apposition.* Repeating the subject for emphasis. This feature is common in Yorube, e.g., "Eya me, ot cu" literally means "My mother, she has died."

The above examples describe what Lewis (1996) said was the actual progression of Africanized speech into a pidgin language that provided the vocabulary for Black English. According to McCrum, et al. (1992), a pidgin is an auxiliary language, one that has no native speakers. Pidgins are speech systems that have been formed to provide a means of communication between people who share no common language. There are three conditions necessary for a pidgin language to emerge: restricted access to the target language, lack of effective bilingualism, and a need to communicate (Landrum-Brown, 1996). A pidgin develops into a Creole when it becomes the first language of an individual, as occurred with the children of the pidgin speaking slaves.

Black English: Not just a matter of words

"Not only does language influence psychology, but psychology influences language."

Joycelyn Landrum-Brown (1996)

Black English made its entry into mainstream American life with the story of Brer Rabbit (McCrum et al., 1992). Brer Rabbit is an example of how linguistics and culture come together to create Black English. Black English is not just a matter of words, but a system with a unique cultural style. Style involves the way speakers put sounds and grammatical structure together to communicate a larger meaning. Style is what one does with the words. Style incorporates the total expression. In Black English, words may become "songifyed." Style encompasses speech rhythms, voice inflections, and tonal patterns (Smitherman, 1977). Like all languages, Black English is kinesthetic, social, emotional, and cultural. Sometimes educators fail to recognize these layers within the communication system. Many of the myths and misconceptions about Black English derive from the fact that most people see Black English as a dialect based solely on words.

Black English incorporates many styles. These styles include: tone, "coolness," signification, and playing the dozens. Black English relies on the tone used to pronounce sounds, syllables, and words. (Landrum-Brown, 1996; Smitherman, 1977). Tonal semantics is what gives Black English its "songifyed" or musical quality. For speakers and writers of Black English, one's verbal performance is a way of establishing a reputation as well as a teaching and socializing force (Smitherman, 1977). Along with superior verbal performance, the "cool" pose that many young African American men adopt is likened to the coolness that is considered an excellent personal quality in many African civilizations (King, 1994). Signification is another way in which one's verbal skills may be displayed. Signification refers to the art of talking negatively about someone through clever verbal put downs. It is a style of communication in which the speaker speaks with innuendo and double meanings and plays rhetorically upon the meaning of sounds and words. Being quick and witty is key to a successful response. Signification is veiled in metaphor; thus, the meaning is not stated directly because the meaning is contextual (Lewis, 1996; Smitherman, 1977). Signification serves three purposes: it saves face, it makes a point, and it provides humor (Flower, 1996). The African epic of *Sundiata* reveals ways in which signification has been used to declare one's grievances, or to begin warfare. The following is an excerpt of the African epic taken from Smitherman's (1977) book, Talken and Testifyn.

"Stop, young man. Henceforth I am the king of Mali. If you want peace, return to where you came from," said Soumaoro.

"I am coming back, Soumaoro, to recapture my kingdom. If you want peace you will make amends to my allies and return to Sosso where you are the king."

"I am king of Mali by force of arms. My rights have been established by conquest."

"Then I will take Mali from you by force of arms and chase you from my kingdom."

"Know, then that I am the wild yam of the rocks; nothing will make me leave Mali."

"Know, also that I have in my camp seven master smiths who will shatter the rocks. Then, yam, I will eat you."

"I am the poisonous mushroom that makes the fearless vomit."

"As for me, I am the ravenous cock, the poison does not matter to me."

"Behave yourself, little boy, or you will burn your foot, for I am the-red hot cinder."

"But me, I am the rain that extinguishes the cinder; I am the boisterous torrent that will carry you off."

"I am the mighty silk-cotton tree that looks from on high on the tops of other trees."

"And I, I am the strangling creeper that climbs to the top of the forest giant."

"Enough of this argument. You shall not have Mali."

"Know that there is not room for two kings on the same skin, Soumaoro; you will let me have your place."

"Very well, since you want war I will wage war against you, but I would have you know that I have killed nine kings whose heads adorn my room. What a pity, indeed, that your head should take its place beside those of your fellow madcaps."

"Prepare yourself, Soumaoro, for it will be long before the calamity that is going to crash down upon you and yours comes to an end."

Thus, Sundiata and Soumaoro spoke together. After the war of mouths, swords had to decide the issue.

(Niane as cited in Smitherman, 1977, pp. 78-79)

Comparisons can be made between this African epic and the exchanges that take place between two teenagers on a street corner or in a school playground.

"If you don't quit messin wif me, uhma jump down your throat, tap dance on your liver, and make you wish you never been born."
"Yeah, you and how many armies? Don't you know uhm so bad I can step on a wad of gum and tell you what flavor it is."

(Smitherman, 1977, p. 79)

Playing the dozens is another form of signification. While signification is the verbal art of insult, playing the dozens is a form of signification were one insults another's family (Landrum-Brown, 1996; Smitherman, 1977)

Shirley (Obviously expressing disapproval): "Girl what's the matter with you today? You look a mess."
Martha (In no mood to be criticized today, not even by a friend): "Aw, yo' momma." [Your mother is the one who looks a mess.]

(Smitherman, 1977, p. 123)

The impact of Black English in the classroom
"Ain't nobody can talk about things being about theirselves."

Student

When talking about the cultural aspects of Black English, the research of Shirly Brice Heath (1982) gives an excellent example of how social experiences of speakers and writers of Black English affect learning styles and school experiences. Shirly Brice Heath (1982) did a five-year study, from 1970-1975, in which she went into a working-class African American community that was located in a moderately-sized city in the Southeastern United States that she called Trackton. She studied the reasons why the particular African American children in Trackton classrooms did not respond as other children did. As her research continued, her focus became the role of questioning in language and socialization. Her study looked at the uses of questions in three different situations: the homes and community of the African American students who lived in Trackton, the classrooms that these African American students attended, and the homes of the teachers that taught in the Trackton community. As Heath began her fieldwork, she saw three main themes emerge: the teachers complained about the students' lack of response to questions, the children said that the teachers asked dumb questions, and the Trackton parents felt that there was little meaningful communication going on between teachers and students in the classroom (Heath, 1983).

The majority of the Trackton teachers were European American middle-class females. These teachers had their own unique way of communicating with their own children as well as the children in their classrooms. When dealing with both preverbal and nonverbal children, the teachers would provide the total content of the question sequences, i.e., they would ask the question and answer it. The questions that the teachers asked of their own children helped to train them to be expert question answerers and experts about specific attributes of objects around them. At the same time they were teaching the children to be expert question answerers about objects around them, they seemed to teach their children not to ask questions that would challenge the authority of adults. They also seemed to teach their children specific types of questions. Children were taught not to ask questions that asked for information pertaining to a person and not to ask too many questions. The Trackton teachers, relying on their own cultural background, could only assume that the African American students in their classrooms learned to use language in the same way their own European American children did. They did not know that within the African American community language was taught differently. The teachers thought that African American parents did not care how their children talked. They assumed that these children did not have adequate exposure to language because of nonverbal parents, and that the African American parents didn't spend enough time with their children to teach them how to speak correctly. Teachers expected African American students to respond to language in the same way other children did (Heath, 1983).

Likewise, Trackton parents had no knowledge of how the teachers of their children used language with their own children. Unlike the European American children, the Trackton children were not required as information givers to adults especially about information already familiar to the adults. Trackton parents never talked about the fact that some things were not to be talked about in the presence of children, yet when a child said something inappropriate, the child would be scolded for it. For Trackton children, it was inappropriate to give personal information to those people they did not know well. Trackton children were talked "at" more than "with." They were given more direct statements such as, "put that away," or "go sit down." When the Trackton parents asked questions they used an analogy type format. Instead of asking, "What's that?", they would ask, "What's that like?" (Heath, 1982). Speakers and writers of Black English seem to be more person-orientated instead of thing-orientated (Hale-Benson, 1986; King, 1994; Ladson-Billings, 1994).

Patterns that Heath (1983) found in the Trackton communities parallel two insights also found by Hale-Benson (1986): cognition is social as well as biological, and language and culture virtually program the mind so that the individual as a learner is bound and shaped by world and life view and the mental processes of their culture. When the Trackton children entered school, there were often conflicts in how the teachers expected the students to process information and how they actually did. Trackton students had little experience with indirect questions such as, "Why don't you hang your coat up?", or "Why isn't your book out?" These types of questions very rarely got a response from the students. Students would not respond until given direct instructions such as, "Put your coat up." or, "Get your book out." Students tended not to respond to personal questions asked by the teacher such as, "Doesn't James live on your street?" When asked these kinds of indirect questions, students did not respond and were often judged as "stupid," "uncooperative," or "pathetic" (Heath, 1982, p. 116). Trackton teachers pulled questions out of context and asked students about specific attributes of characters or objects. Trackton parents tended to ask questions that required an analogical comparison. Therefore, when Trackton teachers would ask questions about things the children had no experience with (such as, queens, elves, walnuts, sleds and wands), and asked the questions out of the context of the total story, the children were unable to respond. Not only were the types of questions being asked unfamiliar to the students, but the content of the questions was also unfamiliar to the students. The Trackton students could provide nonspecific comparisons without explanation; thus, in the classroom when asked such questions as, "What's that like?", they would often give responses that seemed too broad or even unrelated to the question as the teachers saw it. Below is an example of a typical Trackton student's response to a question asked by a teacher.

Teacher: (pointing at a symbol to be used in arithmetic)
         What is it we said earlier this sign was like?

Expected response: The mouth of an alligator. (an explanation used earlier in the day by the teacher)

Trackton student's response: Dat thing up on da board. (The student looks at a bulletin board for Social Studies, which has yarn linking various cities, the yarn forms a shape like the symbol).
                              (Heath, 1982, pp. 117-118).

The interaction of learning styles and dialect
"Knowledge is like a garden: if it is not cultivated, it cannot be harvested."
                                    An African proverb

There are two basic learning styles: analytical learning style and relational learning style (Hale-Benson, 1986). Children who lean toward the analytical learning style tend to be "splitters" (p. 30). These children think of the attributes of a stimulus as having significance only in relation to some total context. Children who lean toward the relational style tend to be "lumpers" (p. 31). They think of attributes of a stimulus as having significance to themselves. Heath (1983) was finding that the Trackton students tended to have a relational style of learning. As Hale-Benson (1986) suggests, most of our schools require the analytic approach to cognitive organization. Thus, those who function within a different cognitive style will not only have lower achievement, but their achievement will decrease as they get older. Children with relational styles of learning will most likely not be rewarded socially regardless of their native abilities. A child's native ability does not determine his cognitive style.

What Heath (1983) found in her study was similar to what Hale-Benson (1986) and Ladson-Billings (1994) have found: African American children have high verbal and reasoning abilities; and they have high levels of expressive ability and tend to be more people-centered than object-centered. However, the high verbal and thinking skills of the Trackton children are not being recognized in the classroom. The types of questions familiar to the Trackton students--questions that ask for analysis, synthesis, or evaluation of lesson data--occur mostly in top-level reading groups and not in the classrooms of the Trackton students. The language socialization of Trackton students had not prepared them to deal with the three major characteristics of questions used in their classrooms: they had not learned to respond to questions that were interrogative in nature, they had not learned to respond to questions that had expectations of feeding back information already known to teachers, and they had not learned how to respond to questions that asked for a display of skills and content information acquired mostly from familiarity with books and ways of talking about books (Heath, 1983).

Misconceptions surrounding Black English
"A log which lies in the river a long time does not become a crocodile."

A West African proverb

The research done by Heath (1983) and Hale-Benson (1986) have connected the positive aspects of the cultural backgrounds of speakers and writers of Black English with negative experiences in school. At home they learn to be persistent and assertive, but when they enter school these positive traits are looked at in a negative light. These children are labeled as having problems conforming to school rules and values. In the schools, the negative stereotypes that are associated with Black English diminish the reality of the superior verbal and thinking skills of speakers and writers of Black English. Time needs to be spent talking about the negative stereotypes associated with Black English Vernacular. The only way for speakers and writers of Black English to overcome their negative school experiences is to realize the falseness of these stereotypes and work to turn the realities of Black English into classroom applications that will enable speakers and writers of Black English to succeed in school.

Smitherman (1977) and McCrum, et al. (1994) talk about some of the public conceptions of Black English. The general public seems to hold the perceptions that Black English is a sign of inferior intelligence and that it is the language of the impoverished. An article in the January 1997 issue of Economist (Ebonics Virus, 1997) referred to Black English as the language of the inner city streets and the speech of the getto. This article also stated that nobody objects to giving "getto children" special help with their English (p. 26). What this article really seemed to say was that only poor people speak Black English. How can all "getto" people be classified as speakers of Black English? Black English does not include all African American heritage people or exclude all people from the macroculture (Flower, 1996). Black English does not just stand for a specific set of language features, it is an indication of a set of complex personal experiences just as we have seen by looking at Heath's research.

In Brian Lewis's (1996) work, he states that *Brown vs. the Board of Education* (1958), which ruled for "desegregation with all deliberate speed," put African American children speaking Black English into the classroom and placed the language at the feet of educators (Lewis, 1996). According to Smitherman (1977), many schools have taken the position that African American children are culturally deprived, and therefore need to be culturally enriched. Cultural differences appear to represent inferiorities that must be eliminated. According to Flower (1996), educators are afraid that Black English will become a different standard of English and that African American children will continue to come to school with speech patterns that are hard to break.

Educators may think that African American children have coding-decoding problems that prevent them from being able to speak Standard English (Smitherman, 1977). Teachers often think that if a student cannot speak a complete sentence in Standard English, he/she cannot think in a complete sentence or cannot think at all.

Conclusion

"Not to know is bad; not to wish to know is worse."
An African Proverb

Black English has its own rich history, carrying with it all of the things that make any language unique unto itself. As well as a rich history, Black English also has its own unique style. Despite all of this, Black English continues to be a controversial topic in the field of education. There have been, and continue to be, misconceptions about Black English. A better understanding of Black English will help teachers develop quality learning experiences for the speakers and writers of Black English in their classrooms.

References

Ebonics Virus. (1997, January 4). Economist, 342, 26-27.

Flower, L. (1996). Negotiating the meaning of difference. Written Communication, 13, 44-64.

Hale-Benson, J. E. (1986). Black children: Their roots, culture, and learning styles. Baltimore, MD: Johns Hopkins University Press.

Heath, S. B. (1982). Questioning at home and at school. In G. Spindler (Ed.), Doing the ethnography of schooling (pp. 102-131). Prospect Heights, IL: Waveland Press.

Heath, S. B. (1983). Ways with words: Language, life, and work in communities and classrooms. Cambridge, MA: University Press.

King, J. E. (1994). The purpose of schooling for African American children: Including cultural knowledge. In E. R. Hollins, J. E. King, & W. C. Hayman (Eds.), Teaching diverse populations: Formulating a knowledge base (pp.25-56). Albany, NY: State University of New York Press.

Ladson-Billings, G. (1994) Who will teach our children: Preparing teachers to successfully teach African American students. In E. R. Hollins, J. E. King, & W. C. Hayman (Eds.), Teaching diverse populations: Formulation a knowledge base (pp. 129-158). Albany, NY: State University of New York Press.

Landrum-Brown, J. (1996). Black English. [Online] Available: www.west.net/~joyland/BlkEng.html [1995, March 24].

Lewis, B. C. (1996). Black English: Its history and its role in the education of our children. [Online] Available: www.princeton.edu/~bclewis/blacktalk.html [1995, September 15].

McCrum, R., Cran, W., & MacNeil, R. (1992). The story of English. New York, NY: Penguin Books.

Smitherman, G. (1977). Talken and Testifyn: The language of Black America. Boston, MA: Houghton Mifflin.

Chapter Twenty-One
Transformative Curriculum Development Through
Exploration of Identities of Self and Others

Irene S. Shigaki
New York University

Kelly Holloran
New York University

Introduction

The purpose of this chapter is to introduce teachers throughout the elementary grades to experiences which will be helpful in the development of a transformative multicultural curriculum--a critical examination of concepts or themes grounded in multiple perspectives integrated in a coherent manner to reflect its complexity (Banks, 1994; Garcia, 1991; Kendall, 1996; Nieto, 1996). After describing the sources for our workshop and this chapter, a four-step process for encouraging participants to engage in transformative curriculum development built on exploration of identities of self and others will be described.

The origin of the ideas which were shared in our workshop stemmed from a course, "Teaching for Multicultural Understandings," which one of the authors created for graduate students in education at a large urban university. Issues regarding many forms of diversity were examined each semester, including race, ethnicity, culture, language, gender, age, sexual orientation, and physical and mental challenges. Class members working in collaborative dyads applied their insights to the development of a variety of curricula appropriate for the early childhood and elementary grades. Subsequently, four teams were invited to continue to develop and refine their curricula with the goal of publication. Our workshop has been greatly informed by our experiences with the publication group where issues including the nature of collaborations, the dynamics of racism, and white privilege were regularly explored. Through the process of dialoguing with the participants at our workshop, our conceptualization was further influenced by their reactions and suggestions. What is reported below is our current synthesis and articulation of a transformative curriculum making process. We gratefully acknowledge the contributions and comments of our participants which strengthen the work..

Employing a four-step process, our workshop utilized a participatory and interactive format within the allocated ninety-minute time period. Promising beginning explorations were made by those in attendance, despite the time constraints. We feel that our four-step process can easily be adapted to other settings with more liberal time allotment thus permitting greater depth of investigation.(See Appendix A for a revised outline of the workshop).

Stage One - Self

The first stage focused on self. Participants were asked to share what meanings their names had for them. For the opening activity, participants worked in triads, a relatively low-risk setting. Conversations emerged comfortably as members of the triads shared part of their heritage with the goal of affirmation of self. The ease with which those in attendance were able to engage in the activities was surely influenced by the fact that our session was scheduled on the third day of a five-day, highly participatory conference where the overall tone was one of collegiality and general commitment to promoting respect for diversity. During our assessment period at the end of the workshop several suggestions pertinent to this stage were made. One participant explained that she was initially uncomfortable since she was unable to say what meaning her name had. Another participant mentioned that he had been asked the same question in another setting thus it lacked freshness for him. We concluded that it would be better to plan for choices to be available in this activity so that participants could select questions to respond to that were both meaningful and novel for them, thus stimulating fresh thinking.

Stage Two - Others

For Stage Two, we had planned on combining two dyads to form foursomes, but since the total number of participants was small, we opted to continue to have them work in the same triads. By doing so the participants were able to build on the initial relationships formed in Stage One. In exploring others, participants were provided with a series of questions regarding their childhood and focusing on their experiences of diversity-especially in school settings. The questions were not intended to be prescriptive but rather suggested possibilities that might be explored in the process of sharing, hearing, and validating one's own life and that of others in the triads. The small groups were also encouraged to reflect on the information shared in terms of unique qualities as well as similarities. Total group sharing followed, where highlights of individual biographies were summarized and patterns across the two triads were further examined. An alternative activity could utilize short stories or excerpts reflecting a particular ethnic or cultural perspective together with a discussion of that literature.

Stages One and Two were viewed as important precursors to collaborative curriculum building, encouraging teachers to reflect on who they are and establish a working relationship open to the perspectives of others. Banks (1994) recommends a process of self-clarification for teachers leading to clarified cultural identity prior to implementation of a transformational curriculum (p. 159). Additional work in this area would undoubtedly be helpful to promote self-clarification and develop tolerance for the many forms of diversity represented in our society.

Stage Three - Transformative Curriculum Development

Banks (1994) has asserted that, "The transformative curriculum changes basic assumptions and enables students to view concepts, issues, themes, and problems from diverse ethnic and cultural perspectives" (p. 10). We would also like to explicitly acknowledge other perspectives associated with sources of diversity due to age, gender, sexual orientation, and physicay and mental challenges. Critical thinking skills are crucial tools for students negotiating a transformative curriculum. In analyzing two accounts of the same event from differing perspectives, students are encouraged to consider the purpose of the author, his or her point of view, and how that perspective compares and contrasts with other sources (Banks, 1994, p. 10). Our experience has been that transformative curricula for the elementary years should include the dominant canon as one of the perspectives to be explored. Given the limited life experiences of elementary-age students, one cannot assume that they have sufficient knowledge of the dominant canon. Ability to critique both the dominant canon and alternate or complementary perspectives is an important goal.

The process described above can be facilitated by appropriate questions to guide the inquiry. Listed in Appendix A are some sample questions designed to encourage transformative curriculum development. These questions should be viewed as advisory and should be adapted to the nature of the theme under investigation as well as the age and capabilities of the students. In the paragraphs to follow, materials gathered for the workshop will be described together with suggestions from the participants.

Sets of children's picture books grouped by theme served as content for curriculum development. (See Appendix B for a revised annotated bibliography). The themes represented by the books can be examined individually or in interrelated clusters. They will be explored in three groupings below: 1) Families, Breaking Gender Stereotypes, and Age Bias; 2) Two Thanksgivings, Immigrants' Recall Their Homelands and Some Views of Life in New York; and 3) The Impact of War. The process of classification can be helpful in providing some focus but can also be somewhat arbitrary. Thus, while the first cluster focuses on the family, one might also examine the family in the context of immigration or the impact of war. These materials represent only some of the possibilities and can be modified, extended or replaced with other themes better suited to the needs of particular classrooms.

Families: The concept of family is often explored in the early childhood grades. The many configurations which families take has been increasingly portrayed in children's literature. Our bibliography includes some of these possibilities: a traditional ethnic intact family, the second family of a divorced parent, a family with two dads, and a multi-racial family through adoption. Other significant dimensions of families such as socio-economic class can also be investigated through children's literature (e.g., Estes, 1944; Thompson, 1983,).

Families are pivotal in encouraging or discouraging full exploration of the potential of both boys and girls. The books included in Appendix B under Breaking Gender Stereotypes explore nurturing, reflective, and aesthetic roles for boys and unlimited possibilities for girls. It is also worth noting, as did one workshop participant, that in addition to expanding gender roles, Oliver Button is a sissy is a good vehicle for examining name-calling and its pernicious effects. Finally, in enlarging options for both boys and girls, their choice of a traditional gender role for themselves must also be affirmed.

Grandmothers commonly intervened on behalf of grandchildren in their quest to be themselves in the books (see e.g., Hoffman, 1991 and Zolotow, 1972). In addressing age bias, such positive interactions may serve as useful bridges in helping children appreciate the value of the elderly. In our highly age-stratified society, children too may have felt unfairly excluded because of their age. Discussing such experiences would be useful in helping them become more empathetic regarding the problem of age discrimination.

Immigration: The pattern of immigration to the United States can be characterized as a succession of waves which continues to provide us with committed new citizens. The on-going nature of the immigration process can be examined through multiple strands, including an historical thread as well as an examination of current issues. Some themes that are relatively accessible to elementary school children include: reasons for coming to the United States, immigrant views of their countries of origin, and experiences of different groups living in the United States. The voyage of the pilgrims and the origin · of Thanksgiving is a common starting point. Representing the dominant canon, the beautifully illustrated (San Souci, 1991) can be juxtaposed with a Native American view of Thanksgiving. Comparing and contrasting the accounts, and considering each author's purpose and basic assumptions, should be a part of the inquiry. A contemporary version of Thanksgiving can be found in (Bunting, 1988) where its spirit is applied to a new context.

Religious and political persecution and economic necessity are often cited as reasons for emigrating to the U.S. What is sometimes forgotten is the nostalgic ties to their birth places that many immigrants still maintain. The books in the set Immigrants' Recall Their Homelands convey these feelings eloquently. Materials expressing a wider range of feelings regarding the homelands including bitterness and anger in addition to nostalgia, should also be made available in the classroom.

New York City has served as the gateway to the United States for many immigrant groups, as well as the destination for internal migration of African Americans and Puerto Ricans. The experiences of recent immigrants as well as those of well-established cultural groups are abundantly documented in books for children which are worthy of study.

Impact of War: Of all the themes explored in the workshop, Impact of War was the most complex. The books selected for this set reflect the complexity of the theme through exploration of many of its facets: the hopes and fears of children living amidst the destruction of war, dreams of freedom nurtured in a Thai refugee camp, the perplexing experiences of Japanese Americans interned during World War II,as well as Jewish refugees befriended by a Japanese diplomat contrary to his government's policy. Workshop participants articulated the theme as: War is a no-win situation; there are only losers.

Strong political and emotional associations covering a diverse spectrum are often made with specific wars. Presentation of the dominant canon to elementary age students as one perspective becomes particularly crucial in this context to provide a point of comparison when exposed to alternate views. For example, using a literature-based approach to the teaching of social studies, one teacher introduced his fourth grade class to World War II through books on the internment of Japanese Americans and the bombing of Hiroshima, reported a graduate student whose son was in the class (e.g., Mochizuki, 1993; Uchida, 1993; and Coerr, 1977). Understandably, her son was confused about the American role in World War II since the bombing of Pearl Harbor and the larger context of the war were insufficiently addressed. The graduate student was advised to speak with the teacher to discuss the importance of providing a sufficient contextual framework for understanding the books. Perhaps, it was suggested, her child's grandfather who had served in the military during the war might share some of his experiences with the class.

Our goal in creating a transformative multicultural curriculum integrating many voices is to evoke the intricacies of human affairs. By providing children with as complete and honest an account as they are able to assimilate, and insuring that they are skilled in critical thinking so that they can process the information thoughtfully, our hope is that our students will come to understand and affirm our commonalities and uniqueness.

Stage Four - Reflections and Assessment

Developing curriculum is an ever-evolving process. Reflecting on experiences in the implemention of a curriculum, and assessing its strengths and limitations are crucial to the process of refinement. The reflection and assessment stage of our workshop provided us with an opportunity to receive beneficial feedback from our participants. Many of their suggestions have been incorporated above. We, too, engaged in a reflection and assessment process shortly after the completion of the workshop, and recorded perceived strengths and limitations regarding the conduct of the workshop and its content. These changes have also been incorporated into this chapter. We recommend that the reflection and assessment process include both teachers and their pupils so that these varying perspectives can inform the development of the transformative multicultural curricula.

APPENDIX A
Workshop Outline

Note: Most of our work will occur in dyads or small groups to encourage as much participation and interaction as possible. As time permits we will be sharing this work with the total group as well so that we can benefit from the thinking of all participants. Please take some notes during your discussions to facilitate the sharing process.

Stage One:

- What meaning does your name have for you? (Kaplan et al, 1997) OR what aspect of yourself has special meaning for you?
- Choose one of the above to share with a partner.

Stage Two:

Think for a few moments about each of the following questions. Then share your answers with the members of your small group.

- Where did you grow up? Describe your neighborhood.
- Describe the first time you interacted with someone different from yourself. OR Describe the first time you felt different from everyone else.
- Where did you attend school? Did you think your teachers were similar or different from you and your family? In what ways were they similar or different?
- Share a significant racial experience that you have had. Why is it significant for you?

Reflect on the responses of your group members to the questions above. Discuss the following:

- What were some of the similarities?
- What experiences were unique? Why do you think they were

unique?
- What patterns emerged regarding the nature of experiences with diversity related by members of your group?
- What tentative conclusions can you draw about how we experience diversity?

Read and discuss a short story or an excerpt from a longer piece reflecting a particular ethnic or cultural perspective (e.g., Cisneros, 1989; Cohen, 1994; Frosch, 1994; Galang, 1996; Ng, 1993; Santiago, 1993; Silko, 1996).

- What insight did the reading provide you regarding the ethnic or cultural group described?
- How does your reading compare and contrast with your experience and the experiences of others in your group?

Stage Three:

Together with members of your small group, select one of the sets of books that is available. OR Select several books that you think may contribute to a common theme. Read through the books together. OR time permitting, create your own set of books addressing a theme your group has identified.

Reflect on the books as a unit:

- What themes do the books explore in common? AND What issues regarding diversity (if any) do the books explore?
- What was the purpose of each author? What assumptions were made by each author?
- What insight does each of the books provide regarding the themes you have identified? What insights do they provide collectively?
- How do the perspectives of the various authors compare and contrast?

- What might account for some of the differences you found in the perspectives of the authors? (e.g. differing experiences; reliability and authenticity of one or more source may be questionable).
- What are some ways that the reliability and authenticity of a source can be corroborated?
- What view or perspective is missing from your current set of books? What additional books or other forms of materials (e.g., interviews, photographs, videos) should be added to provide the most comprehensive collection of materials for exploration of your theme?

Stage Four:

Take a few minutes to reflect on your experience in our introductory workshop. Respond to the following in writing:

- What value did the workshop have for you? What insights were gained from your participation?
- What additional thinking/preparation must you do to develop a viable piece of curriculum that will be of use to you?
- Additional comments:

APPENDIX B
Annotated Bibliography

Families:

Estes, Eleanor. (1994). The hundred dresses. New York: Harcourt, Brace & World. (Louis Slobodkin, illustrator). *Despite her claim that she had a hundred dresses all lined up in her closet at home, Wanda wore the same faded blue dress to school every day.*

Garza, Carmen Lomas (also illustrator). (1996). In my family. San

Francisco: Children's Book Press. (In English and Spanish). *Growing up in a traditional Mexican American community, including eating empanadas and witnessing the blessing on her cousin's wedding day.*

Hoffman, Mary. (1995). Boundless Grace. New York; Dial Books (Caroline Binch, illustrator). *Grace is reunitd with a father she barely remembers who now lives with his new wife ane children in Africa.*

Say, Allen (also illustrator). (1997). Allison. Boston: Houghton Mifflin. *Allison is upset that she and her adopted parents differ racially.*

Valentine, Johnny. (1994). One dad two dads brown dad blue dads. Boston: Alyson. (Melody Sarecky, illustrator). *A lighthearted account of two children--one with blue dads, one from a more traditional family--who compare notes about their parents.*

Breaking Gender Stereotypes:

de Paola, Tomie (also illustrator). (1979). Oliver Button is a sissy. New York: Harcourt Brace Jovanovich. *Oliver Button is teased for enjoying walks in the woods, jumping rope, and especially dancing.*

Hoffman, Mary. (1991). Amazing Grace. New York: Dial Books. (Caroline Binch, illustrator). *Grace shows she can do anything she puts her mind to by portraying a fantastic Peter Pan.*

Zolotow, Charlotte. (1972). William's doll. HarperCollins. (William Pene DuBois, illustrator). *Though William was good at basketball and enjoyed his electric train, he still wanted a doll to care for.*

Age Bias:

Say, Allen (also illustrator). (1995). Stranger in the mirror. Boston: Houghton Mifflin. *One morning Sam wakes up to find that his hair has turned white and his face is wrinkled. Although he feels the same inside, everyone treats him differently.*

Scott, Ann Herbert. (1967). <u>Sam</u>. New York: McGraw-Hill Book. (Symeon Shimin, illustrator). *Each member of Sam's family is too busy to play with him. When he begins to cry, they stop to notice and find the right job for him.*

Two Thanksgivings:

Bunting, Eve. (1988). <u>How many days to America? A Thanksgiving story</u>. New York: Clarion Books. (Beth Peck, illustrator). *Caribbean refugees survive hardships at sea to land in America on Thanksgiving Day.*

San Souci, Robert. (1991). <u>N.C. Wyeth's Pilgrims</u>. San Francisco: Chronicle Books. (N.C. Wyeth, illustrator). *Recounts the coming of the Pilgrims to America.*

Immigrants' Recall Their Homelands:

Bunting, Eve. (1996). <u>Going home</u>. HarperCollins. (David Diaz, illustrator). *When Carlos' farm worker parents decide to take their family back to La perla, Mexico for Christmas, he learns of their special ties to their birth place.*

Linden, Anne Maria. (1994). <u>Emerald blue</u>. New York: Atheneum. (Katherine Doyle, illustrator). *The author evokes memories of the sweetness of life in Barbados and the loving Grandma who cared for her.*

Say, Allen (also illustrator). (1993). <u>Grandfather's journey</u>. Boston: Houghton Mifflin. *Like his grandfather, a young man comes to love both America and Japan. Both feel the moment they are in one country, they are homesick for the other.*

Some Views of Life in New York:

Dorros, Arthur. (1991). <u>Abuela</u>. New York: Dutton. (Elisa Kleven, illustrator). (Spanish introduced in context). *While riding on a bus with her abuela (grandmother), a little girl imagines that they are carried up into the sky and fly over the sights of New*

York City.

Harvey, Brett. (1987). Immigrant girl: Becky of Eldridge Street. New York: Holiday House. (Deborah Kogan Ray, illustrator). *A Jewish family from Russia living on the Lower East Side of New York City in 1910.*

Ringgold, Faith. (1991). Tar beach. New York: Crown. *This story quilt describes Cassie's dreams of flying above her Harlem home and easing the lives of her family.*

The Impact of War:

Mochizuki, Ken. (1997). Passage to freedom: The Sugihara story. New York: Lee & Low Books, Inc. (Dom Lee, illustrator). *A Japanese diplomat in Lithuania expedites the travel of hundreds of Jewish refugees fleeing from the Nazi threat.*

Shea, Pegi Deitz. (1995). The whispering cloth: A refugee's story. Honesday, PA: Boyds Mills Press. (Anita Riggio, illustrator; You Yang, stitchery). *Mai's embroidered tapestry relates the story of her life as a refugee living in a camp in Thailand.*

Uchida, Yoshiko. (1976, 1993). The bracelet. New York: Philomel Books. (Joanna Yardley, illustrator). *Emi receives a bracelet as a gift from her best friend when she and her family are sent to prison camps during World war II because they are Japanese Americans.*

UNICEF. (1994). I dream of peace: Images of war by children of former Yugoslavia. HarperCollins. *Drawings and writings by children from former Yugoslavia reveal their hopes and fears amidst the destruction of war. The book constitutes their weapon of peace as they cry, "Enough!"*

References

Banks, James A. (1994). Multiethnic education: Theory and practice (3rd ed.). Boston: Allyn & Bacon.

Bunting, Eve. (1988). How many days to America? A Thanksgiving story. New York: Clarion Books. (Beth Peck, illustrator).

Cisneros, Sandra. (1989). The house on Mango Street. New York: Vintage.

Coerr, Eleanor. (1977). Sadako and the thousand paper cranes. New York: Dell. (Ronald Himler, illustrator).

Cohen, Leah Hager. (1994). Train go sorry: Inside a deaf world. New York: Houghton Mifflin.

de Paola, Tomie (also illustrator). (1979). Oliver Button is a sissy. New York: Harcourt Brace Jovanovich.

Estes, Eleanor. (1944). The hundred dresses. New York: Harcourt, Brace & World. (Louis Slobodkin, illustrator).

Frosch, Mary. (1994). Coming of age in America: A multicultural anthology. New York: New Press.

Galang, M. Evelina. (1996). Her wild American self. Minneapolis: Coffee House Press.

Garcia, Ricardo L. (1991). Teaching in a pluralistic society: Concepts, models, strategies (2nd ed.). New York: HarperCollins.

Hoffman, Mary. (1991). Amazing Grace. New York: Dial Books. (Caroline Binch, illustrator).

Kaplan, Justin & Bernays, Anne. (1997). The language of names. New York: Simon & Schuster.

Kendall, Frances E. (1996). Diversity in the classroom: New approaches to the education of young children. (2nd ed.). New York: Teachers College Press.

Mochizuki, Ken. (1993). Baseball saved us. New York: Lee & Low Books, Inc. (Dom Lee, illustrator).

Ng, Fae Myenne. (1993). Bone. New York: Harper Perennial.

Nieto, Sonia. (1996). Affirming diversity: The sociopolitical context of multicultural education (2nd ed.). New York: Longman.

San Souci, Robert. (1991). N.C. Wyeth's Pilgrims. San Francisco: Chronicle Books. (N.C. Wyeth, illustrator).

Santiago, Esmeralda. (1993). When I was Puerto Rican. New York; Vintage.

Silko, Leslie Marmon. (1996). Yellow woman and a beauty of the spirit: Essays on Native American life today. New York:

Simon & Schuster.

Thompson, Kay. (1955, 1983). <u>Eloise</u>. New York: Simon & Schuster. (Hilary Knight, illustrator).

Uchida, Yoshiko. (1976, 1993). <u>The bracelet</u>. New York: Philomel Books. (Joanna Yardley, illustrator).

Zolotow, Charlotte. (1972). <u>William's doll</u>. HarperCollins. (William Pene DuBois, illustrator).

Chapter Twenty-Two
A Multicultural/Multilingual University Urban District Partnership that is Working

Nancy Smith-Dramis
National University, Sacramento, CA

Maria Natera-Riles
National University, Sacramento, CA

Rosendo Garcia
Sacramento City Unified School District

===============================

    The distance between the attitudes reflected in the comment "Many students came in rigid, complaining, whining" and those expressed in the comment "How am I impacted? I'm not the same teacher I was last February. Even after twenty-one years of teaching students, I'm different. I see growth in myself. I see a change in myself. I see a change in my students. My teaching strategies have changed." Is a journey of only four months. In terms of changed hearts and minds, it is a journey of light years! The journey has been win-win-win for the students, the teachers, and the administrators of the Sacramento City Unified School District (SCUSD) and National University's (NU) School of Education and Human Services. A minor miracle? A miracle, perhaps, but anything but minor.

    The journey started in the 1994-95 school when the SCUSD found its teacher ranks, especially at the secondary level, woefully thin in terms of teachers with certification for teaching second language acquisition and sheltered (CLAD) content classes. Such certification in California is through additional training leading to a Cross-Cultural Language Academic Development credential. SCUSD was to undergo a State Department of Education review to evaluate how the district was complying with the need for equal access to education for non-English speaking students. A determination of non-compliance could have resulted in a loss of state funding not only in the area of multilingual education but in all categories, a potential disaster of enormous proportions.

In fact, some of the high schools were found to be in non-compliance due to a lack of teachers with training and certification in teaching sheltered or English as a Second Language classes. Because some progress toward training goals and a demonstration of good faith in accelerating provisions for further efforts were in process, the district was given extended time to correct the non-compliance issues. The statistics for the district dictated a need for teachers capable of teaching students representing fifty-one different languages. For Director of the Multilingual Department, Rosendo Garcia, finding these teachers in all the necessary languages was an impossibility. The next best solution had to be providing the opportunity for training as many teachers as possible in the strategies effective for teaching students in English and content area classes, especially at the high school level. These special teaching methods and strategies were called SDAIE (Specially Designed Academic Instruction in English). In addition, where possible, provision would be made for the use of paraprofessionals who were speakers of the fifty-one different languages. Boiled down to essentials, it would mean that large numbers of teachers would have to enroll in classes in Schools of Education at the surrounding universities for certification for the CLAD credential. The logistics were staggering. Clearly time was a critical factor.

Fortunately, Rosendo Garcia remembered a parting dialog he'd had with a high school administrator leaving SCUSD for a position as a full time instructor in the School of Education and Human Services at nearby National University. The administrator, Nancy Smith-Dramis, had indicated an interest in remaining in touch with SCUSD to informally serve as the district's connection to National with regard to encouraging student teachers to consider SCUSD as a viable location to do their practice teaching experience. Rosendo Garcia was determined to pursue the possibility of collaborating with National because of the unique month-long format of the university's classes. This would mean that the upgrade to the CLAD credential would only take four months.

With this positive time line in mind, Garcia contacted Smith-Dramis requesting a meeting with National's Regional Dean, Dr. Sue Cooper. After a series of ground-breaking discussions, National agreed to collaborate with the district in offering a special four-month educational program to provide the classes for the CLAD. This marked the first collaboration of any size between National and the public schools in the Sacramento area. With a possibility of between twenty-five and thirty teachers being trained several times a year, Rosendo Garcia had reason to be hopeful.

The details to be worked out between the two entities were all that were left to conclude. The university's policy of offering a 30% lower fee to students in cases where the classes could be held away from its campus interested the district for two reasons: the appeal of a lower fee and a more accessible location to district personnel at a centralized school location. As a further benefit, SCUSD's Garcia decided to use his categorical moneys to purchase the textbooks for the students so that the fees would be lowered even further. SCUSD agreed to National's stipulation that the instructors be from the university's staff and that the course syllabi be those used in the regular credential classes offered at the university. Coincidentally, some of the district's teachers with the CLAD credential already were part of the adjunct faculty teaching at night at National. This was an unanticipated bonus for it showcased the instructional talent both at National and on the SCUSD staff. This again was win-win for both parties.

Perhaps the biggest surprise was the turn around in attitude on the part of the teachers who enrolled in the classes. It is an understatement to say that there was a distinct lack of enthusiasm on the part of the teachers at the prospect of attending class for four and one-half hours twice a week after having taught all day. What transpired was a tribute to the talent, patience and caring attitude of the university teaching staff and to the diligence of the district's teachers. The statement at the beginning of this article provides an example of a reoccurring theme in the evaluations of each class by the participants. There was almost a quality of awe in their comments at what they had learned and at their own abilities to change. Not a minor miracle!

We are now in the third year of the collaboration. Rosendo Garcia is now able to smile at the numbers of teachers who have successfully completed their CLAD credentials and are out there connecting with students who so badly needed their skills in learning English and other subjects. So far, over 120 teachers have participated in the program with the possibility of another session due to earn the CLAD during the spring of 1998.

Chapter Twenty-Three
Write From the Edge

Derek Smith
Bluebonnet Montessori School, Austin, TX

=========================

In American classrooms in the late 1990s, educators have identified a new and growing population of students. Presently, the predominate label ascribed to these students is "at-risk." The first question we must ask ourselves as educators is, At risk of what? The most general answers seems to be failure: academic failure, social failure, economic failure, and cultural failure. And who are these students? How do we identify them? There is certainly no shortage of tests; however, the pragmatist need only look out over the classroom and detention hall to see that they are easily identifiable. They are the slack-shouldered and the rowdy, the very timid and the dangerous, the latch-keys and the left alones, the black and the white, the rich and the poor, the intelligent and the dull. They are a broad mix of individuals, but over the years, what has marked these students without exception is their finding no value in our educational system and not, by any means, being impassioned by it.

In my early teaching years, I tried every gimmick and new trend in education to reach these students. And though a few methods did perk the students' interest, nothing seemed effective in the long term. Finally, as many mentors before me, I returned to my own experiences for a clue.

I was thirteen years old at the time, and I had already seen enough trouble and failure to know that I was skirting the edge too closely. From my posture to my pastimes, I was certainly "at risk." On my way to the bus stop to skip another day of school, I ran into Johnny B. Goode in the driveway. Johnny B. was a friend of my father's who would drop in on us occasionally during his cross-country travels. This particular morning, he was seated on his '67 BMW motorcycle, his back leaned against the sissy bar, and his feet propped up on the handlebars. He was writing in a worn out old leather book and seemed a million miles away. When I stopped to ask him what this was all about, he slowly closed his book, carefully folding his hands over it as if he were holding some sacred text full of secrets and spells. He told me that this was his personal journal--the one place he kept all the things that tormented him and the things that made him feel most alive. He told me it was the "mythology of his life's journey," start to finish and no bars held.

The idea of actually recording my thoughts and perspectives was more than daunting at first. But as an impressionable boy, the motorcycle, the leathery face, the wild eyes of this writer, and the romantically worn text were incentive enough to get me started on my first journal. What was to follow changed my life in ways unforeseen. In the daily ritual of writing, I began to see myself coming into focus as I had never before experienced. I began to discover the calm associated with reflection. In this calm, I slowly realized that I could do more than just be—I could become.

As a thug turned teacher, I have come to rely on these pivotal moments in life for insight into what can potentially be transformative for my students. The principles which frame this writing program, *Write from the Edge*, are very simple and are based on my own experience with the empowering effects of creative writing.

Write from the Edge is a creative writing seminar designed specifically for students who are courting the fringes. *Write from the Edge* speaks to the youth who will not listen, the youth who is unmotivated, and the youth who has not challenged him/herself.

The educational objective is to provide an opportunity for teenagers to define for themselves what they value and to translate these values into concrete goals. This work begins the creative process of self-determination, self-expression, and self-actualization.

Though informative, *Write from the Edge* focuses less on

imparting knowledge and more on providing a deeper experience of discovery. These students have demonstrated by their truancy and disinterest that being instructed concerning their life situations is ineffectual. They simply have lost confidence in their instructors and their grasp on issues facing youth today. Whether their assessment is accurate or not, it is clear that an alternative approach must be employed if educators and students are to meet and discover value in their discourse. Hence, rather than telling students who they are and what they should do, *Write from the Edge* challenges students to set aside their routine perspective and to independently question why they are here and what they will choose to do now. The focus shifts from teaching to discovery.

In small discussion groups, students engage in peer-to-peer dialogue. In this way, students begin deconstructing the walls of separation. Telling their own stories to one another allows students to gain diverse perspectives on their individual realities. Oftentimes, this is their first opportunity to genuinely be listened to, heard, and empathized with by their peers.

After this community building experience, students begin drafting their highest personal life vision through creative writing. Students who are generally intimidated by writing assignments become engaged in this exercise before realizing that they are, in fact, writing two page essays every two hours. Using a unique method of Poetic Visualization, students easily overcome fears of writing as they begin describing the interior of their imagination. These "imaginations" lay the groundwork for each student's exploration of his/her role in the rhythmic journey of life. As the heroes in their own myths, students begin sketching how their unique qualities of character and courage can determine their success in achieving their long-range, value-based goals.

Write from the Edge is not a magic cure the wandering youth. However, the program meets students at eye level, challenges their ability to rise to their own aid, and begins a process of creative writing that lends an opportunity for positive change in every student.

Session I: *I am . . . I am . . .*

The first session is designed to begin breaking down the barriers of self-protection that separate one individual from another. By telling their own life histories and listening to those of other students, they begin to discover the similarities and differences that define us. Students are astonished by this glimpse into the cultural diversity that exists from one family to another, while also finding empathy with the synchronous elements of all human culture which define our need for one another. This exercise also initiates the development of the fundamental trust among peers necessary for the genuine exchange of ideas and personal vision.

Session II: *Reality as I See It.*

This session offers every student an opportunity to discuss the external world they see around them: their families, friends, school, city, and world. The focus of this round-table discussion is to explore the direction in which they see humanity moving, as well as the power they have as individuals to influence and/or contribute to this direction. This exercise further extends the hand of trust among peers and affords an opportunity for students to own the responsibility of their choices.

Session III: *I'm Gonna Fly.*

The I'm Gonna Fly session gives students their first opportunity to write. Having discussed at length where they have come from and what avenues they see the world offering them, students create their greatest personal vision for the future. The two prewriting exercises have given students a peer or group-based context from which to forge their own insights and prescriptions. Emphasis is placed not on the product of this exercise, but on the process of recording original thought and planning. For many students, this is their first chance to dream their biggest dream on paper. Students are encouraged to embellish their writing, dreaming dreams unfettered and writing with liberated gusto.

Session IV: *Between Here and There*

Session IV is an exercise in pragmatic problem solving. In the previous writing session, students have proposed lofty goals and now must analyze and plan the steps that will lead toward achieving these personal goals. This is a very eye opening activity -- a self-inflicted reality check. Techniques such as visualization, story-boarding, journal keeping, and networking are discussed as means to improve their rate of mastery. Students conclude this assignment by challenging themselves to record these goals in their personal journal and to diligently pursue them in their daily choices.

Session V: *Poetic Visualization*

Poetic visualization is a technique used by writers to initiate spontaneous creative writing. Through oral storytelling, students are led along an artist's pathway. They enter into rich gardens that stimulate their senses with lush color, soft sounds, and the aroma of spring foliage. Here they are invited into the poet's domain. Once inside the weathered wooden doors, worn by the passage of generations of earlier poets, students write what they discover in the world of pure imagination. This is a dynamic technique that stimulates the listener's imagination and inspires a wide range of artistic expression. Students are instructed in the use of this writing technique for their writing assignments in school, thus taking the focus off of their fear of writing and placing it on concentrated writing readiness. By pealing the layers of their everyday reality, students are able to experience the ritualistic quality of creative writing. The calm felt during this exercise is instrumental in drawing students back to the writing table for moments of self-directed introspection and growth. For many students, this is a pivotal experience. The experience of having quieted their minds and journeyed through imagination in full awareness is very powerful. Particularly, students experience the Muse in this session. The realization that this experience can and does occur is dynamically instrumental in helping students find their own voices, and value their own recording of it.

Session VI: *The Mythic Journey*

Through a variety of media, students are introduced to the Mythic Journey and its heroes. Visiting the circumstances, trials, and triumphs of heroes ranging from Odysseus to Martin Luther King Jr., students begin to parallel their own life struggles with the hero's . The central theme of this session is the importance of following one's bliss, making decisions based on values from the heart, and following these decisions with unabashed enthusiasm and courage. This session is vital to the dissolution of conditioned paradigms and the construction of new self-visions, placing the responsibility for positive change and action on each student-hero.

Session VII: *I am the Hero*

The I Am the Hero session is perhaps the most empowering of the *Write from the Edge* seminar. This creative writing experience involves the student writing his/her own personal myth. By casting oneself as the hero, students begin the initial phase of positively transforming their self-image and self-concept with real, pro-active steps. This exercise allows students to creatively "plan" for the fulfillment of previously unattainable goals while directly influencing their ability to see themselves as successful, heroic individuals. This session literally causes students to take a step back from the edge in order to see the difference (one they have determined for themselves) between falling and flight.

Session VIII: *Myself, My Art, My Community*

The concluding session opens with a round table discussion of the day's experiences. Students have an opportunity to discuss new insights, commitments, and discoveries about themselves, their art, and the community as a whole. Emphasis is placed on discovering personal talents, refining them, and then sharing them with the community at large.

The seminar is closed in song:

"All I ask of you

is forever to remember me
as loving you."

Singing creates an intimate atmosphere as students sing eye to eye in revolving circles, engaging voice, physical contact, and movement. The resulting mood is quite humbling, leaving students with the distinct impression that they have traveled to unknown regions of the self and returned richer and more prepared for the challenges of living and changing. Of equal value, students take home three original essays by which to structure the achievement of value based, long-range goals.

Write from the Edge is designed as a one day, eight hour interactive seminar; however, school administrators or group coordinators may choose from any of the eight *Write from the Edge* Seminar sessions with a minimum of 2, one-hour sessions. Aspects of this program may be used by teachers to promote and create an anti-biased environment in which students from diverse cultural backgrounds may experience one another in an intimate and meaningful way.

In order to reach to these students, who by choice and circumstance have left our ordered halls of learning, educators must reevaluate the premise of our task. Unless we can truly demonstrate that there is something of value to be gained through writing (or any other educational endeavor), we will have lost those who skirt the fringes and teeter on the edge. Writing must become a tool of self-affirmation and creative change. According to my own experience, the only method of effective change is experience itself. We must initiate this creative experience and then allow our students to take the responsibility for redefining life's opportunities and purposes.

Chapter Twenty-Four
Crime: The Neglected Area of Multicultural Education

Fred Stopsky
Webster University, Webster Groves, MO

==================

Crime dominates the media and is a key issue in society, but rarely is the history of crime explored in multicultural studies. The relationship between crime and multiculturalism is a fascinating and complex story whose origin in the early history of America offers insights into the persistent strain of prejudice which has impacted our nation. Our failure to address this issue distorts the history of multiculturalism and fosters a crime mythology that erroneously links contemporary cultural groups with criminal behaviors. Studying the history of crime enables youth to understand the complex factors by which the media and those in authority propogate imagery that transforms poor people into criminals.

Young people have been innundated with a plethora of media images linking particular ethnic or cultural groups to crime. Crime, however, is a social definition and the rise or fall of crime rates is as much related to the act of definition as it is to the act of commission. What constitutes crime in American history has always been integral to the conflict over power. Native Americans had their lands legally stolen, their children placed in boarding schools and their language and customs taken away under pressure from forces of law and order. People who resisted were classified as criminals, particularly parents who did not want their children educated in ways other than those supporting traditional Native American values. Law in American history has been used to transform innocent people into criminals because they refused to accept dictates from those in authority.

The history of crime is a neglected curriculum in schools and the absence of information about this topic hinders endeavors to understand the multicultural heritage of our society. We cannot understand contemporary multiculturalism unless we understand that crime has been an important variable in the mix of how cultural groups have been perceived in American history.

Multiculturalism and Urban Violence

The arrival of poor Irish immigrants in the 1800s led to the creation of the first urban slums in American history. The Irish were fleeing from poverty, British hatred of the Catholic Church, and denial of the basic rights of citizenship. America was a promised land offering opportunities for Irish people to become participants as free and equal citizens. However, poverty and confrontation with extreme prejudice against Catholics forced Irish people to live in crowded sections of New York City such as "Five Points," which shortly became famous as centers of urban crime. The Irish, later joined by other ethnic groups, were clustered into crowded tenements in lower Manhatan. One study indicated that of 103 buildings on a single street, there were about 57 "grog" shops which dispensed liquor. The Irish were the first victims of the anti-Catholic core of American nativism.[1]

The Jacksonian Era is frequently taught as a time when democracy was being expanded in America, but rarely is the violent anti-foreigner flavor of this period discussed in classes. The 1830s witnessed an outburst of anti-Catholicism which was most directly aimed at Irish immigrants. Urban mobs attacked Catholics and their churches while the press spewed forth continual stories about Irish criminals. Irish immigrants were portrayed as criminal elements whose presence made city life dangerous for middle class Americans. This imagery provided justification for mobs to vent their fury upon Irish Catholics.

Abraham Lincoln, in 1837, captured the spirit of these times when mobs roamed city streets attacking Catholics and blaming urban ills upon newly arrived immigrants:

There is even now something of an ill omen amongst us. I mean the increasing disregard for law which pervades the country -- the growing disposition to substitute the wild and furious passions in lieu of the sober judgment of the courts, and the worse than savage mobs for the executive ministers of justice.[2]

This anti-Catholic bias was directed mainly at the Irish, and to a lesser extent toward German Americans.[3] Nineteenth century American history cannot be fully understood without studying the history of crime as manifested in viscious attacks upon Catholics in many American urban areas. Catholicism was viewed as a foreign-led religion controlled by criminal elements. The extreme poverty of Irish immigrants undoubtedly led some into a life of crime. The presence of Irish criminal gangs enabled urban mobs to sanction attacks upon Catholics, destruction of their homes, and even murder on the grounds that Protestants were merely defending the existing culture. "The settling of the frontier and the influx of non-Protestant cultures increased the symbolic importance of morality and religious behavior in distinguishing the reputable and the disreptuable."[4]

The influx of large numbers of Irish people in the 1840s who were fleeing the devastating impact of the potato famine rapidly expanded urban slums, which lead to even more virulent attacks upon Catholics. Mobs in 1842 burned a convent outside of Boston while rumors of a Catholic plot to overthrow the American government led to viscious attacks upon the Philadelphia Irish that led to 10 deaths and the forced expulsion of hundreds of people. History books ordinarily do not classify such actions as examples of "crime," but simply as manifestations of disorder. Killing people, wrecking their homes, and forcing them to flee are criminal actions by any standard.[5]

Nineteenth century America depicted the Irish as the mainstay of urban crime and the press continually portrayed them as violent, degenerate savages bent on crime and violence. Assault and battery in South Carolina was frequently classified by the police as "an Irish dispute." In the minds of many Americans, being Irish was synonymous with being a criminal. This attitude denied Irish people opportunities for work and led to fierce competition over low paying jobs between themselves as African Americans.

Upon their arrival in America, the Irish were thrown together with black people on jobs and in neighborhoods. A common expression among white nineteenth century Protestants was that Negroes were "smoked Irish" while the Irish were referred to as "niggers turned inside out."[6] The Irish responded to prejudice as other groups have so frequently in American history: by expending their fury on African Americans. Minority group versus minority group was a nineteenth century theme as people competed for work and social status.

Ironically, African Americans and Irish people cooperated most effectively while incarcerated within jails. Noel Ignatiev's study of the Philadelphia Walnut Street Jail from 1790-1835 indicates a remarkable degree of solidarity between both groups which, between them, made up a high percent of all prisoners. "In the larger society, while Afro-American and Irish-American workers often, and quite militantly, opposed established authority, they rarely collaborated to do so, yet that collaboration was common among the prisoners in the Walnut Street jail."[7]

Until modern times, criminals have demonstrated less prejudice than what was found in American society. Ignatiev points out that there was not a single example from 1815 to 1830 in the Walnut Street jail of a fight between black and white prisoners. Irish prisoners considered themselves "convicts," not white men. Prisons were not centers of racial harmony, but race as a social definition was less important to Irish prisoners than to their fellow countrymen living on the outside.[8]

Bigotry and prejudice, however, were rampant in nineteenth century America as Protestants clashed with Catholics, Irish Catholics fought Germans, and African Americans struggled with all other groups with whom they competed economically or socially. Nineteenth century crime and violence stemmed from poverty and the clash of cultural values. Irish gangs like the Pug Uglies and the Bowery Boys not only engaged in criminal activities, but assumed the role of defending their neighborhoods from Protestant-initiated violence.

Unlike today, rich and poor in the past lived in close physical proximity to one another. Few, if any, middle class New Yorkers ventured among Irish immigrants for fear of being robbed or violently assaulted. The stereotypes of Irish people as criminals and violent drunkards who love a good brawl became embedded in nineteenth century American thinking, and even today on St. Patrick's Day vestiges of this attitude can be seen in the media.

Anti-Catholic urban riots prior to the Civil War and fears of Irish criminals were major factors in the emergence of organized police forces in most American cities by the 1850s. It was clear to local political leaders that existing police forces were not capable of handling mob actions and a new institution had to be created to maintain safety in the cities. Ironically, the low pay and prestige of this new occupation led to the hiring of Irishmen as policemen.

The failure of textbooks to discuss urban violence in prior American history creates images among students that urban violence is a creature of the twentieth century and stems from cultural groups presently inhabiting cities. Textbooks ignore the most violent riot in American history -- the Draft Day Riots of July, 1863 when angy Irish people rebelled against what they claimed was blatant bigotry and prejudice (similar riots also occurred in Boston, St. Louis and Detroit). Irish people believed the Draft had been rigged to select Irishmen for service in the Union army. During the ensuing riots over 1,000 people died, including two dozen African Americans who were lynched by the rioters. The Draft Day Riots are a classic example of how oppressed minorities vented their anger at other minorities rather than uniting to collectively fight against prejudice.

Many Americans have images of African Americans rioting in

Watts or Harlem but few have learned about white American riots against other minorities. In March, 1891, after eleven Italians were acquitted for the murder of the New Orleans police chief, the district attorney of that city cajoled a mob with lurid tales of Italian gangster organizations such as the supposed "Black Hand," and then led the men into the jail were they killed and lynched all eleven Italians. A few years later, the entire Italian population of the city of Buffalo was arrested and brought to the police station for questioning about a murder. The assumption was that Italians were murderers and thieves. Few Americans are aware that of the 5,000 people lynched from 1865-1940, approximately 1,000 were White or of Asian ancestry.[9]

Crime has been a mainstay of urban life throughout American history. Conflicts over morality and behavior invariably have resulted in ethnic and racial clashes within urban areas. Violence more readily occurs in urban areas because of the ease of organizing people and focusing their anger upon a distinctive cultural group. It was common until the midpoint of the twentieth century for White-led urban mobs to attack ethnic and racial minorities. Discussions in the latter half of this century about urban problems unfortunately have focused upon recent inhabitants of cities rather then on examining urbanization and crime in an historical context. Urban areas in American history have been the focal point of clashes between cultures and attempts by oppressed minorities to assert their right to equality of treatment.

Prohibition: A Case Study in Multicultural Bias

In the fall of 1926, a lone plane circled a house in southern Illinois, and then one of the pilots dropped a bomb. This was the first example of aerial bombardment on American soil. The object of the bomb was the home of Charlie Burger, a Jewish gangster who had earned the wrath of the Ku Klux Klan for selling liquor and being openly contemptuous about the Klan's bias and prejudice against minorities. Burger derided the Klan's bigotry toward African Americans and its prejudicial attitudes toward immigrant groups such as Italians.

The Prohibition Era is ordinarily studied in schools as an example of the rise in crime and gangs. Few teachers explore the historical dimensions of the Temperance Movement or even raise questions as to the prejudice inherent in defining drinking alcohol as a crime. Humans have been drinking alcoholic beverages throughout history without being defined as engaging in criminal activities. Prohibition is a classic example of socially defining the actions of ethnic groups as "criminal," and then subjecting members of the groups to prison sentences for failure to adhere to societal laws. The multicultural bias of the Prohibition era is a precursor of contemporary bias toward ethnic minorities. The rich and middle classes drank during Prohibition without being termed criminal, just as today those groups use drugs without ending up in prison. Also, ethnic groups and minorities were more frequently subjected to punitive actions during the Prohibition Era, just as today they more frequently receive jail sentences for drug use.[10]

Slaves and Native Americans were the initial groups forbidden to consume alcohol and subjected to criminal penalties for engaging in a normal social activity. Whereas Whites could drink liquor, slaves were beaten or branded for daring to drink alcohol at a time in history when there were few non-alcoholic beverages. The rise of the Temperance Movement in the early years of the nineteenth century was led by Protestant ministers who wanted to establish a uniform code of morality that was consistent with their own values.

The influx of Irish and German immigrants during the 1840s and 1850s directly impacted the Temperance Movement, since the use of alcohol was part of their cultural mores. Germans enjoyed the social dimensions of Sunday afternoon beer drinking at taverns, and many Irish people regarded drinking whiskey as an integral part of their culture. Temperance advocates linked immorality and crime with newly arrived urban immigrants. "The Irish and German immigrants were the backbone of that industrial expansion. Wherever cities developed so did the complex of criminality, intemperance, poverty and ill-health."[11] Temperance was as much related to anti-alcohol motives as it was an attempt to cleanse America of immoral ethnic groups which were viewed as the sources of crime and immorality. Temperance, from its origin, was a Protestant movement seeking to save the soul of America from the evils of Catholicism.

The thrust of the Temperance Movement was to criminalize immigrant cultural mores regardless of how important alcohol was to German and Irish cultures. The moral fervor of Temperance supporters ranged across a host of issues, making them at the same time anti-liquor, anti-Catholic, and anti-slavery. They both wanted to end the spread of slavery and end the influx of German and Irish immigrants who were viewed as drunkards and criminals. The American Republican Party (nicknamed the Know Nothing Party), which arose in the 1840s, was openly anti-immigrant and drew considerable support from Temperance advocates. The Temperance/Know-Nothing alliance won victories throughout the north in the 1850s, including the election of dozens of Congressmen.

John Dow, a prominent Temperance leader, both opposed slavery and intensely disliked Irish Catholics. As Mayor of Portland, Maine, he launched an attack upon the "Irish cattle" who he believed violated state liquor laws. Dow and the Know Nothings attempted to deny Irish people the right to vote on the grounds that they were ignorant. Dow became known as the "Napoleon of Temperance," and was hailed by Horace Mann as a "moral Columbus." Dow and his supporters regarded Irish and German Catholics as leading culprits in propogating liquor. He criminalized their culture and drove many into financial ruin with the justification that their behavior violated existing moral and legal standards.[12]

Temperance remained a middle-class Protestant American movement throughout the nineteenth century. Its supporters became increasingly concerned about the growing influx of immigrants from southern and eastern Europe, for whom consumption of alcohol was a normal daily activity. Republican Congressman Albert Griffin, writing in 1889, decried the influx of these new immigrants: "Where they constitute one tenth of the population, they run nine tenths of the saloons and furnish a very large part of their patrons and of the voters who willingly vote as their owners command. This is the element that paralyzes so many office holders and seekers who would prefer to do right." Since temperance supporters blamed alcohol for crime, they invariably accused its consumers of being criminals, or as Congressman Griffin noted, of being "depraved."[13]

The Temperance Movement did not achieve its final success until the advent of World War I when Germany became America's enemy. America's entry into the war provided Prohibitionists an opportunity to link temperance with the prevailing anti-German spirit. As John Kobler notes, "it was not hard to whip up popular hatred of the big brewers with their German names and background. The U.S. Brewers' Association, purblind as ever, facilitated the assault by contributing large subsidies to the antiprohibitionist National German-American Alliance."[14]

Prohibition was more than an endeavor to improve American morality. It was a concentrated attack upon minorities designed to transform their cultural beliefs into criminal actions. The rise in crime during the 1920s stemmed from prejudice toward ethnic minorities as the views of Protestant Americans rode roughshod over cultural diversity. Behaviors that had been legal became transformed into crimes because of America's inability to accept differences in cultural practices. Prohibition is the story of blatant prejudice against Catholics and Jews by legalizing cultural bias, and subsequently punishing those who continued practicing their cultural mores.

The famous gangsters of the 1920s, not surprisingly, represented ethnic groups. Al Capone, Lucky Luciano, Meyer Lansksy, Bugsy Siegel, and the O'Banion boys eptiomized to many Americans the Irish, Italian, and Jewish immigrants who refused to accept "American" values regarding the consumption of alcohol. Many young ethnic males discovered in crime opportunities for the social mobility that was denied by the existing economic and social order.

The dramatic rise of the KKK in the twenties coincided with the criminalization of ethnic values. The KKK in the twenties was concerned with ridding America of immoral foreigners, Catholics, and Jews who defied existing cultural values. Prohibition was created by WASP's imposition of their morality upon ethnic groups, and when these people rebelled by defying this new morality, they were termed criminals. Upper-class Protestants, who had created the crime era, then led the anti-crime fight by wrapping themselves in the flag of morality and condmening Jews, Italians, and the Irish as criminals.

"Finally, the history of Prohibition and the mobs it created cannot be understood without careful attention to ethnic aspects. . . . The ethnic patterns of Prohibition endured for at least forty years afterward. The gangsters remained Irish, Jewish and Italian. The would-be gangsbusters remained mostly WASPs and Protestant consciences."[15]

Prior to the twentieth century, famous criminals were White Anglo Saxons. Billy the Kid, Butch Cassidy and the Sundance Kid, Jesse James, and the Dalton boys were portrayed as young White American males fighting to uphold traditional values. Even such twentieth century criminal heroes as Pretty Boy Floyd and John Dillinger were frequently excused on the grounds that they stole from the rich to give to the poor. There is a vivid contrast between the portrayal of Jewish, Italian, and Irish Prohibition gangsters as violent deviants from the glorified presentation of white Anglo Saxon western criminals. Ironically, Jewish, Italian, and Irish gangsters entered crime to fulfill a social need -- alcohol-- while WASP western gangsters sometimes financially ruined towns when they robbed banks.

A significant difference between ethnic criminals and western crime "heroes" is that many Jewish and Italian boys entered crime in response to bigotry. For example, Jake Zelig, a Jewish boy from lower Manhattan, organized a group of Jewish boys to fight against Christians who entered their neighborhood and terrorized Jewish adults. His experience in these fights eventually led Zelig to create a gang that extorted money from the very Jewish storekeepers he once defended. Zelig later worked with Meyer Lansky and Busy Siegel. Al Capone also organized teen-agers to fight against attacks upon Italians.

Throughout the twentieth century, young males in ethnic groups have used physical violence to protect their people, and this training unfortunately led some to enter crime.

There is a need in education to raise new questions about Prohibition in order to understand contemporary times. Seventy years ago, immigrants from German, Italian, Jewish, and Irish backgrounds bore the brunt of prejudice from a dominantly white Protestant middle class which imposed its cultural will and in the process fostered urban crime. The Italian-Jewish criminal coalition which dominated many urban areas initially arose in reaction to Protestant bigotry. The rise in crime rates also represented a clash of cultures in which Protestant America, by criminalizing mores of ethnic cultures, forced people to engage in criminal actions.

Conclusion

The failure to address the history of crime in school curricula distorts the development of multiculturalism in American society. Minorities have often been classified as criminals for engaging in activities that in most parts of the world are considered legal. In the process of defining cultural beliefs as "crime," America has transformed ethnic and cultural groups into criminals. Throughout American history the clash over crime and justice has also been one between dominant values and cultural mores.

Young people today need a broader perspective on issues of crime and punishment in order to comprehend the complex issues confronting contemporary society. The presence of over 600,000 people in jails due to drugs (a majority being people of African American or Hispanic background) must also be addressed in terms of a clash regarding cultural beliefs. To what extent is the war on drugs a war on ethnicity and race?

NOTES

1. Gilje, Paul. The Road to Mobocracy, Chapel Hill, University of North Carolina Press, 1987.

2. Williams, Harry, ed. Abraham Lincoln Selected Speeches, Messages, and Letter, NY, Alfred Knopf, 1957, pg. 7.
3. Nativist mobs in Louisville killed twenty Germans in 1856.
4. Gusfield, Joseph, Symbolic Crusades, Urbana, University of Illinois Press, 1961, pg. 5.
5. Culberson, William, Vigilantism, NY, Greenwood Press, 1990. The author notes that between 1828-1833 there were 20 riots, in 1834 at least 16 and in 1835 about 37. By 1835 at least 61 people had been killed in riots and by 1840 about 120. "More than one thousand people were killed in antebellum riots", pg. 77.
6. Ignatiev, Noel. How the Irish Become White, NY, Routledge, 1995, pgs. 40-41.
7. Ibid., 47.
8. Al Capone in the 1920s was an equal opportunity employer whose gang included men of virtually every ethnic group in Chicago. His right hand gunman, Jack Guzig, was an Orthodox Jew who did not kill on Sunday.
9. White, Wlater, Rope and Faggot, NY, Arno Press, 1969, pgs. 238-244.
10. Fox, Stephen, Blood and Power, NY, William Morrow, 1989.
11. Gusfield, pgs. 55-56.
12. Kobler, John, Ardent Spirits, NY, Putnam Sons, 1973, pgs. 80-90.
13. Chatauqua, July 1989, pg. 590.
14. Kobler, pg. 206
15. Fox, pg. 51.

Chapter Twenty-Five
STAR
(university Students Talk About Race with secondary students)

Douglas F Warring
University of St. Thomas, St. Paul, MN

Sally Hunter
University of St. Thomas, St. Paul, MN

Kerry Dean Frank
University of St. Thomas, St. Paul, MN

==================

Introduction

A six-month study of race relations in three public schools was conducted by People For the American Way in 1994. This study was entitled Invisibles: A Study of Racial Division and the Challenge of Building Bridges in the St. Paul, MN Area Schools. This study took place in three public school districts in the Midwest, and found deteriorating race relations and disturbing tensions in the schools. There were also high rates of harassment, a tenuous peace, a lack of a sense of community, and the experiencing of unfair treatment. Out of this study came The Invisible Walls Project where university students are paired with a partner and trained to be facilitators of weekly discussions about racism, sexism, prejudice, and discrimination in secondary school classrooms. This article outlines the program, discusses some of the issues, and highlights some of the comments made by students and teachers.

Overview

STAR was created by People for the American Way in North Carolina as a tribute to the university students who led the Greensboro civil rights sit-ins. Today, hundreds of university students and youth of all races and backgrounds are volunteering their time with STAR. After being founded in North Carolina, STAR was brought to California in 1992 and Minnesota in 1996. Other states are becoming involved in this exciting project as well.

This midwestern university presently has students participating in this program in the local area public middle and high schools. In addition to a local program coordinator, three faculty from the university work with the students and provide training and ongoing support each semester. The students receive special training in group facilitation skills and a curriculum which they use for each week's activities and regular meetings to discuss issues and assist each other. These university students become valuable role models to the younger students, according to Pederson & Carey (1994).

The STAR curriculum guide serves as a basis for leading students successfully through the weekly discussions. As Tiedt & Tiedt (1995) state, discussions are essential in combination with other methods of dealing with topics of this nature. The guide includes icebreakers, lesson plans, historical and descriptive overviews, and techniques to promote productive conversations among students. The weekly lesson plans have several areas of focus according to People for the American Way (1995). Through the weekly lessons the students should be better able to: distinguish between fact and fiction; understand concepts such as prejudice, stereotype, discrimination, pluralism, etc.; identify and formulate appropriate generalizations and inferences; and understand perceptions other than one's own.

Teachers, principals, parents and students begin preparations for a multi-program strategy to promote respect and tolerance in their schools, and to continue collaborative efforts to improve intergroup relations across geographical and sociopolitical boundaries. Nieto (1992) discusses the need for this as a way to increase positive communications as well as to improve the chances of success for students.

STAR Training

STAR recruits and trains university students to be the facilitators of lively and engaging discussions about racial, ethnic, and other differences in both middle school and high school classrooms. The program's goals are to provide a forum for youth to (a) share their personal thoughts and experiences, (b) reflect on complex issues like prejudice and citizen responsibility, and (c) learn the value of tolerance in today's society, all of which are essential according to Adler (1993), Atkinson & Hackett (1995), Delpit (1995), Gay (1994), and others. As part of the training, university students are provided a curriculum and participate in ongoing seminars. Using university students increases program effectiveness. As noted by Allport (1954), Deutsch (1949), Cohen (1986), and Johnson and Johnson (1977), peers are known to be effective role models and teachers for young people as they demonstrate and discuss critical issues central to a commitment to social justice, multiculturalism and democracy through the building of coalitions across groups.

Key Components of STAR

There are four components of the STAR program that lend to its success.

1. *Volunteer Recruitment and Training.* University volunteers are recruited from a variety of higher education institutions. The university submitting this paper has 14 students participating this semester. All are university students who volunteer and are trained by experts in prejudice reduction and group facilitation.
2. *University/School Partnerships.* The involvement of the university volunteers in leading discussions in high school and middle school classrooms encourages the development of strong partnerships between the secondary school and the higher education community.
3. *Curricular Materials.* Both the university volunteers and the STAR school students receive educational materials that provide a

context for discussions dealing with prejudice, discrimination, and other related topics including sexism and racism. These materials include historical background information and examples of active citizenship.

4. *Evaluation.* All program participants are asked to assess the program by completing evaluations designed to measure the impact of STAR on attitudes, perceptions and understanding. The coordinator and university faculty also visit the classes and complete assessments.

Outcomes

Comments from students and teachers in the STAR Program.

According to the participants in many school districts, Invisible Walls has been a good project to improve inter-group relations. The project's multiple-program strategy utilizes (a) whole-school conflict resolution, (b) community service learning, (c) performing arts and (d) dialogue to break down the invisible walls that separate people and that create barriers. These complement the university curriculum and help to show the interrelationships between schools and families (Martin, 1995; Chavkin, 1993).

An assistant principal at one of the schools reported that one of the best things about Invisible Walls is that it makes the school aware that there is more out there than just their community. This reasoning seems to fit with some of the essential issues raised by Gollnick and Chinn (1998), who state that we need to be continuously aware of the changing nature of our pluralistic society. The principal described a few activities that he really enjoyed. One of these was when students of different communities were involved in short skit performances that he felt really opened the eyes of many of the "Norwegian kids." Students were able to see how much alike they all were. One student responded, "I don't care what color their skin is. I just care what kind of person they are." The principal also indicated that he enjoys the networking part of this program. He likes to meet others, see what they are doing in their schools, and discuss how they handle different situations. He plans to continue the program at his school and would like to see it expanded.

An assistant principal from a high school shared that the program sends a message that the school cares about diversity issues. The students were enthusiastic about becoming involved, and this offered another positive way for them to become involved. A weakness of the program is that it takes extra time from the staff and students who both have very booked calendars. According to Baker (1994), planning and organizing take time that is essential for positive multicultural outcomes. The principal said that the anecdotal data indicate a positive impact on students and that they generally want to see people getting along with each other. He would also like to continue his involvement with this program next year.

One of the STAR facilitators related the following experience: It was not until we showed the movie *Not in our Town* (Condeni & Vallejo, 1996) that a real breakthrough occurred. The movie talks about a small town in Montana where hate crimes suddenly erupted and about how the town fought back. We stopped the movie a few times for questions, and that was how we opened the flood gates. First the students wanted to know about the Nazis and the Ku Klux Klan, and then they got angry. Chris, a boy with autism (which I thought meant he was going to be introverted. I was proven wrong.), yelled out, "Why can't we kill those bad people?" Jesse, the only African American girl, had the same question. Brice told the story of how his new step mom was Jewish and that actually, "she was kind of cool." When the outrage finally settled down and everybody agreed that hating people just because of their religion or skin color was, in their words, "dumb," I reminded them of something. Weeks earlier students were asked what they did and did not want to talk about. They did not want to talk about Martin Luther King because he had already been talked about, as had homosexuality. Students were confronted about this attitude which resulted in a fiery and worthwhile discussion. The outcome was extremely positive. Students were able to openly discuss ideas that previously were held to a whisper.

Another facilitator commented, "I have learned a lot about myself from STAR. In every exercise I did with the students I found something that I did not know. I found out that at first I paid more attention to the boys because they were more demanding as our instructor had told us and we read in Banks & Banks (1997). When I realized what I was doing, I was able to give more equal time to everybody."

"Overall, I think that my STAR experience was very beneficial to my future," said one university student facilitator, "and it is something that I will never forget. I was really glad and proud that I took the opportunity and it turned out very beneficial. It really made me look at the different sides and perspectives of issues that teens in an inner city school have to deal with and live with every day. It was definitely a great experience that no one could ever take away from me!"

Discussion

We realize that this project is one of several attempts that are currently being made to ease tensions among different groups, to accentuate disparities that exist among different groups in our society, to recognize the role of schools in addressing certain issues of concern, and to show how the educational system is inextricably linked to political, social, and economic structures. It should be noted that a large number of approaches that attempt to address issues of racism, sexism, sexual orientation, homophobia, and sexual preference attempt to do so through two general perspectives--a psychological or cognitive perspective, and a structural perspective (Brewer, 1979; Brewer & Campbell, 1976; Deutsch, 1982; Johnson, Johnson & Maruyama, 1983; Grant & Sleeter, 1986; McLaren, 1991; Nieto, 1992).

The psychological/cognitive perspective focuses on developmental changes that the student/child goes through. The use of intelligence facilitates the child's ability to negotiate changes in his/her environment. Much attention is focused on the individual learner, the exception being Vygotsky's focus on the role of culture (Piaget, 1960 & 1971; Flavell, 1963; Vygotsky, 1986). The structural perspective focuses on facilitating students' understanding of the social, political, and economic factors that contribute to their learning. Understanding power relations is a major focus of such work (Sleeter & McLaren, 1995; Goldberg,

1994; Leistyna, Woodrum & Sherblom, 1996).

One argument is that one's psychological/cognitive development enhances one's understanding of power relations. Another argument is that persons can understand power relations that have an impact on their lives whether they fit the traditional (read psychological/cognitive, reductionistic) definition of intelligence or not. This argument lends itself to an understanding of two competing views; one espousing the psychological/cognitive perspective, the other espousing the structuralist perspective. A larger percentage of today's school systems favors the psychological/cognitive perspective.

In the STAR program we feel that both the psychological/cognitive perspective and the structural perspective are necessary. It is necessary for individuals (students) to recognize the cognitive factors which contribute to the formation of negative attitudes toward others. Additionally, students need to understand that cognitive development and/or intelligence are/is situated within certain social, political, and economic contexts. It is the interplay of cognitive development and power relations which historically have affected, and continue to affect, learning. Trainers, facilitators, and school personnel need to be aware of this.

There is a constant change of numbers and cultures of students. We believe that if students are given a multicultural education starting from a young age, they will be more aware of the diverse society in which they live. Hopefully, their life styles will be much different from fifty years ago, and this is why we need to help to make them aware of these issues.

Teachers should also try to influence the parents of their students because responsibility needs to be shared by the community as well (Martin, 1995; McCaleb, 1994). Multicultural education requires support from an empowering school culture and a social structure.

Summary

People For The American Way is an organization of over 300,000 members and activists who are committed to promoting American values like freedom of religion and expression, personal liberty, and opportunity for all. Central to the People For the American Way's vision is the founding American principle of e pluribus unum – out of many, one. The STAR project reflects the belief that America's diversity is America's strength. Our nation must be able to accept, respect and celebrate our differences and understand how these differences, as they exist within certain contexts, affect people's lives. When Americans are able to do that, we will be able to come together as one nation. That is the best of the American way. It is worth fighting for.

> The American ideal is not that we will agree with each other, or even like each other, every minute of the day. It is rather that we will respect each other's rights, especially the right to be different, and that, at the end of the day, we will understand that we are one people, one country, and one community, and that our well-being is inextricably bound up with the well being of each and every one of our fellow citizens.
>
> People for the American Way, 1995, p. 82.

References

Adler, S. (1993). Multicultural communication skills in the classroom. Needham Heights, MA: Allyn and Bacon.

Allport, G. (1954). The nature of prejudice. Boston, MA: Anchor.

Atkinson, D. & Hackett, G. (1995). Counseling diverse populations. Dubuque, IA: Wm C. Brown.

Baker, G. C. (1994). Planning and organizing for multicultural instruction (2nd ed.). New York: Addison and Wesley.

Banks, J., & Banks, C. (Eds.). (1997). Multicultural education: Issues and perspectives (3rd ed.). Boston, MA: Allyn & Bacon.

Brewer, M. B. (1979). Ingroup bias in the minimal intergroup situation: A cognitive-motivational analysis. Psychological Bulletin, 86, 307-324.

Brewer, M. B., & Campbell, D. T. (1976). Ethnocentrism and

intergroup attitudes: East African evidence. New York: Halsted Press.

Chavkin, W. F. (Ed.). (1993). Families and schools in a pluralistic society. Albany, NY: State University Press.

Cohen, E. (1986). Designing group work: Strategies for the heterogeneous classroom. New York: Teachers College Press.

Condeni, Vivian & Vallejo, Joan (Producers), & Shiedel, Gary (Director). (1996). Not in our town local response [Film]. (Available from Oregon Public Broadcasting, Portland, OR)

Delpit, L. D. (1995). Other people's children: White teachers, students of color, and other cultural conflicts in the classroom. New York: The New York Press.

Deutsch, M. (1949). A theory of cooperation and competition. Human Relations, 2, 129-152.

Deutsch, M. (1982). Interdependence and psychological orientation. In V. Derlaga, & J. Grzelak (Eds.), Cooperation and helping behavior (pp. 15-42). New York: Academic Press.

Flavell, J. H. (1963). The developmental psychology of Jean Piaget. New York: Van Nostrand Reinhold.

Gay, G. (1994). At the essence of learning: Multicultural education. West Lafayette, IN: Kappa Delta Pi.

Goldberg, D. T. (Ed.). (1994). Multiculturalism: A critical reader. Cambridge, MA: Blackwell.

Gollnick, D. M., & Chinn, P. C. (1998). Multicultural education in a pluralistic society (5th ed.). Riverside, NY: Macmillan College Publishing.

Grant, C. A., & Sleeter, C. E. (1986). After the school bell rings. London: Falmer.

Johnson, D. W. & Johnson, R. (1977). Cooperation, competition, and individualization and interracial, intersexual, and interability attitudes. Paper presented at the annual meeting of the American Psychological Association, San Francisco.

Johnson, D., Johnson, R., & Maruyama, G. (1983). Interdependence and interpersonal attraction among heterogeneous and homogeneous individuals: A theoretical formulation and a meta-analysis of the research. Review of Educational Research, 53, 5-54.

Leistyna, P., Woodrum, A., & Sherblom, S. A. (Eds.). (1996). Breaking free: The transformative power of critical pedagogy. Cambridge, MA: Harvard Educational Review.

Martin, R. (Ed.). (1995). Practicing what we teach: Confronting diversity in teacher education. Albany, NY: SUNY Press.

McCaleb, S. P. (1994). Building communities of learners: A collaboration among teachers, students, families and community. New York: St. Martin's Press.

McLaren, P. (1991). Decentering culture: Postmodernism, resistance, and critical pedagogy. In N. B. Wyner (Ed.), Current perspectives on the culture of schools (pp. 232-257). Boston, MA: Brookline.

Nieto, S. (1992). Affirming diversity: The sociopolitical contexts of multicultural education. New York: Longman.

Pederson, P., & Carey, J. C. (Eds.). (1994). Multicultural counseling in schools: A practical handbook. Boston, MA: Allyn and Bacon.

People for the American Way (1995). STAR curriculum guide: Students talk about race. A Project of People for the American Way. Washington, DC: People for the American Way.

Piaget, J. (1960). Psychology of intelligence. Paterson, NJ: Littlefield, Adams.

Piaget, J. (1971). Science of education and the psychology of the child. New York: Viking Press.

Sleeter, C., & McLaren, P. (Eds.). (1995). Multicultural education, critical pedagogy, and the politics of difference. Albany, NY: SUNY Press.

Tiedt, P. L., & Tiedt, I. M. (1995). Multicultural teaching: A handbook of activities, information and resources (4th ed.). Boston, MA: Allyn and Bacon.

Vygotsky, L. S. (1986). Thought and language (Rev. ed.). Cambridge, MA: MIT Press.

Chapter Twenty-Six
"Classroom Techniques and Behaviors that
Can Be Utilized by Teachers to Meet the
Diverse Needs of Students While Enhancing the
Teaching Learning Process"

Glenn A. Doston
Ohio University

Samuel H. Bolden
University of West Florida

As the educational systems of the United States prepare to organize to deliver and ensure a better education for all students, the goal of preparing teachers who are culturally responsible should be at the top of the list. The authors of this paper contend that educators who are culturally responsible are absolutely necessary to reduce the huge disparities in academic achievement among students from diverse backgrounds. Teacher preparation programs must understand that they play a major role in the lack of academic success for many students.

Recent literature in education is full of examples of techniques and behaviors that can be utilized by teachers to meet the diverse needs of students while enhancing the teaching/learning process. Many scholars suggest that educators who are responsive to the cultural backgrounds of their students as well as to their diverse learning styles, increase the level of learning (Delpit, 1988; Ladson-Billings, 1994; Nieto, 1994). Harste and Burke (1988), suggest that the key component in effective instruction in multicultural classrooms is the teacher. Harste and Burke suggest that the teacher's "theoretical orientation" guides the style of pedagogy of many educators (p. 112). They go on to maintain that a teacher's theoretical orientation is made up of:

1. Particular knowledge
2. Life experiences
3. Personal belief systems

which lead teachers to interact and behave toward students in specific ways (p. 113)..

Ladson-Billings (1992) suggests that pre-service educators enter their classrooms with such huge knowledge deficits that they needed to participate in "multicultural remediation," which challenges them to develop multiple perspectives and informed empathy. Ladson-Billings suggests a need to rethink what it means to be "culturally literate" in a multicultural society and improve the modeling of the kind of classroom interactions educators want to see in pre-collegiate classrooms as well as find ways to integrate teacher-trainees into both the communities and schools in which they will teach.

Many in America's teaching force are victims of the same system that continues to victimize today's young students. The problem of preparing teachers who are predominantly white to work with a diverse population is becoming more difficult. Student populations are growing ever more multicultural and are even more culturally different than the current generation of teacher education trainees.

However, Giroux and McLaren (1986) suggest that teacher educators and pre-service teachers develop a "language of critique and possibility," which empowers and encourages teachers and students to analyze and evaluate the school and society in a democratic context (p. 231). Included in the "language of critique and possibility" is a deep regard and respect for diversity.

The authors suggest that teacher educators focus on a model

which places language and culture oft the center in the lived experiences of student teachers and the students they serve. This can be accomplished by providing a more participatory education which would examine multiple alternative realities in order to understand their own perspectives and those perspectives of others in a diverse society. Through integration, mission, methodology, and outcomes, student teachers should be provided the opportunity to examine, critique and evaluate the moral, political, ethical and educational implications used in their everyday thinking as teachers.

For general guidelines we suggest that colleges and universities can benefit from most of the curriculum guidelines as outlined by James Banks (1992); namely:

1. A school's staff should reflect the ethnic and cultural diversity within the United States.
2. The curriculum should help students understand the totality of the experiences of ethnic and cultural groups in the United States.
3   The multicultural curriculum should explore and clarify ethnic and cultural alternatives and options in the United States.
4   The multicultural curriculum should promote values, attitudes, and behaviors that support ethnic pluralism and cultural diversity as well as build and support the nation state and the nation's shared culture. E Pluribus Unum should be the goal of the school and nation.
5. The multicultural curriculum should help students develop their decision-making abilities, social participation skills and sense of political efficiency as a necessary basis for efficacy citizenship in a pluralistic democratic nation.
6. The multicultural curriculum should help students develop the skills necessary for effective interpersonal, interethnic, and intercultural group interactions.
7. The multicultural curriculum should be comprehensive in scope and sequence, should present holistic views of ethnic and

cultural groups, and should be an integral part of the total school curriculum.

8. The multicultural curriculum should include the continuous study of cultures, historical experiences, social realities, and existential conditions of ethnic and cultural groups, including a variety of cultural groups.

9. Interdisciplinary and multidisciplinary approaches should be used in designing and implementing the multicultural curriculum.

10. The multicultural curriculum should use comparative approaches in the study of ethnic and cultural groups.

11. The multicultural curriculum should help students to view and interpret events, situations, and conflict from diverse ethnic and cultural perspectives and points of view.

12. Schools should provide opportunities for students to participate in the aesthetic experiences of various ethnic and cultural groups.

13. The multicultural curriculum should provide opportunities for students to study ethnic group languages as legitimate communications systems and help them develop full literacy in at least two languages.

14. The assessment procedures used with students should reflect their ethnic and cultural experiences.

We also believe that teachers and pre-service teachers should be monitoring their own behavior in order to become aware of their own prejudices, stereotypic perceptions and behaviors. However, we realize that becoming aware isn't enough, since the very structure of society supports certain basises. Real behavior change requires determined effort over time.

Some valued techniques and behaviors that can be utilized to meet the diverse needs of students are included from Grossman (1995).

1. Discussion of similarities and differences.

2.   Inclusion of a student's culture in the classroom.
3.   Emancipitory and Tranformational Approaches
4   Learning and teaching style incompatibilities (i.e. accommodation)
5.   Empowerment
6.   Biculturalism (home, school)

In part two of this paper, come with us, if you will, as we take you on an educational journey to the next millennium by describing to you, *Classroom techniques and behaviors that can be utilized by teachers to meet the diverse needs of students while enhancing the teaching/learning process* (kindergarten through Professional School).

1.   *If you are a teacher*, as you go on this journey we are going to stop in a lot of cities, towns, villages, and make a few rest stops. Each of these cities, towns, villages and rest stops will represent certain classroom techniques and behaviors that you should possess. If you do not possess these techniques and behaviors, you need to back track, go back to your home city to acquire and learn these essential techniques and behaviors because you *will not be ready for the next millennium.* You must re-examine your own skills and techniques and retool for a different journey to the twenty-first century.
2.   If you are going on this journey as *a person connected with (or responsible for) the recruitment, hiring and retention of quality teachers for your school system, college or university,* and the teachers you are seeking do not possess at least 90 percent of these techniques and behaviors, pass them up, don't recruit them and don't hire them. If you do, your particular educational setting will suffer from the maintenance of the *status quo* by hiring teachers who will prevent your institution from providing quality education in the next millennium.
3.   Our first stop, just five miles out-of-town, is Curriculum City. This is our most important stop because all teachers for the next

millennium should be trained in colleges and universities that utilize a multicultural curriculum which should also be developed for K-12 settings. We agree with James Banks' suggestions from his (1992) *Curriculum Guidelines for Multicultural Education* in which he outlines the following:

a. Ethnic and cultural diversity should permeate the total school environment.

b. School policies and procedures should foster positive multicultural interactions and understandings among teachers, students and support staff (including custodians, cafeteria workers, school bus drivers).

c. Schools should have systematic, comprehensive mandatory staff development programs for all those involved in the education process.

d. The curriculum should reflect the cultural learning styles and characteristics of students in the school community.

e. The curriculum should provide students with continuous opportunities to develop a better sense of self.

f. The multicultural curriculum should help students understand that a conflict between ideals and realities always exists in human societies.

g. The curriculum should conceptualize and describe the development of the United States as a multicultural society.

h. The multicultural curriculum should make maximum use of experiential learning, especially local community resources.

As we prepare to leave Curriculum City, please keep in mind that many in America's teaching force are victims of the same system that continues to victimize today's young students. And, while the problem of preparing teachers who are predominantly white to work with a diverse population is becoming somewhat more difficult, *it can and must be done*! Student populations are growing more multicultural and are even more culturally different than the current generation of teacher trainees.

Now that we are on our way to Behavior Branch, we would recommend an approach suggested by Herbert Grossman in his 1995 book, Teaching in a Diverse Society, wherein he suggests the Proactive Antibias Curriculum Approach:

a.   Eliminating teacher bias.
b.   Eliminating curriculum bias.
c.   Teaching about prejudice.
d.   School-wide approaches (p.99).

As we approach Behavior Branch, we see a big information sign that says, "Warning!   Teachers must observe these classroom techniques and behaviors or they may lose their licenses or teaching certificate's:"

Effective communication (both oral and written).

a.   Teaching rests on communication. Human beings communicate both verbally and non verbally, by their attitudes and behavior. All of these forms of communication are important in the classroom because they help students and instructors understand one another.
b.   Correct grammatical usage is a teaching imperative.
      Over the years, we have met too many teachers who have yet to fully grasp (nor speak) Standard English. Nothing probably bugs us more than to hear teachers in the presence of their own students, (parents or others) *issing* where they should be *areing* (terms coined by Doston and Bolden).

No teaching of Ebonices!

a. We are sure you have read about the Oakland, California school decision to teach Ebonics (so-called Black English).

b. Ebonics is a fake word, a blend of "ebony" and "phonic" used to describe the style of English spoken by many African-Americans. You won't find the word in any dictionary.

c. Examples, the verb "to be" is not conjugated and may be dropped entirely: "She be home"; "You bad." Absence of a third-person-present tense: "she walk."

d. Proponents say the idea is to help students make the transition to standard English by understanding and translating their mother tongue.

e. *Give us a break!* The fact of the matter is that most of the African-American students have not been taught standard English by that system's cadre of teachers. What's to assure that even Ebonics will be taught. However, being the pragmatist that we are, if it works, we'll support it, although it will be tantamount to an educational miracle!

f. It was reported in the media on January 1 that black students in Oakland admit their teachers sometimes have trouble understanding them, but many say they are perplexed by the school board decision declaring black English a second language. In addition, the Los Angeles City Schools System is considering a similar proposal to teach Ebonics.

g. To us, there is a far more disturbing scenario in the Oakland schools. District records show that although 53% of the districts 51,000 students are African-Americans, they account for 64% of those retained, 71% of those in special-education classes, and 80% of those suspended. Almost 20% of African-Americans in grade 12 do not graduate. What accounts for these atrocious facts? Outright, rampant racism? Inability of all teachers to teach African-American students? Ebonics? Does 71% of a particular racial or ethnic group really require special education?

As a footnote, the Associated Press reported on January 13 that an Oakland school task force that proposed recognizing Ebonics as a second language clarified its policy on January 12, dropping any suggestion that black English is genetically based. Instead, the policy now states that Ebonics is traceable to African languages that slaves bought to the United States.

1. Be culturally responsive in the classroom.
2. Be able to respond to the educational needs of diverse learners.
3. Interpret culture beyond black history month.
4. Respect values, attitudes and beliefs that go beyond those of middle class Americans.
5. Help students develop the skills necessary for effective interpersonal, interethnic and intercultural group interactions.
6. Learn major tenets underlying the cultural history of all students in your classes.

Our first rest stop is <u>TEACHER TOWN</u>, which deals with specific, individual teacher behaviors/attitudes:

a. If someone asks you, "What do you do for a living?" don't just say, "I'm just a teacher." If we were asked the same question, we'd say, "We are *teachers*! We are competent, effective teachers, who can make a difference in the lives of those we touch. Be proud of what you do!

b. Be able to teach reading! Reading is the key to all students' learning. Without adequate reading skills your students will be lost.

c. Involve everyone in your classes (questioning, projects, special activities, etc.)

d. Do not make assumptions.

e. Give students an opportunity for success while previously they had none.

f.   Do not be afraid to give your opinion or take a particular stand on controversial issues. However, make it clear that there are other positions.

g.   Constantly strive for creativity to avoid burn out or stagnation.

h.   Project a sensitive attitude, without can lead to the social estrangement of some students.

i.   Challenge your students to make sure they understand.

j.   Offer suggestions and constructive criticisms even though they might be outside your area of expertise or subject matter.

k.   Don't be afraid to say "I don't know" when appropriate. However, be sure to research the correct answer and bring it back with dispatch.

l.   Correct and appropriate advice are essential for career building (also making referrals to designated resources).

Our second rest stop occurs at TECHNIQUE TOWN which includes:

a.   Motivating students. This rests almost exclusively with the teacher although other factors come into play. Many minorities, particularly African-Americans and Hispanics, are more easily motivated when the purpose for learning relates to the needs which they perceive as real and immediate. By contrast, middle-class white students, whose achievements orientation begins early and is reinforced continuously by family lifestyles, respond to such purposes as preparation for college or scoring well on standardized tests. It is important for teachers to have an extensive repertoire of motivational skills to fit the cultures of their classrooms.

b.   Planning, organization and time management. These are important techniques for success which every teacher must utilize on a daily basis.

c.   Managing classroom behavior. In general, teachers receive some training in the principles of behavior management, but far too many are ill-equipped to deal effectively with behaviors that represent conflict between what is expected in the home and the community. Generally, an atmosphere of mutual respect is engendered when teachers seek information about minority cultures from all available sources, verify the information obtained to form a knowledge base, and develop from that knowledge base a set of understandings which modifies their own behavior.

d.   Inviting students to collaborate and be part of the learning process. The uninviting teacher is a major inhibitor to learning.

e.   Developing your individual style of listening rather than hearing.

f.   Making a special effort of establish rapport.

g.   Re-examining your expectations and student achievement.

h.   Utilizing effective introductions to various lessons, units, themes, etc.

I.   Being prepared to deal with ever-changing student demographics.

j.   Considering peer coaching or colleague evaluation to develop new or innovative teaching techniques.

k.   Where applicable, encouraging students to take a foreign language.

l.   Learning the basic elements helping students negotiate standardized tests.

m.   Varying the types of quizzes, examinations, oral exams and other forms of assessment while being aware that fairness is a key to success for your students.

n.   Keeping abreast of technological advances. Being

computer literate means going beyond understanding the keyboard and word processing. You must learn how to utilize and incorporate technology in your teaching.

o. Don't have a "teacher's pet," the students will immediately begin to resent you.

6. Our next stop is in <u>HISTORY HAMLET !</u>
In History Hamlet you must:

a. Do your part to correct historical facts and to dispel historical myths. Teachers must set the record straight on many of the direct lies and distortions that permeate most history in general.

b. Tell your students that blacks have a distinguished history before the Mayflower came to these shores in 1619.

c. Tell them that ancient Africans were creative contributors to Egyptian civilization. We were once Kings and Queens.

d. Tell them that our ancestors were the strongest of the strong that were forced to this country in chains as slaves. Tell them that slavery in one form or another has been practiced in every country known to man. Also tell them that our strength is related to our perseverance and survival.

Don't be afraid to discuss black history and if you don't know it, learn about it. *READ! READ! READ IT AND DISCUSS IT WITH YOUR PEERS!*

f. Tell your students that Columbus did not discover American------that native Americans, Mexicans and Eskimos were here centuries before Columbus arrived.

g. American history books have longed been enamored with white authors' biases about the American West. The books are long on folklore and, until relatively recently, the roles of blacks in the west were virtually ignored.

h. For a sterling historical account of the black west let me suggest you read "The Black West" by William Katz. In this work for example, you learn about Isaiah Dorman, Sioux and African-American ancestry, who served as a scout for General Custer at the battle of Little Big Horn. A courier for the War Department in the Dakota Territory for many years, Dorman was transferred to General Custer's Seventh Cavalry only a month before the battle. His orders stated that he was to "report for duty to accompany the expedition as interpreter" into Montana. He died in battle with 264 cavalrymen.

i. Tell your students that Thomas Edison invented the light bulb and also tell them that each time they come to a traffic light, they should think about a black man, Garrett Morgan, who invented it, November 20, 1923.

j. Tell your students that Dr. Christian Barnard performed the first human heart transplant in 1967, but also balance that with the fact that Dr. Charles Drew, a black man, invented the blood plasma bag in 1939.

k. Discuss how Henry Ford manufactured the Ford auto in 1904, but also tell them how a black man, Edmond Berger invented the spark plug on February 2, 1839.

l. Tell them that blacks have graduated from every major university in North America and Western Europe.

m. Do not shy away from racial history in the U.S. History never changes but it tells us about our past, helps us to understand the present, and it give us some good clues to our future.

n.   Tell them about two recently (1996) published books (which you should read) by highly respected journalists who paint a bleak picture of life in America's Twenty-First century.

Our next to last stop is Sin City! Teachers that exhibits the sins that are described are courting disaster with their students. Such teachers will become the major cause of "students being forced out" of school rather than being "drop outs." Teachers must avoid:

a.   Kenneth Eble's (1976)"Seven deadly sins of teaching: arrogance, dullness, rigidity, insensitivity, vanity, self-indulgence, and hypocrisy.

b   Hiding behind tenure's door (i.e., taking a "I've got it made, I don't care attitude)."

c.   Exhibiting a personal character that is perceived by students to be negative.

.   The last stop on our journey to the next millennium is a <u>One Horse Town</u>, but a very important town for successful, effective, competent teaching.

a.   Greet students by name, smile and offer words of encouragement.

b.   Show some enthusiasm! Rotate (physically move) around the classroom!

c.   Avoid lecturing! Lecturing! Lecturing!

d.   Students at every level (k-professional school) imitate and emulate you. Look the part, talk the part and act the part.

e.   Respect yourself, then students will begin to respect you, which in turn leads to their self-respect.

For many of you, this journey may not have been new but it was intended to be a restatement of teaching behaviors and techniques that can make a real difference in the classroom. We shoulder a large responsibility for providing education to an ever-increasing, diverse student population in the next millennium.

References

Banks, J. (1992). Curriculum Guidelines for Multicultural Education: National Council for the Social Studies.

Delpit, L.D. (1988). The Silenced Dialogue: Power and Pedagogy in Educating Other People's Children.

Giroux, H. A. and McLaren P. (1986). Teacher Education and the Politics of Engagement. The case for democratic schooling. Harvard Educational Review, 56, 213-238.

Grossman, H. (1995). Teaching in a Diverse Society. Boston, MA: Allyn and Bacon.

Harste, J. C. and Burke, C. L. (1988). Understanding the Hypothesis: It is the Teacher that Makes the Difference, 111-123, in "Multicultural Education: A Global Approach" as cited by Dillard, C; 1992.

Katz, W. (1987). The Black West. Open Hand Publishing, Inc.: Seattle, WA.

Ladson-Billings, G. (1994). The Dreamkeepers: Successful Teachers of African-American Children, Jossey-Bass: San Francisco, CA.

Ladson-Billings, G. (1992). Coping with Cultural Illiteracy: A Teacher Education Response in "Multicultural Education": A Global Approach.

Nieto, S. (1994). Lessons from Students on Creating a Chance to Dream. Harvard Education Review (64), 392-426.

Chapter Twenty-Seven
Multicultural Perspective Transformation of Teachers: The Impact of Cultural Immersion

Angela V. Paccione
Colorado State University, Fort Collins, CO

Barbara A. McWhorter
Colorado State University, Fort Collins, CO

===========================

Linda Darling-Hammond (1997) articulated it clearly: "To this day, most schools in the United States do an extraordinarily poor job of educating students of color" (p. 1). Significant in this quote is the phrase, "To this day . . .", for it alludes to the history of inequitable education for minority students in the United States. While facilities and finances play a role in the equitable delivery of education, the role of the teacher is paramount (Darling-Hammond, 1997; Joyce & Showers, 1988; Kozol, 1991). All things being equal, individual teachers make a significant difference in the learning processes of all students. Therefore, creating equitable education for students of color must begin with individual teachers.

A 1989 survey of a representative sample of members of the Association for Teacher Education revealed that the third highest rated critical issue facing teacher educators was preparing teachers for diverse student populations (Buttery, Haberman, & Houston, 1990). The changing demographics of the nation's schools have intensified the need for preparing teachers to work effectively with students from a variety of cultural backgrounds. Reed (1993) states emphatically that teachers "must be taught that they have a legal, ethical, and moral responsibility to provide the best education they possibly can to members of all racial, ethnic, and cultural groups" (p. 28).

The Demographic Imperative

As we rapidly approach the new millennium, we are witnessing the fulfillment of the demographic predictions of diversity in American classrooms. From his analysis of the 1990 U.S. census, Hodgkinson (1993) predicted that from 1990 to 2010, the number of European-American youth in the United States would decline by 3.7 million while the number of Hispanic-American youth would increase by 2.6 million, and African-American youth would increase by 1.2 million. Others have forecasted that by the year 2010, one in three Americans and approximately 40% of U.S. students will be from a racial minority group (Thornton, 1995; see also Pallas, Natriello, & McDill, 1989). These figures have significant implications for educators and are some of the reasons for multicultural interventions in school districts across the country.

In 1979, the National Council for the Accreditation of Teacher Education (NCATE) included multicultural education amongst its criteria for accreditation of teacher preparation programs. With this impetus, many colleges and universities have included multicultural education in their requirements for preservice teacher preparation. Still, Gollnick (1992) found that only 56% of universities were in compliance with the NCATE mandate for multicultural education. Evans, Torrey, and Newton (1997) conducted a national survey of State Departments of Education to identify the requirements in multicultural preparation for certification or licensure. With a 100% return rate on the questionnaire used in the study, the researchers were able to determine that only 25 out of 50 states and the District of Columbia require coursework in multicultural education for prospective teachers to be certified/licensed. Almost twenty years after the NCATE mandate, it appears that neither states nor teacher education programs have made substantial progress toward complying.

The NCATE mandate addresses the cultural disparity between the teaching force and the student population. In 1991, the K-12 teaching force was approximately 84% White (Bennett de Marrais & LeCompte, 1995). During 1993-94, that number rose to approximately 87% (National Center for Educational Statistics, 1995). There is little evidence that these numbers will change significantly in the near future (Grant & Secada, 1990), as the typical teacher education student is White (Darling-Hammond & Sclan, 1996; Zimpher, as cited in Fullan, 1991). As the K-12 student population grows increasingly diverse, the nation's teaching force is on track to maintain a profile that is overwhelmingly White (Bennett de Marrais & LeCompte, 1995; Darling-Hammond & Sclan, 1996).

Garmon (1996) gives three reasons why these demographics present a compelling reason to prepare preservice teachers for a diverse student population: (a) the potential cultural mismatch between teachers and students may result in lower achievement for some students; (b) students from different cultural groups may have different learning styles than students from the majority cultural group, and teachers typically are taught to teach in the learning styles that accommodate majority culture students; and (c) teachers may hold negative racial attitudes towards and beliefs about culturally/ethnically different students (p. 4). Garmon suggests that,

> a largely white and female teaching force may bring negative, unaccepting attitudes toward the growing numbers of students of color in their classrooms; these attitudes, coupled with the attendant lower expectations, are major contributing factors to the widespread academic failure among minority students. (p. 5)

The pedagogical and interactional styles of teachers could still be in conflict with culturally diverse students, even if teachers do not hold negative racial attitudes toward such students. It is appropriate to assume that a lack of cultural awareness, and a lack of specific instruction in culturally relevant pedagogy, may create a classroom environment that fails to facilitate the success of culturally diverse students. However, assuming, as Garmon (1996) does, that *all* teachers who are White have inherently negative or racist attitudes towards minority cultures is inappropriate. Research consistently indicates that teacher perceptions of students based on race, class, and gender influence their expectations for behavior and academic performance (Gollnick & Chinn,

1998; Sadker & Sadker, 1994; Sleeter & Grant, 1992). Many White teachers have lower expectations for students of color, although they are often not aware of these lower expectations (Bennett, 1995; Hinchey, 1994). Gay (1997) reports:

> Because teachers' cultural backgrounds and value orientations are highly compatible with middle-class and European American culture, they can use these cultural connections to facilitate the learning of White students. This is done routinely and without conscious or deliberate intentions. It is their shared cultural orientations that make instruction more relevant and personally meaningful. The absence of these for students of color places them at a learning disadvantage. (p. 211)

This, however, is not an indictment of *all* teachers. Certainly there are some, perhaps many, teachers who possess a commitment to facilitating the success of *all* students. Not every preservice teacher nor every inservice teacher is unaware of the cultural differences that impact student learning. Still, statistical analyses indicate that by and large, students of color do not succeed in American schools. Consider the following statistics: Approximately 32% of all students ages 5 to 17 are from minority cultures and 68% are White (National Center for Educational Statistics, 1995). Among persons 16 to 24 years old, the percentage of dropouts in 1994 were as follows: 8% White and 43% non-White (National Center for Educational Statistics, 1995). While dropout rates for all students have fallen over the past 20 years, the differences between racial groups remain disturbing. Marable (1997) further emphasizes this point: "Across the United States, more than fifteen hundred teenagers of color drop out of school every day" (p. 155). He also noted that "between 1981 and 1995, the actual percentage of young African American adults between the ages 18 and 26 enrolled in colleges and universities declined by more than 20%" (p. 155).

In addition, students of color repeat grades more often than do

White students (Gay, 1997). A recent report of student grade retention in grades 1-8 of the Denver Public Schools revealed that 156 students of color were retained compared to 62 White students (Weber, 1997). Approximately 48% of the students in Denver Public Schools are Hispanic, 26% are White, 21% are Black, 4% are Asian and 1% are American Indian. The 1996 graduation rate for Denver Public Schools reported 74.3% White, 73.6% Asian, 67.7% Black, 46.8% American Indian, and 45.9% Hispanic (Colorado Department of Education, 1997). If students of color are being retained in grade in such numbers at the elementary school level, it is no wonder the graduation rates are discouraging for students of color.

Teacher Education for Diversity: Becoming a Multicultural Person

The numbers above concerning students of color in U.S. public schools are discouraging. There are numerous avenues which the educational community can explore to combat the inequities and injustices that exist in the present system. A focus on preservice teacher preparation is just one of the many avenues. Knowledge of diversity, skills for effectively working with diverse populations, and transforming attitudes toward diversity are all necessary goals for the preservice teacher (Banks, 1997; Bennett, 1995; Gay, 1994; Nieto, 1996). As Garmon (1996) indicates, two of the three most compelling reasons to prepare preservice teachers for student diversity can be addressed in the cognitive domain: that is, acquiring new knowledge about different cultures and learning pedagogical skills related to learning styles. The third, and in his view the most compelling, reason to prepare preservice teachers for diversity lies in the affective domain: racial attitudes and beliefs about culturally diverse students. Attention to this domain shifts the focus from knowledge and skill development to personal beliefs and attitudes. Thus, the process through which individuals change their personal beliefs and attitudes becomes an important element of preservice teacher preparation. This article is about that process.

Nieto (1996) asserts that multicultural education includes the process of becoming a multicultural person. Yet, Boyle-Baise (1996) contends that, "any process of becoming assumes willingness for self-change . . . it demands a caliber of personal engagement foreign to most school experiences (p. 5) Many of the leading scholars in the field of multicultural education assert the need for critical self-reflection as a vital component of the process of becoming a multicultural educator (Banks, 1997; Bennett, 1995; Gay, 1994; Nieto, 1996; Wurzel, 1988). This self-reflection requires that individuals examine their actions, values, beliefs, and perspectives with regard to issues of diversity. Individuals' perspectives on the world are rooted in their life experiences (Boyle-Baise & Sleeter, 1996; Mezirow, 1991). Becoming a multicultural person, especially if one begins as a monocultural person, requires exposure to and affiliation with diverse cultural groups. Many of these groups have been conspicuously omitted from the mainstream academic canon or left on the margins. Multicultural education promotes the movement of diverse groups from the margins of curriculum to the center.

Ideally, multicultural education is a transformation of the practice of educators and the institution of education. There is an underlying and motivating belief that understanding cultural differences and becoming culturally competent will lead to respecting and appreciating differences, rather than marginalizing cultures that are different from the predominant Eurocentric culture of the United States. Cultural competence has been described as "the ability to understand another culture well enough to be able to communicate and work with people from that culture" (Kivel, 1996, p. 207). As Kivel describes, becoming (multi) culturally competent is difficult for White people because they are the majority culture. He says:

> Wherever we look we see ourselves, our language, our values, our images, and our history. We are given little sense of the importance of cultural competency and an over-inflated sense of the importance and centrality of our culture. We have learned how great European-based American culture is. (p. 208)

Often, the rights and privileges that are inherent in a person of the majority culture are invisible to the individual (McIntosh, 1989; see also Lawrence & Bunche, 1996). This invisibility is one of the reasons why effective teacher preparation for diversity is so critical.

Powell, Zehm, and Garcia (1996) present seven objectives for making diversity a central component for teacher development. They say that educating teachers for diversity will:

1. Facilitate successful learning for all students.
2. Consider the human dimensions of teaching.
3. Assess the impact of global and local demographic changes on teaching.
4. Address the growing disparity between the cultural backgrounds of teachers those of and students.
5. Move multicultural education from marginal status to central status in teacher development.
6. Examine teacher biases, stereotypes, and misconceptions about cultural groups.
7. Make classroom curriculum culturally sensitive (pp. 9-12).

As teachers examine their biases, stereotypes, and misconceptions about diversity, change may occur and individuals might become multicultural persons (Powell et al., 1996). However, the ability to change one's biases, stereotypes, and misconceptions is more than simply a change of mind. Biases, stereotypes, and misconceptions are one's perspectives-- constructs that develop over a period of time. Once developed, perspectives are difficult to change (Zimbardo & Leippe, 1991).

Perspective Transformation: A Model for Change
Mezirow (1991) describes "meaning perspectives" as the very components of how an individual perceives, comprehends, remembers, and interprets information. That is, individuals develop a habit of expecting the world to be as they have conceived it and subsequently they view all

information through their frame of reference--their perspective. In his theory of perspective transformation, Mezirow (1991) suggests that the process of changing one's meaning perspectives includes experiencing "disorienting dilemmas." He describes these dilemmas as experiences in which new knowledge contradicts existing meaning perspectives. In these situations, the new knowledge is sufficiently strong to cause a dilemma for the individual. Accepting the new knowledge will initiate a change in the meaning perspective. Mezirow's theory of perspective transformation provides a tentative theoretical framework from which to examine the process of change that is anticipated through preservice multicultural education.

The goals of multicultural education include a transformation of the policies, practices, and structures of education (Banks, 1997; Bennett, 1995; Delpit, 1995; Gay, 1994; Grant, 1995; Ladson-Billings, 1994; Nieto, 1996; Sleeter, 1996). However, as Mezirow (1990) says, "we must begin with individual perspective transformations before social transformations can succeed" (p. 363). According to Mezirow (1991), critical reflection on one's life experiences is the central dynamic involved in perspective transformation. The specific type of reflection that promotes transformation is "premise reflection," which is described as "our becoming aware of *why* we perceive, think, feel, or act as we do" (p. 108). Through premise reflection one becomes aware of the presuppositions, biases, and perhaps prejudices formed through prior learning. Transformational learning occurs when these presuppositions and presumptions are found to be incongruous with new knowledge. Therefore, in an effort to assist preservice teachers in perspective transformation, teacher educators should create experiential activities through which students have the opportunity to confront the incongruity of their beliefs. Then, through guided reflection and praxis, students may be able to change their perspectives. Clark (1993) adds, "transformational learning *shapes* people; they are different afterward, in ways both they and others can recognize" (p. 47). This is the sort of change that is hoped for through multicultural education and the training of teachers for diversity (Huber, 1996; Nieto, 1996).

One of the desired outcomes of multicultural education is a change in student perspective, therefore it is imperative to understand the conditions under which that change may occur. One place to begin the examination of multicultural perspective transformation is with those who have already undergone such change. This article will address the impact of field experiences using cultural immersion as an impetus for perspective transformation and the source of the motivation to become a multicultural educator.

Description of Project Promise

Preservice teacher education continually comes under attack for its lack of rigor and its failure to prepare teachers for the "real world" of education. Casual conversations with inservice teachers reveal a universal disappointment with their preservice education. Most teachers report that the only value in their preservice education was the actual immersion of student teaching. The frustration with the status quo in teacher education led to the development of an experimental program at Colorado State University called *Project Promise*.

Because of its success, Project Promise was designated by the Colorado Commission on Higher Education (CCHE) as a "Program of Excellence" in teacher preparation (Richburg, Knox, Carson, & McWhorter, 1996). The purpose of the project is to use "best practices" in the training of future teachers. We begin with an intense selection process during which we select a cohort of twenty students. The students all possess bachelor degrees in content areas that will permit them to be licensed in secondary Math, Science, Social Studies, or Language Arts. They typically have experience working in their content area and come to us as career-change professionals. Therefore, many of the students are older than traditional students, and they often have families. Our students have experienced success in the "real world" of work and their motivation to succeed in teaching is extremely high. The program is a fast-track; students complete the program in ten and one-half months.

The success of the Project Promise Model can be attributed to many factors. Primary among those factors is the purposeful integration of theory and practice. Students in Project Promise receive instruction/coursework in 3 – 7 week "chunks," after which they are engaged in field experiences. The "chunks" of instruction are taught from 8 a.m. until 4 p.m. during the week. This requires a full-time commitment from the candidates. In addition, there are four field experiences, one in each of four different contexts: rural, urban, junior high, and senior high. The typical rural field experience provides diversity by way of a large immigrant farming community. Those who own the farms trace their ethnic origins to strong enclaves in rural Europe, while those who work the farms are often Mexican immigrants to the U.S. Meanwhile, the urban field experience provides a rich exposure to Black and Hispanic cultures in an inner city environment.

Method: Cultural immersion field experiences

The persistent failures of present educational systems to meet the needs of their multicultural student bodies suggest a compelling need for revolutionary teacher training in multicultural education. Teacher education curricula attempt to promote multicultural understanding in preservice teachers. This training often includes activities designed to increase teachers' pedagogical understanding of multicultural education in an effort to increase minority student achievement. Yet all of this training doesn't appear to have made a difference commensurate with those efforts. The difference may be that "doing" multicultural education without a requisite perspective transformation is not as effective as "becoming" a multicultural educator.

There are a variety of studies which have traced preservice teacher development through the use of journals, case studies, interviews, reflection papers, and life-history accounts (Calderhead, 1988; Deering & Stanutz, 1995; Rice Jordan, 1995; Garmon, 1993; Banks & Stave, 1996). Many of these and similar studies focus on the "doing" of teaching or the "doing" of multicultural education. While these studies make significant contributions to the knowledge base of preservice education, a void exists in the area of personal perspective transformation. Banks & Stave (1996) investigated the attitudinal change that occurred in two preservice teachers as they completed a two week experience in an urban high school. This sort of research advances the dialogue toward perspective transformation.

Clark (1993) reminds us that virtually everyone experiences transformational learning through those events which we report, "changed our life."

> In all cases, we can look back on these or similar marker experiences and identify the effects that they have had on our development, on who we are as human beings. They have changed us. Before the experience we were one sort of person, but after we were another. (p. 47-48)

After the first seven weeks of instruction, Project Promise students embark on their first field experience. This first attempt at student teaching is purposefully designed to be conducted in a small, safe community in order to facilitate the success of the preservice candidates. Still, the level of anxiety is raised because we move our students to the rural environment for the entire week. Project Promise students live with host families in the rural community for the duration of the field experience. Meanwhile they engage in student teaching in the local schools. Because our group of twenty students often overwhelms the rural community, we assign our students to K-12 classrooms. This is particularly effective in emphasizing the range of developmental issues pertinent to the classroom.

The urban immersion field experience is conducted in a similar fashion. However, it occurs after a long term (10 weeks) junior high student teaching experience and an intensive three week training through the Project Promise Diversity Institute. The students are better equipped to embark on this field experience due to the training they have received and the exposure to diversity that they experience in the junior high field placement.

During this immersion experience, Project Promise students are housed in a bed and breakfast in the heart of downtown Denver. Rather than actually teaching, students participate in Denver schools by assisting teachers and shadowing students. In addition, they are required to participate in cultural/city activities such as: using public transportation, visiting local museums and galleries, eating in ethnic restaurants, and the like.

Prior to embarking on the field experiences, students are given a pre-test to determine underlying stereotypes or biases toward rural and urban communities. A post-test is also conducted upon their return. The results will be discussed later in this article.

Student Reflections

We attempted to determine whether the theory of perspective transformation provides a sufficient framework from which to examine *multicultural* perspective transformation. The explicit nature of research that investigates the personal construction of knowledge through individual life experiences poses difficulties in understanding a phenomenon through a framework that can then be generalized for many populations. The motivation that inspires one teacher to become a multicultural educator may have no relation to the motivation of another. Still, an investigation into the sources of motivation for preservice teachers to own the value of multicultural education may reveal particular experiences which provide the impetus for transformational change.

The results of the pre/post tests for the rural experience indicated that before the immersion experience many students believed that the teaching strategies used by rural educators would be progressive, upon return they reported that the strategies were conventional. Another significant finding indicated that upon return students reported that the schools had more resources than expected. In addition, students found more cultural diversity in the rural community than they had anticipated. However, they also received an impression that the communities were less accepting of diversity than they had indicated on the pre-test. Overall, Project Promise students were quite accurate in their preassessment of the rural experience. Fort Collins, the location of Colorado State University, is a relatively small community (approximately 100,000) and this may contribute to the student's accuracy of perception. The rural experience is not far removed from the life experiences of our students.

However, the urban experience provided rich evidence of transformation. Few of our students had spent significant time in urban communities, thus some were apprehensive as the time approached to actually engage in the field experience. One student put it this way in her journal:

> I felt like such a hypocritical person the day I couldn't understand why Kristie (not her real name) and Jason (not his real name) had some reservations about spending the week in Denver. Here I was, trying to be an open-minded teacher for my students and I didn't realize I was being close-minded with my peers. It never occurred to me that as much as many urban people probably never get exposed to the suburbs or the country, these educated, broad-minded peers had rarely been exposed to the city. I realized in those moments that as much as I've moved and traveled and adapted to numerous environments, I had remained close-minded in the sense that I took those experiences for granted. I had never looked at things from "their" perspective. I've thumbed my nose at conservatives, suburbanites, ruralites - whatever label I'd given to people who had limited exposure. I was the one with limited thinking. These types of people just may make up the majority of my student's family population. THAT was important for me to realize (her emphasis).

This is the sort of perspective transformation that we hope for in conducting immersion experiences. The realization that this student arrived at occurred even *before* we left Fort Collins. The processing and diversity training that Project Promise students receive prior to the immersion experience are critical to their preparation. For two weeks prior to the immersion experience, the Project Promise students receive specialized training in all measures of diversity. This includes face-to-face experiences with children with physical disabilities, gifted and talented students, students with learning disabilities, and Baseline training (training in dealing with children from chemically dependent families or with chemical dependencies of their own). Students are introduced to theories of multicultural education, including the work of Banks (1997), Sleeter and Grant (1992), Ladson-Billings, (1994), Gay (1994). In addition, students experience a prejudice reduction workshop using the film *The Color of Fear* (Mun Wah, 1994*)*. This training, along with daily processing and reflective journaling, assists in preparing students cognitively and emotionally for the immersion experience.

Still, with all the cognitive and emotional preparation, the transformations occur most dramatically during the actual immersion. One student wrote, "I thought that these three weeks in January were absolutely wonderful. I cannot express in words how they have changed my life except to say that I feel very honored to be a part of a program that values these types of experiences." Another student wrote about his fear for his safety. He had been one of a few White students at a predominantly Black high school when he was an adolescent. At that time he had experienced discrimination and mistreatment based on his skin color. It was easy to understand his apprehension about the urban immersion experience. He wrote:

> I had a great walk/run through downtown and was heading NE on California Street when I began to feel somewhat uncomfortable with my surroundings. I became keenly aware of the fact that there were several tough looking teens around and that I was the only visible Anglo (on foot anyway). While my first instinct was to be careful, my second one was probably one of confidence. I was simply a human being walking with other human beings. I observed the graffiti, broken glass, disrepaired houses and wondered what it would be like to live in this environment which seems so far away from the one in which I currently reside.

In describing the importance of reflection, another student wrote,

This past month has been a great opportunity to reflect on my own values, beliefs and emotions. The more I get in tune with myself and deal with my own issues, the more I can empathize with others and their issues. The month was intense, but invaluable to me.

During this time in Denver, we were fortunate to have Nikki Giovanni come to town for the Martin Luther King, Jr. Celebration. She gave a performance that many of our students attended. One student described his reactions this way,

> The two events I'll remember most about the week in Denver are the poetry reading by Nikki Giovanni and working with the elementary school kids and Reverend Leon Kelly. The poetry reading was at times awkward for me but very satisfying. It was awkward because I felt in the minority. Not just from being White in a mostly Black audience and from being male in a mostly female audience but also from finding myself questioning many of the preconceived notions I brought with me to the reading. The satisfaction came from the fact that although I went with some preconceived notions, by attending the reading I developed a more in-depth awareness and knowledge of concerns that some African Americans have towards "our" society's power structure. I try to convince myself that I am fully aware of how racism (whether institutional or individual) is pervasive in our country but until one deals with it directly, it is difficult to fully comprehend.

These examples are representative of the types of responses we have received over the past five years of conducting cultural immersion experiences. Students are changed by these experiences. It is our belief that seeing and being in the communities with people of color through an immersion experience has the greatest potential for perspective transformation.

Discussion

In his theory of adult learning, Mezirow (1990) states that meaning perspectives (referred to in related literature as frames of reference, paradigms, world views, etc.) influence what we remember. The rural cultural immersion experience does not "shake" the meaning perspectives of our students. There is little, if any, conflict in the world view between our students and the people who live in rural communities. Therefore, the experience serves to reinforce the meaning perspectives as they relate to the rural environment. However, when our students enter the inner-city of Denver, they are met with tremendous challenges to their assumptions, stereotypes, and biases. Mezirow (1991) states that, "Reflective learning becomes transformative whenever assumptions or premises are found to be distorting, inauthentic, or otherwise invalid" (p. 6). He suggests that transformative learning results in transformed meaning perspectives when reflection on premises occurs. We encourage and require students to maintain a reflective journal throughout the entire 10 and one-half month program and especially during the immersion experiences. This has proved to elicit the kind of introspection that results in transformative learning.

One of the limitations of this study is the quantity and quality of the journaling by the students. Some students prefer to talk through their experiences rather than write them down. Others get so caught up in the process of immersion that they prefer to write after the experience. Often students writing after the experience do not capture the depth of emotions that they may have experienced during the cultural immersion. The Project Promise students are not aware that we are researching the transformative learning experience. For them, the cultural immersion activities are simply another in a series of innovative strategies to facilitate their success as preservice teachers. Project Promise is an experimental program by design and therefore the students are accustomed to extensive processing, reflective journaling, and consistent integration of theory and practice.

While we know that this January experience is worthwhile, it is not without its sacrifices. Students over the past five years have consistently reported feeling exhausted and overwhelmed. This year a student wrote,

> January was tough for me. It was exhausting and challenging. While I realized that everything we did was valuable and necessary, it was almost too much, too fast. It felt like a lifetime of therapy packed into one month, in one little room, with twenty people who weren't sure if they wanted to ever know or feel or think as much as we did. I explored, examined, learned, and grew more in that month than maybe ever before.

And another wrote,

> The first three weeks of January consisted of a variety of rich experiences. The month and various experiences were emotionally, mentally, and physically exhausting at times. Realizations made or re-emphasized were powerful, to say the least. One was continuously processing and reflecting.

Most students echo these statements, adding that the experience was invaluable. Shortly after returning from the immersion experience, the students embark on their final field experience, a 10 week senior high student teaching experience. During this time, they are acutely aware of the variety of "differences" in their classes. Students make extra efforts to modify lesson plans for students with learning disabilities, begin to infuse their lessons with a multicultural perspective, and make special attempts to reach students who were heretofore deemed "unreachable."

Implications

Our experience in conducting cultural immersion field experiences has the potential to significantly impact teacher preparation programs in the United States. During the past five years, we have found that these particular experiences can and often do lead to a transformation of students' perspectives on multicultural education. As teacher educators develop curricula for preservice teachers, we recommend that serious consideration be given to the impact of cultural immersion field experiences. Such curricula would provide opportunities for teachers to experience events which have life-changing potential. Those who then become multicultural educators may have a greater potential for affecting change within their classrooms. This change could significantly impact minority student achievement in American schools.

REFERENCES

Banks, D. N., & Stave, A. M. (1996, February). Changes in preservice teacher attitudes concerning urban teaching: A case study. Paper presented at the Annual Meeting of the American Association of Colleges for Teacher Education, Chicago. (ERIC Document Reproduction Service No. ED 394 913).

Banks, J. A. (1997). Multicultural education: Characteristics and goals. In J. A. Banks & C. A. McGee Banks (Eds.), Multicultural education: Issues and perspectives (3rd ed., pp. 3-31). Boston: Allyn & Bacon.

Bennett, C. I. (1995). Comprehensive multicultural education: Theory and practice (3rd ed.). Boston: Allyn & Bacon.

Bennett de Marrais, K., & LeCompte, M. D. (1995). The way schools work: A sociological analysis of education (2nd ed.). New York: Longman.

Boyle-Baise, M. (1996, April). Finding the culture in multicultural education: A theoretical exploration. Paper presented at the Annual Meeting of the American Educational Research Association, New York.

Boyle-Baise, M., & Sleeter, C. E. (1996). Field experiences: Planting seeds and pulling weeds. In C. A. Grant & M. L. Gomez (Eds.), Making schooling multicultural: Campus and classroom. Englewood Cliffs, NJ: Prentice-Hall.

Buttery, T. J., Haberman, M., & Houston, W. R. (1990, Summer).

First annual ATE survey of critical issues in teacher education. Action in Teacher Education, 12(2), 1-7.

Calderhead, J. (1988). The contribution of field experiences to student primary teachers' professional learning. Research in Education, 40, 33-49.

Clark, M. C. (1993, Spring). Transformational learning. In S. B. Merriam (Ed.), An Update on Adult Learning Theory (pp. 47-56). New Directions for Adult and Continuing Education, no. 57. San Francisco: Jossey-Bass.

Colorado Department of Education (1997). website: www.cde.state.co.us/dist0880.htm#students.

Darling-Hammond, L. (1997, February). School contexts and learning: What is needed to give every child the right to learn. Paper presented at the Cross-Cultural Roundtable, Teachers College, Columbia University, New York.

Darling-Hammond, L., & Sclan, E. M. (1996). Who teaches and why: Dilemmas of building a profession for twenty-first century schools. In J. Sikula (Ed.), Handbook of research on teacher education, (2nd ed., pp. 67-101). New York: Macmillan.

Delpit, L. (1995). Other people's children: Cultural conflict in the classroom. New York: The New Press.

Deering, T. E. & Stanutz, A. (1995). Preservice field experience as a multicultural component of a teacher education program. Journal of Teacher Education, 46, 390-394.

Evans, E. D., Torrey, C. C., & Newton, S. D. (1997, Spring). Multicultural education requirements in teacher certification: A national survey. Multicultural Education, 4(3), 9-11.

Fullan, M. G. (1991). The new meaning of educational change. New York: Teachers College Press.

Garmon, M. A. (1993, April). Preservice teachers' perceptions of the first year of a teacher preparation program. Paper presented at the Annual Meeting of the American Educational Research Association, Atlanta. (ERIC Document Reproduction Service No. ED 359 187).

Garmon, M. A. (1996, April). Missed messages: How prospective teachers racial attitudes mediate what they learn about diversity. Paper presented at the Annual Meeting of the American Educational Research Association, New York.

Gay, G. (1994). A synthesis of scholarship in multicultural education. Urban Monograph Series. Oak Brook, IL: NCREL.

Gay, G. (1997). Educational equality for students of color. In J. A. Banks & C.A. McGee Banks (Eds.), Multicultural education: Issues and perspectives (3rd ed., pp. 195-228). Needham Heights, MA: Allyn & Bacon.

Gollnick, D. M. (1992). Multicultural education: Policies and practices in teacher education. In C. A. Grant (Ed.), Research and multicultural education: From the margins to the mainstream. London: Falmer Press.

Gollnick, D. M., & Chinn, P. C. (1998). Multicultural education in a pluralistic society (5th ed., pp. 218-239). Upper Saddle River, NJ: Prentice-Hall.

Grant, C. A. (1995). Praising diversity in school: Social and individual implications. In C. A. Grant (Ed.), Educating for diversity: An anthology of multicultural voices. Boston: Allyn & Bacon.

Grant, C. A., & Secada, W. G. (1990). Preparing teachers for diversity. In W. R. Houston (Ed.), Handbook of research on teacher education (pp. 403-436). New York: Macmillan.

Hinchey, P. H. (1994, Fall). Introducing diversity: We don't have to wait for a program. Action in Teacher Education, 16(3), 28-36.

Hodgkinson, H. C. (1993). A demographic look at tomorrow. In Reflecting Diversity: Multicultural Guidelines for Educational Publishing Professionals (pp. 5-15). New York: Macmillan/McGraw-Hill School Publishing Company.

Huber, T. (1996, November). Attitudes toward diversity: Are we preparing future teachers to be responsive to cultural pluralism in the classroom? Paper presented at the National Association for Multicultural Education Conference, St. Paul, Minnesota.

Joyce, B., & Showers, B. (1988). Student achievement through staff development. (ERIC Document Reproduction Service No. ED 240 667).

Kivel, P. (1996). Uprooting racism: How white people can work for racial justice. Philadelphia. PA: New Society Publishers.

Kozol, J. (1991). Savage inequalities: Children in America's schools. New York: Harper Collins.

Ladson-Billings, G. (1994). The dreamkeepers: Successful teachers of African American children. San Francisco: Jossey-Bass.

Lawrence, S. M., & Bunche, T. (September, 1996). Feeling and dealing: Teaching White students about racial privilege. Teaching and Teacher Education, 12 (5), 531-43.

Marable, M. (1997). Racism and multicultural democracy. In C. Hartman (Ed.), Double exposure: Poverty & race in America (pp. 151-160). Armonk, NY: M.E. Sharpe.

McIntosh, P. (1989, July/August). White privilege: Unpacking the invisible knapsack. Peace and Freedom. (ERIC Document Reproduction Service No. ED 335 262).

Mezirow, J. (1990). A guide to transformative and emancipatory learning. San Francisco: Jossey- Bass.

Mezirow, J. (1991). Transformative dimensions of adult learning. San Francisco: Jossey- Bass.

Mun Wah, L. (Producer). (1994). The Color of Fear. [Videotape]. Available from Stir Fry Production, 470 Third Street, Oakland, CA 94607).

National Center for Education Statistics. (1995). Mini-digest of educational statistics. United States Department of Education. Office of Educational Research and Improvement. Washington, DC.

Nieto, S. (1996). Affirming diversity: The sociopolitical context of multicultural education (2nd ed.). New York: Longman.

Pallas, A., Natriello, G., & McDill, E. (1989). The changing nature of the disadvantaged population. Educational Researcher, 18 (5), 16-22.

Powell, R. R., Zehm, S., & Garcia, J. (1996). Field experience: Strategies for exploring diversity in schools. Englewood Cliffs,

NJ: Prentice Hall.

Reed, D. F. (1993). Multicultural education for preservice students. Action in Teacher Education, 15(3), 27-34.

Richburg, R. W., Knox, K. A., Carson, S. R., & McWhorter, B. A. 1996, Spring). Adding power to our ability to develop outstanding new teachers. The Teacher Educator, 31(4), 259-270.

Rice Jordan, M. L. (1995). Reflections on the challenges, possibilities, and perplexities of preparing preservice teachers for culturally diverse classrooms. Journal of Teacher Education, (46), 369-374.

Sadker, M., & Sadker, D. (1994). Failing at fairness: How our schools cheat girls. New York: Scribners.

Sleeter, C. E. & Grant, C. A. (1992). Making choices for multicultural education: Five approaches to race, class, and gender (2nd ed.). Columbus. OH: Merrill/Macmillan.

Sleeter, C. E. (1996). Multicultural education as social activism. Albany: State University of New York Press.

Thornton, M. C. (1995). Population dynamics and ethnic attitudes: The context of American education in the twenty-first century. In C. A. Grant (Ed.), Educating for diversity: An anthology of multicultural voices (pp. 17-32). Boston: Allyn & Bacon.

Weber, B. (1997, October 23). DPS flunks 214 summer truants. Rocky Mountain News, Denver, CO.

Wurzel, J. S. (1988). Toward multiculturalism: A reader in multicultural education. Yarmouth, ME: Intercultural Press.

Zimbardo, P. G., & Leippe, M. R. (1991). The psychology of attitude change and social influence. Philadelphia: Temple University Press.